MW00489716

The
CAMINO
PROVIDES

a curious guide to the camino del norte

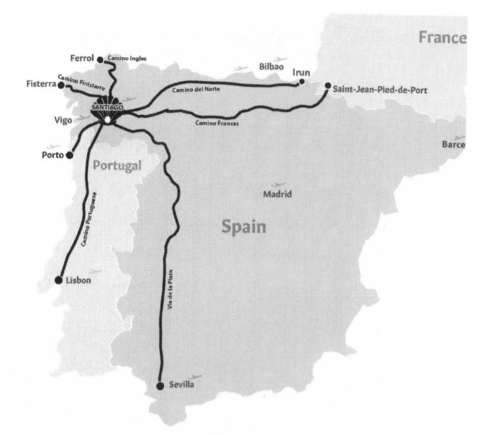

The CAMINO PROVIDES

Camino del Norte

a curious guide to the camino del norte

James Ryle & Cassie Childers

2020

Copyright © 2020 by James Ryle & Cassie Childers

All rights reserved. This book or any portion thereof may not be reproduced or used in any manner whatsoever without the express written permission of the publisher except for the use of brief quotations in a book review or scholarly journal.

First Printing: 2020

ISBN: 978-84-09-23516-2

Edited by: Ivan Broadhead & Tom Button
Cover art: Bob Thompson
Photography: Cassie Childers

thecaminoprovidesbook.com
caminocoaching.org
ascensiontherapyclinic.com

In order to maintain anonymity, in some instances we have changed the names of individuals and places.

Although the author and publisher have made every effort to ensure that the information in this book was correct at press time, the author and publisher do not assume and hereby disclaim any liability to any party for any loss, damage, or disruption caused by errors or omissions, whether such errors or omissions result from negligence, accident, or any other cause.

for Tiago

and our grandmothers,

Dora and Dorothy
&
Pamela and Jacqueline

acknowledgements

Steve Weiss, Bob Thompson,
Melissa D'elia
& Alex

the human elevator, Tom Button

&

the legend himself, Ivan Broadhead

...and to our parents,
Helen, Joe, Wendy & Lee

THANK YOU

practicalities

CAMINO DEL NORTE 5

ACCOMMODATION 6

MILLION EURO QUESTIONS 7

BUDGET 8

ULTIMATE PACKING LIST 56

ALBERGUE ETIQUETTE 57

KNOW THE BASQUE 58

SAN SEBASTIÁN BASICS 59

JAMES THE SAINT 99

THE AUDACITY OF NOT FOLLOWING THE STAGES 100

BASQUE COUNTRY HIGHLIGHTS 101

LOSING WEIGHT ON THE CAMINO 138

EUROPE'S WEB OF FOOTPATHS 138

BEAT THE BLISTERS 139

ROMA PEOPLE OF SPAIN 140

CANTABRIA HIGHLIGHTS 141

CAMINO FITNESS 180

CAMINO SAFETY 181

LEY LINES 182

ASTURIAS HIGHLIGHTS 183

CULINARY HIGHLIGHTS 217

USEFUL PHRASES 219

GALICIA HIGHLIGHTS 220

RECOMMENDED MEDIA 221

SANTIAGO BASICS 265

OFF THE BEATEN PATH IN SANTIAGO 266

FINISTERRE, MUXÍA & THE COSTA DEL MUERTE 267

ROUTES OF THE CAMINO 323

introduction

Cassie

Wine and sleeping pills will save me. I was on edge from whiskey fumes wafting into my airspace from the large man in the wrinkled suit seated behind me, and being crushed into the middle seat wasn't helping.

For comfort, I snuggled closer to my husband, nestling into his shoulder as dusky light glowed through the airplane window. 800 kilometers of walking ahead of us and I was already exhausted.

As I was drifting off, the whiskey drinker coughed uncontrollably. The heightened stench took me to a time and place I didn't want to remember.

Seven years earlier, on the other side of the world, we'd found his father hunched over the bed. Bodily fluids and cheap Indian whiskey melded into a sweet and sickening perfume. I'd never seen a dead body so raw. Such a contrast to carefully manicured corpses at wakes back home in the States. But this was India – a Tibetan refugee settlement – and after years of living here, this may have been the only thing left with enough clout to shock me.

An hour earlier, my bag was packed, ready to finally leave Pemba - the man I'd fallen in too deep with. Too much. Too fast. A relationship built on big dreams and shared by perfect strangers. The day I moved in with him, my gut churned. I knew deep inside I was trying to build a life with a man in no way suited to me. Two months later, looking out the window of the Rajdhani Express with tears streaming down my cheeks, I was completely gone. Unrecognizable from the young, empowered woman I used to be.

I was stripped down to the primal level. A newborn baby, with no parents to bring me clarity, remind me who I was, or tell me I was loved. Dying was easier than living. I was nothing, Pemba told me. I didn't matter. Everything that went wrong was my fault. And somehow, I believed him.

But I knew I'd never survive and I had to go. So I packed my bag. And then the phone rang.

Tibetans in-exile prefer not to involve the local Indian authorities in matters such as death. Instead, an unidentified Tibetan man arrived to guide us through the next three days. He instructed us to pull up the carpet and drag it to the river bank to burn. We undressed Pemba's father and threw his clothes in the flames, along with the stained stinking sheets he'd died on. We tugged his gold rings off swollen fingers, and searched for other valuables, which I was instructed to hide. We cleaned his body as best we could. And then the monks arrived. For three days and nights, we sat with them as they prayed for a more auspicious rebirth of this dreadful man's soul. When demanded, I boiled water and served the assembled guests salted butter tea and cookies as the corpse looked on.

Then came the first punch, square in the jaw. But I couldn't leave him now. I couldn't leave him to deal with the grief and liturgy of loss on his own. Pemba couldn't read the legal documents. He couldn't pay for the funeral rites. Someone had to serve the tea. Rub the sugar on the corpse. Pour the whiskey on the body as it crackled on the funeral pyre. Someone had to dig through the ashes with their bare hands, searching for bone fragments and molars. Someone had to cook him dinner before giving a thought to washing off the dead man's ashes that dusted her skin. That someone had to be me.

Somehow I survived another couple of months with Pemba. My sanity only preserved by morning walks up into the heavenly Himalayan foothills, and subsequent sprints back down to my own personal hell.

I thought I had blocked all that out. *Why was I thinking about this now, on the airplane to Spain?*

James

Dreading interacting with those god-fearing fitness freaks that called themselves pilgrims, I'd hoped my brother would ease my burden by walking some of the Way to Santiago with us.

"So, any plans for you and the new wife?" Graham asked, shouting obscenities at the football we kicked against his mud-splattered wall.

"We're going to walk the Camino de Santiago," I said excitedly, hoping my exaggerated tone would peak his curiosity.

"What's that?"

"Well, there'll be all sorts of drinking and fun."

He put his foot on the ball. "Go on."

"We'll be on a bit of an adventure. A holy walk like when they used to do a pilgrimage to Jerusalem. But this is to Santiago. In sunny Spain. Cassie wants to walk it. Might be all sorts of interesting fanatics to interact with."

Seemingly unimpressed, Graham wiped a muddy splatter on his bald head. "A holy walk? Sounds like something you'd do during a midlife crisis. Are you okay?" He shook his head. "How long is this walk anyway?"

"About forty days or seven weeks or something." Saying it out loud made me aware of a pain in my chest.

You'd think Graham had sucked a lemon. "Are you serious? That sounds really shit. And boring. There are enough weirdos around here. I don't need to go looking for them on some holy quest."

I understood completely, but had to feign more enthusiasm in the slim hope he might still join us. "But it's the thing Cassie wants to do most in the world. The 'last great adventure on Earth' she calls it. Wouldn't you like to meet up with us for a few days? We'll have a laugh. Eat good food. Drink too much wine?"

Again he shook his head. "Jimmy. Jimmy. So that's what marriage is all about for you? I thought it would settle you down, but you get married then take up walking the world like some kind of Jesus Forrest Gump. Is that how it goes? You know what they say these days?" He tapped his forehead. "It's people with the real serious issues that need to take up walking and running. So what's your big issue?"

Deflated and annoyed by his insightful ridicule, I told him to pass me the ball. Graham rolled it towards me. I smashed it back in his general direction.

Nimbly, the fecker jumped out of the way, letting out an evil laugh.. "You expect me to walk on a holy pilgrimage for forty days? That sounds like torture. Marriage isn't a penance, you know?"

Graham looked to the sky. "Why, God?!" he shouted, pretending to kick an imaginary ball into heaven.

"That's what the wife wants to do," I said. "It's part of the honeymoon."

"Honeymoon? Just take her for a long walk to mass. Tell her to confess everything. Maybe she's guilty or angry about something? You *do* know? That's why most people walk. Too much pent-up emotion. They push it down. Pretend they're fine. But they're not fine. That's why they have to take up walking for forty bloody days across a foreign country. You haven't been with Cassie very long. She could be crazy and you still don't know it." Sagely, he tapped his mud patch. "Up here for thinking." He pointed at his feet. "Down there for dancing." He did a little jig in the wet grass. "Anyway, when did you get so holy?"

"I'm not holy," I said defensively.

Quietly laughing, he jogged away to retrieve the ball.

Discomfort in my chest made it sore to breathe. This was going horribly wrong. It felt like a confrontation. I hate confrontations. Cassie had meticulously planned our trek to Santiago. I hadn't thought much about it. Now hearing my brother's evil laugh, I realized this Camino could be a nightmare. My intestines twisted as I thought about forty days trapped on the road, in cramped dormitories and pilgrims rattling on about the significance of every minor detail. Everything will be a sign. Or worse, a miracle! I cringed at the thought of how many times I'd have to hear, "It all happens for a reason."

Already I felt like shaking them and shouting, "Nobody knows what's going on. We live on a spinning fireball in the middle of nowhere. Not everything has a reason."

I hadn't been able to say all this to Cassie. We were still caught up in our whirlwind romance.

Graham arrived back with the ball.

I gave it one last try. "So. Can I tempt you to walk with us awhile? Once-in-a-lifetime opportunity? Could be amazing ..."

"Piss off. You know it's going to be shit. No way am I walking that weird thing. Besides, I've got the kids and my head's already wrecked just walking them to school. Tell you what though. I'll buy you a few beers if you finish. But don't bring back any pedophile priests!"

In startled agony, I dropped to my knees after he smashed the football right into my balls. He laughed maniacally. "See. You're praying for it to be over already."

Camino del Norte

Spain's northernmost route of the Camino de Santiago is also believed to be the oldest. There is a considerable amount of evidence that the Camino del Norte actually predates Christianity in the region, serving as a spiritual road for nature-worshipping pagans traveling to Finisterre, believed at the time to be the edge of the world.

During the 9th century the grave of Saint James was discovered in present-day Santiago by two shepherds, and King Alfonso II (c.759-842), ruler of the kingdom of Asturias, was notified immediately. He commanded that a chapel be built over the site, and shortly after, made the first known pilgrimage on what came to be known as the Camino de Santiago. The seat of King Alfonso's kingdom was Oviedo, one of the most important cities in northern Iberia at the time.

As word spread of this new holy site, throngs of devout Catholics from around Europe began to make the pilgrimage, most opting to pass through Oviedo on their way. It was perfect timing, as the more traditional Catholic pilgrimage route to Jerusalem had become too dangerous due to the Crusades. Different routes of the Camino began to connect Europe's main cities with Santiago.

Meanwhile, Islamic Moorish invaders began spreading north through Iberia, making the new southerly routes of the Camino too dangerous. Thus, the Camino del Norte only grew in popularity, as it was mostly out of the Moors' reach.

Over time, the Moors fell away south and the significance of Oviedo waned. Eventually, the more southerly Camino Frances gained in popularity due to economically-fueled publicity drummed up by King Sancho the Great of Pamplona, and the Norte fell into its shadow.

Accommodation on the Camino

camping	campgrounds are not common along the Camino but do exist in places. camping at unofficial sites is illegal in Spain.
albergue 'donativo'	public, simple, and often unmanned dormitory that accepts a donation of your choosing. rarely includes breakfast or linens.
albergue municipal	publicly run dormitory for a fixed price, usually €5-€8 pp. usually includes breakfast, a disposable sheet, and pillow.
private albergue	privately owned accommodation with a higher level of comfort & privacy, usually €10-€15 pp. usually includes breakfast & linens.
hostel	accommodation open to all travelers and not necessarily Camino-oriented. found in the bigger towns and cities. prices vary.
pensión, casa rural, hostal	small hotels, inns & bed and breakfasts with private rooms only. usually includes breakfast. €30-€45 per room. some have self-catering facilities.
hotel	high quality hotels and inns can be found along the Camino, a treat for a special night. the Parador chain is a Camino favorite. prices vary.

Million Dollar Questions

How do I get money?

Traveler's cheques are relics, and carrying a lot of cash is foolish. The only way to do it on the Way is by ATM. Machines are plentiful on the Camino. Alert your bank before you leave that you'll be using your cards in Spain. Many banks reimburse customers' ATM fees now. Credit cards are also widely accepted, though not everywhere. The only currency accepted is the euro.

How do I get my phone to work?

Some people can get away with only using wifi. Almost every bar, restaurant and albergue will have free wifi you can use to make calls and check email. If you want to be making posts in real time, though, you'll have to get a European sim card or pay a hefty daily fee to use your non-European card from home. Sims are easy to get before you begin. We recommend Vodafone, which works anywhere in Europe for a standard fee.

How do I get to Irun?

Irun is well-connected by train, bus and air. From Madrid, we recommend the direct bus. Note that San Sebastian airport is actually in Irun.

Will I be lonely on the Camino?

Absolutely not! So many pilgrims fear this route will be long and desolate, but if you're walking anytime from April-October, you'll be in the company of many others. The social atmosphere on the Camino is much more open and welcoming than footpaths back home, and you will most definitely find that you're making friends faster than you ever have in your life. Don't be too quick to link up with strangers online or on your first day of walking. Give yourself a couple of days and you'll find your tribe.

How do I train for my Camino?

The more you train, the more enjoyable the first week of your Camino will be. However, many people don't ever train at all. For most, the first week serves as your training for the remainder. Training could consist of walks of ever increasing length and incline, preferably with your loaded pack and in the shoes you plan to wear. This will help, but you won't truly be ready until you're walking full stages, with a full load, for several days in a row. Very few people have the time to do this at home before they leave, hence, the first week of the Camino can be a rude awakening. We strongly recommend taking it slow the first week, gradually building up to the speed and daily distance you want to maintain for the rest of the Camino.

How much does it cost?

This can vary greatly based on the individual. There is no fee for walking the Camino. It is usually possible to stay in a municipal albergue and eat off pilgrim's menus, which can keep the budget very manageable. We've put together two different daily budgets as examples. Most people will fall somewhere in between. (printed in 2020)

Camino Minimalist Budget

€6	bed in a municipal albergue including breakfast
€10	pilgrim's menu dinner
€5	sandwich or small lunch
€8	beverages or snacks
€29	**TOTAL PER DAY**

Camino Comfort Budget

€30	private room in a pensión including breakfast
€16	dinner at a mid-range restaurant
€5	sandwich or small lunch
€8	beverages or snacks
€59	**TOTAL PER DAY**

...butterflies

-

Cassie

For the first time in my life, I was nervous as the plane descended. I've traveled solo all over the world, to places considered much more dangerous and challenging than.... drum roll please... Spain. This was probably the 10th time in the last year we'd been on an international flight. So why this anxiety?

At least I was feeling something. For the past year, I'd hardly felt anything. Our bodies and minds are so seemingly kind in this way. When the pain is too much, they can shut it all off. No more crumbling under the weight of suffering, our minds free themselves to do what they need to survive.

So kind, but at what cost?

James was furiously rearranging bags of nuts and crumpled up travel tickets into our bags.

"Dude, relax. You're freaking out," I grinned.

Half the stuff in a bag fell onto the floor.

Earlier, James' anxiety was clearly exposed as we approached passport control back at the airport departures terminal. Instead of handing his passport and boarding pass to the security officer, (like every other person), he decided he needed to stick his passport into a machine to be scanned. A machine that didn't exist. When the officer outstretched his hand to receive the documents, James' eyes focused on a dusty receptacle instead. It was a mailbox gap filled with exposed wires and crumpled arrival forms and James forced his passport into this crevasse. Noticing the officer's confused expression, he realized what he'd done. But James was panicking; his brain and hands no longer communicating. Now he was elbow-deep into the hole, his sleeve caught on the wires and unable to release his grip on the documents. His face turned red and he was shaking, unable to control either body or mind. Watching events unfold, I looked at the officer and laughed.

He looked at me sympathetically. "First time flying?"

It was actually his millionth. As James composed himself, the guard cracked a smile. He knew I'd need all the support I could muster on this journey with my beautiful, befuddled Irishman — a journey that had scarcely begun.

James continued to clean up the stuff he'd spilled beneath our airplane seats.

"You know," I said, "we can quit if we don't like it? It's fine with me. If you get injured, or your ear infection won't go away. I won't mind. We'll just head south. Find some Spanish beach town and hang out for a month."

A few seconds of silence as he finished repacking. He plopped down hard in his seat.

I sat back as the plane touched down. My body wouldn't settle. I was focusing on James' well being, but who was I kidding? My stomach churned as we taxied to the gate. I looked back at my husband. "But what if you get injured? Or your ear infection won't clear up? What if my knee gives out? And blisters? Who wants to walk with blisters?"

I was looking for an out. James clearly wasn't buying it. Or maybe he just couldn't hear through his pus-filled ear.

He snatched my hand and held it tightly. I lowered my head onto his shoulder and closed my eyes. The Camino would make me forget these bad feelings.

The Camino de Santiago is an ancient pilgrimage path that began in the Middle Ages, leading the devout to the apostle Saint James' resting place in the far northwest corner of the Iberian Peninsula. The violence of the Crusades had all but removed the possibility of pilgrimage to Jerusalem, so Europe's millions of devoted Catholics needed a new destination. A network of trails developed, branching from all corners of the continent, and all leading to the same place – Santiago.

For hundreds of years pilgrims have trod the Camino. And in recent years, promoted by the Spanish government, it has experienced resurgence. Now more than 300,000 people walk some part of it every year. Arguably, it's become much less a religious journey, and more a spiritual one. People of every nation, race and religion ply the paths, following the scallop shells that are the official blaze of the trails. When they finally reach Santiago, many after walking hundreds of miles, the pilgrims arrive at the foot of the city's stunning gothic cathedral and kneel at the grave of Saint James - where many deep epiphanies are experienced.

Miracles are said to occur on the Camino. I heard whispers that it's one of the most poignant and powerful healing journeys anyone can take. Some form of alchemy happens once you've committed to walking long distances each day with only a small bag of basic possessions. Every night you share a sleeping space with others in the extensive network of pilgrim-only hostels that has developed along the routes. Your 'stuff' begins to surface, and the Camino presents situations and people to provide opportunities to learn and heal.

People have all sorts of reasons for walking the Camino – but as the old adage says, the *real reason* presents itself along the Way. *Here's hoping*, I thought, as our plane taxied to the terminal.

We chose the Camino del Norte as our route mostly because of the weather. Walking in June and July, most of the more popular routes, leading through the high altitude desert of Spain, would be too hot at this time of year. Influenced by the Cantabrian Sea, the Camino del Norte stays relatively cool and green. It's also the most challenging route, with lots of ups and downs and fewer services for pilgrims, which makes for longer walks each day.

I first met James on a stormy night in the Himalayas. It was a night that bridged the hopeful emptiness between a previous life I'd just deconstructed, and the promise of a new one I was about to create. He was put in my path in this neutral ether, and seven years later we found ourselves in this same neutral ether, this time newlyweds. The evening we met he was leaning over the railing in an empty rooftop bar as snow began to fall. James' sad eyes watched the people pass below as his wispy auburn hair became ever more tangled in the wind that whipped down from the mountain.

It was me who started our first conversation, for a reason I could never understand. It wasn't like me to start talking to sad-looking hippie guys in freezing-cold bars. It would take six years working together in India for us to realize we loved each other. Within weeks of that eureka moment we were married. Now we'd left India for good and were travelling on an extended honeymoon with no ambition or end date. One country to the next, searching for the next distraction, the next cheap thrill. Maybe one day we'd find a place that felt like home.

My dreams on the plane were feverish. Shadows of demons and devils laughing at me and my fears, daring me to give up. It had been a year full of such dreams.

11

Dawn finally crept through the sides of the window shade as the plane came to a halt at the gate. All my thoughts and fears were quickly compressed inside. I sat up straight. We were in Spain.

Despite our lack of sleep, James and I easily navigated through Madrid to store our few possessions - which were too much to carry on the Camino. At the transport interchange, we boarded a seven-hour bus to the French border at the town of Irun, the starting point of the Camino del Norte.

A long bus ride is one of my favorite things about travel. The journey facilitates mental transformation. You are no longer yourself. On the road to Irun, you're now a pilgrim. Your house, bed, food, laptop, sofa are all gone. You are bonded to the Way now. You will not stray. You will walk, and keep walking, whatever may come, until reaching your goal.

Away from the *autopista*, crumbling castles lined rocky ridges marking the northern reaches of old Iberian kingdoms. These fortresses would be considered a treasure in America, where Cinderella's Disneyland pad is as real as it gets. Here, they look long forgotten, the local villagers barely aware they exist.

The bus pulled into Irun. Too tired to be excited, we stumbled to our room in some nondescript pensión, oblivious to the fact that tomorrow, we would start walking.

Our own castle, forgotten.

James

I'm one of those annoying folk who avoid doctors. I think any sickness will just magically clear itself up. Give it time and I'll be fine. Normally this works, but not with this festering ear infection. How long had it been this time? Three weeks? A month? Plenty of time for parasites to wine, dine and get intimate with my inner ear.

The plane landed in Madrid with a soft judder, then sweetly skimmed the tarmac. I tapped the sensitive skin of my ear for the hundredth time. A wall of fire erupted in my head, leaving a scorched barrier against sound. Poor Cassie was hoarse repeating herself. I had to remind her to speak into my good ear. You'd swear we were nearing our 50th wedding anniversary, not our first.

People were getting up, but my mind flew back into the clouds. Anniversaries made me worry about time. *Are we really going to walk across a country the size of Spain? That's absurd.*

12

"Get up," said Cassie into my non-infected ear. She thumbed her finger over her shoulder to the aisle but it got stuck in her long, luxurious hair. Patiently I smiled, pretending I wasn't stressed as she disentangled hair from her raw opal wedding ring. Knowing I'd probably lose my wedding ring on the Camino, she kept it on a chain around her neck. Triumphantly she puffed out her freckled cheeks. "Aisle free. Can you hear me? Get your stuff. We're going to be late."

Tired as usual, I just looked out the window.

"Are you pretending not to hear me again? I know which one is your good ear." She gave me a playful flick on my bad ear. Pain nearly seared my soul away. I hopped up in an inferno of annoyance, but her sweet smile cooled my irritation. "Come on. And promise you won't make us late by sticking your passport in random holes."

To finally cure my infection before starting the Camino, I was supposed to find the address of a *Centro de Salud* (hospital chain that accepts the free European Health Insurance Card) in Madrid. Not wanting to visit a doctor, I told Cassie I'd forgotten to search for one. "We have no time now," I suggested.

Dubious, she squinted at me while tapping her foot in frustration. "This is ridiculous. I'm not going to shout for the whole Camino. No more suffering. We're going to the doctor!" She whipped out her phone, and quickly found the address.

It was close. With minimal pain and fuss, I was in and out. Cost for the visit and medication was about 3 euros. The card came in the mail. I'd advise any European get one. I'd be covered if I hurt my back, got sick or suffered from Pilgrim Interaction Syndrome.

On the bus to Irun, something strange was happening in my ear. A cracking noise, like bursting parasite eggs. I moaned as the doctor's liquid dribbled out my ear then down my face staining my green jacket. *Damn doctors!* Suddenly the pain took an exquisitely sharp texture as it scraped its nails across the blackboard of my brain. In my mind sentences glowed in disappearing red dust.

You are an idiot.

You don't even want to be here.

You are already hungry. What would Saint James's bones taste like?

You are an idiot.

Life is too short for this Camino.

If you want to get fit - join a gym.

13

If you want some therapy - go to a therapist.
If you want spirituality - go meditate.
Why walk across a country?

WEEK 1

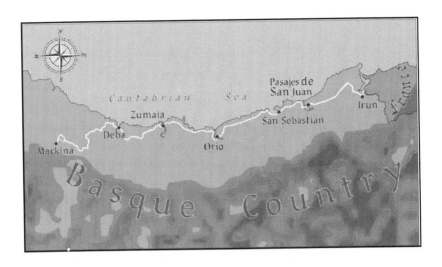

...the secret german

–

Day 1 - Irun to Jaizubia
5.4km

Cassie

Many pilgrims spend their first day walking the 22km from Irun all the way to San Sebastian, which is the official first stage. We chose a different approach to the traditional stages for a few reasons. First, we had plenty of time. We wanted two months in Spain, so why walk fast? We had nowhere else to be, no home to return to. It was possible to finish this Camino in three weeks, but we would aim for seven. This would also allow us time to break in our feet and avoid injuries, which we seemed prone to after years of playing soccer around the world. Second, not being totally exhausted at the end of each day would give us energy to see and experience the places we visited along the Way.

We slept in until 10:30, feeling like we'd left random neurons and synapses sprinkled across the Atlantic, yet to catch us up. We headed for the *Iglesia Pasionistas*, a church that distributes the official credential that pilgrims need to get stamped daily along the Way. This proves we have earned our *compostela* — the certificate issued by the Catholic Church at journey's end in Santiago. Honestly, I couldn't have cared less about getting a piece of paper issued by a religious authority. But I did care about discounts, and life becomes so much cheaper in Spain once you flash your pilgrim's credential.

The stone church loomed ahead. Nothing to distinguish it from the thousands of other small-town Catholic churches in the world. Doors locked. We scurried around the back down an alley to a small office building. Entering, we saw no sign of any other pilgrims.

I giggled, and elbowed James as a priest studied our passports at his desk. "What if we're the only ones walking?"

We burst out laughing, which made James wince as he tapped his earlobe.

The priest abruptly stood up, pushing our credentials to us across the table. We'd receive no blessings here. Just a booklet and a single stamp.

Our new pilgrim passports in hand, we grabbed a quick bite to eat in a nearby Peruvian restaurant. Marveling at the Basque people rushing through the streets, we scanned for signs of pilgrims as we slurped down our ceviche.

Tummy full and a sparkle in my eye, with yesterday's anxieties behind us, we stepped out and took our first steps on the Camino del Norte, well-marked by yellow arrows and scallop shell blazes. They led us right out of town through a beautiful estuary, where we quickly started climbing a hill through Basque pastoral perfection.

After the priest's indifference to the fact we were about to walk across Spain, the solitude and bucolic peace of the first section of the Camino served as our true initiation. The gulls hailed our departure with their screams overhead, the sun shone its spotlight on our sense of courage and the wind shifted to our backs, nudging us forward.

After 5km of jet-lagged walking, *Capitan Tximista Albergue* came into view. The setting couldn't be more perfect. The hostel was set inside an old mill, with a stream running underneath. Downstairs was a simple lounge with ageing furniture and a dining room with a solitary long table lined with benches. Upstairs was a large attic with sloped ceilings, filled with cheap metal bunk beds smashed in so tight you'd surely be able to feel your neighbor's breath in the night. The sound of the rushing water underneath would surely drown out any snorers, I hoped.

16

Finally, we sighted our first pilgrims. First day of school butterflies fluttered in my stomach. Several men and women straggled in as the day darkened, all a good bit older than us and seemingly alone except for a quiet Swiss couple with their heads down. No one made eye contact.

One by one, after removing their shiny, heavy boots, they took turns buying cans of beer from a small glass refrigerator, sipping in solitude on the wooden deck over the millstream. I watched with self-awareness as, furtively, they took turns comparing themselves to one another. *Look at his boots. Ankle-high. Am I supposed to have those? Her pack - it's huge. What could possibly be in there? Are they taking sleeping pills over there? God I hope my ear plugs work. What the hell language are they speaking?*

Over our first communal dinner on the Camino, the ten pilgrims sitting at the long, wooden table courteously introduced themselves, formally stating names and places of origin. Our soup was slurped in uncertain silence. This was not exactly the 'Camino family' vibe I'd heard about. Were we entering a geriatric treadmill of unfriendly couples desperate to save their souls as death drew near? A beach in southern Spain suddenly felt very appealing.

James

Dark clouds within my chest began to rain worry when I saw we'd all be eating dinner at the albergue's communal table. "Buen Camino!" our fellow pilgrims chorused. Confused by their overly enthusiastic greeting, I tentatively said, "Hello." Their frozen smiles revealed my response was disappointing.

German was the most common tongue. At least if everyone spoke in a language I couldn't understand, it might save me from endless tales of 'Camino miracles' and how 'it's all meant to be'.

Opposite me was a solitary, wrinkly-skinned German. She leaned over the table, then said, "I've been on the road for 72 days." She sat back. Blue veins throbbed in the black bags under her milky blue eyes.

Holding my breath, I waited for more. Uncertain how to respond, I smiled. Under her stern gaze, I began to sweat. Was this some kind of pilgrim greeting code? Should I congratulate her or commiserate? Should I announce to the table I've been on the road for one day?

She nodded. I nodded. We both nodded. Is this pilgrim etiquette? Am I doing all this nodding wrong? I nodded again. She nodded back. I didn't know what was going on, but she wouldn't stop staring at me. I felt judged. My throat became dry, causing me to cough up a morsel of food. Silently I pleaded, can't someone else interact with the Secret

German who has been on the road for 72 days? I don't want to crack her enigma code.

Sometime after another coughing fit, my idiotic anxiety surprised me by blurting out a question. "Where have you been walking for the last 72 days?" *Damn. Why did I ask that!?*

Skin rippled as she leaned in close. Deep breathing tickled my ear hairs, as if she was telling me something so important that even she was afraid to hear the words. Her moist lips touched my ears, making me shrivel up inside. Finally I made out the words, "It's fresh in here."

I whispered, "I don't know what you mean? Why is it fresh in here?" She pulled away. For the longest moment she interrogated me with her piercing gaze. In hope of relieving the tension, I nodded. Mercifully, she nodded back, then got up to leave the table. I nodded as she departed. She didn't nod back.

The Secret German's bed was next to mine. Even my aching ear couldn't keep the sound of her snoring at bay. All night she thundered and plundered my sleep. At 1am, moonlight crept into the room.

In the dim glow I saw a little crucifix on a silver chain hanging from a pilgrim's bed. It reminded me of my grandmother who'd been a full-time Catholic and loved a bit of mass. Actually, I think she had a serious addiction, attending seven days a week - twice on Sundays.

Religion wasn't a relief. My mind galloped to the little horses in an overgrown field full of messy briars I'd seen today. Disentangling their luscious coats from the brambles, they ambled over to investigate us. No doubt in their minds, our backpacks held all sorts of delights.

In bed I relaxed a little as I felt again each horse tentatively nibble the cashew nuts I brought for the journey. They were impressed, banging their furry heads in hope of more. In the brief moments we touched, I felt a centering strength that helped me breathe easier.

By 4am, I was rattled from sleep deprivation. At 5am, the Secret German emitted a walrus-like screech that rattled the room. This seemed to be her dawn chorus, accompanied by a dramatic stretch. Unsteadily, she got up. She glanced at me, but I closed my eyes in case her morning greeting was another nodding contest. Relieved, I took a deep breath as she limped away.

Unable to sleep, I went into the common room to find her poring over maps. Pencil notes were scribbled into her waterproof notebook. Soon the Swiss couple was up. They nodded at the Secret German.

Nodded at me. Nodded to the map. With a sweep of my head, I tried to nod to everyone. Compassionately, they smiled - as if I was a buffoon.

Intent on capturing some sleep, I got back into bed, but was irritated by every knot in the mattress.

Then I was provoked by a waking dream. I was in a mud-strewn mountain village in Guatemala. Rain hammered hard upon a soccer match. Gunshots were fired. Death, the referee, brandished a red card. Shocked, the offending player fell onto the mud and died on the spot. Death placed the red card into his mouth and play continued.

A chorus of yawns and stretches from my fellow pilgrims awoke me from the death match.

This was going to be a long walk.

...bed races

-

Day 2 - Jaizubia to Pasajes de San Juan
14Km

Cassie

I woke startled at 8am, a good hour after the other eight pilgrims. My earplugs and eye mask had allowed my jetlagged body to believe it was still on Guatemala time. James was sitting up in his bunk, but I could tell from his eyes he hadn't slept a wink. As he furiously stuffed random items into his pack, nuts went flying everywhere. He kicked them under the bed in frustration. A moment later, shaking his head, he was on the floor to retrieve them. "Horses be hungry," he muttered in his beautiful Irish brogue.

There was no reason to rush today. The next albergue, 14km away, wouldn't open until 4pm. We calculated we would walk at 4km an hour even, so no point leaving at the crack of dawn.

We were given decent *café con leche* and bread for breakfast (typical Spanish), and headed off by 9am, the albergue attendant confused by our lateness.

Up we climbed, through a cool, mossy forest. Up, up. One foot in front of the other. I'm a lowland girl, through and through. Born and raised at the Jersey Shore, flat as a pancake. The mere sight of a hill was awe-inspiring. But moving to the Himalayas changed all that, real fast.

At least once every day, I'd walk up a hill too steep for cars to reach my little apartment in the forest. My only neighbors were a band of monkeys, some Tibetan spiritual hermits who woke me up each morning with their thigh-bone trumpets and guttural chanting, and James. I felt my body slowly change in those Himalaya years, gradually adjusting to the inclines, until I barely noticed them.

We opted for the more challenging *alpinista* route for the day due to perfect walking temperatures with no wind or rain. On our climb (of approximately 1,500 feet), we realized just how gloriously beautiful this Camino thing was going to be. Little medieval port towns came into view below, the full vastness of the Cantabrian Sea to the north and the foothills of the Pyrenees to the south.

Following a high coastal ridge, we came across four different watchtowers built of ancient stone, relics of some long forgotten kingdom. My daze from the previous night wore off as the hiking endorphins kicked in. Another night of the bad dreams about soccer, Tibetans and hysterical crying, that had been plaguing my sleep.

I'd spent much of the past year walking alone. Dodging landmines and bears in Bosnia; through hurricane-strength storms in the Irish highlands; circumnavigating a crystal-clear crater lake in Guatemala; up a snow-laden volcano in the Cascades. I couldn't get enough. Just walking, walking, as much as possible. In the Andalucía hills, I encountered an Iberian lynx one sunny winter afternoon. There are less than 500 left in the wild. She crossed the trail five strides in front of me, pausing to look deep into my eyes before calmly sauntering off in her noble feline way. I still felt nothing.

We rounded a bend, and a rock monolith that seemed almost Celtic came into view. I knew this was the spot.

"We'll break here a minute, alright?" I asked James.

Our packs were downed and James rounded a boulder to take a leak and talk to cows. I had already written most of them on a slip of paper. The things, the people, that kept barging into my dreams and making my life a special kind of hell. I quickly submerged the list into the small bag of black salt I'd found deep in a labyrinthine, smoky market in Guatemala...

In the same country, I watched Mayan families visit the graves of their ancestors, tending small fires with sprays of whiskey, sprinkles of black salt, and cracked eggs. All to help banish bad energy from their lives and those of their children.

At the foot of the monolith, I hung my last string of Buddhist prayer flags (known to Tibetans as *lung ta*, or windhorses) and emptied the bag of salt and slip of paper into a fist-sized indentation in the rock. *This is it. Please, god, or goddess, or whatever - let me feel again. I'm tired of just walking for no reason.*

Up the slope, we heard singing. I could see a young woman in her twenties, slim with reddish hair and a backpack that looked like it weighed more than her. In a squeaky, Germanic pitch I could make out, "I love the mountains, I love the rolling hills, I love the fireside when the lights are low..." Her voice wavered as she maneuvered the steep path. The song was her point of meditation, keeping her focused so she wouldn't trip and tumble into the Cantabrian Sea. She staggered by us quickly without a glance. Tangled hair whipped in the wind as she swiftly descended towards the village, holding back tears as she sang.

14km felt enough for the day. Good news was no sign of 'hot spots' on our feet, so no pending blisters - at least for now. My weaker right knee shook slightly, but the new brace appeared to help.

As we meandered down the only street in Pasajes de San Juan, we were surprised to suddenly see so many pilgrims. Most head 8km further to San Sebastián, following the official guidebooks stage. We were nervous we wouldn't score a bed in the village's only hostel which only had 14 bunks. After gobbling down salad and cod, we camped out on the steps of the hostel where a line of backpacks was already forming. The first 14 would be allocated a bed tonight. By 2pm, seven pilgrims were already ahead of us.

"Ughhh," I groaned sitting on the stoop out front. "Is every day going to be a race to find a bed? Doesn't sound too spiritual to me."

James sighed and picked up a stick. You can take the Irish out of Ireland, but you can never efface their memories of the Troubles. "Don't worry," he said, with mock menace. "If there are too many pilgrims racing ahead of us meaning my wife won't get a bed, I promise you now, I'll romantically break someone's kneecap. That's real Irish Republican love." He gave me a wink and pointed his stick at a passing pilgrim. "Slow down, yer bollocks!"

The hostel was a municipal albergue. Simply put, a hostel specifically reserved for pilgrims walking the Camino de Santiago, usually operated by a local church or town association. More often than not, the price is a modest 5 euros (less than $6) per bed per night. This one, like many others, was housed in a ridiculously charming old church, probably in the area where monks or nuns used to live. The view of the quaint harbor below was worthy of the Ritz Carlton, and a slight distraction from the sardine-tin atmosphere of the bunk room.

After they opened the doors at 4pm, we got our credentials stamped, claimed bunks by spreading our crap over them, showered, washed today's clothes in a sink and put on tomorrow's. The hostel issued a disposable sheet and pillowcase, made of very thin fabric, which we augmented with light sleeping bag liners we carried with us.

The singing redhead was lying on the bunk across from me, her face jammed into her guidebook. I tried to make eye contact, wondering what her story was. I was certain it was sad. Feeling my attention, she stuck her face further into the pages. *Geez. Was this chick planning to walk the whole Camino not speaking to anyone?*

The rest of the day consisted of tapas (called *pintxos* in Basque Country) and sampling the local alcoholic cider. After the tough hike and lack of food or water, we quickly realized we were pretty drunk. Under normal circumstances, we could hold our own on the grog front. James is pure Irish, a champion of the bar stool, and I can normally keep up with the best of them. I could tell from our heightened queasiness we needed to be more careful on the Camino. Hangovers don't mix well with hours of sweaty walking and mandatory early morning wakeups.

James

My leg muscles burned as we reached the muddy peak. Along the ridge, I was intrigued to see crumbling, medieval watchtowers. With the last of my energy, I clambered to the top of the first tower only to have my senses assaulted by the potato-like features of an irate man with onion breath. In a thundering Welsh accent he shouted into my face that I was disturbing his work, leaving my beard covered in breadcrumbs.

Startled, I stepped back. "Calm down," I said.

His bushy brown eyebrows flapped from me to his fallen sandwich. He bent down to pick it up. "Ahh, will you look at that," he said. "Ruined. My fault." He brushed some dirt off the top of his half eaten cheese and onion sandwich. "Sorry, boyo," he said. "I'm waiting for the damn light. I need to get the right photos for the boss. But the light is never right. He's one of those pompous English types, you know? Couldn't you see I was up here from below?" He pointed to his expensive-looking camera equipment strewn atop the grassy tower.

22

My heart jumped as my foot slipped. Flailing my arms in wide-eyed panic, he pulled me back from the brink.

"Jesus, boyo!" he shouted. "You nearly died."

Shaking a little, I looked down. Poor Cassie would have taken the brunt of my fall.

"Relax," he said, then smiled. "It can't be that bad to be jumping at your age."

I shrugged.

He put his hand on my shoulder. "I think we're both done for today. I'm done with walking anyway. I'm sick of it."

"Are you okay?" I asked.

Annoyingly, he responded by picking up his camera and poking the long lens towards my head. "You have an interesting face. Especially that little hole on your forehead," he said in his rolling Welsh lilt. "Care if I take a snap of it? Looks like something burrowed in there to lay eggs."

"No," I said, self-consciously rubbing my birthmark with one hand and pushing the lens away with the other. I really needed to get away from this guy. Only then I noticed his sleeping mat laid out next to his backpack. *Could he have slept up here all night waiting to get the perfect picture? Shit. I really could be getting in the way of his work and messing up an already agitated mind.*

"Look," I said. "I'll leave you to it. I'm in the middle of this Camino thing, too. Actually, I'm only at the start. Which is obviously a lot worse."

Sympathy softened his brow. "Yes. Best if you go. Just tell me. Where are you from?"

"Ireland."

"I know. I can hear that. But what's your heritage? Your roots? I'm supposed to take notes in my diary about a pilgrim's lineage for the boss."

Noticing his tree trunk legs, I swallowed down a bit of stress. An ancestral bind held my tongue. He'd seemed upset that his boss was English so he might kick me off the tower if I didn't answer correctly. My mother is Welsh, while my father, though extremely Irish, was born in England. Would he embrace me as a fellow Celt, or be incensed by my oppressive English ties? Worse, he could throttle me on the spot for being a half-blood. A treacherous Englishman in Celtic disguise.

I stuttered. "I'm... I'm." In my mind's eye the Secret German nodded. "I'm German."

"What?" he said.

"I mean. I'm not German." All that stupid nodding last night came rushing back. Could I now be the secret Celt? With as much authority as I could muster, I nodded at the Welshman. He nodded back. I nodded again. He nodded to the path, in a way that said, 'Get off my tower you idiot, I'm trying to work.' As I was about to climb down, he laughed. "Look at these two giddy bugs." he boomed.

A male and female trekker approached our tower. I wondered if it was a sleep deprived mirage, for the two were so alike. They wore matching blue outfits, with the same short, black haircuts and plump dimpled cheeks like two identical puppy dogs out for a walk.

I watched Cassie wave at them as they passed the tower. The woman had a monopoly on clam shells. Or were they scallops? They're clams in my mind. I was never sure what a scallop was. Cassie told me pilgrims in the olden days used the shells to scoop up drinking water. I didn't have a clam. Maybe because this woman had hoarded them all. Dozens dangled from her bag. To add to this crustacean jamboree, the couple was adorned in matching clam-design t-shirts, clam pouches and clam-shaped hats. Clam patches were sewn all over their clothes and packs and printed on their t-shirts were images of each other's smiling faces. Truly, puppy love.

"Why do you have so many breadcrumbs in your beard?" Cassie asked after I'd clambered down the tower. "It looks like a bread bomb went off in your face." Like a duck, she pecked at the debris with her fingers.

"Weird story. I'll tell you on the Way. No time for talking now. We've got to catch the walking clams. They seem intriguing enough to help the day go faster."

Quickly we caught up with Mr. and Mrs. Clam. I was not disappointed. Mr. Clam was one of those people who looked at his map at every turn, dramatically pointing and shouting as if he'd just discovered the New World. I enjoyed his manic enthusiasm until he became exasperated with Mrs. Clam's continual stopping because of a worsening limp. That was until he also succumbed to a limp. Their distress helped me realise Cassie definitely had the right idea to walk slowly and not too far in the beginning. We asked if we could help them carry anything but they waved us away with a beaming smile.

Nestled by an inlet below us, the jaunty, nautical town of Pasajes de San Juan appeared, decorated with fishing nets streaming from three-story buildings. A merry meandering atmosphere prevailed. Salty old men washed up and down the harbour, pushing and shoving each other like children into reclining couples who relaxed with glasses of wine in the evening sun.

Night brought winds that rattled the albergue's windows. Pilgrims' snores forced me out of bed to seek comparative peace in the howling gale. From the balcony, the lamplight created a watercolor palette far below that made the boats appear to dribble away from the dock.

What were all these people getting from the Camino? Wind pushed the boats from the harbor, but their moorings ensured they couldn't float too far. That is just like the Camino. These pilgrims think they're free, but they are tied to the Way. Like the boats, they surely need something else to untie their minds from their troubles. Surely walking can't be the answer?

...parts unknown

-

Day 3 - Pasajes de San Juan to San Sebastián
12 Km

Cassie

The sea breeze hitting my face was a welcome relief from the smell of ten other people's dirty socks. Feeling refreshed after a solid night's sleep, I could see James hardly able to lift his head as the dormitory came to life. Poor guy. His earache was worse. We needed to leave this fishing village for the city of San Sebastián. The mere 12km/8mile walk was sure to be vastly more difficult after the previous night's cider over-indulgence.

Off we went, no breakfast or coffee, again the last to leave. First we boarded a little dinghy that took us across the inlet to pick up the Camino. The grey sky, on the verge of rain, led us to a path that meandered along a high cliff for the length of the walk, the placid sea below us gently undulating to the rhythm of James' ear fluid. The familiar feeling in my gut began to stir. That acrid heaviness trying to convince me that something bad was happening, though as usual, I couldn't identify what it was. I daydreamed about my next glass of wine.

A spectacular sight awaited, as we descended into San Sebastián. It's an idyllic city, set on two beautiful bays with long clean beaches, filled with a greatest concentration of Michelin-starred restaurants on Earth. My excitement to explore its culinary alleyways and remove myself from the reality of the Camino took over.

I learned about the area on a 2017 episode of Anthony Bourdain's 'Parts Unknown,' and was majorly stoked to go *pintxos* hopping. The superstar traveling chef claimed there was no better European city to eat in. So we'd get this ear thing under control, and then eat!

Pilgrims on the Camino often find they have the eating inclinations of a truck driver, never fully satisfied. Yes, you're burning many more calories, but your body makes up for it by giving you constant hunger pangs and an insatiable appetite. Plus, you're in Spain - a country that's fully mastered the art of snacking. And nowhere in Spain does it better than the Basque Country. Chefs here seem to take more pride in finger food than main courses.

We checked into our room for the evening, a private bedroom in a local apartment. Perfect night to go for this option, since James needed a good sleep to kick the infection, plus deal with being on antibiotics. San Sebastián is a great excuse not to stay in an albergue, since the main ones are quite a distance from the alimentary action in the city's old quarter.

We'd just walked 12km and still hadn't had a single bite to eat. My stomach rumbled, calling for fuel. We shuffled directly to the famous *Borda Berri*, and broke our fast with squid ink ravioli and veal cheeks in red wine sauce. Breakfast of champions. Paired with a couple glasses of wine, my gut was numbed.

Pintxos are the ultimate snack. They are served as small portions, and in San Sebastián are laid on platters along the bar. You either take what you want, or point to it for the bartender to heat up for you. A *pintxo* can be anything - there are no rules. The bar staff are amazingly skilled at keeping a tally of what everyone eats. Somehow the bill is always accurate, despite nothing being written down. The key is to be assertive. Elbow your way to the bar, and use Jedi mind tricks to make eye contact with a waiter. Shout or point, just don't be shy.

We hopped around a few more places, trying unique anchovy spirals, stewed hake cheeks, and an array of flavors that explode in your mouth creating a complexity of tastes us non-Basque mortals have been deprived of our whole lives. Full, but not ready to give up, we searched

San Sebastián's back lanes for the famous burnt cheesecake from *La Viña*, which was the best cheesecake I've eaten. Not too sweet; creamy and slightly uncooked in the middle, burnt and creme-brûlée-esque on the outside. A hint of lemon, a dash of sea salt in the crust. I ate slowly, with long, languid movements of my fork, exaggerated 'mmmms,' and a starry-eyed look as I fell in love with a piece of cake. Perfection - somehow satisfying every taste bud in just one bite.

Next, as the Spanish do, it was time for siesta. In our plush bedroom, with total privacy, James curled up and tried to sleep. I sopped up some alone time, laying down with my device to catch up on the news.

Shit shit shit, NO.

It couldn't be. *Anthony Bourdain dead from suicide.*

A lump formed in my throat and I couldn't help but cry out a little. Anthony Bourdain was my hero. He lived the most inspiring life, with a job the stuff of dreams. His New Jersey snark mixed with his ability to authentically connect with anyone, anywhere, (usually over a beautiful meal and plenty of drinks), had me follow him for years. I always checked his recommendations for any place I visited. And he dies the very same day I'm in San Sebastián?

How can a guy, who seemingly had it all — fame, fortune, looks, genius, and admiration from millions – end his own life? It was easy for me to pose this question as I lay there in San Sebastián, one of his favorite places, but I already knew the answer.

For most of us, it's more important to concentrate on tangible struggles in life – earning a living, maintaining relationships, keeping your body healthy, and being a successful, productive member of a material society. But when you strip all that away, and you should have nothing else to worry about, perhaps that's when the gravity of the reality of existence sets in. At the end of the day, it's actually very difficult to be happy in this world.

I could understand how he must have felt, along with the countless others having a hard time being alive. Reading this, in the centre of carefree San Sebastián, a place I'd only heard about from Bourdain, I was reminded of why I was walking the Camino.

James woke up and looked livelier. There we were. And there was no better way to celebrate the life of my idol than eating *pintxos* and making new memories. It felt like sacrilege to be sad in San Sebastián, with a world of possibilities and food right outside our door. Bourdain wouldn't have stood for that.

As we wandered the cobbled alleys of the old city, exotic smells wafting from kitchens as friends shared drinks and laughter on the streets, I shed one final tear for a man I deeply admired. His story was part of my story, and I was determined to figure out why.

I'd begin over another piece of cheesecake.

James

A gleaming mane of greasy hair bounced before us. This creature was more mullet than man. Portly of face, round in the belly, but strong in the arms, he placed a foot on the edge of one of San Sebastián's stone fountains. His dark eyes, keen, scowled at passing citizens as if they were peasants.

Again, my gaze greedily drank in his hair. Like an ever-expanding black hole, it seemed to capture light. The man glowed, leaving all other mortals in his shade. Except one. For by his side stood a remarkable fellow whose angular face could have been etched from the steep cliffs protecting this land.

Daunted by their aura, I wanted to dodge this duo.

Fate intervened. A car next to us honked, drawing their attention. The mulleted man nodded at us to approach. I declined, but the angular man beckoned us seductively with a wave and a hawkish whistle. Wary but intrigued, I quelled my better judgment and let his beck and call guide me to the fountain. I was in disbelief. Not only was the mullet massive but, the man himself, enormous.

"Have you seen my horse?" The density of his black hair made his rumbling voice echo as if inside a cave.

Overwhelmed, my voice croaked. "I don't know. What does it look like? I've fed a few horses along the Way. "

"Ahhh, pilgrims," he said. He leaned forward towards the fountain to give his beefy calves a flex, then whispered something to his companion. Both men pursed their lips.

The thin, cliff-faced man looked to the sky, then pierced the air with another whistle. "How far have you walked?" His voice was fast and free flowing, the words were like wind whipping down the steep features of that face. "Tell me? Tell me your story?"

Before I could answer, he leaned down behind the little fountain to pick something up. Worried we were about to be robbed, I tried to diffuse the situation with a joke.

"We walked from Ireland."

Mid-motion he stopped. My plan was to throw a stone at him if he produced a knife. Instead, he slowly got up holding a guitar. He pursed his lips and words flew. "Ireland. Good. Green. Rain. Dublin. Drinking. Guinness. IRA. Cold. Fuck England."

Before I had time to reply, the dark-eyed Mullet was clapping an extravagant, clattering beat. What happened next rejuvenated my love of music. Cassie, with her rock n' roll soul, was our connoisseur, and I rode her coat-tails with no real musical taste. This Jersey girl's highest form of art was flamenco so the men's impromptu show wowed our jaded souls. I was lost in flamenco's hypnotic highs and melancholic depths.

Eyes closed, the Mullet seemed possessed as his deep voice resonated through the air. The angular man's features transformed from cliffs into soft rolling hills as he strummed, then furiously loved his guitar. Electrical energy danced around the duo. Suddenly in a flash of lightning foot stomps, they were still. "AY!" We were humbled. In silence they both bowed.

Energized, I couldn't wait to give them some coin.

"No money," said the Mullet. "That was for my horse."

"What?"

"You fed a horse. It could've been my beautiful beast. For this, I thank you. She is lost. A Breton horse. Her name, Canción. She's the colour of ripe chestnut. Blond mane. With a white streak down her face. Under moonlight white becomes silver. Have you seen her?"

Horses flashed. "I'm not sure..."

"Think hard, for we may talk again. Your journey leads you to Santiago, no doubt. We go that Way. But before you and behind you. My horse will not tread the beaten path for long. The ley lines criss-crossing this land lead her." Hair alight under the morning sun, he brushed the strands from his red cheeks then looked to the mountains. "My horse. She is wild. Wild like the storm winds. Wild like my friend here, Nicu." For no apparent reason the man mountain punched his companion in the shoulder, causing him to almost drop the guitar.

Nicu said nothing, just stared into the distance.

I found myself following Nicu's gaze. Horses grazed on the hills.

"Your horse?" I asked. Their eyes cut me deep. I lowered my head in shame. "So your horse escaped towards Santiago?" I asked.

"She is not ready," said the Mullet.

"For what?"

"For the Way."

"Okay." These guys had some deep horse empathy going on.

"How do you know when a horse is ready? Isn't it illegal to let your horse run around by itself?"

"She escaped," replied the Mullet.

Nicu lowered his guitar, then pulled a rolled-up cigarette from the case. "Smoke?"

"No, thanks."

"So," said Cassie, "It's time for breakfast. We've got to get to the doctor's... What are your guys' names anyway?"

Names were given reluctantly. Handshakes were not offered. "My name is Fonso, but people call me Gypsy Mullet, and this is Nicu." Gypsy Mullet began to scan the mountains. "I'm sure you need to get to Santiago. Good health for your journey."

With that, I knew we had been dismissed. Our farewell was not acknowledged.

...lsd

-

Day 4 - San Sebastián to Orio
16.3Km

Cassie

I enjoyed our glorious sleep-in until ten, though I don't think it did James much good. Still in agony with his ear infection, I drugged him to shut him up. It was easy to get prescription painkillers without a prescription in Guatemala, which proved helpful in a country where ear infections were also easy to pick up.

The first hour of today's walk took us along an expansive beachfront promenade in cosmopolitan San Sebastián. Our grungy clothes, backpacks and sneakers were totally out of place surrounded by all the designer bikinis and shiny metallic sandals. We reached the edge of town and climbed up through an old hardwood forest. Ramshackle lean-tos erected in the bushes clearly indicated people lived in this park, such a contrast to the row of mansions below.

We passed a scrappy tall guy with an olive complexion and moppy brown hair carrying a large backpack. He was talking to a man living in one of the shacks, in an eastern European language I couldn't place. Was he a pilgrim? He could've just as easily been a forest dweller.

30

As our path wound up the hill, the tall guy, now quite a way below us, shouted "Are you walking the Camino?!" at the top of his lungs in our direction

James said, "Yes!"

He said, "Wait!"

James said, "No!"

He yelled he'd catch up with us in a second. James and I looked at each other like, *Oh boy. Here we go. Some young fool wants to interrupt our existential brooding with his naive optimism.*

We walked on quickly, silently hoping he wouldn't catch us. But before too long we heard someone behind huffing excitedly.

"So, you guys are walking the Camino?" His tone was exaggerated, full of wonder, as if talking to a couple of five-year-olds. Kind of weird, although I didn't think he meant to be.

"I just started walking, and couldn't find any mates. I really want to meet people. That's why I'm here. So I saw you guys, and, well... Now you're my mates." Victorious, he smiled a ridiculous grin. This 20-something gangly guy had his head in the clouds. He was a puppy let out to play in the snow for the first time.

Before we could all properly introduce ourselves, he pulled out a sheet of LSD tabs and offered them to us. "Wow," I said, nodding in approval. "You're really trusting the flow."

"Well, yes! Of course. I live in Austria, it's different there. Everyone is so proper, and expects me to live my life in the proper way. I keep thinking I'll do it, but then... I don't know. I just can't. Started feeling a bit dead, ya know?"

"Yes, I know. So you said 'fuck it,' started taking LSD, and decided to walk across Spain instead?"

"Exactly!" he shouted, as if I was the only person in the world who ever understood him. "My girlfriend... she's beautiful. Want to see a photo?" he asked, continuing his habit of over-sharing. He whipped out his phone to show us a picture of an attractive young brunette.

"I love her. I'm going to marry her. She's the one. We've been together since we were 17 - that's seven years! She's so beautiful, right?"

"Yes, she is," I said. "But why didn't she come with you on the Camino?"

His shine dimming for just a moment, he said, "Well, she actually wants me to get a job. A career. Go to university. So we can get married, have a house and a bunch of kids and stuff like that."

"And you don't want that?" I probed.

31

"Well, I don't know what I want. Know what I mean? So I'm going to walk the Camino then go back and figure out what to do."

"You know," I said, "there are all kinds of studies coming out saying depression can be treated with psychedelic mushrooms."

"Really?!" he replied excitedly.

"Yeah. One study out of Oxford shows just one session with psilocybin can lead to six months free from depressive feelings."

"But how?!"

"They're not exactly sure how," I said, pausing as I stared at the distant sea. "But I think it's because the mushrooms have a way of reminding you of the unseen world of energies and entities all around us. That there's so much we don't understand, so much more out there, and *in* there. They somehow make us feel more connected to all of that. Plus, they get the old neurons firing, you know what I mean?"

"Guys, I lost my hash. I smuggled it in through Barcelona airport in my hair. Stolen in the hostel, man," he said in wonder as we walked. "Can you believe that?"

"Yeah. I believe it," said James. "Most people are terrible creatures."

Twitching his nose in shock, he pulled away from my husband. "Really? You think that?"

"Yep. Bastards the lot of them. Especially pilgrims."

He took a deep breath to steady himself. "So why are you walking the Camino with pilgrims?"

"Can you see any pilgrims with me?" asked James.

"No. But why are you walking?"

"To make new enemies."

Our companion scratched his tidy little beard. "What do you mean, man?"

"Well," James said seriously, trying not to smile. "It's too easy to be out here making connections and fair weather friends. But I say, trust no one. It's survival of the fittest. Remember first one to the albergue gets the bed and doesn't freeze to death. Take my advice. Take no prisoners. Probably one of us won't make it to Santiago. I am James and this lass is Cassie, by the way."

In awe as he digested James' words, he slowly reached into his shoulder bag, and offered James LSD again. It was a funny old moment. Like two curious tribesmen meeting for the first time, each giving a gift of their mind.

"I'm Luka."

We three began to walk in unison, discussing maladies and cures of the spirit and mind. A lone sheepdog began to follow and a little terrier marched by our side. Our merry band reached a highway where we parted ways with our animal companions. A goat and a blackish horse stared from behind a fence and nuts and fruit were shared. The goat's eyes rolled in the same way our Austrian friend's did on LSD as it gobbled down a sweet, sugary plum. James showed me how to feed a horse out of my hand. My worried squeals made him laugh as the horse's wet tongue raked up the nuts.

"Don't spike his nuts with LSD," James said.

Luka placed the almonds in his open palm, then tentatively tried to feed the animal. Chomping sounds of the horse's teeth brought him to an uncontrollable girlish giggle.

As we walked, rain began to fall, with a distant rumble of thunder. The Way was peaceful on this misty afternoon as we traversed a steep coastal ridge. We didn't pass another human soul for hours, or at least we didn't notice any. Luka's energy was contagious. We talked all day, swapping human observations and psychedelic tales. He knew all about my favorite band, the Grateful Dead - maybe the only European I've ever met who did. Turned out he was Serbian, raised in Vienna - completely broken free of the ice-cold-stoic-emotionally-dead-former-Yugoslavian mold I had come to know during my travels. The woodsy man he'd been talking to on the edge of San Sebastián was an ex-Serbian soldier who'd come to live free in Spain, where there was better weather and better heroin.

15km into the walk, I noticed I hadn't experienced a bad thought or feeling all day. This gangly guy had somehow restored a sliver of my innocence. He was so excited about everything. It was irritating, but hell, it made me feel young again. Luka was my therapy dog.

Finally, the three of us rolled into the *Orioko Aterpetzea Hostel*, wet to the bone but smiling. James tried to nap while Luka assaulted a new crop of pilgrims. I took the opportunity to grab a can of beer and sat outside on the deck overlooking the expansive green valley, reflecting on how different I felt. This kid was having the same effect on me as psychedelic mushrooms.

Dinner was served family-style at a long wooden table, and we were laughing heartily with a herd of new pilgrims as the wine flowed. The sad, singing redhead was there. She was sitting next to Luka, blushing as he asked her prying questions and cracked friendly jokes as she answered between giggles.

Our first few nights on the Camino had been pleasant, but in a way lonely. On this night, though, everything changed. We sat and mingled with this large group of lively pilgrims, all strangers to each other. The energy was there. Everyone's eyes were more open, and quick to share a tale or insight. We were the only couple, surrounded by solo travelers.

Luka buzzed around like a honeybee, weaving in and out of conversations, asking everyone the same thing. "So why are YOU walking the Camino?"

Out of anyone else's mouth, this question would sound contrived and cringe-worthy, even prying. But Luka's authentic juvenile curiosity allowed him to pull it off, and people answered earnestly. I sat back and listened, sipping my wine. Everyone had their reasons, their stories for coming. As varied as they were, they all had one common thread, a truth I could only sense, not yet identify.

The young Tuscan blacksmith was walking to figure out if he wanted to retrain as a psychologist. Misha, the German, wanted to prove her knee replacement couldn't slow her down. Nicole, the bleach-blonde pensioner, walked every year, and was just plain addicted. Roberto, the gay shaman from Capri, was sure he was going to find his soulmate along the Way. Simone was hoping to finally lose the weight. Finnish businessman Boils was walking to get away from monotony and his wife, though he wouldn't say it outright. Patrick, the Irish schoolteacher, was making a grand attempt to end a 17-year cycle of social isolation. The singing redhead, Gerta, only answered Luka with a giggle, but I could still see the pain in her eyes.

It was exciting to have so many new people to talk to. Those long days of walking might be a lot more interesting with a variety of companions. Bring on the distractions.

I fell asleep to a chorus of snores, smiling as I pondered my new name…

James

As the stars dimmed in Luka's eyes, they glowed brighter in the night sky. We three sat as the lone occupants on the wooden benches in the albergue's dining room. Dinner long finished, the other pilgrims milled about inside or were tucked up in bed. Still, bits and pieces of pilgrim paraphernalia lay about. A battered walking stick in the broom basket in one corner. Stacked against a cupboard, was a blue plastic jacket, green baseball cap and some dubiously smelling socks.

A gust of wet wind swept in the door, bringing a newcomer hidden under a black umbrella. I thought it strange a pilgrim, hauling his grungy pack of possessions, would arrive so late on a rainy night.

Without acknowledging us, he put the umbrella in the basket with the walking stick. Rain trickled down his weathered face like he'd been crying into his gingery, scraggly beard. Wild blue eyes suddenly darted to me. My chest tightened as he measured me for a moment. A wolf observing his prey. He shot a hungry glance at Cassie. A pungent smell accompanied his peculiar etiquette.

Sweaty pilgrims have this scent but his was sharper, like when a normally mild smelling horse finishes galloping and its sweat becomes prickly sweet. The odour quickly filled the little room, making it feel like a barn. Maybe he'd been sleeping rough in barns of late? His green trekking ensemble was stained with patches of mud.

He looked up, stroked his beard and glanced us over in a heartbeat. "No wine and no words?" he said. "I should have kept walking."

LSD Luka bounced into action. "Hello. Helloooo," he said. "My traveling wet man. You want words. I'll give you words."

"Maybe they're words I won't like?"

"You'll love my words. Everyone loves me and my words. Right, James?" Before I could reply, Luka erupted, "Except James. He's my enemy. He could be your enemy, too? Would you like to be our enemy?"

The newcomer squinted at me, then smiled. "I like enemies." His voice was smooth like water washing over flat stone. "Bastian is my given name. I'm Dutch. I'm walking the wrong way. From Santiago to Istanbul."

"Istanbul?" asked Luka.

Momentarily, Bastian's eyes danced. Disconcertingly, his attention drifted to the ceiling, until he began to nod slowly. Gathering wind rattled a loose window pane.

To alleviate the weirdness, we all simultaneously blurted "Why are you walking the wrong way?"

Instead of answering, he waved away our question and sat at the dining table. We tried to engage with him but he was vague and aloof until our conversation turned to Christianity. His wandering eyes suddenly pinned us to our seats.

"Thank God," he said with a relieved sigh. "Do you know I'm a bit like John the Baptist? Except I just do names. Not total religious conversions."

Perplexed, we nodded, politely waiting for more. But he stayed quiet. "So are you saying you are the reincarnation of John the Baptist?" asked Cassie.

"I never said that."

"He never said that, Cassie," interjected Luka. "That was rude." Cassie gave Luka a playful whack across the back of the head.

I knew it wouldn't take long to find a religious nutter on the Camino. My brother Graham would do a little jig in delight if he could see us now. Did this Bastian think he was a saint with holy powers, or a sinner out for redemption? I looked at the water in my glass. We needed a change of vibration. He could do with some Jesus-juice to oil his conversation gears.

Straight faced, I asked, "Bastian, I suppose you're not holy enough to turn water into wine?"

To my surprise he shot back, "My price. My extremely low price. Is to simply convert you. Then I can turn anything into wine." Biblical miracle in motion, he pulled two full bottles of red wine from his backpack. Showing off his sharp incisors, he smiled, then repeated, "My extremely low price is simply to convert you."

In anticipation, a metallic taste settled in my mouth as if real blood lay within the bottles.

"Don't be scared, James," he said. "You are going to be my miracle in motion. Look at me." Eyes fluttering, he seemed to be trying to communicate with some higher power. Dim red patches on his face began to glow angrily. "I've found no one really knows how to care for the dead," he whispered.

Sweat patches formed on my back. *What is it with these pilgrims making me sweat? If it's not the Secret German, it's this Dutch nut.*

"I got you by the bones," he said slowly. "I got you right where you need to be. Your new divine Camino name is..." He smiled. "Bones. Your name is Bones. After the bones of Saint James you walk towards. Let me baptize you, fellow pilgrim."

To humor the guy because he might bludgeon us to death with his wine bottles, I agreed. He inhaled, making his face glow even more terribly crimson. Dramatically, he quickly made the sign of the cross millimeters from my face.

36

Panicked, I whipped my head back as his finger brushed my eyelashes.

"Be still, Bones," he hissed. "Closer to the eye. Closer to the soul." Adrenaline stirred within me. My body clenched, fearing a confrontation was nearing.

"Now, young lady. Are you ready to seal the deal?" Cassie did not seem at all ready to seal the deal. "Stop shaking your head," he said. "No can still mean yes. You are just confused by your faith. Maybe more confused than you know." He squinted. "Interesting." Face reddening, he theatrically took a breath. "Be reborn to the name... Saint Michael!"

Cassie's confused pout prompted an urge within me to protect her. *Should I stop him mid-miracle?*

"Do not mourn the passing of Cassie, for we do not know what kind of Michael you may become. For you are a dazzling, glittering lady." He clicked his finger at my wife. "I feel it. You are now Young Mike. A young pilgrim." I took a deep breath of restraint to stop me grabbing his arms as he almost hit Cassie with his whipped blessing.

She shook her head and mouthed at me, "Young Mike?"

"Young Mike," I mouthed back, with a half smile.

Unaware of our silent communication, Bastian turned his attention to Luka, tapping him on the forehead. Luka lifted his chin. "Who's a pretty boy, then?" asked Bastian.

Luka's nose twitched. Unable to hold his delight, he cracked a smile. "I'm a pretty boy."

"Steady. This is not the time for indulgent matters of the flesh. Remember, I see who you really are." He opened his arms wide as if to hug Luka, but at the last moment pulled back. "Luka, you are not just this sack of blood and blasphemy. You, too, are my pilgrim soldier." Skin blotching red, Bastian's eyes flickered. He inhaled steadily through a whispering grin, and announced the name, "Bill."

Luka's face drooped. "Bill?" he asked, throwing his arms into the air. "Just Bill?"

"Luka is now dead and has arisen Beautiful Bill. Don't be afraid to cross back over."

Luka looked at me. Raised his chin. "Beautiful Bill." He basked in Bastian's blessing. "I feel beautiful, Cassie. I deserve this."

"Miracle pilgrims," said Bastian. "Now you are forever bound to this Camino family. The deal is sealed. All your days belong to God. Now if you don't mind. Will we drink the wine?"

Later that night, Bastian, after polishing off plenty of his wine, shook his head in disgust when he heard I disliked the mere utterance of the term 'Camino miracle.' He branded me a heretic of the Way, even going so far as to try to rebaptize me 'Judas.'

This got Luka animated. Waving his hands maniacally, he tried to rebaptize me the Irish name for James, 'Seamus.' Bastian was having none of it, slamming his fist onto the table to reinforce his point.

Cassie and I took this as our cue to leave.

...peanut butter

-

Day 5 - Orio to Zumaia
17.3km

Cassie

As day broke and the early birds packed, LSD Bill seemed flustered. He looked back and forth between the other pilgrims, laced up and ready to go, and James and me, taking our sweet ass time. He was visibly torn as the singing redhead slipped out the door.

"Cassie. I mean Young Mike..."

"Yes, Bill?"

"Should I wait for you guys?" he asked as the last of the others departed.

"Well, we certainly don't expect you to," I said, "I'm not sure what James thinks." I knew exactly what James thought. I secretly hoped he'd stick with us. The guy gave me energy. Luka deeply exhaled, threw his pack down with a thud and ran off to find James.

It was a common dilemma on the Camino. Uncertainty surrounding new friendships, loyalties and the commitment to newfound friendships. You may walk an entire day or two with someone. Is there an unspoken agreement that takes hold after walking a certain number of miles together? Are you officially bound as Camino partners, doomed to spend every waking moment of the next month together? What's the etiquette of parting company when you're done with their blisters, complaints and life story, and are ready for your next candidate for secret psycho-analyzation?

Today the Camino sun showed us its full face for the first time, and the Basque people were taking full advantage. James, Bill and I meandered along sandy beaches and rocky bays, through medieval seaports and past loud, bustling seafood restaurants.

By noon we noticed that something unusual was happening. Huge numbers of people were appearing on the coastal road the Camino was hugging, all wearing white bandanas around their necks or heads. Seemingly all at once, as far as we could see, they all fell into line, removed their bandanas, and formed a chain holding the corners of each other's fabric. People of all ages, even in strollers and wheelchairs, were joining in.

As we walked awkwardly alongside the human chain, I asked a young person what was going on. Turns out we had walked into the heart of a demonstration for political autonomy in the Basque Country, officially a part of Spain but very much its own state in most ways.

For 200km uninterrupted, from border to border, the Basque people stood in this chain united as one.

The Basques are a people all to their own. Physically, they look like others from this region nestled between northern Spain and France, but their hearts burst with exceptionalism, their minds and identity course in a permanent state of separateness. Their language will be unrecognizable to you, even if you're mildly familiar with French, Spanish or Italian. It's a true language-isolate, a mystery, but perhaps a relic from the ancient languages indigenous to this region long before Romanization thousands of years ago. Surrounded by the powerful Catholic kingdoms of Europe, the Basques resisted religious conversion until the 10th century, and today some of their animistic worship rituals still exist in folklore and song.

I felt the stirring of affinity. Tibetans are much the same, existing for eons in isolation between the cultural strongholds of India and China, their spoken language related to neither, their religion pure and unique. Like the Basques, Tibetans are forced to exist within the borders of an invading country of superior military might. But despite Chinese attempts to suppress every vestige of Tibetan-ness, Tibetan hearts remain unwavering, their spirit unyielding. They are Tibetan, pure and simple, and no matter what the map says, they always will be.

In modern years, the Basque Country finds itself in a new era of peace, granted a high level of autonomy by the Spanish government. Basque culture is once again allowed to flourish, despite the fallout from years of heavy terrorism that marked the separatist movement. I wish I could say the same for the Tibetans, whose situation remains grim. I thought back to my friends in Dharamsala regularly mourning the self-immolation of yet another Tibetan making the ultimate sacrifice in the protest against Chinese hegemony and cultural genocide. An ongoing tragedy that no longer made the news in Europe or North America.

As we walked our final miles of the day along the Basque human chain, I wondered what would happen if Tibetans performed a similar act of defiance, perhaps spanning the city of Lhasa, or encircling the Potala Palace. *It would be a bloodbath*, I knew. Any Tibetan who shows the slightest hint of dissidence disappears or is murdered by the state.

We pilgrims on the Camino were making our own human chain. Each morning you leave new friends behind, and catch others you haven't seen for days or weeks.

See, what happens on the Camino is that people walk at different speeds, different distances, take rest days, get injured... All sorts of things can happen and you never know when you're going to make or lose friends.

I felt a tinge of panic when we arrived at the old stone convent that evening. Would we again dine with the ten people we met yesterday? Walk in stride tomorrow? Stay at the same albergue together again? The ease with which we conversed with these virtual strangers was magical. The group always had me laughing. Walking along shooting the shit with just James had a way of bringing up lots of bad memories. I'd rather be distracted by this motley crew.

There might be some value in staying with this core group. For me, anyway. James was a different story. He was so socially awkward most of the time, in between bouts of extreme charm. I knew he'd be more comfortable walking in silence all day, remaining unbeholden to expectant pilgrims. I wanted a Camino family. James, well. He wasn't exactly a family man.

James

With those most interesting lads, Bastian and LSD Bill literally sleeping next to me, I'm surprised I even woke to day five.

In the night Bill bounced into the dormitory then fell into the bed next to mine with a satisfied sigh. Bastian glided in much later. He stood still in the dark for a long while then slowly climbed to the bunk above me. The weight of his presence hung heavy, a shadowy layer smelling wild. The scent crept down my throat and forced me breathlessly awake from forgotten dreams.

Eyes still closed to the morning, my good ear was assaulted by the coughs and splutters of pilgrims. Aching limbs were stretched. Guttural curses in German, Italian and Spanish. A steady chorus of poetic pain.

Something scratched my mattress. I growled, then opened my eyes. John the Baptist himself, Bastian, was standing above my bed, water dripping off his glistening beard. Not saying a word, he seemed content to watch. Uncomfortable with the smile forming on his face, I told him neither James nor Bones were morning people.

Hastily I sat up to another delightful morning on the Camino. I brushed past him to get my backpack. A little hum emanated from the Dutchman as I riffled through its contents, followed by a steady flow of idle chit chat about his interest in murderers. Jolliness in his voice, he began to explain about the 'peanut butter murder'. Such was his excitement to finish the story, he even followed me into the bathroom.

As I brushed my teeth, I learned about a man who injected his wife's food with concentrated doses of peanut particles. Every day for months, he slowly poisoned the highly allergic woman. Bastian gave minute details describing how it was the perfect crime. A lump formed in my throat as I wondered how someone could be so cruel. The husband slowly overdosed his partner, until eventually his meticulous attention to detail triggered her massive peanut allergy. Anaphylactic shock, then death. Bastian showed no empathy, just childlike delight in recounting the murder. As if he was proud someone was smart enough to pull it off.

On finishing, he declared, "I was the guy!"

I brushed my teeth slower. What's he telling me? *Would I have time to defend myself with a toothbrush?*

"The guy what?" I asked.

"No. You don't understand. I was the guy. Let me explain. I'm a chemist."

"Really...?"

"Yes. The peanut butter murderer. He asked me to send him journals."

"On what? How to kill people?" I took out my toothbrush in self defense. I'd seen those prison movies.

Bastian rubbed his palms together. "No. Not exactly how to kill people. He was in prison for some previous crime, and told the authorities he wanted to study to be a chemist when he was released. He sent his request for science journals to my lab. And some of them were

41

about poisons." Bastian smiled. "I was the deciding voice on his case. I made the choice to send the journals. Sometime after he was released from prison, he poisoned his wife."

Still wary about where the conversation was going, I put the toothbrush back in my mouth. His eyes flickered. I had an uneasy feeling he wanted something. Foam fell from my brush. He looked at the white froth and smiled. Strands of blood lay within.

"Foam," he said, "is unfathomable, don't you think? Like a brain disintegrating into acid." We both stared at the mess on the floor. I felt trapped in the empty bathroom. Why did he smell like horses? Quickly I spat the rest of the paste into the sink.

"Well, Bastian. Thanks for the morning update. You're my new guy for gruesome chats before breakfast. Maybe send me your podcast and I'll listen to you before bed. Would you like that?" He didn't answer. Lost somewhere, he kept staring at the foaming mess.

"Bastian? Hello. Bastian?" He just looked at me then smiled. "Are you waiting to use the shower or do you want to baptize my toothbrush?"

With a sigh, he said, "No. Nothing for me. Just. This is fun, isn't it?" He swirled my bloody toothpaste foam around with his bare toes. "I like the inner workings of the Camino. There is a depth. A dread. A death to it all. I think that's why I can't stop. I'll die if I finish. I've got to keep going."

"Sounds like you're a bit too infatuated by the Camino?"

"Brother, I'm just trying to walk the straight and narrow." With a wink he walked out.

A while later, the four of us stood at the crossroads on the cobbled path outside the albergue. Bastian scratched at his beard, seemingly conflicted about leaving us.

"Istanbul is a long way, baby," said Beautiful Bill, "but if you walk with us to Santiago, it's closer than Turkey. You can nearly touch its sweet sunrise. It's going to be so good. Think about it. You could baptize the bones of Saint James."

Bastian puffed out his cheeks. "No, Bill. No, I feel not. I've seen all the blood and bones I need to see in my lifetime."

A chill touched the back of my neck. His words reminded me of something my father had said years ago. People could tell you anything if they think they'll never see you again. They feel relief to share. On a train journey, a man once admitted to Dad that he'd murdered someone.

The incident left my father shaken as the man described a heinous crime of passion.

Bastian stared at us for a long moment, then nodded to himself. "Istanbul it is. For now at least."

"I'll stay off the peanut butter just in case," I said.

He laughed. "Good idea. You just never know. But now you're blessed. So we are family. Family takes care of each other."

"The Manson family," I muttered.

Turning to walk towards Santiago, I glanced back at him a couple of times. Strangely, he jumped over a wall into a field instead of following the Camino route along the road.

After another day's trek with Luka, Cassie and I fancied dinner alone. At a streetside dining table, in the chilly air, we toasted with a glass of wine then devoured a substandard meal of fish and runny potatoes.

Luka wandered past. He appeared to be the leader of a bunch of pilgrims that trailed in his wake. He didn't see us because his phone was stuck so close to his eyes. Did he need glasses? Presumably, he was trying to locate a restaurant using Google maps, but maybe he was high and watching an episode of Pokémon.

Suddenly, he pulled a move that would have made the exclamations of Mr. Clam-Hoarder proud, extravagantly pointing and giving a triumphant shout. The only problem was, his destination appeared to be up in the sky. Hungry pilgrims looked to the heavens. Expectant faces quickly became confused.

Oh, ye lost flock. You know not the way of LSD Bill. Embarrassment etched onto the pilgrims' faces. Muttered excuses. No one making eye contact. Slowly, everyone wandered off leaving Bill looking at the beautiful clouds. An awkward end to his brief leadership.

Forlorn, he looked around then spotted us. With a whimper of delight he rushed over. Immediately, he ranted about Google maps. Maps. Google. Google monks. Pilgrims. Priests. Nuns. Jesus. Toast. Hash. High Kings and sore feet. Finishing his stream of consciousness, he concluded breathlessly, "I'm utterly disgusted you ate without me, guys."

"Calm down," I said. "I didn't want to eat with anyone. I just wanted to enjoy my food in peace."

He looked inwards. Brown eyes searching his memory banks. "Alone," he nodded. "I get it." He sighed. Shoulders relaxed. Tension drained from his face. "I'm sure I need it, too. Buen Camino."

"Buen Bollocks," I replied.

...time travel

-

Day 6 - Zumaia to Deba
19km

Cassie

It's strange to wake up surrounded by your newfound Camino family, earplugs still half inserted and drool dried on the side of your mouth. Coffee and any sense of privacy are distant possibilities as you realize where you are and that you're supposed to walk 19km before lunch.

A wave of social panic reminiscent of middle school sinks in when your friends are already packed and headed out the door. Will you catch them? Will you ever see them again? Will we make new friends? Am I cool? Am I popular? The tendency of my mind to regress like this made me laugh out loud.

As I brushed my teeth to a chorus of morning ablutions, I briefly contemplated the unique social fabric that makes up a Camino family. There is really nothing else like it. I could see why most pilgrims do the Camino alone, and are usually in their 30-50's. I can't think of another place or activity where it's so easy to meet new people and make new friends. Back in real life, once you reach this age, it's much harder to initiate meaningful connections. And if you're socially awkward to begin with, it's nearly impossible.

On the Camino it was like being a teenager again. People strike up a conversation with a stranger without flinching, and if you walk together a while, forget it. You're friends for life by day's end.

As usual, James and I were last out the door around 7:30am. We couldn't get used to the morning rush to get on the road, so decided to rebel against it. We walked very fast, though, so despite leaving last, we were usually among the first to arrive at the end of the day.

About an hour into this day's walk, dark clouds starting to build on the horizon, James muttered, "Damn it!"

He knelt down in the grass, and rummaged wildly in his pack. He was looking for his poncho. As the unmistakable scent of fresh rain built around us, he realized his mistake. The next town was another 10km away, and there was nowhere to go but forward. Still searching, James discovered that in addition to his poncho, half of his clothes and twenty bucks worth of nuts were missing. As the rain started to fall, so did my spirits. I looked around for my puppy dog Luka, but he'd gone ahead with some other pilgrims.

Negative forces took over. My mind latched onto this small setback, using it as fuel to indulge in other topics deemed life-crushing enough to dominate my otherwise perfect day. I slogged forward in silence for the next couple hours, up and down a series of steep inclines, moving fast and breathing hard. I started feeling sad about Anthony Bourdain again, moved on to the state of American Trumpian politics and ended up exhausted, wanting to give up this whole Camino thing.

Giving up would prevent me from having to think about the shit that was *actually* upsetting me.

We'd decided to walk the Camino at the end of a long year of introspection. I imagined it was the kind of year old people look back on, remembering how tumultuous it was, and see how its events could change the course of an entire life. Introspection in retrospect.

India was still raw. I'd spent seven long years living there, and started a girls' soccer team for Tibetan refugees. This quickly grew into a social and geopolitical force so strong it attracted the attention of CNN, BBC, sports stars and major politicians. The wave of publicity, drama and personal intensity swallowed me whole, consuming every aspect of my life.

Things actually kicked off a decade earlier. Just out of university, I'd traveled to the Himalayas as a backpacker, looking for adventure and to study Buddhism in Dharamsala, home to the Dalai Lama and thousands of Tibetan refugees. My initial visit lasted six months, and I became more interested in the human rights situation than the religion. I met so many young Tibetans who'd trekked, on foot, with no possessions, over the highest peaks in the world, to reach the relative peace and freedom of India. Life in Tibet, under Chinese occupation, had become so terrifyingly oppressive, many Tibetan families preferred to send their children alone over the mountains rather than suffer under the yoke of Chinese rule. Hunted by PLA border guards and running the gauntlet of deadly snowstorms and avalanches, the risks were enormous but worth taking for the chance of freedom. Planned escapes continue to this day. When the children reach India, they're taken under the wing of the Tibetan government-in-exile, and raised in boarding schools where they get a decent education, and are free to practice their religious and cultural traditions. Most never see their families in Tibet again.

In 2010, years after my first visit, I returned to Dharamsala during my summer holidays while teaching high school history in California. After watching a World Cup match, a Tibetan friend dragged me into a ragtag photo exhibition put on by the Tibetan National Sports Association (an organization loosely tied to the machinery of the government-in-exile). As I surveyed the photographs and old trophies, I realized there was no sign of women playing the sport anywhere. In fact, there was not even a single female in the exhibition hall besides myself.

I already knew that gender inequality was a pressing issue in the Tibetan community. Among other indicators, friends and I had been appalled witnesses to extreme domestic violence with no intervention from authorities and no support offered to the victims. Many other observations from my visits came rushing to the forefront of my mind. Why did I never see young Tibetan women out socializing at night in the scores of cafes and pubs that festoon Dharamsala? Why were female Tibetans so quiet and shy compared to their brothers, lovers, husbands, fathers and male colleagues? Had I ever seen a Tibetan girl with a football or basketball playing in the street alongside the boys? There was a Tibetan national football team for men. Why wasn't there one for women?

Standing there, the photo exhibition enveloping me, I had a moment of pure epiphany. It would alter the course of my life, the lives of scores of young Tibetan women and, I'm told, the historical fabric of Tibetan society in the exile community.

Driven by a primal force, I approached the visitor book and wrote the words; *If you would like a women's football team, I would like to help you. Cassie Childers.*

After my signature I left my email address, then walked out. A month later, back home at my teaching job in America, I received a message from the Tibetan National Sports Association. They invited me to come back to Dharamsala full time to start a women's soccer team. Only, I'd have to do all the work, and raise all the money myself. There was no funding for such pursuits outside the men's game.

I spent the remainder of that school year planning how I'd approach this amazing but massively daunting opportunity. I sold all my worldly possessions, resigned from my job and bought that one-way ticket back to India. What happened next would prove so unexpected and intense,

46

that it was only now, eight years later on the Camino, that I felt able to process the seismic events that followed.

When we made it to the next town I was breathing heavily and shaking, trying to hide my emotions. James and the contents of his backpack were drenched. After reassuring each other with a long hug that I'd be okay to continue the last 5km alone, he decided to hop on a train back to Zumaia to get his poncho.

Unable to assuage the emotion coursing through my veins, I took my first steps on the Camino alone. In the pouring rain.

As James' train chugged into the distance, I saw my three Camino pals - LSD Bill, Tomasino from Tuscany and Boils from Finland - about to head up the path. As if sensing my turmoil, the three humongous men beckoned me over and embraced me. It's moments like these that make the Camino family so important. Despite not seeing me all day, they could somehow knew I needed them. And as much as I hated to admit it, we all need people sometimes. These dudes were into walking slow and singing that day. Finally able to slow my furious pace to match their more relaxed gait, my breathing calmed. Listening to their sampling of 80's hits sung with operatic bravado in the echoing forest brought a hint of a smile to my face. By the time we reached the albergue, I was singing, too. These boys were the balm I needed.

We spent that evening high on a hill overlooking the Cantabrian Sea, feeding bananas to a trio of adorable pigs, ignoring the new band of dark clouds on the horizon…

James

Do you ever go sideways in reality? If you're a bit older perhaps you even remember doing the time warp again…

Today I jumped into another multiverse. I assure you, Bill did not spike the water… that I know of… so I achieved this feat unaided. Using only a train as my time machine, I moved through space-time to glimpse how my life could be changed in the present for us pilgrims.

On the trail this misty morning, dark clouds rolled over the mountains so I naturally reached for my poncho. "Damn!" I must have left it at the convent in Zumaia. And this wasn't just any poncho. It was 'The Bourbon Street Poncho.' A plastic tourist heirloom from New Orleans that Cassie's mom gave me, covered in the iconic Bourbon Street sign.

The bloody convent was miles back. Clarity dawned as memories emerged from the fog of last night's wine. I remembered the blue paint flaking off the old cupboard in our spartan bedroom. Its dusty confines still held not only the poncho, but most of my nuts! It was a long way back, but even farther to the next stop. "Feck it."

Feeling guilty at the prospect of buying new stuff but mostly happy to roam alone for the day, I decided to return to the convent. But it wasn't so easy. First, I had to go another 8 kilometers onwards to Deba, to catch the train back to Zumaia.

Cassie and I held each other tight in the thundering downpour at the station. Her embrace fizzled my senses into life because I suddenly noticed I was on the wrong side of the tracks to board the train. The stop signal was already blaring red as the engine rushed towards us. Instinctively, I ran down the platform to make my connection, not realizing how much my backpack would slow me. I barely made it across the track without being squished. Passengers shook their heads in disdain, but the adrenaline was flowing and I had nuts and my neck to save.

It was a good day for the ducks in Zumaia. Puddles everywhere. Rain lashing the streets. My soaking feet were beginning to freeze when I saw the notice outside the convent gates. The place didn't open for another two hours. So I did what my brave Irish ancestors would have done. I took refuge in the local pub. Even getting in a game of pool with the proprietor.

Mildly intoxicated, I walked back to the convent. As I stuck my head around the wall I had my first jarring sense of time travel. These pilgrims, in this haphazard line, waiting for a bed, could've been part of *my* life if I'd started the Camino a day later. Part of each new high and low. All my world and stories.

Acting like I owned the place, I pushed through the throng of my alternative travel companions to the front door. We shared curious glances. Their eyes shouting, 'Who is this bastard interloper looking like a drowned rat?' I could sense that my Camino experience would've been totally different with these people. *Same, same, but different...*

At the door, I turned and noticed their bonds, smiles and winks. How they hugged and cheered the late arrivals. Each person glanced at me as if I'd jumped out of my storybook and into their fairytale. I felt wrong, but my nuts and poncho quest felt right.

An overpowering curiosity kept me studying these Past People to see if I'd like them to be my Future Folk. They were Americans mostly. Twenty-somethings. Strong, athletic. A smattering of older Europeans with limps. Others looked like they were from somewhere recognizable, but sounded like they were from nowhere in particular. This group even had a little dog, and a woman clutching a child's hand. Such different tales from around the world I would have heard. Our individual realities would create new tangents and facets to forge our communal atmosphere. I only needed to wait a day and all this could be mine. Or speed up one day to meet new pilgrims ahead of our group, to share another part of the world.

Tagging along behind a loud group checking in, I managed to sneak past the clerk. As gently as possible, I tried the latch on the door of the room where we slept last night. Unlocked, it clicked open easily. Inside, the saints painted on the walls witnessed my sin. *Had anyone ever broken into this convent before?* I studied their accusing eyes, daring them to alert the Vatican police. None moved in their frames, so I opened the cupboard. It was bare bones! My stuff had been snaffled. Most likely put in the lost and found box? I tipped my imaginary hat to the saints, thanked them for their shelter and was gone.

In my pilgrim disguise, I was able to mingle easily. Finding the lost and found box, I rummaged through its moldy interior. My nuts appeared but not my poncho.

Hmmmm...? I remembered Cassie reading on Camino message boards that many pilgrims reported thefts along the Way. Could someone have gone into my bag while I was sleeping, or while I showered, and stolen my poncho? Now I thought about it, I'm pretty sure I'd never taken that poncho out of my bag to put it in the cupboard... But if someone did steal from me, why just take a poncho?

Whatever the story, I thought, best just tell Cassie's mother I donated the poncho to a wet monk. No new son-in-law wants a New Jersey matriarch on their case any sooner than necessary.

Enjoying my nuts on the train back to the future, I smiled at the nature of Camino connections. The Way is so simple. If you don't like what you have in the present, you can easily peer into your life a day in the future or past.

So relax. Investigate the possibilities of your alternative lives. You can do this until you find your perfect day and continue on with your favorite family.

Raucous cheers from my pilgrim crew heralded my arrival at the albergue.

"Buen Camino," they chorused.

"Buen Bollocks," I replied with a smile.

Cassie beckoned me to sit next to her at the wooden table that everyone sat around.

David, the recently retired English gent, with a succulent voice fit for radio, put it to good use by commanding his subjects to make way for me. I squeezed in as the playful groans of rebellion rose up faster than the bits of bread thrown at David for his haughtiness. A glass of red wine was poured from one of the many bottles on the damp table. Cassie and I held hands under the table as Nicole and Misha, the two middle-aged Germans and slowest of the group because of their bad knees, argued about something that threw them into fits of laughter.

Squished in next to David was Patrick, the bespectacled, serious history teacher from Ireland. Anxiously he tore at bits of a paper while he left his wine untouched. Tomasino, the 19-year-old Italian blacksmith took up the space of two. Young Lina, who shone like the moon if it wore a blond wig and had plump red cheeks, said something in German to me that I didn't understand, so she stuck her tongue out. In excited glee, she reached into the bag on her lap then placed a little stuffed unicorn on the table.

"I love your t-shirt," she squealed. I looked down to see I was wearing my strange space-cat-sitting-on-a-unicorn shirt. "It's such a magic day," she said smiling, then went back to whispering into the ear of a much older Finnish guy with an enormous bulldog head. His eyes twinkled like a naughty school boy as he listened to whatever tales she told.

Slowly, I began to relax a little in their company. A fast splash of silly and serious conversations rippled. It was refreshing how easily honesty flowed here, becoming ever more free-flowing with each subsequent glass of wine. Tomasino, the giant youth, stood up then tapped his glass with a spoon. We were expecting another toast, but he burst out into Italian opera. David, who couldn't get the wine down fast enough, was the first to try to match Tomasino's high notes, followed by the baritone voice emanating from the acoustic setting of the Finn's large head. Suddenly, the Germans were at it, and soon our whole table was operatic. Except for me. The close proximity of the people made me feel unsafe. Also, it didn't help that 5 minutes before, I'd somehow managed to spill half a bottle of wine, splattering its contents over a few people at the table.

In the end though, I did join in for a few bars of a Frank Sinatra tune. I know it's the Way of Saint James, but I'm sure the apostle would have been okay with us all singing, "My Way."

...bin bags

—

Day 7 – Deba to Markina-Xemein
16km

Cassie

Our albergue was a converted cattle shed, so the torrential downpour reverberating on the corrugated tin roof prevented any of the usual lively conversation over the usual breakfast of packaged cakes and instant coffee. I purposely slowed the pace of my morning routine, knowing that this was bound to be a long, wet day for poor James. Maybe the rain would calm down a bit.

It wasn't hard to slow down, as the 20 people we shared a room with were practically out the door by the time I'd removed my eye mask. The albergue was without a morning host, leaving it to pilgrims to show themselves out, so we relaxed until 9am, two hours after everyone else left.

Our tall friend LSD Bill stayed behind with us again and found some garbage bags in the back of a high cupboard. I cut them up and we constructed a makeshift waterproof pack cover for James.

As we walked out the door, we saw the sun emerging through the clouds. We only walked through the drizzle for about 10 minutes before the rain stopped completely. The benefits of starting late paid off.

Today we decided to stay off the Camino proper, and instead followed a network of single-lane farm roads. We heard this part of the trail was extremely muddy even on dry days, and also very windy. Being that it rained all night and the wind was still howling, we didn't want to risk a filthy, miserable mess. It's always smart to check Camino message boards for trail conditions, especially on the Camino del Norte, which is infamous for mud and rain. There are almost always alternative routes

51

you can muster up. I simply used the maps app on my smartphone to navigate a new route for the day.

It was the right decision. We spent the day walking lonely lanes past deserted old farmhouses, feeding horses and admiring the gorgeous Basque mountains.

James was acting strange, like he had something to tell me. I could sense the wheels of his mind were spinning, and trusted he'd share what he was thinking about when the time was right.

When we rolled into Markina, we were dry as a bone. And the first to arrive, despite our delayed departure. Touché.

We checked into the private albergue. I heard the owner was a trained chef and constructs magical dinners for guests. Private albergues differ from municipal. The latter are usually owned and operated by the town council or local church parish. They are normally more barebones, and costs are cheap or by donation. Just a simple bunk, with only a disposable sheet provided, or none at all. Private albergues generally are a higher standard. Maybe they include sheets and pillows, offer more sophisticated food and service; stronger wifi, lockers, and usually better showers. Typically, the price is only slightly higher and well worth it.

In this case, the Camino rumor mill was wrong about the food. Totally decent pilgrim menu of salad, pasta, and fried fish with chips, but it was nothing special. However, the owner does shout at you like a real chef (you know what I'm talking about if you've ever worked in a restaurant).

James

I was still poncho-less, despite yesterday's travel back in time. However, Cassie and LSD Bill had cut up a black bin bag so I could brave the torrential rain that battered the northern Way. Pulling the bag over my head, the acetate smell of plastic immediately flooded my mind with memories.

I'm eight years old staying with my grandparents. My spritely, gnome-like grandmother would dress my brother and me up for Halloween. Other kids would be dressed as superheroes or a leprechaun, but the adults dressed us in black bags with dark boot polish smeared on our faces. I never figured out what we were supposed to be, although my grandfather did once refer to me as "Binman"... so I went with that, even if Marvel never would.

Looking back, I think this unintentional racism gave us extra reign to run wild through the neighbourhood. With our innocent black faces and our flautist friend Nigel, the plan was to trick or treat our way to sweets and money. But never fruit. Upon the door opening, Nigel would play his flute badly while we did a weird, jive bunny dance that made us look like two racist, dancing hobos.

Thirty years later, Binman had made a glorious return. Except now under the weight of my backpack, each labored step created stifling heat causing sweat to ooze down my torso, soaking my clothes.

Mud puddles were thick enough to suck our shoes off, so we were constantly jumping here and there. Bill fell on his arse a few times, soaking his cigarettes. He was not a happy bunny.

An abandoned farmhouse looked like a good place to relieve myself. As I got closer I saw footprints, little and large, leading towards the rubble-strewn building. "I'm going to drain my weasel," I told the others.

"We're coming, too," they chorused.

"Can't a man piss in peace?" I muttered to myself, feeling claustrophobic in the bin bag. Alone time would be good.

Rotting beams of wood, doors barred with rusted nails and windows broken. Only the wind whistled within. Clusters of nettles grew around the house, a natural defense against soft-skinned humans. Rain made the jagged leaves emit a dangerous scent, pricking my throat in warning.

Hair stood up on my neck. Someone was watching from the top window. Light and dark danced in the house. My chest constricted. Claustrophobia overwhelmed me. In panic, I tried to pull the bin bag over my head but filth washed over my face in the slick darkness. Somehow the bag had bunched up and I couldn't get it off my head. Blind, my ears pricked up. I froze. Someone was tapping on the window. Was it coming out? I tore at the bag and daylight streamed in as I pulled off fists full of plastic. Blood thumping, I wiped away the bag sweat to see shadows retreat from the window.

"Guys," I shouted without turning. "Come over here."

Cassie was soon at my side. "What's up, honey?"

"Look."

Cassie stared at the window. "What?"

"I think there's someone in there."

"No," she said. "That house has got to be empty." Again, shadows danced over light within. Clasping my hand tight, she peered a little closer. "Okay. Let's go. That guy did tell us about those hermit, homeless people moving into these abandoned houses. Don't really want to disturb them, do we?"

Only yesterday we learnt an American woman was attacked years ago on the Camino. Some local guy moved the clam signs so she ended up at his house. Later her body was discovered buried in the wilderness. Her hands were missing. Cops only found the culprit after he aroused suspicion trying to change hundred dollar bills at a nearby village market.

"Where's Luka?" I asked. We turned. Only swaying nettles guarded the grounds. Footprints dotted the muddy area. I didn't want to call out again in case someone came barreling out the door. Both our hands were clammy as I pulled Cassie along to find Bill. Crushing each other's fingers in shock, we found him lying motionless on the grass. His eyes were closed. "Bill!" His eyelids shot open.

"Shhhhh," he whispered.

"What?" I said.

"They know you are here. Look."

I looked around then back at him. "Who?"

He pulled up his jacket. On his bare belly he'd arranged three cigarettes. "I'm trying to dry them. You'll wake them. Shhhhh."

What a bollocks. "Get up. We're going."

"Why?"

"Cause there's someone in the house."

"Really?" His eyes widened in interest. "Who? I'm going to ask them for tobacco."

"No. Private property. Could be some crazy guy." Bill nodded as if this were a good thing. Finally he realised we just wanted to leave.

Each of us confused in different ways, we hurried back to the path. Little and large footprints that led to the house also now headed in the direction we were walking. *Why did the footprints make me so anxious?*

"Stupid question," I said. "But did you see these little footprints going away from the house earlier?" Cassie shook her head. Bill blew on a damp cigarette to dry the tobacco then looked down at the prints.

"Why? You're acting a bit strange, Seamus. Did you make a new enemy-friend in that house?" He lunged in to tickle me under the chin. "Did you make a cute little enemy? You're so cute. We have bigger problems, you know." He waved a damp cigarette at me.

They must have seen the stress in my face, because they both looked at me with worried expressions. What was I supposed to say? That I felt a deathly connection to the scary shadows, and I think the little footprints here are from the same person in the house? Anger and resentment began to course through my veins. This felt confrontational.

54

I needed them to stop looking at me. Their stares made me feel so unsafe.

This insecurity wracks my mind and body at times, making me act crazy. It's so hard to talk about mental health. I've only been married to Cassie a year. I've not told her how overwhelmed I can get. I can't be seen to be so weak.

We walked on in silence for five minutes. The little footprints abruptly vanished, greatly disturbing me.

Cassie rested her head on my shoulder. "The footprints," she said. "I don't think it's really a mystery. The child just got picked up. Someone just picked up the child and carried her is all that happened."

Of course. I'm so stupid. Wrapped up in my own world, I was adding all sorts of supernatural layers. The child just got lifted up. We could even see where the adult prints looked heavier from the weight where they both continued on.

Bill coughed out cigarette smoke and tried to speak but just sputtered unintelligible words before clearing his throat. "When did James become scared of footprints? What are you? Afraid of kids? Come on, man. I'm hungry. I could eat a horse. And a beer always seems good medicine for you."

Cassie and I discussed the footprints as we trudged. "What if the footprints are of some ghostly little pilgrim?" I asked, joking. She loved the question as she believes in all manner of unseen creatures and energies. Her words began to relax me as we all talked about multi-dimensions and unseen realities. She even offered to go back to the house with me to ask about the child. But, despite my fixation on the prints, we kept plodding forward.

The winds picked up, bringing the serrated scent of nettles. Again, little footprints began to appear beside the adult prints in the mud. Ahead, rain caused a little river to flow across the path. I stopped dead when I saw the adult and child footprints went into the river but neither walked out. What could we all do but shrug in surprise and continue on our way? Except I couldn't shrug off the sense of worry that drained any enjoyment from the rest of my day.

Ultimate Lightweight Camino Packing List

Start with a backpack of about 32-liter capacity. Waist straps are important.

Fill it with:

- sleeping bag liner
- quick-drying pack towel
- two complete walking outfits (top, bottom, underwear) of quick-dry material
- pajamas that can double as loungewear
- lightweight jacket
- flip-flops
- hat
- waterproof trail runner sneakers
- heavy duty socks with a high % of wool. avoid cotton.
- heavy duty poncho
- earplugs & eye mask
- sunscreen & sunglasses
- smartphone & charger + earbuds
- shampoo & conditioner bars + containers
- toothbrush & toothpaste
- blister kit with Compeed & Engo Patches
- rehydration salts for summer walkers
- naproxen & other medications as needed
- water bottle
- hand sanitizer
- passport, insurance info, ATM card
- small, foldable handbag to carry valuables during evenings out

Albergue Etiquette

❖ Ear plugs, eye mask and a small torch or light are absolute necessities.

❖ If you snore, consider skipping the albergue, and carry extra earplugs for your bunkmates who may have forgotten them.

❖ If you come back to the room late at night, or leave very early in the morning, do NOT turn on the lights. Have your clothes and everything you need laid out in advance, and use a small torch or your phone's light instead of waking up the whole room.

❖ Rustle through your bag and pack somewhere away from sleeping heads.

❖ Whispering is a thing. Do it.

❖ When you arrive, claim your bunk by spreading some non-valuable belongings on it. Never put your dirty pack on the mattress.

❖ Leave your stinking shoes and socks outside somewhere.

❖ Don't use up all the hot water. Take quick showers.

❖ Leave space on drying racks and clotheslines for others.

❖ Theft is common. Never leave your valuables out. Use a small bag to carry them everywhere you go, even the shower.

❖ If the doors are still locked when you arrive, get in line for a bed by placing your pack or your shoes in a queue outside the door. Take turns keeping watch with others.

❖ Always be considerate of others, and put the good of all above the good of yourself. It's the choice you made when you decided to stay in an albergue.

Know the Basque

Basque is one of Europe's most fascinating subcultures, and often overlooked, even by pilgrims who walk clear through the region from one end to the other. They are one of the only surviving examples of pre-Christian heritage on the Iberian Peninsula, and the continent as a whole. The Basque language is so ancient that no one can even begin to trace its origins, and much of its culture is tied to a rich, animistic nature-worship the Popes would have had a major problem with.

There are whispers that the Basque are descended from the inhabitants of the lost city of Atlantis itself, lending to their unique genetic makeup. Today, Basque people consider themselves wholly different from the Spanish, a country with an independent heart and soul swallowed up by its more powerful neighbor. For centuries the Basque people have fought to regain independence from various foreign powers, most recently via a long series of violent separatist protests ending in 2011.

Today Basque Country maintains a certain level of autonomy within Spain and a peaceful balance has been struck. Don't hesitate to ask the Basque people about their country, and while in this region never assume the locals you're interacting with are Spanish.

San Sebastián Basics

Skip the municipal albergue & stay in the Old Quarter where the center of the foodie & cultural action is.

Instead of big sit-down meals, hop from one bar to the next sampling *pintxos*, (pin-chos). Pick up a map at the tourist office to guide you to the most popular places.

If you want a rest day to give your new blisters a chance to heal, don't hesitate to do it here. It's an amazing city worth your time.

Double your budget for San Sebastián, it's the most pricey stop on the Norte.

Be sure to sample *sagardoa*, Basque alcoholic apple cider, served dry and poured from a height with great pizzazz.

Steal half a day on San Seb's *La Perla Beach*, urban beach elegance at its best.

Take a short boat ride to Santa Clara Island, and have a drink and some seafood at its waterside *chiringuito*.

Many pilgrims opt to start their Camino in San Sebastián after flying into its airport. We recommend starting in Irun, though, because that first stage is perhaps the most dramatic of the entire Norte. Most pilgrims don't realize the airport is *actually in Irun.*

This is your last chance to stock up on major supplies/equipment until Bilbao.

Dine at one of 7 Michelin -starred restaurants for a splurge.

WEEK 2

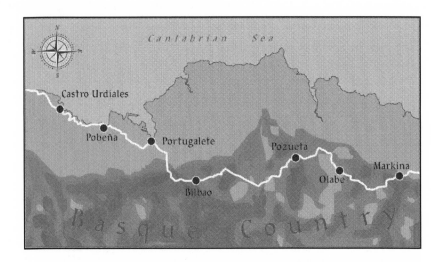

...breakup ballads

-

Day 8 - Markina to Olabe
16km

Cassie

Walking along, I knew things would be changing soon. Our group of 14 was closer than ever, but I could sense our Camino family would start unraveling. Not only did everyone have different schedules for reaching Santiago, but it also seemed we'd energetically fulfilled the purposes of the new friendships. The time to part ways was drawing near. The fast companionships brought much comfort and support to everyone during the Camino's first week, but sometimes for real significant transformation, we must shove out from the safe harbor and sail the open seas alone.

Today happened to be our one year wedding anniversary, and I made the mistake of mentioning it to Bill. Eyes wide with wonder, he immediately started giddily hopping around the albergue, spreading the news to our fellow pilgrims as they bandaged feet and brushed teeth.

People seemed surprisingly excited. I mean, who cares? But then I realized, everyone else was walking alone. All these other pilgrims in our Camino family, are off alone, with little or no mention of a significant other elsewhere. *Maybe they need to believe in love*, I thought.

Before long, I noticed some whispering amongst themselves. A party was in the works, I was sure. Oh, well. James and I decided to enjoy it and make it a double celebration. For I predicted it would also be our last big hoorah with the gang, though no one had actually said it out loud.

LSD Bill was scuttering around me all day. Rushing up ahead on the trail at times, doing god knows what, he'd then fall back again to 'check' on me and James. He was like a child on the playground, delighted to be running free and meeting new kids, but occasionally looking back at mom and dad for reassurance.

"So, uh... how's it going, Bill?" I asked on one such occasion, curious to hear what he'd say.

"Oh, you know. You know, Cassie. I mean... Young Mike. Just enjoying the beautiful day and the beautiful walk and the... beautiful girl." He grinned maniacally and bounded off ahead at rapid speed before I could respond.

Ahhhh. Beautiful girl. I'd noticed him cozying up to Gerta, the singing, redheaded German chick ten years his senior. I had attempted to connect with her a few times, but found her guarded. She had a story to tell, for sure, but wasn't ready to share it. She always lit up when Bill was paying her attention, hanging on to his every word and laughing at all his ridiculous jokes.

I thought back to the day we first met Bill. Within five minutes he'd offered us LSD and shown us a picture of his Austrian girlfriend, gushing about her beauty and how much he loved her. *So much for the innocence of Bill*, I thought.

To ensure we all stayed together for the impending party, James and I called ahead and booked beds at a small albergue. Meanwhile Tomasino, the young blacksmith from Tuscany, volunteered to cook dinner – pasta, of course, helped by eager English David.

First in the door, I saved a bunk for Bill next to ours. When he showed up a few minutes later, he politely pulled me aside. "Cassie. I mean, Mike. Thank you so much for saving me the bed. But, I'm going to sleep on the floor."

"Sleep on the floor?" I inquired. "Why? There's a bed for you right here, man."

He fidgeted as he looked around the room, lowering his voice. "I'm going to sleep on the floor next to Gerta. In the game room. Like a campout. Just for fun. Right?" He raised his eyes, searching for my approval.

I stared back at him deeply, his eyes transfixed on mine. I wouldn't release him from my gaze. I didn't need to say anything. He could feel it. His shoulders began to slump, begging me for moral emancipation.

It was an evening that produced the kind of warmth usually reserved for intimate occasions with your dearest friends and family. Everyone pitched in, much wine was poured, and we took over the entire hostel with our Camino family, pulling in stragglers we'd only just met.

Everything perfectly fell into place. The owner of the charming *Albergue Andiketxe* was the coolest guy ever and went out of his way to accommodate our party. A bottle of champagne appeared, a guitar materialized, and good vibes were so thick you could cut 'em with a knife.

After an animated dinner that would make pure Tuscanos proud, I felt a wave of emotion come over me. I knew that even though it was time to say goodbye, I would still miss these folks on the road ahead. I wondered how many of them could feel it, too.

I stood up and banged my wine glass with a knife. The speech that followed acknowledged the truth that no one wanted to say out loud. Yes, we were all going to have to split up – but I also honored the incredible fortune we'd fallen into, meeting each other and sharing our first week on the Camino together. Tears filled the room. Even the faces of the manliest of the men were awash with emotion, and I could see they had all known in their hearts it was time to start splitting up. As I stood there in front of them at the head of a long wooden table, I reminded everyone of the human chain we'd seen the other day. I let them know James and I would be falling back tomorrow, intent on slowing down, but we'd be the final link in our own human chain that was now forming along the length of the Camino. No matter what troubles they might come across, we were just behind, ready to back them up.

We can't remain innocent forever. We are destined to make mistakes. I knew Bill was making one. But I also realized he had to play this thing out, whatever it was, in order to learn what he needed to move forward in life. It may turn out that someone gets hurt in the process, but I somehow knew he wouldn't regret it, either.

The evening was the perfect ending to a beautiful series of interactions with a diverse group of people united by the love of freedom and the willingness to do what it takes to truly feel it.

One year ago, James and I had eloped on the southernmost point in Spain, alone and in love. Now, on the northernmost point in Spain exactly a year later, we were more in love than ever and surrounded by true friends to celebrate our bond. Through the trials and tribulations of love and romance, we'd both hurt so many people along the way, and been hurt ourselves. But without those experiences, we'd never have learned what we needed to know to come together as we had.

As the music lowered and punch-drunk pilgrims headed off to bed, I looked into the starlit hills and said a little prayer that it would turn out as good for Bill as it had for me.

James

Pilgrims awoke. I felt them flow past. Bill shook me but I didn't open my eyes. Pressure from my blocked ear threatened to burst my brain. Infection ran rampant. The left side of my face was tenderized, sizzling meat.

In a daze, I finally got out of bed. Dark bags bloomed under my eyes reflected in the mirror. Snot dribbled from my left nostril. I blew my nose. "FUCK!!" I keeled over. Did I just have a mini stroke? The pressure had practically blown out my eardrum. I pulled myself up to the mirror. My right eyelid drooped while the left eye streamed tears. *What was the point of this fucking Camino?*

Pockets of pilgrims trekked up the ancient tree-lined path towards Olabe, chattering madly or puffing hard, depending on their age and injury. I tried walking with my eyes closed to get some extra rest, but jumped back in fright when I found myself too close to the edge. The rocks below our dusty path would release me from life and splatter my memories. A horrid compulsion pushed me to jump.

Maybe it was my bad ear trying to listen too hard. Stupid mind. This cliff is not a siren song. Re-calibrate. What's so interesting down there anyway? Below, horses talked conspiratorially while a dog chased some sheep around black plastic cylindrical bales of hay. None of the horses seemed to match Gypsy Mullet's description.

Horse scanning and avoiding a fatal fall were the themes of the morning until idyllic harp music washed over our sweaty group from a whitewashed cottage that dotted the Way. LSD Bill was a little ahead, deep in conversation with the willowy Gerta. This German pilgrim spoke perfect English, and seemed open yet vague on why she walked. A sadness appeared on her face when she thought no one was looking. Although, Bill's force of friendliness had her laughing now.

Serenity shifted to chaos when a flock of sheep burst onto the path in front of us. Packed cloud-tight, dozens of woolly creatures bleated as they bounced up the road. Bill began to visibly vibrate. Gerta tried to pull him back but it was too late. Arms flailing, he turned to us looking awestruck as if he had seen a giant, fluffy joint. "Sheep!" he squealed. Heavy backpack no deterrent to his glee, he bounded after the creatures with a girly giggle.

Like a little old woman worried about her grandchildren, I clenched up in fear when the sheep scattered dangerously close to the cliff's edge, trying to avoid crazed Bill.

"Stop, you stupid bastard!" shouted Tomasino, breathing heavily under the weight of his giant pack, as he jogged past me to try to catch the manic Austrian.

In no time, three more pilgrims were huffing past to stop Bill. This was turning into The Running of the Pilgrims.

From an open gate higher up the path, a snarling, bushy-bearded farmer appeared. Brandishing a glimmering pitchfork, he smashed the steel prongs into the path. Sheep surged around him into the field. Bill slowed, but this friendly force of nature couldn't stop his exuberant momentum.

Like Poseidon with his mighty trident, the farmer dared Bill to come closer by smashing the pitchfork into the ground even harder. LSD Bill could not be slowed. He was next to the farmer in a flash, arm extended in such a happy greeting that it momentarily shook the farmer's resolve. The man looked at his own hand in disbelief as it reciprocated Bill's greeting. But at the last moment he came to his senses, whipping his hand back then pointing the fork towards the exuberant wanderer. The frothing farmer spat a barrage of guttural Basque obscenities. This just made Bill beam brighter, driving the farmer into hysterics. The prongs were thrust forward to skewer Bill.

Coming from behind, Tomasino's massive arms swung Bill away. Again the farmer erupted and banged the fork against the ground while his other hand pointed to the sheep, then to the steep edge.

Bill began to apologize, finally realizing the precarious position he'd forced upon the sheep. The farmer spat on the ground. Astonishing us all, Bill snapped. His jolly nature evaporated as he morphed into a fist-pumping fool shouting about his freedom of expression and right to walk where he wished.

What do these rural people think of us pilgrims? We're holy shit to some of them. Trespassing on their lands. Worrying their animals. Disturbing the peace. Singing stupid songs.

Cautiously, the rest of our group neared the glaring farmer. Embarrassed, some offered more apologies, but I'm sure he'd seen it all before and was no doubt expecting trouble again. Based on his occasional spitting into the ditch as we walked by, nothing could've been said to help the situation.

A little later we rested to eat whatever food we'd brought. I munched on some nuts while the sour juice from an unripened orange stung my throat. Heavy weariness took me and I felt the power drain from my body and seep out from my feet. I sat with my eyes closed against a mossy tree a little away from the group. Cassie gave Bill a good whack on the back of the head for crimes against sheep. I was happy with that. It reminded me my wife takes no bullshit. I'm proud of the woman I met in the snowy Himalaya. I could easily have missed Dharamsala and my neighbor the Dalai Lama. Such thoughts took me down memory lane.

Ten years ago, lost in the Ladakhi mountains of Northern India, I accidentally ended up in a restricted zone where foreigners were not permitted. Not knowing I risked deportation, I hitchhiked deeper into ancient tribal lands. Tradition was strong in the village of Turtuk. Women did the manual labour, hauling rocks on their backs to build the foundations of new houses, while men looked on smoking copious amounts of marijuana. Custom decreed I was fed and sheltered. I heard how Turtuk was designated Indian territory at partition. But after the First Kashmir War, the locals woke up one morning to find they were part of Pakistan until India retook the area again in 1971. My days were spent listening to melancholy music sung by shy children, eating delicious apricots, marveling at the village's irrigation or heating systems, and finding burial sites scattered among the mountains. But I was so busy searching for a way to not feel so constantly stressed, I couldn't relax with these peaceful people.

An ancient man wrinkled in so many folds of time that I could barely see his eyes, would follow me as best he could. Eventually, someone translated that he wanted to tell me about Vipassana meditation. A Buddhist practice, chased out of India a thousand years ago by Hindu priests because, the locals said, it actually worked. These were greedy priests who only wanted to treat mental issues for money and on the basis of returning customers. But if you had a meditation that actually helped the mind... well, that was like giving away free health care! These Hindu clergy wanted respect, wealth and power. Effective treatment didn't fit into that equation.

Vipassana has crept back into India in the last hundred years. After navigating my way thousands of kilometers south to find a meditation center, I finally reached Dharamsala, the seat of the Tibetan government-in-exile. Damp moss clung to the tall trees surrounding the wooden huts of the Vipasanna centre, situated on a windswept hill inhabited by wild monkeys. I learned Vipassana consisted of ten days of total silence, practicing the strict meditation technique twelve hours a day. Up at 4am. Finishing about 9pm. And that's just the beginners' course! I struggled deeply. People left every day, teachers admonishing them for quitting because a fallen student had taken the place of someone who had the mental strength to endure the training and achieve a sense of inner peace.

Mental and physical pain were constant. Teachings were tedious and deep. I thought my knees would blow out sitting cross-legged as my brain trickled out my ears. Liberation is the desired state that one needs to be aware of constantly. Remain equanimous to all. I went as deep as I could, but mostly, all I learned was how to meditate, not the deeper levels of true Vipassana.

Paradoxically, I nearly got into a fight with a fellow practitioner in those peaceful confines. I had even more trouble sleeping than I do now. At the centre, I shared a tiny, freezing room with a tough, little Spanish guy. I thought everything was okay between us. Of course I didn't have much to go on. We never spoke and were forbidden to make eye contact. On the seventh day, I returned to our room to find his bag packed. Obviously he'd had enough. Curiously, he was scrawling endless words on reams of toilet paper. We made eye contact.

"What's wrong?" I asked, my voice weak from lack of use. "Are you okay?"

"I'm leaving to see the fucking Dalai Lama!" His anger boiled over and his next words hissed out. "His teachings are on in Dharamsala and they don't want me to go. And you... What's wrong with you?" He threw some pebbles, barely missing my head. "Why didn't you just tell me to stop snoring? Instead of banging around in bed and breaking the door. What's wrong with you? Just tell me to stop. Wake me. Why did you punish me!?"

Going from complete silence to confrontational overload took time for me to process. Slowly it dawned on me I must've been thrashing around in bed. When trying to sleep, I suffer from this incredible pain in my shoulders and arms that forces me to violently jolt to ease the pain. Since I'd been practicing at the centre, Vipassana put me in a state that helped release my emotional energy. At night, the pain became unbearable as the energy coursed through my arms and out my hands. Constantly, I slammed myself around the bed, then would rush out into the freezing dark night to cool down, only to return and repeat.

"Give me the toilet paper," I insisted. Reluctantly, he passed it to me. Angry words scrawled all over. All against me. I must've totally messed up his meditation. His sleep. His life. In his mind, I was banging around to be vindictive because he kept me awake snoring. I felt terrible. By luck, he was an understanding, forgiving man and after I'd explained myself, we were both laughing at the absurdity of it all. If nothing else, we learned if people don't communicate, that's when the real trouble starts.

I kept the toilet paper as a souvenir, and we've kept in touch since. I even bumped into him months later and we had a few pints. Putting aside the rules of the centre, we didn't shut up for hours.

It was around this time in Dharamsala that I met Cassie. Still searching for all sorts, little did I know I'd found my future wife on a snowy night in a refugee colony.

Now on our first anniversary, on a cold evening on the Camino, we're celebrating with more wandering seekers.

At the albergue on the cracked stone balcony overlooking the terraced green hills, we found chairs and low walls to mingle and rest. A heady smell of marijuana wafted up from the apple trees. A little drunk, I half expected to see the wrinkly mountain man of Turtuk, but it was just the proprietor smiling up at us. Bill rushed down in a flash, tapping him for some sweet smoke.

Boils the Bulldog, our fearsome Finnish comrade, found a guitar. He beckoned us all to sit, then commanded Cassie and me to hold hands while maintaining uncomfortably deep eye contact with us as he sang entirely ill-chosen songs about breakups and broken hearts. We smiled and swayed, but needed another drink to wash down his bitter melancholy.

Pulling Gerta along, Bill bounded back onto the packed balcony. Both red-eyed and laughing, he had her instantly dancing to Boils' breakup ballads.

"Boils, man," said Bill, whirling around. "You're killing us all. I'm so happy I could cry. Let me play one song." Bill turned out to be a guitar expert. Head bopping, foot stomping, he attacked a symphony. "And this one is for my favorite enemies, James and Cassie." Nirvana's *Smells Like Teen Spirit* crashed over the balcony causing dogs to howl. Everyone loved it. If I had a bin bag, I'd have gotten up and done a little Halloween hobo jig.

Last ones standing were Cassie, me and English David, his voice for the radio now tuned to slobbering baby-talk directed at the dog by his feet. Away from prying eyes, Bill and Gerta were sleeping upstairs on the floor. It's interesting. All these pilgrim people are searching and hoping to find something. Most of our Camino crew had left relationships behind. Spouses and partners, all left to wonder what's happening on the holy road.

Silently I toasted the Universe, by tipping some wine onto the Earth. With one last whispered toast to love, Cassie and I watched the stars twinkle. It was her greatest dream to walk the Camino. Doing it while celebrating in style made us glow. Hopefully, I could make a few more of her dreams come true as the years roll by. Tonight she drunkenly whispered she wanted a pet pig called Augustus Disgustus the Turd, and a Pomeranian dog called Puff. I was told we'll need a motorbike with a sidecar so the animals can travel with us for our new life on the open road. How can you not love a woman who has such dreams?

...hangovers

-

Day 9 - Olabe to Pozueta
12km

Cassie

Emotions banged out. One foot in front of the other. Things come up. Desperate anxiety like someone is holding a gun to your head. So grateful I can separate the feelings from reality now. There was a time when I couldn't. Every anxious pang felt like a sign my world was about to end.

The simple act of walking all day, every day, with little to distract you, allows the negative emotions to work themselves free from your cellular structure. When we act strong and stuff our feelings inside, they don't dissipate. They get stored in our muscles, nerves and organs. Walking, walking. One foot in front of the other. The stored feelings loosen up, begin to circulate through your body again. Hands shake one moment, a stomachache the next. Heart races. Face turns red. A long forgotten situation from years or even decades ago, finally comes back to haunt you because you were previously too scared to let yourself feel it. Up another hill, around another bend. You have to keep walking. Don't try to push the feelings back inside again. This time, allow them to course through your veins, feel them. Cry, scream if you need to. Do not be afraid. They can't hurt you anymore, unless you keep letting them live inside you.

Nothing is wrong. Healing is happening through a process of release. It requires feeling the uncomfortable sensations again, maybe a few times, but not reacting to them and just letting them pass by.

You keep walking through the emotion. You breathe heavy, it's released and gone forever. You're a little lighter, a bit more free, and you have faith that the Way is providing.

Too much wine for the anniversary. So much joy last night. Why do I feel this gun against my head today?

A very quiet night in the very small *Caserio Pozueta* albergue followed, allowing space to ponder after a long day of quiet walking. We had hung back again in the morning, deliberately walking slower, allowing the others to majorly move ahead of us. We wanted a clean break - to release them to find their own paths forward, and to release ourselves, sensing there was more to this than just fun and games. Like clockwork, with the distractions of Bill and the others in the distance, the anger started coming up. And oh so angry I was.

A few days ago, next to a crumbling fountain, we passed the two Spanish travelers whose performance made me cry. An ancient, haunting ballad echoing of gypsies, late nights under the stars, lost love and hopelessness. Their song transfixed me, sweeping me away to another time and space. My tears were wrenched out by some unstoppable force, rising through me like a freight train. I couldn't follow the meaning of the words, but it dripped with hot anger and a sadness so deep it rendered me frozen. I knew this emotion. This raging grief. My mind was searching for the source. When had it started? How long had I been carrying it?

Caserio Pozueta has just 7 beds. Outside, right on the edge of the Camino, sits the grandmother, advanced in her Alzheimer's and unable to walk. She sells drinks, fruit, and slices of cake to passing pilgrims on this lonely, desolate hilltop. Everything costs one euro, probably because she can't remember any other prices.

Her daughter and her husband run the place, and care for a myriad of thriving children, chickens and dogs. In the silence of its old stone walls, *Caserio Pozueta* provided us with the perfect amount of hospitality and a home cooked meal unrivaled by any Michelin starred restaurant.

It was like visiting grandma's house – old and quiet and existing outside of the busy world reserved for youth. In stillness, surrounded by these ancient stone walls, I was able to rest and think.

What had it felt like for Zomkyi to walk across the Himalaya? She had to endure her own trek aged just eight years old. A Tibetan refugee travelling through brutal snow and ice wearing nothing but thin, cheap plastic shoes, sent by her parents to seek freedom in India. She carried a plastic bag of roasted barley, her only food for the month-long journey, and little else. What had Zomkyi felt, walking under cover of the darkness, compelled to silence, avoiding the snarling guard dogs and the strident searchlights of the Chinese soldiers looking for her, and too many other children? Knowing she may never see her parents again as the cold numbness set into her toes, was she able to stuff her feelings down inside, or did her endless walking not allow her to? I wonder if she cried during those long nights, having no idea what awaited on the other side of those magnificent, daunting mountains. Or had her mind shut itself to extraneous thought, too numbed by fear, pain, or just bloody-minded determination and the need to survive each moment?

As a young woman, Zomkyi didn't show her anger. There were no signs on her face, or in her actions. I felt it for her; angry at an entire nation. Angry at the entire world for letting it happen. Angry at her own

70

people for teaching her to stay silent, to stop dreaming so big. Angry at myself for not being able to help her.

She had to walk. She was given no choice.

James

I croaked for some water but after forcing my eyes open, found I was alone in the dorm. My parched throat could ask nothing more. A pounding headache made me wonder, was it worth it? Laughter cut through my dry lungs as fragmented memories flooded back and I knew it was definitely worth it. Now stop laughing, you idiot, and get up.

Our departed comrades had left us alone in the albergue. My hangover, which masked some of my earache, dictated what kind of day we needed this to be. For sanity's sake, we would surf the quiet waves between pilgrim groups, finding a serene spot where no one could wreck our sore heads with incessant chatting. So we tried to time our trek perfectly, looking for that sweet spot that would help us avoid catching up with our slow moving group, while staying ahead of the pilgrims coming up behind. From my revisit to the convent in Zumaia, I knew the group a day back were accompanied by kids and dogs. Dogs I could handle. Kids I could not. We hurried out the door.

After miles of road, a pub was needed as a medical hub to take away my hangover. Hair of the dog. The cure. Whatever you want to call it. I needed it to soothe my soul.

After leaving our new albergue that evening, a lonely back road brought us to a creaky public house. Empty patio out front. Ivy terrorizing the walls. A blast of heat welcomed us as we pushed in the heavy door.

Surprisingly, sitting by the roasting fire was Patrick, the Irish history teacher who'd been in and out of our Camino crew. Alone and in deep thought, his knuckles were white from tightly holding his half drunk pint. He'd struck me as paranoid. Worried that people weren't taking him seriously. It can be a thankless job being a teacher. Maybe the poor guy's students had bullied him over the years.

Suspicion took me when I noticed his beer was flat. It's a stupendous, sacrilegious feat to let a good cold pint go warm. I wondered, was he Irish at all with that lack of alcohol etiquette?

Bringing our own beers to his fiery nook, I tapped him on the shoulder. "Buen Bollocks, Patrick. Hope you're doing good man? Are you warming your pint up for later?"

71

He barely registered our presence. A few tears glinted, running down his cheeks as he stared into the crackling flames. "Jeez," I said rubbing his shoulder. "Are you alright, Patrick?"

In response, he gave a slight nod to the other wooden chairs surrounding the fire. Heat forged into our bones as we took our seats close to the inferno. Flames reflecting in Patrick's thick reading glasses made him look like a demon mourning the death of the Devil. He looked so lonely, resigned to a fate of eternal depression. Sighing heavily, he wiped the tears from his eyes, then smiled sadly.

"Cassie. James. How are you? I let the others go today. Don't worry about me. I'm alright. Silly, really. Just my mother walked with me today. I mean. Today is the... it's the anniversary she walked with me. She was sick. It's the day she died. And before you ask. No. I don't want to talk about it."

His eyes lost focus, as if he'd forgotten where he was. It was then I noticed all the empty pint glasses stashed under his chair. Patrick had been boozing away his troubles. I nudged Cassie. She spotted the pile of dead pints. For some reason, Patrick slowly leaned so far forward I was afraid he'd fall into the fire. He then jolted himself back from the brink, to resume his fiery gaze.

"Any chance," he said slurring a little, "you two love birds could tell me anything interesting? You know. Take my mind off it." He unfolded his boney frame and stretched his legs out, then made me squirm by drinking deeply from his hot beer. "Walking has been torture today, lads. So don't tell me anything boring. I find boredom brings up the bad memories. So don't be boring."

Jeez. I'd forgotten how judgmental he could be. I could've said, 'Isn't that the point of the Camino? Stuff comes up and we process.' But it obviously wasn't the time. I could tell him something amusing about Bill. But something interesting?... "Now that you ask. I did see something interesting. Did you notice a couple days just before reaching Markina, the tracks of a small boy disappearing into a river? Walked in but didn't come out."

Inquisitively, Patrick's eyes wobbled in his head.

"You think it's a boy now?" asked a sweating Cassie while removing layers of clothing. I stayed sweltering in my jacket, perhaps subconsciously trying to burn out my ear infection.

"Did I say 'boy'? I mean. It could be right?"

"I don't recall any disappearing footprints," said Patrick. "James. My dear man. Is that what you call interesting? Footprints on the most

72

walked pilgrimage in the world? Are you serious? Cassie must be arousing herself in bed if that's any measure of your pillow talk."

Cassie spluttered beer through smiling lips while I tried to cut into the conversation, but Patrick wanted to hold court. He waggled his finger at us as if we were bold children. "The Camino is an interesting place. Brings out the best in the worst kind of people. Do you even know how all this Camino stuff started? You two probably don't."

"I know some, I suppose," I said. "But enlighten us if you like." This was perfect. No interacting. My hangover could settle. Just sitting back by the fire drinking beer while listening to stories. Thank you Lord God above."

Patrick's voice took on the nature of a drunk school teacher. As a boy, I had a teacher that would sip from small bottles of whiskey under the desk. Sometimes he wouldn't even make it to class, the principal telling him at the school door he was too drunk and to come back after lunch when he had slept it off. Under Patrick's fiery gaze, I slumped to attention then closed my eyes to stop them from drying out.

"This pilgrimage," he said unsteadily. "Began in the year of our Lord." He started chuckling to himself. "Ah forget it. You know the story I like the most is that one time the Pope had a proper long chat with God. Do you know it? Anyway, afterwards the Pope pops up and decrees that God told him anyone walking to Santiago would be cured of eternal damnation. Now that's a real good promise!"

My cheeks were on fire, so I rubbed my cold pint glass over my face as he continued his slurred lesson.

"God is mysterious. He, or she said that you don't even need to be the one to walk to save your soul. That's the important part. You can pay someone else to do it for you! So of course the wealthy paid some peasant to walk the Way for them so their souls would be saved. Well, I'll save my own soul. Thank you very much."

"James! If you're not going to open your eyes to listen I'm going to bed."

It took me a few moments to raise my eyelids to see he'd begun staring into the flames again. Melancholy had returned to his face. "I'll save my own soul and mother's," he said to the fire. Studying his pint glass, he gave it a squinty-eyed appraisal and shrugged. Unsteadily he stood up. "Give us a hug, you two. I'm leaving early. Probably never see ye again."

Cassie got up to hug him. Patrick had to bend down to hug me. If Cassie hadn't held my hand and spoke sweet love lullabies, I'd have stayed by the fire.

...limited anonymity

–

Day 10 – Pozueta to Lezama to Bilbao
23km

Cassie

The solitude began to set in. We'd finally broken away from the group. In a way I was relieved. He wouldn't say it out loud, but James was having a difficult time being with people all day. He's always preferred the freedom of anonymity, never beholden to interacting with those who know him. Now we'd dropped back from the Camino family, I detected a new pep in his step. Most of them had return flights booked and needed to finish the Camino earlier than us, so it was inevitable we'd eventually fall out of step. For me, I craved the extra company. Anything to distract from hearing my own thoughts. A good dose of brouhaha would always accomplish that.

We started our day marching through beautiful pine forests spread over high inland hills, taking us to Lezama, which is essentially a suburb of Bilbao. Its sudden commercial ugliness was shocking after days in the idyllic countryside.

So little was Lezama's charm, we decided to keep going another 12km to the Basque capital. Our aching feet weren't happy, but it meant we got an extra day's rest in Bilbao. More anti-inflammatory tablets would help. As we walked, I booked a couple of bunks at a large city center hostel. It looked geared towards college students and young people on drinking holidays – the most decidedly non-Camino place I could find online. We needed a break, and James needed more anonymity.

As our feet finally hit their first urban pavement in more than a week, I felt terribly out of place. Chic Bilbaoans rushed to and fro with high street shopping bags, or enjoyed wine and cocktails at outdoor hightop tables. The distinctive architecture, framed with beautifully manicured flower boxes and dabs of street art served as a stark contrast to the cow sheds and crumbling old villages out on the Way. Though a city girl, I immediately felt out of place, an impostor without my flouncy dresses and conditioned hair. I missed my makeup. I caught my reflection in a shop window, and could barely believe my eyes. Shabby, yes. But nowhere near shabby-chic.

As we continued through the posh shopping streets, dribbling sweat and wreaking of the trail, I started to gush over the summer dresses on the mannequins. I'd never felt like such a girl before. I had two unattractive hiking outfits, and zero time or space for primping in the mirror, which was actually starting to get to me. Only I didn't realize it until I was back in the "real" world. Nothing to do. Any dress bought would be carried on my back for the next month. On the Camino you are faced with your own vanity, and then forced to abandon it for utility.

Our rucksacks were some of the smallest we'd seen on the Way. Some people were truly crushing themselves. It was an endless source of wonder at what they could be carrying in their packs. Within a few days of setting foot on the Camino, our packs, weighing in at around 8lbs (3.6kg), were no longer noticeable to us. This is what all pilgrims should want to achieve. But such aspirations leave no room for flouncy dresses.

We arrived at the huge city hostel in central Bilbao. After stepping off an elevator into our bunk room, low and behold, Bill was sitting in the middle of the floor. Legs akimbo and wearing a headlamp, he was earnestly engaged in cutting up little papers of LSD. *You've got to be kidding me.*

Of all the hostels in this heaving metropolis, of all the bunk rooms, on all the days, we were sharing space with Luka again... by chance. The other five beds in the room were filled with the rest of them. We found out later that as so many pilgrims stayed here, they were put into dedicated rooms because they got up earlier than hungover college kids. Our plan to fall behind wasn't exactly panning out. I couldn't figure out why.

As Bill looked up and saw us, his long body heaved towards James, finally collapsing on him in a giant bear hug. Little tabs of paper went flying across the room. Through his forced grin, I could hear James let out a stifled sigh.

James

Reruns of the Portugal versus Spain football match were on TV, its crackling glow flashing over each drunk, smiling face that piled into the hostel's common room. Back from a raucous night of Karaoke, I got a

75

hearty hailing of, "Buen Bollocks." Karaoke wrecks my head, so I'd stayed in to watch the World Cup.

Bill strutted up and down doing a Mick Jagger impression until Tomasino jumped on his back causing them both to crash to the floor in laughter. A few pilgrims piled in next to me, while the more disheveled slumped on the red leather couches to catch a breath.

Linked arm-in-arm with some guy I'd never seen, Lina was the last to arrive. He wobbled then staggered about in a right mess. Lina kissed his perfectly trimmed black beard that tickled his grey scarf. Make-up ran down her flushed cheeks where she must've been crying. From happiness or sadness, I couldn't tell.

Did she ditch Boils? They had gone out together and he'd seemed very keen on her the last few days. She stuck out her tongue at me as if to say 'I can do what I want.' I wasn't going to argue. Good for her. Although, she could have made a better choice. The guy had begun to drool while leaning heavily on her broad shoulders.

Tired and beginning to shake a little from all the chatting in my close proximity, I got up to leave just as Lina's guy's phone rang.

Rudely, her companion told us all to be quiet, then answered loudly. Energized, he scampered off down the hall and within seconds brought back three more disheveled dudes covered in beer stains. Suddenly, the room turned tense as they sneered at us, demanding drinks and cigarettes. Lina shook her head in despair when she comprehended the mess that was brewing.

"Out! Out!" she yelled in her thick, German voice, barreling into the guy she'd brought, sending him staggering backwards towards the door. The torch paper had been lit. Shamed that a woman had pushed him, his eyes burned. Furiously, he swung his arm at Lina, but us pilgrims moved as one and pushed the guys out the door. A fist flew over my shoulder. I heard a meat-smacking thud, then the groan from behind.

Thankfully the night watchman appeared. Shocked, he quickly assessed the situation, then roared at the drunk guys that he'd rung the police. Talk of the cops calmed the situation much faster than I anticipated. Their worried eyes darted everywhere. It was only then I noticed how young they looked. Maybe still teenagers. All that beer, bravado and acting like hard men had made them look weather-worn. They probably couldn't hold their drink.

Adrenaline pumped as I lay in bed. Not even the duets in the dark Bill and Tomasino sang could lull me to sleep....

So I left to walk the streets of Bilbao. This was supposed to be my rest day, but here I was, wandering again. Under the street lamps, I realized that my perception of walking had already altered. A mental barrier had been broken with time. Moving felt right. Perhaps I was now more in sync with the perpetual motion of the Universe? Nothing stands still, why should I? To be still may just go against the very laws of nature. So I walked.

...jazz hands

-

Day 11
Bilbao Rest Day

Cassie

I awoke to the sounds of the city, a far cry from the morning hum of the Basque countryside. Horns outside honked as the internal doors of the huge hostel opened and slammed to the rhythm of an endless stream of backpackers using the toilets. The excitement of last night introduced plenty of welcome distractions from whatever was alchemizing within me out on the trail. Comfortably numb once again.

As I sat up and swung my legs over the side of the upper bunk, someone grabbed my ankle.

"Cassie! I need to talk to you." Bill must have been loitering on the bunk below for a good while, waiting to pounce.

"OK... can you give me a minute?" Geez, I hadn't even had my turn in the bathroom yet.

I made my way down the hall in my pajamas and quickly brushed my teeth, then detoured into the communal kitchen to fill a styrofoam cup with some burnt coffee. Back in the room, Bill was perched, staring at the door waiting for me.

"What's up, man? How goes it?"

Bill looked at me sideways, then nodded towards the door.

"Can we go somewhere?"

I followed him into the emergency stairwell. Something was majorly up.

"Ok, I need your expert advice," Bill began. "I don't know what to do. I'm so confused. Do you think it's possible to love more than one person at the same time?"

77

Wow. I could write an entire self-help book on this topic, I thought to myself.

"I used to think so, but I didn't know then what I know now."

"And what is that? What do you know now, Cassie?"

"I know that I would never, and could never, lie to the one I love. When I realized that, that's how I knew I loved him."

"But I think I love them both. My girlfriend and Gerta."

"Does either of them know about your ability to love them both?" I asked.

"Well... my girlfriend doesn't know anything, anything at all, Cassie. And Gerta, she knows about my girlfriend."

"And she says she doesn't mind?"

"Well, I kind of told her that I'm planning on breaking up with her." He bit his lip. Saying it out loud clearly made the gravity of his dilemma sink in.

"OK. So both girls are under the impression you love only one girl, not both. Do you think they both love you?"

He smiled for the first time today. "Yes! I do! I think they both love me. I know they do." *Ass,* I thought.

"And do you think they'd still feel the same if they knew that you loved both of them?"

His face turned grey. "Probably not. My girlfriend would *not* be happy, not be happy *at all* if she knew. And Gerta, I don't know." I could see by his eyes, he knew.

"So there's your answer, dude. They both love you, but the *you* they love is not really *you*. The real you thinks he loves two girls at the same time. Do you want to be loved for the real you? Or do you want to live a lie?"

Bill was holding his head in his hands. He was no longer able to look at me.

"I know there's a part of you that wanted me to say, of course it's possible to love two people at once. To give you permission to carry on like this. But I also know there's a part of you that chose to ask me of all people for advice, full knowing that I'm going to tell you the absolute truth."

"Cassie....." he groaned, still not able to look up.

"Bill, you know what to do. I'm not going to make you feel better about it. Bottom line - if you really love them, you'll tell them the truth."

He sat in silence.

"Just remember, I'm here for you." He got up and slowly walked back into the hostel. I knew I didn't give him the satisfaction he was after, but I'm not going to enable a friend to turn away from the truth, or continue in a course of action that would hurt innocent parties. But I could already see that Bill was too caught up in the drama of his own story. This love triangle would have to play itself out. Having me around to watch would probably be too much for him. I didn't expect to see him for a few days at least.

Bill's situation is not uncommon on the Camino, I sensed. The majority of pilgrims, middle-aged and walking alone, likely had partners of some sort back at home. Walking the Camino is often an act of self-discovery, perhaps subconsciously designed to test these relationships. The long days on the road, the people and the experiences, would be almost impossible to relate to a partner who was not present to share them. The very nature of the Camino, which somehow transforms people into their true selves, rapidly and often dramatically, could leave one feeling naked and vulnerable. Ripe for attracting a new person who may be better suited to their more authentic self.

So, was it valid to say, "What happens on the Camino stays on the Camino?" Was there some unspoken law of the Way that allowed for free love and romance, all in the name of spiritual ascension?

Ha. Bill would certainly hope so. I, however, didn't buy it.

James

The receptionist had been right to put the early risers in the same room, for goodbyes were whispered loud enough to wake me at about 6am. A pilgrim I barely knew called Danish Hans had taken the punch in the eye. Swelled blue before he got into bed, I wondered if the ordeal hastened his departure. He rustled in that immensely irritating way that people trying to pack a backpack in the dark always managed to achieve, no matter how quiet they strived to be. Each rustle of his plastic bags sounded like corn popping in my overheated brain. Why not just do it outside? I'm sure he wasn't trying to be inconsiderate, but like so many people on the road, he'd just never thought to have his stuff ready the night before.

An hour later, abnormality surged in the room as Bill awoke in song. He must've heard me groan as I tried to block him out.

"Seamus?" he whispered furiously. "Seamus? Are you awake?" He began to make a chirping noise. "It's the dawn chorus, Seamus. I'm a bird. A beautiful, plume-feathered friend. Now I'm a stork with a baby. I'm all birds to all men. Wake up."

He must have mistaken my tired groan for a cheery good morning because he hopped out of bed, then assaulted my face with his jazz hands. Those dirty, wiggling digits were bothersome. "Look at my wings. Feel my feathery finger-wings beat the air above your head. Joy."

I rolled over. His breath was hot on my neck. I heard him whisper, "I love you, Seamus. Don't you love me?"

"No, I don't. Please piss off." Sulking because no one would play with him, he scuttled out the door. I tried to sleep but my mind played a game to see how many things sounded like Bill. *Bilbao. Bill. Butter. Barbarians. Boondock. Blarney. Buttocks. Bollocks. Bloated. Beetlejuice. Beetlejuice. Beetlejuice. Bitchin. Bill. Bilbao...... Shhhhh. Shut up, stupid mind.*

Minutes later, Bill burst back in the door with his headlamp on full blast. Shielding my eyes from the glare and Bill's manic smile, I asked, "What's the story with the lamp?"

"I'm going to the Guggenheim with Gerta. We're going to microdose LSD for breakfast and check out the exhibits."

"That's not the proper pilgrim menu, now is it, Bill? Do you think there's enough protein in LSD for an entire day?"

"It's brain power, Seamus. Who needs fatty fish omega 3 oil when I've got mind-expanding consciousness?"

"Do you take it with milk and sugar?"

"Stop wrecking my buzz, man. I love LSD and I need it to concentrate."

I rubbed my eyes until they hurt, then opened them again to find mad scientist Bill, sitting cross-legged in the middle of the floor. He used his tiny beard scissors to cut up the tabs of LSD into what he thought must've been smaller, more romantic pieces for him and Gerta.

A loud groan from another bunk let me know the bear Tomasino had awoken. Shaking his head in horror, he rumbled at Bill. "I've never seen this before. I don't even know what you are cutting. I don't want to know. But I know it's evil." He glanced nervously at the door. "What if someone comes in? Someone famous?"

Even Bill stopped for a moment. "No, man. It's fine. I'm sure no one famous will come." Then Bill went back to preparing breakfast. "Sure you won't join us, Seamus?"

Bill's invite was intriguing. I'd spent time in countries where it's normal for spiritual ceremonies to be intertwined with hallucinogens. One time I got lost sailing down some tributaries of the Amazon River,

80

later finding myself taking Ayahuasca with a shaman. Moonlight streamed through holes in his hut as I drank the sacred brew. He chanted for hours, holding space with his song as my consciousness journeyed. Bill's synthetic LSD would be sugary cereal compared to the shaman's organic oats. What really stopped me, though, was I was totally peopled out. I felt like a full bucket of water. One more intense interaction would spill my emotions out over everyone. Waking like this is never good for my sanity.

The rest of the day unfolded fast until we bumped into English Dave on a busy street on our way to watch France versus Peru. Dave was just rambling alone, so he was glad to join us. I didn't mind too much, as we'd be drinking beer, and I knew the relaxing liquid would push some of the negative emotional water out of my stressed body.

Dave, balding and always smiling inquisitively like a skinny Buddha, was wearing the sandals-and-socks combo that people in their 60's find so appealing, and others find a crime against fashion. I actually liked the look of his yellow, woolen socks. My toes were catching a chill in my smelly flip flops. Weird sleeping patterns seemed to make me feel too hot at night, then too cold in the day.

It was not easy to find a place showing the game but I spotted some men puffing cigarettes and drinking full pints of beer outside a bar. Spanish people don't normally drink full pints. So it was good odds these guys were UK or Irish and getting in the mood for the match.

Inside, *pintxos* of all shapes and sizes adorned the glass bar. Tuna covered in some pink sauce took my fancy, but I was trying not to eat so much white bread because it irritates my skin, so instead ordered three glasses of beer from the jovial bartender with the Freddie Mercury mustache. Dave drank deeply from his glass as soon as it hit the table, then gave a satisfied sigh. He licked the froth off the top of his lip, then rumbled the timbers of my tummy with his luxurious Shakespearean actor's voice. "I'm trying to escape my personality. At times, I'm so elated that I'm worn out. Do you understand?"

"Sorry. I don't really know what you mean, Dave." After feeling so anxious all day, I couldn't connect with that. "You're just too damn happy, is it?"

"Well, yes and no. I'm in the cult of my own personality. I can't escape it. I'm tormented by fits and starts of happiness. It shocks me. I'm walking along relaxed. Then, bang! I get this enormous explosion of happiness. Incredible amount of positive chemicals flowing. Sends my

81

mind into a spin. Totally takes me out of the Camino. I may as well be walking in the clouds."

"You sound rather happily lost, Dave."

"Young man. I've lost nothing but memories. Mostly the negative ones." He squinted at the TV. "I hate football. Did I mention that? Give me Rod Stewart over the blasted beautiful game any day. Anyway. The bad memories are still there. I just have no connection with them. I'm like a TV that's always on. A conduit for pictures in my mind."

Shadows jumped from a dark corner of the bar and flashed into my chest. Momentarily shocked by the weird sensation, I almost crushed my glass. My mind leaped to the shadows in the crumbling house where the little footprints had entered. In the bar a swinging door caught the sun. Tricks of the light. I picked at my beard. Jeeez, I could be so on edge sometimes.

"That describes humans well enough, I suppose," said Cassie.

Taking a long gulp of beer, I tried to tune back into the conversation.

"We're all just conduits for memories, you mean?" she asked. "For feelings?"

"I agree," he said tapping his bald head, "but I must have short circuited. I don't feel the negatives anymore. Just overpowering positives. It's clouding my expression of self. Distracts me from walking. I suppose what I'm trying to say is… I'm not balanced, but in the best possible way."

"Cheers to that," said Cassie. Glasses clinked and Dave gave us a toothy smile of too much satisfaction. "Is that a scallop tattoo?" she asked.

As if only just realizing he'd had his body inked, Dave looked at the inside of his wrist. "Ah, yes it is. Observant young lady you've got there, James. A keen woman. I present you with the gift I gave to myself." He extended his arm to show us a faded green and black clam on his wrist. "Seen the world, this shell has. Been on four Caminos with me. Knows more secrets than a saucepan of ears."

"Four Caminos?" Cassie asked. "All the length of the Norte?"

"Oh, much further than that."

"That's pretty impressive."

"Thank you. That's right. I did them all alone. Need something to keep me going." He dazzled us with another award-winning smile then pointed to his teeth. "These shiny choppers would fall out if I get frail. What you see is what you get from me. I just love it. The walking. The talking. The sights. Sounds. The beer. I don't think I'll ever stop."

82

"Happy to die on the Way to Santiago?" I said.

"No. No. You got me wrong. I don't mean it like that. If Death comes for me, I'll fight him tooth and nail. Like Dylan Thomas, I'm going to rage, rage against the dying of the light." He sat up straight as if on stage, then spoke deeply in that luscious baritone. "Do not go gentle into that good night. Good men, the last wave by, crying how bright their frail deeds might have danced in a green bay. Rage, rage against the dying of the light." He nodded in a way that may have been a slight bow, then took a sip of beer.

Impressive. My Welsh mom was a proud Dylan Thomas fan. I wanted to ask him for an encore, but he continued to talk.

"See. I can't tell you if that was me or the happiness talking. Either way, let's toast to Thomas." Another tinkle of glasses. "You know it was the demon drink that killed Thomas? Died in New York after seventeen whiskeys and more. But it could all be a conspiracy, too, you know." He tapped his nose. "It's a pity alcohol has wrecked so many careers. Mind degrades from the drink. Look at Thomas's career. His work deteriorated like his liver. Other greats went the same way. Hemingway couldn't lift a pen in the end. F. Scott Fitzgerald fell out with nearly everyone. His funeral was poorly attended. The Camino will catch up to you if you are not careful. It's a hotbed for raucous interaction. Liberated as we are from home and family, we disguise ourselves to our new companions day after day. As they slow or speed up, we shed ourselves of their burdens, ever moving on to collect more light and free trinkets of the soul."

Swirling the end of his beer, he smiled. "I'm a relic of time, but the Camino is timeless."

...irish funerals

–

Day 12 - Bilbao to Portugalete
15km (by train!)

Cassie

Something didn't feel right. It was a glorious day yesterday, taking a day off from the Way and wandering the bustling city with no real purpose. But on the morning of the second non-walking day, I felt lost. I wanted to get back out onto the road. My very soul, now committed to

83

its journey, felt betrayed by the lack of forward motion and the obstacle that Bilbao had become.

Alas, we'd also combined two days of walking into one before we entered Bilbao, effectively catching up with the Camino family, whose spell we were once again under. If we continued walking again today, we'd never lose them. I didn't particularly want to separate, but I knew James was about to explode with his need for more solitude. So we decided to progress to the suburb of Portugalete, but do our aching bodies a favor by taking one more day of rest and utilizing the city train. Many pilgrims choose to skip this portion of the Camino. The Way takes you through a long 15km stretch of urban sprawl and rundown, dangerous neighborhoods, with no charm or nature to speak of. It's easy to hop on the subway in central Bilbao. We'd take it to the end of the line at Portugalete harbor, famous for the Vizcaya Bridge, a space-age looking contraption that transports an aerial pod on wires back and forth across the river.

Sitting on the train, I remembered the day this all began. A year ago, on our delayed honeymoon in Ireland, James and I had wandered into a pub in the far back West of Kerry. Considered by the Irish to be the end of the world, it's an area where people still spoke Gaelic as their first language and sea salt seeped from their pores. The dark, wood-trimmed pub was filled to the brim on this foggy summer's day, men in suits revealed we'd mistakenly crashed a funeral party. Sitting down for one pint anyway, an old man with a white beard bid us hello.

"Who died?" asked James.

The old man replied in such broken, heavily accented English, James needed to translate for me.

"He says the guy who died, Danny Sheehy, was rowing a boat and it tipped over."

"Wow, that's terrible," I said.

The old man must've seen the interest in my eyes. A good death at sea story never failed to capture my imagination. He went on.

"Them local lads, four of 'em, built themselves a boat and rowed it all the way to Spain. They made it to Spain, then decided to row to Morocco. They only made it to the Portugal border, then Danny drowned at the mouth of a river."

"Good god, you'd be crazy to row a boat through these waters," I spluttered. This stretch of the Irish coastline was called the Wild Atlantic Way, and rough and roiled it was indeed.

84

"Crazy, maybe," he replied. "But it was the call of God himself that made them do it. Their faith. They were rowing to catch a glimpse of Saint James in Santiago."

A flicker of recognition registered in my brain. "You mean they were rowing to Santiago? They were doing the Camino by boat?"

"Indeed they were, young lady. Indeed they were. And they made it. Should've called it off once they'd made it that far. Who wants to go to Morocco anyway? No bones of saints there."

Later that evening in our room in an Irish country inn, I spent some time researching the old man's story. Sure enough, a group of Irish villagers built a traditional wooden boat and rowed it all the way to Ferrol, the closest port to Santiago. What strength of character, what longing for adventure had these men possessed to make them attempt such an impossible task? The romance of it all, the sheer challenge of it, swept me away.

As James and I enjoyed a nightcap at the inn bar, I looked at him with a seriousness he found startling. "What is it? What's up?" James asked.

"Nothing," I replied, trying to catch the bartender's eye to order another round.

We kept on drinking, as they tend to do in these parts. Enjoying the evening, the local lads who must sit in this pub every night pulled us into their jolly fray.

At some point James went to the bathroom. A dark man with a large, crooked face approached me and placed his hand high on my thigh. "I love you," he said forcefully, as his hand jerked deep into my lap.

My mouth dropped wide open in shock. He leered closer, nearly knocking me off the barstool as his hand further invaded my private space, penetrating me.

Suddenly my world went dark except for the pink neon from the cheap disco ball spinning in the corner. *Dancing queen… young and sweet, only seventeen, oh yeah…* ' Blood began to pool in my cheeks, in my eyes, in my throat. My heart was pumping out of control. I was not safe. *You can dance, you can jive, having the time of your life…* '

Frozen darkness. My soul had taken flight. Only my physical body remained, unable to navigate, unable to feel.

James reappeared at the bathroom door. Suddenly I could see. Suddenly I could move. Dodging the drunk man still at my side, I jumped up from my stool and ran over to him. When I reached James, instead of embracing him, I began to swat furiously at his chest and his handsome face in a maniacal frenzy, all the while desperately trying to contact him through my pleading eyes. I couldn't get enough air into my lungs. I gasped for oxygen as I continued to slap him, the neon light still revolving, the song still pumping. *'Oh, see that girl. Watch that scene...'*

I must have been screaming as I attacked my sweet husband. Somehow he pulled me outside onto the sidewalk and sat me down on a stoop.

"Cassie! Cassie!" he shouted. "What the fuck happened? What's wrong? What the FUCK!"

The trance suddenly broken, I startled at the terrifying realization of what just transpired. From within the darkest crevice of my guts, a wail arose as I collapsed into James' strong arms.

"It's ok. It's ok," he said. "Let's go home now. It's ok. It's alright."

He led me to bed and held me close all night.

When I emerged from a deep sleep the next morning, I knew what had happened, yet couldn't remember it at the same time. James' serious eyes at breakfast let me know it hadn't just been a bad dream.

"What happened last night?" he asked.

"I'm not so sure." I took a long sip of coffee. "Everything was fine. Obviously. Until you went to the bathroom."

"Yeah, it seemed like you were having fun," said James.

"Yes. I was. But then some guy came over and touched me... and I'm not really sure what happened next. I don't know why I was swatting at you like that."

James' lip was quivering ever so slightly. We got up, and he took my hand in his, letting me know with a squeeze that everything would be ok.

I'd narrowly escaped from India with my last shreds of sanity only a week before, and had no plans ever to return. In fact, I had no plans for anything. Life was a clean slate, but I was lost. I think James may have been worried about me.

Leaving the inn, we walked hand in hand back to our car. "You once asked me what I want to do more than anything," I said.

James glanced at me.

"Well, I know what it is."

His eyes twinkled for the first time that morning.

"I want to walk the Camino. It's like, a long walk. But let's do it. I want to do it."

James knew even less about the Camino than I did, and enjoyed hiking a whole lot less. But as only a truly wonderful friend and husband would, he made up his mind on the spot. "Cool. When do we leave?"

A year later we woke up on our last morning in Bilbao, only about 15 percent of our journey complete. Bill and the others were gone ahead of us. I was quiet on this day, which felt like a Sunday of the soul. The true break of Saturday had passed, and you know it's back to work on Monday. You're supposed to be enjoying your rest, but a bit of the mad rush of the workweek is seeping in.

Your physical body mirrors your subconscious mind. When you start pushing and challenging yourself on a physical level, you're bound to agitate the hidden pain and fears all humans carry. Whatever I'd been holding and hiding deep in the darkest corners of my psyche was slowly rising to the surface as I walked further down the trail. I knew a storm was coming.

I still wasn't sure why I wanted to walk the Camino, or even why I had told James it was the thing I wanted to do most that terrible morning. All I knew was, I wanted to keep going.

James

Bill never made it back to the hostel before we left. Perhaps he was still on his romantic trippy adventure. Or in prison.

Under racing clouds threatening rain, we walked through Bilbao. An urbanite scraped her umbrella against the side of my eye. Images of Dave's clam tattoo flashed through my vision. Intriguingly, it brought my attention to other symbols and iconography scattered around the city. Saint James' clam adorned many walls and nooks, along with swirls, curls, stars, crosses, bosses, scythes, suns, moons, dicks, doves, loves and my favorite, turtles.

Before this trip, I never knew the former home of a crustacean would dangle reverently from pilgrims' backpacks. Wandering folk wearing a clam are seen to be making a sacrifice; walking these hundreds if not thousands of kilometers to find something... or just for the love of walking ... or to take LSD and risk arrest in a world-famous museum. Or to find love. Indeed, half the time the Camino felt like the rambling world's dating app.

Cassie and I still didn't own a clam between us. So this made us inconspicuous. Also, we didn't overdo it with all the serious trekking gear, so we could blend in with any typical backpacker, except we were dripping with sweat, sunburnt, limping and a little hungover. So, I suppose, exactly like most backpackers.

We decided, well, more like I pushed, to get the hell away from our Camino group. I couldn't do another day of waking up anxious and having to deal with people sticking their jazz hands into my face.

Thank God she could see I needed a break! I just couldn't tell her if I didn't get away, I'd have some real mental issues. So we boarded the train to escape my emotional baggage.

Listening to the click-clack of the tracks, I closed my eyes. As people say, it doesn't matter *how* you get to Santiago. What matters is that you get to Santiago... But the guilt I felt all morning from taking Cassie away from her Camino family, now soaked from my mind into my soul. Feeling guilty robs one of any enjoyment of the moment. I knew interacting with this extra pang of culpability for taking the train was so juvenile. Did this guilt stem from my Catholic upbringing? Am I still riding the rails of Catholicism? How many people like me are indoctrinated at a young age, until guilt is so ingrained into the fabric of living it becomes hard to enjoy anything without a tinge of regret?

Guiltiness first appeared at about the age of five. My grandmother made my younger brother and me pray on our knees before bed. Looking at that blue bedroom wall, I felt odd trying to project people onto its blank surface to pray for. Surely they could take care of themselves? Is it really my fault if something goes wrong in their lives? How terrifying is this world if they need me to help them and I can't even help myself? Finishing my prayers, I'd not have a feeling of inner peace because I had prayed for the souls of my family, but of guilt, for the people I'd not prayed for. It would prey on my impressionable mind all night, scraping thick furrows in which to plant, then cultivate my emotional worries as I tried to sleep. Eventually, worry became a daily part of my early life. At only age six, I felt sure that if I didn't pray for someone, they would get sick and die or something horribly worse. Either way, it would be my fault if they went to agonizing hell. I learned guilt well over those years, and was quite the expert entering my teens.

As potentially corrupting, my grandmother would bribe us with raw blocks of lemon jelly if we said all our prayers before bed. This gave me the impression you only did good to get something in return.

So Catholicism taught me guilt, worry, sleep sickness. And trained me to think I should be rewarded for any good deed. Also, the agony of jelly-induced tooth decay.

Don't get me wrong, my grandmother was a wonderful woman. She just loved mass a bit too much.

...the matrix

–

Day 13 - Portugalete to Pobeña
13.8km

Cassie

For most pilgrims, walking the Camino is the toughest physically demanding challenge of their lives. On average, 1500 extra calories are burned per day. Appetites fight back in response, and many find themselves with a hunger so strong, it's hard to find enough food to shovel into your mouth.

Almost two weeks in, and I was struggling with the food on the Camino. Breakfast is usually provided by the albergues, and is almost always restricted to simple carbohydrates, commonly a packaged muffin or a piece of cake. Sometimes you'll get sliced white bread with butter and jam. Spanish cafes and bars along the way mostly have the same menus. Breakfast is extremely limited and virtually never consists of protein. Spanish people eat cake and cookies for breakfast, fried dough *churros* sprinkled with sugar being particularly popular. Oh, and they dip those in hot chocolate thick as motor oil. I'm not kidding. I'm accustomed to eating an egg or two in the morning, or yogurt or oatmeal. Two weeks of sugary breakfasts were weighing on my energy levels.

For lunch and dinner we were usually stuck with some very oily meat or fish with potatoes. The mainstays of the widespread *menu del dia,* a set meal found in nearly every eating establishment in Spain at lunchtime. If lucky, we could get a salad of iceberg lettuce, canned corn, and canned tuna. Vegetables were almost impossible to find on a menu, except for fried green peppers. On the bright side, almost every bar makes fresh squeezed orange juice to order, which often felt like the only healthy option available.

Just as I found myself really starting to drag, we discovered the Spanish tortilla. It's not the same thing as a tortilla in Latin America – it's essentially a thick egg omelet with potatoes and sometimes peppers or onions. It's tasty, full of protein, and gives you good power to walk. They're available at almost every bar you pass and are super cheap and fast to be served. I decided to skip the muffins and cakes at the albergues, and stop at the first bar we passed each morning for a tortilla instead. For me, it changed everything. I even carried a small jar of hot sauce with me as an accompaniment.

We also started stocking up on cheese, nuts and brown bread whenever we passed through a town, which was often enough for us to skip lunch completely and walk straight on through until dinner. We needed to concentrate a lot of effort on getting enough protein and complex carbohydrates. Once we did, we felt our energy levels soar and bodies grow stronger.

James was taking his sweet time getting out of bed this morning, still moaning about his ear. My blood sugar wouldn't allow me to start yet another beautiful day listening to his complaints. I excused myself and walked down the block to a café for my morning tortilla waiting for him to shake off the terrors of his sleepless night.

I was worried about James. I hypothesized months ago that this Camino would be good for him. It would take his mind off whatever thoughts were haunting his existence, and beneficially exhaust his body so he could enjoy more restful sleep. For the first few days I wanted to believe it might be working, but lately I could sense his anger and frustration building again. I prayed the Camino wasn't doing him more harm than good.

As I sprinkled my pocket hot sauce over a fresh slice of glistening tortilla, the door to the café swung open. It was Lina.

"Cassie!" she squealed in her thick German accent. "I saw you through the window. Thank GOD!"

I tried my best to mask my disappointment at being interrupted. "Lina, hi. How's life on the road treating you?"

She threw down her backpack, covered in an array of unicorn keychains and assorted rainbow-colored talismans. "Wow!" she exclaimed, rolling her eyes dramatically towards the heavens. "You won't believe!"

"Try me," I told her.

"I'm totally in love, Cassie. I really mean it. I just have a feeling, you know? A feeling that he is the one. Didn't you ever have that feeling? This is it!"

Oh, boy. Was it another Spanish guy she brought back to an albergue? This should be good. "Tell me, which one is it? What did he say? Tell me everything," I egged her on.

90

"Well, I had been feeling something from him for days. He was always trying to talk to me, always laughing at my jokes and asking me about my unicorns. I could tell he liked walking with me," she gushed.

OK. I guess it's not one of the random Spanish guys from the karaoke bar. "Who is it, Lina?"

"It's Boils!" she squealed like a schoolgirl.

"Boils? Really?!" Wearing yet another mask, I feigned happiness at the news.

"Yes!" she went on. "Last night he came into my bunk and woke me up. He took me into the stairwell and told me everything."

"What did he tell you?"

"He said he couldn't stand seeing me with other guys, and he thinks we met for a reason. He said he wants to keep walking with me til Santiago, Cassie!"

Thump. I took a long, slow sip of my café con leche. This was one of those moments in life that every woman must face at some point. *Do I tell her the truth about the guy she likes?*

Lina was sitting at the bar, chin cupped in both hands, staring off into space with a grin. She was absolutely childlike in her preoccupation with the man, who must have been at least 25 years her senior.

"I love him, Cassie," she said. "I just know it this time."

"Did he tell you that he loved you?" I asked.

"No, but I can feel it. He even said I should visit him in Helsinki this winter."

If this was you, Cassie, would you want to know? Hell, yes.

"Um, Lina. I'm happy for you. But I have to ask, did you know he's married and has kids and stuff?"

The rainbows and unicorns that had been spewing out of her eyes suddenly dropped dead in a pool of fantastical carcasses around her. "What? What do you mean?"

"I was walking with him the other day, and he told me all about his family. His wife and children, and his life back home. He even showed me a picture. Did he not mention them to you?"

"No. No, he hadn't mentioned it..." Lina's face had turned grey.

"Well, who knows what the situation is. Maybe things aren't so rosy back at home. Maybe you changed things for him." I was trying to cheer her up, but I knew that wasn't true. I was well versed in men like Boils, and I could feel his vibe from the start. A man's man, uber masculine and overconfident, clearly overcompensating for some insecurity, some dire need to feel adored and in control. These types often look for

91

women who'll love them without asking too many questions, and pretend to be single when they're definitely not.

"Cassie, are you certain he showed you photos of his family? His wife?" she asked.

"Yep, I'm sure."

"But I could really feel it this time…" Lina was staring off into space again.

"I know you felt it, but listen, you deserve better. You still have practically the entire Camino in front of you. Just forget him and walk forward. Don't let it affect you too much."

She took a deep breath and looked at me, hopping off the stool as her eyes welled up. She embraced me in a huge hug. "Thank you, Cassie. See you further down the road. Buen Camino." She snatched up her bag and was out the door. She hadn't been expecting that for breakfast.

James

We found ourselves lost in super highway hell. Hemmed in on all sides by decrepit cars and shuddering juggernauts. Trying not to die, we timidly tip-toed along the thin margin of the steamy road as the sun fried our pasty skin. Cassie's map on her phone had led us astray. Far as we could tell, her shortcut had disappeared.

"Statistically," she said trying to reassure me, "only a few pilgrims are killed by traffic each year." Moving carefully, we soon became ever more trapped inside this matrix of roads and ramps. A tractor trailer bounced by inches from our heads. There seemed to be no way forward that didn't involve hiking down a six-lane highway. Stress lines crisscrossed Cassie's sweaty face as she took out her phone again.

Disgusting smoke spewed into my face from the exhaust of a beat up car. This chaos was no place for the pilgrim. Packs on backs, we're just not nimble enough to dodge the mayhem. To relieve the tension, we needed to quickly find a holy clam to lead us back onto the path to the promised land.

Around the next bend, we knew the highway had beaten us. Thundering traffic raced from the gaping maw of a polluted tunnel. To enter would be suicide. *Ohhh magic clam, where art thou?*

Heat rose within my chest from waiting for Cassie to check her phone again. Roaring traffic made my bad ear feel like it was bleeding. *What the fuck are we still doing here?* "If you hadn't been so sure to follow that shortcut, we wouldn't be trapped," I snapped.

"If you hadn't made me leave the rest of our group, we'd be safe with them," she retorted.

Hot silence steamed between us.

My body tensed. "This Camino is a mistake, you know."

"Oh, shut up. Your mother made a mistake giving birth to you." Cassie tried to whack me on the back of the head, then screamed in fright as I jumped back into oncoming traffic. Barely in time, she tugged me from obliteration as I was nearly hit by an irate driver, madly honking at our stupidity. "Let's not fight here," she said.

"Okay, darling," I agreed sarcastically. "You know best."

"The only other option I can see," she said wearily, "is going all the way back to where we started."

One of the first lessons I learned about my wife was she's a stubborn woman. Cassie scanned the area. Pursed her lips then wiped sweat from her eyes. "But there must be another way to maneuver through all this asphalt to meet the Camino." She pointed. "It's just over there. On the other side of that highway, I'm sure. A few hundred meters as the bird flies."

I couldn't tell if that bit of dirt on the hill was the Camino or a goat track. Horns blared. At least we agreed that definite injury, if not death, awaited us if we continued into the tunnel.

Cassie went on a mission to find an escape route. Like the manic roadrunner, she darted from one side of the road to the other, eventually finding a series of parking lots leading to road ramps that eventually led through several dank, dark, albeit quieter tunnels. Finally, we found a hallowed clam shell etched upon a murky wall. Sweaty exhaust fumes oozed from our overworked pores as we hugged each other in greasy relief.

Lesson learned. Watch out for shortcuts, especially when there is a series of superhighways in the vicinity. On the Camino forums, maps and directions can become quickly outdated as new roads are built and traffic patterns change.

Hours later, we made it to the outskirts of Pobeña. Cresting a sand dune, I marveled at the serrated cliffs that looked as if a giant had taken an enormous bite out of the mountainside. Following the trail along a bouncing, wooden boardwalk, we made our way into the bay.

Pobeña's shore reminded me of the Dingle Peninsula in Ireland, where my grandparents would take me on holiday. At the beach they lived a peculiar life, far removed from their conventional norms.

For instance, to everyone's surprise, my grandmother became something of a nudist in later life. A devout Catholic topless sunbathing in 'ye olde' conservative Ireland required a suspicious type of bravery.

As if to compensate for Nan's nudity, my grandfather would come to the beach immaculately dressed in a pinstriped suit with large lapels. He resembled a 1950's mafia don. That suit was even worn going into the sea. He would take pride in rolling up the trouser legs just above his knees, then take me by the hand and wade into the freezing water. Beachgoers gawked. I'd always try to pull him further into the ocean by his tie, but he just swatted me away.

Inevitably, Irish rains would fall, causing my topless grandmother to jump up and scream as if a shark had appeared from the deep blue. "Get out!" she'd shout. "Get out! You're going to get wet! You're getting wet!"

Always, my grandfather would just roll his eyes, straighten his tie and pretend to ignore the crazy woman's absurd yells about getting wet in the ocean. But she would never stop shouting about the wetness of rain.

Sulking, me and my mafioso minder would wade back to the beach. I always enjoyed how she'd rush to me with a bright red, fluffy towel, drying me so hard it would scrape off my skin.

Besides the memories of my grandparents, there was something else peculiar in Pobeña's atmosphere. A magnetic storm of dusty energy was billowing and bustling around the town's little square of overgrown weeds. Hair stood up on the back of my neck. *What the hell was going on?*

In a frenzied moment, music, lightning sharp and splendid, ripped through the world. Gypsy music. Dueling guitars and thundering handclaps. Could it be? Gypsy Mullet and Nicu were near! Music engulfed me as an open-backed, blue van rounded the corner. My heart skipped a beat. Gypsy & Nicu, in all their pomp, were in the back, playing a sweaty storm to tease the elements. I wanted to race towards them but the van sped away, throwing up a wall of dust that left me coughing and spluttering. Gypsy Mullet noticed me, then nudged Nicu. Both squinted and nodded in acknowledgment. My heart sang. *They know me!* Our momentary connection raised my spirits for the rest of the day.

...space babies

—

Day 14 - Pobeña to Castro Urdiales
16km

Cassie

I only had to roll over and see James' eyes for a second to know he had a disastrous night's sleep.

The beachfront albergue felt more like an overcrowded geriatric ward than a beach resort. As the hostel manager looked over us at 7:30am, practically pushing us out the door, I remembered we'd booked a private room for tonight in the gorgeous town of Castro Urdiales, a short 16km walk away.

Last to leave again, James spent the first 10km going on about 'space babies' or some shit. He might have been hallucinating for all I knew. As we walked along clifftop paths in a misty rain, I realized he couldn't hear me properly, which meant his Guatemalan ear infection had struck again. No bueno.

Somewhere along the line we unceremoniously crossed from Basque Country to Cantabria, a decidedly more Spanish province. It felt we were making progress, though.

Today we deviated from the Camino proper to take a recommended shortcut, despite the previous day's woes. This shortcut is one of the most useful to consider on the Norte. Basically you have the chance to shave off seven kilometers from the route if you're prepared to divert along a highway for a short while. I can't compare the two, but the highway kind of sucked. The asphalt seemed to stretch on forever. There wasn't much traffic, but if it were a hot day, with summer weekend congestion, it might be entirely unpleasant and even dangerous. Maps of the shortcut were not needed, as the deviation is very clearly marked.

I was beginning to learn you don't need any kind of map or guidebook for the Camino, really. The Way is marked extremely well, including the albergues and restaurants. You can't go wrong as long as you stay on the path and follow the scallop shells or yellow arrows.

"James?" I asked as we trudged single file along the side of the highway.

He didn't hear me. Ear must've been completely clogged.

Waiting until we were off the highway to talk to him, I noticed how relieved I felt to be released from the energy of the Camino family and all their drama. Despite all the fun and camaraderie, there was a heaviness to my interactions there. I missed Bill, but yet I didn't.

Finally rejoining the Camino proper, I decided to ask James what he thought.

"How do you feel being apart from the Camino family?"

"Hmm. Feels pretty good, actually." He squinted into the sun muttering again about space babies.

"I'm trying to figure out why I feel so relieved being away from him."

"Away from who?" asked James.

"Bill. I love him like a brother. But I feel more relaxed now he's left us."

James smiled in his all-knowing way. "It can feel pretty uncomfortable being around someone who reminds you of some aspect of yourself you might not want to see."

Humpf. We walked on in silence. *What the hell was he getting at? Bill reminded me of some aspect of myself? My yoda-husband could somehow see this?* My mind twisted and turned as James' words stewed on the outer edges of my consciousness.

We sauntered into Castro Urdiales, a perfectly manicured seaside heaven. Complete with an old beautiful lighthouse and a cliffside Gothic cathedral, it was a welcome distraction from the unfamiliar sensations rumbling around my gut.

Over the best lunch we've had so far at Sidrería Marcelo, I schooled James on the historical significance of flying buttresses. He wasn't listening.

"Do you think we're going to find a new Camino family?" I asked the all-knowing one.

"I hope not," he said smiling. "Actually, I have a feeling we won't. That Camino crew was maybe as good as it gets. They are lost to us now. Others will stop to adopt us, or us them, but perhaps the first family cuts the deepest."

We walked on, holding hands for a while.

James

Another bed-rattling, horrid thud from the old guy above me stretched my sanity to breaking. Exasperated by exhaustion, I clawed at my face in the darkness, then made a fist to punch the idiot. Countless times he'd rattled me awake by swinging his legs off the top bunk then flopping back onto his back. One time he started flapping around like a dying fish. I wanted to debone him.

I'd noticed the old geezer about 5pm as he limped in with a load of elderly trekkers. At the time I thought he was cute with his wispy beard and blotchy skin. Now the memories of his shriveled head sticking out of his blue rain cap made me think of a deformed potato that I wanted to squash.

On one occasion, I hopped out of bed to check he wasn't having a heart attack as he wheezed like a boiling teapot. Immediately he stopped moving. Even in the darkness, I'm sure our eyes met. I had to force my hands not to shake him and say, "Will you just shut the hell up before I mash you!" Instead I growled, slapping my throbbing ear infection in the process, thus generating enough lightning pain in my skull to clear the man from my mind. Dazed, I went back to bed.

Oh, God. Not a minute later he was flailing around again. Slowly at first, but then he revved up through the gears until he was like an 80-year-old space baby, thrashing about in outer space. "Please stop," I whispered, which eventually turned into, "Please die."

Dawn peeped in the window as he continued his crazy space adventures. Dim light illuminated the dorm. No one else had an old space baby above them. No one else was gnashing their teeth and balling their fists in frustration. Just the usual annoying rustlers and snorers. Suddenly he flopped so hard on the mattress our entire bed jolted sideways. My fist just flew. All that angry exhaustion smashed into the bottom of his mattress. My wrist crumbled in pain as it hit the wooden slats. I felt the tops of my knuckles slice off. I bit my tongue to silence a scream.

My punch didn't stop him. Just slowed his perpetual motion. He was now a slow-motion space baby wobbling about up there. I looked at the blood dripping from my knuckles. *Do I want to go to jail?*

Suddenly, defying the laws of nature, the old man hopped off the bunk with the grace of a gymnast. Thick, blue varicose veins bulged from the back of his legs. If I could just get a knife, I could slice an artery causing massive blood loss. Imagining his pain made me feel a little better. I half-heartedly reached out a bloody hand to crush his calf, but he ambled towards his backpack.

Of course he rustled in his backpack for 10 minutes. Of course plastic bags were involved. Of course he dropped coins everywhere. Of course one rolled under our bed. Of course he muttered loudly about his loss while scratching around beneath me. This was my moment. Right now, I could stamp on his back. I would feel so much relief. I took a deep, murderous breath. Held it. But I just didn't have enough energy to release the killing blow. To quell my blood lust, I licked the blood off my knuckles, savoring each iron-tinged corpuscle, and the thought of his bloody demise.

Triumphantly, he gave a squeak, then pulled himself up onto the side of my bed, by sticking his nails into my arm. Our eyes met. His face reared back in horror at my murderous stare. Quickly, he backed away. I stuck out a bloodied tongue. He scampered off with a whimper.

But of course he was one of those people that waltz in and out of a dorm four times. Of course he repacked his backpack three times. Of course I didn't get back to sleep.

By this stage, it was so bright the other pilgrims were clambering down from their bunks. Morning was filled with groans of octogenarians complaining about their dilapidated limbs. Laying in my bunk, I kept thinking if I saw that old space baby again he better have a good explanation for all the thrashing around, or else he'd be cashing in his travel insurance.

I closed my eyes. I'd been walking for fourteen days and been to the hospital three times with my ear. My head pounded. My knuckles bled. My wrist throbbed. My ear roasted. Spain was pain.

When I finally peeled myself from bed, I discovered I'd lost my baseball cap plus another t-shirt. At this rate, I'd end up going full Binman and have to walk into Santiago wearing only a flimsy, black plastic bag.

James the Saint

James, also known as Jacob, is believed to have been born in Judea in around 3AD. The New Testament explains that he was beckoned to by Jesus, along with his brother John, as they stood on the shore of the Sea of Galilee. They bonded, and James and John became the first disciples of Jesus, witnessing the transfiguration and other miracles.

Tradition recounts that James later traveled to the Iberian Peninsula to preach the teachings of Jesus. When he returned to Judea in 44AD, King Herod Agrippa ordered him beheaded as part of his efforts to quash the burgeoning Christian movement.

It is believed James' followers smuggled his body back to Iberia, burying it in present-day Galicia, where it was discovered centuries later in 814AD by two shepherds after seeing strange lights in the sky above the site. The presiding ruler of the kingdom ordered a chapel be built over the grave immediately, which eventually and gradually was replaced by the grand cathedral you see today.

The idea that James' remains were ever buried in Iberia is not unanimously accepted by Biblical scholars and historians, but is accepted as truth by the Catholic Church. The name *Tiago* means James in the local dialect, hence the area became known as *Santiago*, or the city of Saint James.

Folk etymology for the name *Compostela* is that it comes from the Latin *campus stellae*, meaning *stars field*, referring to the legend of lights appearing in the sky. Some scholars say a more probable etymology relates the word with Latin *compositum*, meaning *burial ground*.

James' relics are housed in a silver reliquary in the crypt beneath the cathedral, which can be viewed by the public from afar.

The Audacity of Not Following the Stages

Every Camino guide out there presents the Way as being divided into specific stages, each with a clear beginning and end. These guides usually focus on the towns and albergues they deem relevant to these stages, often ignoring or underreporting on the numerous towns, hamlets, albergues and other services found in between. So many first-time pilgrims, unsure of how things work on the Camino, think they must follow official stages, not yet understanding that the real magic of the Camino happens when things don't go according to plan, and you're free to follow your whim.

Dare to reject the idea of following the stages. This will allow you to slowly build up your fitness in the beginning, listening to your body. This will also give you the freedom to speed up to find a new walking partner, or drop back to ditch a crew of snorers. This provides the opportunity to explore an amazing town for an extra day, relax on a beach longer than planned, or have a rest if you fall ill.

We recommend not making reservations more than a couple days in advance, except in extreme situations when you know you'll be in a sold-out town due to a holiday, etc. Leave it all open. It might feel a little scary in the beginning, but we promise, you'll be glad you did.

Leave space for the legendary Camino magic to enter.

Camino Tip: if you meet someone on the Camino you want to stay in touch with, NEVER assume you'll see them further down the trail- get their contact info ASAP.

Basque Country Highlights

Le Train de la Rhune

If you're taking a day to rest in Irun before you begin your Camino, this authentic cog railway and its wooden train can sweep you up a peak in the Pyrenees with expansive views over the mountain range and the Bay of Biscay from more than 900 meters high. You can reach it via public transport from Hendaye, just over the French border from Irun. To extend, stay a night in Ainhoa, probably the *most beautiful village* in the French Basque Country...its cemetery, right by the church, deserves a visit, as well as its main street, surrounded by beautiful Basque-style houses in perfect condition.

Pintxo Hopping in San Sebastián

Satisfy your culinary curiosities in the official 'European Capital of Culture.' The art of the hors d'oeuvre is best enjoyed with new friends, wandering the alleys of the old city with no particular agenda. Budget a bit extra money and time to stay in this area of town and enjoy it without restrictions.

San Juan de Gaztelugatxe

Fans of HBO's 'Game of Thrones' will recognize this dramatically situated seaside shrine as Dragonstone, where scenes were filmed for the hit series. Its history spans back to the time of Saint John, who is said to have visited the small island, which has been transformed into a man-made peninsula by a long, stone staircase that's the stuff of fairytales. It's a 3km round trip walk to the hermitage and back. The path of the Camino del Norte passes within 25 km of the site, and it is well worth working it into your schedule. You can reach it via public transport from either Guernika or Bilbao. We recommend taking a rest day in Gernika and doing it from there, as the trip is shorter and the landscape more beautiful. You can connect via bus or train to the town of Bermeo, from where you can catch a shuttle to the site.

Guggenheim Museum

This world-class museum of contemporary art serves as a welcome departure from the pastoral beauty of the Camino for a few hours. The building itself is a work of art, considered widely to be one of the most important examples of modern architecture of the modern era, designed by Frank Gehry. Closed most Mondays.

Vizcaya Bridge

Vizcaya is a 164 meter transporter bridge, listed as a UNESCO World Heritage Site. Its gondola can transport six cars and several dozen passengers in one and a half minutes over the Nervion River. The Camino del Norte proper passes just steps from it in the town of Portugalete, but there is a variant that enlists the use of the bridge as part of your route leaving Bilbao, and also shaves 7km of unpleasant urban walking off your day.

WEEK 3

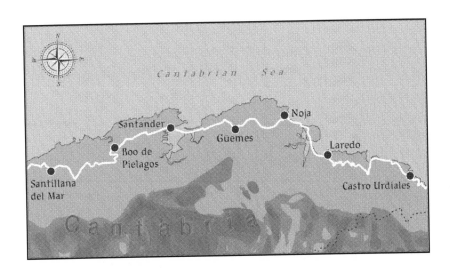

...inquisition

Day 15 – Castro Urdiales to Laredo
25.9km

Cassie

Well. This was quite a day to walk one of the entire official stages for the first time. If you're going to walk the Norte, I fully recommend breaking this section up, and definitely don't take the shortcut all the locals suggest. There are actually two potential shortcuts on this day. The first allows you to shave quite a bit off the journey, but it's miserable, leading you along an endless tarmac highway. However, the second shortcut is my most beautiful stretch of the entire Camino del Norte. Heaven and hell on the same walk.

Over tortilla breakfast, I checked my email. Two in one day, both from journalists asking me about a past life. A life that I was trying hard to forget.

As the sun beat down, on the hot, black asphalt, I felt the emotions gather force in my throat and jaw. It had been a year away from my other life in India, and I was still so mad and so disappointed. I timed

103

my next few steps to avoid earthworms that had squirmed onto the road after the early morning rains.

Tibetans make a point of not stepping on bugs and crushing mosquitoes. Kalsang la always made a point of stopping me dramatically in my tracks when we were walking together. He'd act like he cared so much for the lives of the creatures, dramatically offering a leaf to escort them to safety.

I couldn't forget sitting across a wooden table from Kalsang, the man charged by the Dalai Lama's government-in-exile with running the Tibetan National Sports Association. Three years into my project, the simple girls' soccer team I aimed to create had grown into 15 teams, feeding top players into the first Tibetan women's national team in any sport. The national team camp was starting the next day. I was anxious for the players to arrive.

"Cassie, there is something important you must hear. Please listen to me," stated Kalsang. His dark, wrinkled face seemed serious, but carried the exaggerated energy of a play-actor. I braced myself to hear some kind of lie.

"As you know, we received a grant for this camp."

Of course I knew. I was the one who applied for it. I was the only person who did any fundraising. And I'd been working hard at it.

"The grant is for $5,000, but I feel we only need to spend about $2,000 for this camp."

"What do you mean, Kalsang la? I've budgeted everything perfectly," I reminded him.

"Yes, well, look here." He pointed down to a printout on the table detailing the camp budget. "You said every player needs a ball. They don't need balls. Only two or three is fine."

What? Two or three balls for a one-month camp for thirty players?

Kalsang went on. "And meat and eggs? They don't need to eat those things. Maybe once a week is fine. We can serve more rice and bread. And milk every second day."

You've got to be kidding me. These players are training 4-5 hours a day, and need protein.

"And uniforms," said Kalsang. "The girls do not need their own uniforms. They can wear the men's jerseys for matches. It is a waste of our money otherwise."

Holy shit. He wants these skinny little refugee girls to wear large men's uniforms for matches when I could easily get them their own that fit them properly?

"But the grant is more than enough to cover these costs, Kalsang la," I said. "I don't understand."

"Well, see," he continued, now lowering his voice. "If we spend only $2,000, then we will have $3,000 left for other things."

"What other things? I've already started raising money for the next camps, and we've got plenty in the bank for now." My cheeks were getting hot.

"No, no, not for the girls. For them, no more money is necessary. For the men's team, I mean. We can use the funds for the men's team. After this camp, we don't think there should be girls' football anymore. It's been decided."

"Kalsang la, what are you talking about?" I was having a hard time keeping my voice from rising. "The program is going so well. We're getting more and more girls who want to play; invitations for matches all over India. And look at the girls on the team - they're absolutely loving it. Soccer's changing their lives. AND Kalsang, those funds were given for women's empowerment. They were raised for the girls, not the men. The organization that gave us the grant won't agree to this!"

I sat there exasperated, my mouth gaping incredulously. This was the moment of truth.

"That's ok, Cassie. The organization will never know. We can change the receipts."

Bam. There it was. A full on, shameless, in-your-face invitation to participate in blatant financial corruption. *You've got to be fucking kidding me.*

When I thought it couldn't get any worse, he continued, "And as I said, it's been decided. No more girls' soccer. And you can never take a women's team to play abroad. So stop saying that. It just isn't possible."

I stood up. Livid. Adrenaline coursing through my body. I needed time to think about how to respond to this, and the first girls were about to arrive for the camp. The whole point of everything I'd been working towards was creating a girls' soccer program strong enough to field a women's national team at international tournaments. This would've been a massively symbolic act of sports diplomacy. Potentially the most empowering way to give young Tibetan women a platform to represent themselves on the world stage, period.

How were Kalsang and his lackeys not getting this? After all, they were Tibetan refugees, too. *He stops everything to bend down and save the fucking ants, but he treats human beings like this? Women like this?*

Kalsang made a huge mistake that day. Telling me I can't do something I believe to be principled and morally correct, is the one sure way to make me do it. I've always been a rebel with something to prove, starting as a toddler who refused to allow my mother to pick out my clothes or brush my hair. I had to do it myself. And there was no greater satisfaction than when I did. That day across the table, Kalsang said I couldn't bring a Tibetan women's team to play abroad? Well now, he'd absolutely guaranteed it would happen, or I'd give my last damned breath trying.

And I nearly did.

It's interesting about feelings. Humans often feel most scared of their own feelings – emotions that can't hurt us unless we allow them to. They can be the easiest pests to get rid of, but the catch is, we have to feel them first. Now on the other side of the world in Spain, long separated from this man and this situation, my body still tensed and seethed as I walked along that hot tarmac highway.

As James strolled up ahead, the heat building as cars whizzed past, I built up the courage to allow myself to feel the whole sorry mess of crappy emotions I'd done everything to avoid. I reminded myself that I was safe. No one could hurt me. It was just me and James on the Camino, not another soul in sight. What was scarier? The intangible emotions gushing through my nervous system, or the actual speeding vehicles rushing inches from my body?

Comic relief allowed me a giggle at this thought. Actually, walking along the shoulder of this road was totally dangerous. So I walked. And I walked fast.

I sweated and breathed heavily. I told my tensed up abdominal muscles to relax and allow the feelings to rise into my chest. Then I told my shoulders to relax and allow the feelings to rise to my throat. Then the tears started to stream down my face, uncontrollably. I allowed them to flow. James was concentrating on not getting hit by a truck, and didn't look back. I was free to cry as much as I wanted, and I did.

Unlike speeding trucks, feelings cannot hurt you UNLESS you keep them inside, covering up, stuffing, and doing everything to distract yourself from feeling what's real. Feel them, and they will feel heard.

106

Once they've transmitted their message to you and you've listened, they'll melt away.

The Way was long and arduous on this day. I was emotionally and physically drained by the time we reached the turnoff for the next shortcut near Hazas. I wanted to lie down in the cow pastures and fall into a deep sleep. But as we climbed over a green hill, I realized we were entering a legitimate wonderland fit for fairies of the highest order. The rolling emerald green valley rose sharply on both sides, culminating in high, jagged rock peaks standing like sentinels on the edge of the roiling azure sea. Slowly I came out of my head and back into the world around me. The sun started to dip after this long day of walking, birds of prey soared overhead, urging us on as we climbed the last steep hill. As we crested the ridge, the dramatic sight of the large town of Laredo stretched out below us. We descended through a charming farming community framed in blooming flowers and kissed by the salt breeze, our aching feet finally feeling the smooth medieval cobblestones of the old city.

Tonight we'd sleep in *Casa de la Trinidad,* a convent albergue run by nuns.

James

Caked in itchy grime from sweat and exhaust fumes, we stumbled into a beat-up old bar called... Bar. At the dingy counter, two older gents, gulping wine and green-colored shots were arguing about the Portugal versus Morocco match on TV. The rowdiest one, with the tobacco-stained mustache, hung a shot glass off his outstretched tongue in an act of defiance. The quieter man swiped at his buddy's tongue, staggering sideways into the bar.

The barmaid, obviously a veteran of diplomatic pub resolution, diffused the situation by reminding them they both hated Portugal. The pair sighed and nodded sadly. The rowdy guy took the shot glass off his tongue, then licked the last of the sticky green liquid out. They whispered and erupted in laughter before ordering more drinks.

Cassie arrived back from the bar with a couple of beers. I needed a pint while putting my swollen feet up for fifteen minutes. "If I wanted to watch two old drunks fighting in the middle of the day, I would have stayed in Ireland," she said.

Quietly sipping beer, I smiled. I was missing the chaotic drunks dancing jigs in the early morning bars, as others slept in the corner.

107

Those fellas would be ready to power into the alcohol again at lunchtime. Some lads I knew would get drunk three times a day.

Taking another sip, I contemplated a further three hours trek. Much of the skin around my little toes was sheared away after massive blisters ruptured yesterday. I'd been walking on putrefying organic matter all morning. Taking my left sock off, I found white, wet bits of skin were plastered all over its insides. Covering my right little toe, was a spongy protector. I'd lost the others. We christened them 'toe condoms.' Rancid fumes wafted up as I took it off. The bottom of the toe was mush. I'd never realized my little toes slightly arch and tuck under the adjacent toes. After kilometers of blistered walking, the skin couldn't take it anymore and gave up. Maybe if I dipped them in a hot whiskey it might disinfect the toes and rejuvenate their spirits. Works on my mind. Could work on the body.

A cavernous convent would be our sanctuary tonight. Cassie was disappointed we weren't greeted and stamped by 'real' nuns wearing a habit. "Next Halloween, instead of Binman, I'll dress up as a nun," I promised her. "But only if you play the flute." This seemed to satisfy her needs.

Our dormitory, with its seven hard beds, was wonderfully simple. Prayer hung in the air. It weighed as much as you wanted. Holy crosses adorned the walls, reminding me of the agonies of Jesus. As I hopped into bed, I thought about the utter torment the Bible tells us he suffered. Good strong Catholic stuff to bring on pleasant dreams.

Dream I did. Of a hairy man, dripping blood from a crown of thorns. But it was not Jesus. It was Gypsy Mullet. In a dark cave, he sang until the dead arose. Nicu was on hand to pass out cigarettes to the animated corpses.

At about 3am I awoke with an urge to wander the foreboding convent. Illuminated by eerie candlelight that flickered over the sinister paintings of dead saints, mournfully looking to heaven, my footsteps echoed in the empty hallways. A clattering noise made my hair stand up. Scared of the shadows, I almost turned back. But then a smell of fresh air, so I followed my nose into darker places.

If I bumped into a late night nun, would she scream for the Spanish Inquisition? Those hooded, holy nutters might stick me on the rack. Stretch me until hamstrung, thus seriously hampering tomorrow's walk.

Eventually my nose found the source of fresh air. Pale light guided me to an ancient picture of a bloody angel with its eyes to heaven.

Beneath the painting, a dripping font of holy water was freezing to the touch. Another dimly illuminated picture showed a woman being dragged towards a burning fire. Strangely, I recognized her terrified face. I peered closer. She didn't look like a witch. Just a woman in shock. In the background, the body of a barefoot young boy lay dead in a river. Crazy thoughts flooded. *That's the boy from the abandoned house we passed about ten days ago! His footsteps walked into the river but never came out.* My mind tried to swim away from reality. How could I pretend to know this was the boy? I never saw him. But this is what I imagined he'd look like, when I saw those footprints disappear. Sorrowful and small. Light snuffed out his hollow eyes. A cruel smile misunderstood.

Behind me a thump in the corridor almost gave me a heart attack. Arms raised, I spun around. I couldn't understand it, but the darkness flashed. A deeper darkness, sending shadows reverberating towards me. The granite basin dug into my back. Tears were in my eyes. I couldn't see. In desperation, I turned to splash freezing water over my face. I turned back. Only shadows. Just the sound of dripping water to accompany my thumping heart.

In the darkness, I dared not move unless something heard me. How would I find the courage to get back?

I threw more freezing, holy water over my face. Immediately, images of my brother and I appeared. We used to go to the local church to fill our water pistols from the font. We didn't think about killing zombies. We just wanted the little thrill of stealing holy water to spray the church goers in the car park. We'd get chased away every Saturday. On Sunday we'd have to sneak in again with our grandmother.

I have no pistol now. Just shadows for company. I would've given anything to have my brother by my side. Someone to pretend to be unafraid with while trying to be quiet as a mouse, but laughing all the way.

...father ryle

–

Day 16 - Laredo to Noja
20.5km

Cassie

Summer solstice was near. Just when all should be light, the world turned dark. Our stroll from Laredo to the ferry dock took us through what felt like an atomic wasteland. Five kilometers of abandoned holiday apartment towers, overgrown playgrounds, tumbleweeds and sick old dogs. Shirtless heroin addicts lined our path. A horde of oblivious shoeless pilgrims threw down their packs in the sand, as the local rig beached and dropped its ramp for us to scurry aboard. Karst formations of what looked like mottled limestone in the gray distance. The captain pathetically tried to sell us jars of anchovies as the ferry made its crossing. Spain's economy was still working its way out of years of recession.

Earlier, James and I hopped out of bed and quickly dressed before wandering through medieval corridors into the inner sanctum of the abbey. We found the sisters sitting in a circle within a small chamber with the lights dimmed, a single candle lit.

Of the fifty pilgrims who spent the night here, we were the only two who showed up for the pilgrim's mass. No doubt I was the least Catholic person on the Camino, but somehow I was offended. These sweet sisters show up every morning to pray with the pilgrims staying in their home, and no one can be bothered to turn up? They prayed and sang in their kindhearted nun voices, but dark was their dirge.

I shed a small tear of gratitude for these gentle ladies. Day after day they tend to the needs of an endless stream of people like us, most of whom seem not to care about the underlying faith and spirituality integral to the Camino.

At the start of their service, one of the nuns handed James, the only male in the room, a small English Bible. James delivered mass for his first time to these pure-hearted sisters, and spoke it in a voice both steady and mystical. I was transfixed by the catechism for the first time in my life.

Throughout Cantabria, the A8 (northern Spain's super highway) threads through narrow valleys between the multiple needles of the coastal hills. You can either walk up and down the steep slopes or navigate your path on hard asphalt next to the highway. The former requires better balance and more nimble feet than Leo Messi. The latter is a world away from the lush turf of the Camp Nou. It struck me that, on the Camino, you'll often be faced with a choice between the two —

110

beautiful and challenging, or ugly and easy. After two weeks, today I'm going with beautiful and challenging. Fuck asphalt.

Best restaurant on the Camino? Maybe. Azafrán in Noja did not disappoint. Prices are so low for the quality of cuisine. For 40 euros we had a salad of local tomatoes, guacamole and fresh cheese, rustic fresh bread, plump mussels in a spicy broth, and perfectly cooked steak *entrecot*, all washed down with a bottle of fantastic white wine.

That night we celebrated summer solstice on a memory foam mattress in a private room at *Hotel Azcona*, watching the Argentina match with 30 cent cans of beer and James' antibiotics.

Maradona was right. Argentina was a disgrace. Despite his thread-the-needle passes, Messi couldn't change the game.

Tomorrow we would avoid asphalt at all costs. And move towards the light.

James

This morning I ascended to the lofty perch of 'Protector of Pilgrims.' My words would bolster the faith of those on the Camino. No one could've been more ill-prepared.

Still sleepy from my nocturnal misadventures in convent-land, we decided to seek out the revered pilgrims' mass. I'm not sure why. I never go to mass anymore, except midnight mass and then only choose it on the stormiest of Christmas Eve nights. I must have a catholic subconscious feedback loop for suffering, then vindication and validation for that suffering. Confession is its own psychotherapeutic technique I suppose.

I expected the church to be filled with pilgrims proclaiming piety. We found it empty. Hollow of worship. Numbers must have become so low over the years, the service was in a darkened chamber next to the glittering altar rather than the main part of the church.

Determined to experience this mass, we sheepishly poked our heads into the room. About fourteen nuns aging from timid youths to dozing elders perked up. "English?" said the youngest nun behind the keyboard.

"Irish," I stupidly answered. Whispers shot through the ladies, asking did any of them speak Irish? Leaning forward onto her zimmer frame, the eldest nun firmly stated the mass must now be said in English. Not wanting to cause a commotion, I protested that, "God's word in Spanish was nearly as good as English." This joke did not earn a smile, only stern stares that left me sweating in my seat.

111

A group of what looked to be young South American nuns riffled through a stack of books, then one confidently strode over and gave me a blue Bible. "You will say the mass in English."

No I won't. You can't make me. Her brown eyes pinned me to the seat then pricked my heart. "Yes," I muttered. "No problem." Cassie giggled at my anguish.

The smiling sister at the keyboard steadied herself, took a deep breath, checked her sheet music then began to play a timeless melody to God. All the other nuns stood, then sang religious passages in soft murmuring lullabies accompanied by crescendos of hallelujahs. Humming tunelessly, we stood as they stood. Everyone sat. We quickly sat. An uncomfortable, expectant silence filled the room. All eyes on me. Cassie gigged again. I began to sweat again. I opened my book. Dropped my book. Cassie burst out laughing. I picked up my book. This was my moment. My mouth dry. Surrounded by the faithful. Being judged by God in his own house. I looked around. Judgmental nuns everywhere.

At that moment I was at my grandmother's funeral again. After eight years, dementia had finally taken her. My uncle was supposed to give a sermon from the Bible in her memory. For some reason, his courage failed a few minutes before, so he asked a young me to do the deed. I was so freaked out speaking in front of people that I knocked the priest's wine goblet off the altar. Being laughed at during a funeral is a strange sensation. I had felt like a clown, sentenced and waiting to be hanged for gallows humor.

Now I held the Bible again. My laughter burst forth because of anxiety. Shocked nuns stared, but quickly smiled. After a couple more false starts and Cassie's whispering words of encouragement, I finally croaked through the first part of the sermon. Nuns even echoed some of my words as if I were a real priest. Everyone smiled at my lowly endeavor. Could I have made it as a priest? Father Ryle. Out on his holy adventures. Converting the heathens and blessing stuff. Then selling the new holy relic for a tidy profit.

Somewhere in the middle of the sermon, my mind drifted to the pilgrims. I realized the weight of my words. *This mass is for the pilgrims!* It's supposed to give energy and protect them on their journey. *I really shouldn't be saying this thing at all.* It would be my fault if a pilgrim broke her leg, lost her passport, lost their way, took a bad batch of LSD or was killed by the peanut butter murderer. *Damn it.* If I knew I'd be saying mass, I wouldn't have been poking around like some weird, medieval thief last night.

I clawed my mind back to focus on the words of the Bible. Back and forth the mass went, words tumbling over each other in metaphoric meaning. Nearing the end, my head hurt from concentrating. All the nuns nodded encouragement as the last sounds played on the keyboard. In a momentary connection that stirred my heart, I loved that these ladies had chosen to give up so much of their lives for the fulfillment and sanctity of God. I hoped it made them feel fulfilled and safe.

On the ferry crossing to the town of Santoña, the bothersome captain would not stop trying to sell us cans of anchovies. Cassie shooed him away again, then smiled. "You know, husband? My grandmother would've been so proud if she was still alive. She was always trying to get me to go to mass."

The thought struck me that my grandmother would've also been proud because I'd led mass. More than proud. She would've been utterly delighted. Mass was her rock concert and her grandson was on the main stage. Her pilgrimages to mass seven days a week made her a holy groupie extraordinaire. If there was a guarantee mass was said at the end of each day, she would've loved to walk the Camino.

Sitting there, bobbing about on the boat, I realized she would've made a much better pilgrim than I ever will.

...cheating spaniards

_

Day 17 – Noja to Güemes
15.6km

Cassie

It takes about two weeks until you're truly broken in. The early days on the Camino are busy and filled with a series of newbie tasks like blister-popping and guidebook checking. It's hard to find time to take a breath and realize where you are and what you've come for. Energy is spent on nursing your wounds and numbing your sore body rather than self-reflection and emotional wave-riding.

For me, Day 17 was the breakthrough.

My body finally felt limber and used to walking all day. My shoes began to feel like a second skin, and my pack's weight undetectable. We gave up navigation long ago, and fully trusted the 'clams' to lead us forward.

This morning, I knew the unseen, magical world that exists all around and within us was ripe to become part of my awareness again. I'd eased into the Camino flow, and had the space to feel the more subtle vibrations of the spiritual side of the Way. I figured I better get on the spiritual path soon, because we received a text from LSD Bill this morning. He was waiting for us one day ahead.

In steps Father Ernesto. Albergue heaven. Get to *La Cabaña del Abuelo Peuto* by 2pm, just in time for lunch, and you won't be sorry. This man is Santa Claus of the Camino. Every pilgrim, up to 80 a day, is greeted with a cold glass of water and hearty welcome at his door. We were some of the first to arrive, and were immediately ushered to the supper table and given a grand three course lunch free of charge.

The house had been an albergue going back many generations. This was the original Way, and you could feel the walls pulsing with the spirit of the Camino.

Father Ernesto feeds every soul who wanders through his door, and never asks for money. There is a simple wooden box in a corner for donations.

The grounds are extensive, every detail perfectly planned to cater for pilgrims. There is a serene meditation room laid with animal pelts and decorated with religious artifacts from Father Ernesto's world travels.

A stolen moment alone in his library. Meticulous records, maps, pilgrim biographies all carefully pasted to cardboard and laminated. Hundreds of them, all testament to this man's fascination, and dedication to the Camino and all it stands for.

He asked where I was from. I sheepishly told him I'm American, and he excitedly scurried over to one of his laminated maps. It was of the San Juan Islands in the Puget Sound near Seattle. One island was circled with red marker. Its name? Güemes.

He had similar maps of all the places called Güemes in the world. There were many. However, he informed us this one, the one we were in, was the first, the original.

This Güemes we were in was barely a village; mostly abandoned stone farmhouses and dilapidated barns. A tall church stood in the distance. There's no supermarket, no bars, and no hint that somewhere along the line, people from this tiny hamlet must have traveled to the New World for a fresh start. Bringing the name of their beloved home with them, leaving the original Güemes virtually empty.

114

I suppose this is the meaning of Old World.

Father Ernesto gathered all 52 pilgrims before dinner. He told us our education means nothing. Family means everything. Put down your phones and walk. The goal is not Santiago. The goal is the Way.

After family-style dining with pilgrims of the world, James climbed a long ladder to his third-tier bunk where the space babies couldn't get to him. I dodged the grimy feet of a pilgrim who tried to play footsies with me in his sleep, as we were laying foot-to-foot.

For the first time on this Camino, I fell asleep feeling connected to the pilgrims of old, who'd undertaken this journey hundreds of years ago, and perhaps slept in this very same house.

James

"All Spanish are cheaters." This information was conveyed to me by Albert, a recently retired factory worker from Devon, England. He spoke slowly, dragging his nasally words out through a face that looked troubled by human existence. His blond-haired wife fluttered around with the face of a startled owl. I kept checking over my shoulder. Were we about to be swooped on by birds of prey? For her miniature size, she carried a giant green backpack. She also assured me all Spanish are cheaters.

This was their third Camino. Which is impressive since most of the time I'm thinking, why am I doing this one? We bumped into them as Albert clambered over a rickety gate that was only feet from the edge of a cliff that ended in the roaring ocean far below. Albert's wife struggled, so I helped by pushing her by the backpack over the fence. Albert immediately told us that this fence was nothing. He'd seen it all before. Not just seen it all on the Camino, but seen it all in life. In less than thirty minutes, we were reminded four more times that he'd seen it all.

Feeling assured he'd seen it all, I asked him, "So why are all Spanish cheaters?"

Albert, lean, veiny and in his mid-fifties, slowed his pace, then rubbed his white beard. "Well, it's like this. Those Spanish are right behind you. Then. BANG. They're in front of you. How, you may ask? The bastards take cars."

"What? They do the Camino in a car?"

"No, you silly sausage. They get a relative to pick them up. You always know a hard walk is coming up because you'll never see any Spanish on that stretch. If they see a steep hill, they ring the blooming family. Up comes the car. They hop in. Next thing you know, we find

115

them relaxing in the bar as we all bloody well come sweating in with swollen ankles. I don't like it." In agreement, his shocked wife nodded furiously.

"So what are those Spanish up to?" I asked as the sun scalded my face.

"That's a fair question. It's good for their CV. Better job prospects if you have a Camino credential. Cheating bastards."

"Really? But what do you mean, exactly?"

"Geez," he said, stamping his foot onto the grass. "You have to open your eyes more." He looked at his wife, then frowned. "It's everywhere. The Camino is a fraud perpetrated by the Spanish, for the Spanish. I'm trying to tell you they only walk the thing so when they apply for a job, they have a better chance of getting it. Any government job or bank or what have you, will look at your application more favorably if you've done the Camino. Get it? Think it's the same for them getting into college. It adds to your grades in school. Could be wrong about that." He nudged me in the ribs with his boney elbow. "Spanish probably cheat on their exams, too." He winked to his wife. "Keep that to yourself, Nora."

"I will, Albert. You know me."

"I know you, Nora. You're my wife" He looked at me "I know my wife Nora well. We've seen it all. She's salt of the earth, my Nora. Never cheated a dog nor man out of so much as a sausage. Now the Spanish. That's different. Don't you see them passing you on the buses all the time?"

"Buses?" I looked down at the sea breaking against the rocks. Green hills stretched off into the distance. This could be the most beautiful part of the Camino so far. "I don't even see any road, Albert. Don't mind any buses."

"Dammit. Use your head. I don't mean here!" He waved his arms around his head. "I just mean everywhere else. Bus loads of Spanish. Sometimes the whole Camino Frances is just full of tour buses with young Spanish jumping out of the bus into the pub." He stamped his foot again. "Stamping their credentials then walking thirty minutes then jumping back on the bleeding bus. It's not right."

Looking shocked, his wife chimed in. "It's not right. Sometimes you see one guy alone in a bar, getting five other credentials stamped at the one time for his family. And the family are just sitting outside in the car, waiting. The worst is when you arrive at an albergue after walking all day to find it full with these people who just got dropped off by bus or car.

116

We had nowhere to stay a few nights. Isn't that right, Albert? Remember that time we had to ask for money from Tokyo Joe and he gave us a bag of rice? Did you know that, James? All Asians carry rice to cook in their packs. Can you believe it?"

"No," I said. "That's probably not true is it?"

"The worst is the internet forums," said Albert looking to the sky as if God was personally listening to his complaints. "I posted my knowledge about the Camino then I got attacked by online trolls. Online bleeding trolls. Boils my blood. I asked the forum members what had happened to all the Camino spirit and camaraderie? Then do you know what happened, James? Those forum members were mean to me. Of course it was the Americans that told me off. They're all so rude. One woman replied that it must be me that was the problem. But I'm telling you now, mate. I'm not the problem. I'll talk to anyone. If you talk to me, I'll talk to you."

As the grassy path became asphalt we bade a hurried farewell to Albert and Nora. But not before Albert had reassured me another time that he'd seen it all and advised me to keep my eye out for the cheating Spanish.

Albert was a fading memory by the time we reached the hilltop albergue in Güemes. It was run by a priest. I hoped he was a dancing priest, jigging away to God's merriment. We were barely in the door when mugs of water and wine were offered, as we happened to be just in time for a hearty lunch. The place was a paradise. Pictures of the priest's far flung adventures from all over the world hung on the walls.

Dozens of us were seated together on long benches as live music played. There were free beds and hot showers. They even had a meditation room and library. Later we sat in the sun, letting our sore muscles relax. People seemed at ease here. Laughter fluttered. It had to be one of the best abodes so far. Then I overheard a familiar voice.

"It's a cult, I tell you. Don't trust anyone. It's always like this. Everyone's happy. Then BANG. This place and all of us are in a sinister, religious Netflix documentary. It's the way here. I'm telling you now. I've seen it all before. Don't trust the Camino. It's a scam. Set up to further the career of the Spanish. All Spanish are cheaters."

At bedtime, I clambered to the safety of my third tier bunk. Tucked up in my sleeping bag, I felt safe in the knowledge I could forget my woes because Albert and his wife were paranoid enough to do the worrying for all of us.

117

...beautiful bill

–

Day 18 – Güemes to Santander
15.4km

Cassie

Within a few meters of 52 people eating breakfast, I found a quiet bench to drink my cafe con leche and watch the mist in the valley below.

Father Ernesto came around the side of the albergue as a pilgrim was throwing his pack over his shoulder to head off. Ernesto embraced him as if he were his own son.

It's impossible for this man to deeply connect to all the pilgrims he accepts as guests each day. But with tiny interactions and his constant vibration of generosity and spirit, he emits enough love and care to fill us with a sense of warmth not easily found while traveling so far from home. I promised the mist I'd keep this in mind as I went forward on the Camino.

We took the non-asphalt shortcut, and although it added 4km, it was the most gloriously beautiful day we've had yet.

The path wound along a high cliff for a couple hours, the sea spread out to our north. Spectacular rock pools filled with turquoise waters fit for mermaids below, and low and behold, the high peaks of the Picos de Europa finally came into view. Far in the distance, they were snow-capped and majestic. Perhaps Father Ernesto walks this way some days after all the pilgrims leave. He must recharge his soul somehow. This would certainly do the trick.

Maybe nothing in this world fills me with as much wonder and joy as seeing snow-capped peaks. I don't know why. Perhaps they echo of some home I had in another life. But on this fine morning, I felt my stomach turn. *Hmmm. Reminds me of looking up at the Dhauladhar Himalayan Range on my morning walks in Dharamsala. No time for this shit now. Stuff it away.*

It's incredible to think we'll be walking up and past this mountain range in the coming week, flanking it and walking clear around it when we finally turn inland towards Santiago. *Hopefully I can keep this vomit feeling stuffed down until these damn peaks are out of sight again.*

The last bit of the walk took us along a wide, hard-packed beach, with people surfing, swimming and enjoying the first official day of the Spanish summer. James got all hyper when he saw the indentation of horse shoes in the sand.

We boarded the ferry to take us across a wide bay to the modern city of Santander. I sat in the bow, the wind whipping me and goosebumps rising on my uncovered arms as we approached.

If you're coming this way, I don't necessarily recommend spending a night in Santander. If you're in need of supplies and other logistical stuff, it may make sense, but otherwise it's a city with little charm, although beautifully placed.

Regardless, we spent the night. And who was waiting for us when we got off the ferry? Bill. Just standing there at the dock, like he knew we'd be getting off at exactly that time.

As James and I hopped off the ferry and started walking towards him, the three of us burst out laughing at the same time. It had only been a few days since we'd parted, but it felt like an eternity.

"Heyyy guys!" exclaimed the man, the myth, the legend himself.

James was smiling big and shaking his head.

I ran the last few steps and gave him a giant bear hug. "What the heck are you doing here, man? We thought you were long gone. Way ahead of us."

"Nah, well, I was, but, I felt like I had to see you guys again, ya know?"

"Yes, I know," I said smiling. I did know. I had felt it, too. "But what happened to your lady friend? Your Gerta? I thought you guys had ridden off into the sunset."

Bill's shoulders immediately slumped, suddenly remembering why he'd decided to avoid me a few days back. I knew his secret, and wouldn't let him forget.

"Well, uh… I guess I just didn't want my Camino to be defined by her, like you said back in Bilbao. I had to feel what it was like to be off on my own again. Plus, she told me she was feeling very attached to me. I can't be having that! Right, guys?!" He skipped off ahead of us with a few giant strides, and when he jumped around to face us, his smile had returned.

I wasn't surprised Bill had experienced a sudden change of heart. The initial thrill of illicit love affairs is usually stifled by tremendous feelings of guilt. But people can't help ride but them out, no matter how self-destructive.

Bill was experimenting with freedom, but couldn't reconcile it with his strong needs for approval, admiration and companionship. I found it interesting that his version of going off alone was falling back to us. My thoughts went back to the day we met, just as he was taking his very first steps on the Camino in San Sebastián. He hadn't walked a single minute on his own since, and hadn't been without a girlfriend since he was 14.

Celebrating our reunion, we drank way too much wine. Bill mesmerized us with tales of his adventures of the past week, and we laughed and sang like old friends. Well, no singing for James, but he enjoyed having an additional drinking companion for the evening. It felt unbelievably good to be in the company of an old buddy again.

Friendship on the Camino is a peculiar thing. Under normal circumstances it takes months or even years to fully bond with another human being in devoted friendship. But out here, people find themselves away from everything familiar. Their homes, jobs, families and communities. In order to fill those gaps, pilgrims are more open to connecting than they normally are. Meanwhile you're on this once-in-a-lifetime adventure laced with thrilling uncertainty, unsure of what's around the next bend and where you'll sleep that night. All the drama and high emotions make for some strong, intense friendships that form very quickly.

I couldn't help but wonder what Gerta was doing, how she was feeling. I didn't know her story, but I could feel she also had a strong need for companionship. Particularly with a comedian like Bill.

Just as I finished my thought, my phone went off. It was a text message from Gerta, who'd taken my number, but never texted me before. *Hey Cassie, just want to warn you, today I saw a flasher on the Way, just outside of Santander. Be careful.*

Wow. Did Gerta know we were with Bill? Was she trying to signal to him?

I replied, *I'm so sorry that happened to you! Where exactly was it? I'm going to report it and try to warn others. Are you OK?*

Gerta informed me it happened as she was exiting a railway tunnel on the outskirts of Santander that morning. Two men had been waiting there, exposing themselves when they saw she was walking alone. It was a desolate area, with nowhere she could hide.

I could feel my ears starting to burn red. Nothing makes me more angry than this kind of bullshit. Some mentally ill jackasses so desperate to expose themselves that they're willing to defile and abuse a female pilgrim as she undertakes probably the most meaningful adventure of her life. I'd love to beat the living shit out of these guys.

Fuming, I took to the internet and started posting warnings on every Camino message board I could find. Private messages and comments began pouring in. I discovered that there had been sightings of two male flashers for a 94km stretch of the Camino, spreading out either way from Santander. In every case, the victims had always been walking alone, and there were always two men.

After a while, the boys noticed I was glued to my phone.

"Cassie! I mean Young Mike. What are you doing?" demanded Bill.

"Well, actually I got a text from Gerta."

His face suddenly looked confused and a bit panicked. "Ummmm?"

"She was warning me to be careful of flashers. She saw two this morning outside of the city."

Several beers in, my male companions initially reacted by laughing. "Flashers?" asked James. "Like guys waggling their willies about?" Bill shrieked with laughter.

But they saw by my facial expression that I did not find their response amusing. Bill sighed. "Is she OK?"

"Yes, she's ok. She was just warning me."

James ordered another round.

James, Bill and I began to devise a plan for the following day. I would walk on ahead a bit and see if the flashers were in the same spot. The guys would sneak up behind me videotaping and trying to get photos of their faces so we could give them a good old-fashioned internet shaming.

Around midnight, we decided to end the evening. Bill realized that he'd missed his 10pm curfew at the municipal albergue, and the doors would be locked.

We had a private room that night. Bill came back with us, and slept in a sleeping bag on the floor next to our bed.

The three amigos, together again.

James

The call of nature became too strong so I clambered down from my third story bunk. Moonlight bathed Father Ernesto's albergue and the surrounding countryside in a light, buttery glow. Stars spun above. Tantalizing glimpses of other galaxies.

Lost in the Milky Way, I let my legs carry me to the front gate. My neck and back were stiff. Breathing into each sore spot, I began to relax.

I was lost to the celestial lights until the sound of footsteps took my attention.

To hide from the night walker, I stepped back behind the low iron gate. As the shadowy shape turned human, I saw a pilgrim concentrating on the Way ahead. Hair tied in a ponytail and a bushy 70's moustache made him look like a lost Woodstock hippie.

"Hello," he said, suddenly stopping.

Hoping he'd move on, I didn't answer.

"Hello, you?" he said louder.

"Who, me?" I said stupidly. "How's it going?" Cold was creeping into my body, so I bounced from one foot to the next.

"You're staying at Father Ernesto's. Good choice." His accent was unmistakably Scottish, mixed with a tired purpose. Like he was excited, but wary of the long journey ahead.

"Are you staying here?" I asked. I took another step back to let him through the gate.

"Here? No friend. I've stayed here too many times. It's no place for the night."

"For the night?"

"Aye. For the night. The day is when I want to sleep." He took something from behind his ear then a bright flame illuminated his face as he lit a half-smoked cigarette. Deep lines around his cheeks and forehead made him look older than he sounded. "Smoke?" he asked, offering me a drag of his fag.

"No. I'm good. Gave them up"

"Life is too short to be giving up stuff, wee man. Half the people I meet these days talk about giving up on the Camino. One thing I've learned in ten years of walking is that if you're happy in life, then that's good enough. So many young fools trying to better themselves these days."

Did he think I was a young fool? "You've been walking for ten years? Not continuously, obviously?"

"Oh. It's obvious, is it?" he said, sounding annoyed. "I've been walking, alright. I'm tired, and I'm still walking." He took a long drag of the cigarette. "The Camino is a guest that won't fucking leave your head. Dogs of war fighting in your mind. Snarling and snapping. Bleeding you so dry that no amount of wine will satisfy. Until you're like me. Just walking." A few sparks flew as the cigarette bounced off the road before he stubbed it out with a heavy stomp.

I didn't know what to say. Maybe he was joking, but the words were spoken with a ferocity that made me feel the Camino had ground him down like the butt of his cigarette. Albert could've learned what it meant "to have seen it all" from this guy. In the cold, I continued to bounce.

"I'm going," he said. "I'm out the gate, as they say. Maybe I'll see you on the way back."

"What will they do?" a German accent rang out. "Murder us?" In mild fright, I turned towards the albergue to see a pot-bellied man in dark glasses, already too close for comfort. Glancing back for moral support, I was relieved the Scottish guy had decided to stay.

"What if we don't leave?" said the German, now so close I could smell the cigarettes on his breath. "Will the old priest kill us?"

The Scottish guy gave a raspy laugh. "Father Ernesto will kill you! He'll stab you with a wee bottle of wine in both eyes. See no evil."

The German rubbed his belly, then laughed. "Too true. I sleep with a bottle of whiskey under my pillow. Maybe I'll hit him first."

"Do you have the whiskey now?" asked the Scot.

"No. Drank it. Do you have smokes?"

"No. Smoked them."

The German leaned so close he could've licked my cheek. "I could hear by your accent that you're an Irishman. I was told all Irish carry a bottle of whiskey with them?"

"Only the real Irish. I'm a plastic paddy."

"A what?"

The Scot laughed.

"A fake Irish," I said. "Plastic. Not real. Also, I'm a plastic pilgrim."

An uncomfortable silence settled. The Scot lit another cigarette, seemingly intent on insulting the German after lying to him, then walked off, glowing until he became shadow. The German went back the way he came.

I nodded to both of their backs. It seemed I still wasn't getting this Camino etiquette.

As we left the holy hostel in the morning, we were joined by a Polish skinhead. Church bells tolled as we descended into the thick fog sitting in the valley below. He informed us that being a chef in London was a stressful job. But he would never ask for help. Never in his whole life had he let anyone help him with anything.

Now he felt detached from himself, cold and withering away from all the city living. He felt the Camino would help him connect with his past

123

and to people. So two weeks ago he left London with sixteen pounds in his pocket and began to walk the Camino. So far he'd managed to survive on the charity of others. Father Ernesto let him stay a few extra nights so he could fuel up on the fantastic free food.

Interestingly, he couldn't stay still. Even when standing, he would make a walking motion. "Can't seize up," he kept muttering. "Can't seize up." And for a guy with no money, he somehow chain smoked the whole time he walked with us.

Upon reaching the ferry to Santander, he moved from our group to others' with effortless transition. Seemingly reading the air as he approached new people, he would morph his body language to suit their atmosphere. Relaxed to concerned. Happy to somber.

I was intrigued by the way he quickly captivated each group, but then I also couldn't help but smile at how some of the people slightly closed their body language as he probed too quickly into their personal circumstances. At times he came across calm, then suddenly desperate. If he was hustling, he really needed to work on his game. Patience is a virtue in the swindling business. He was changing the pilgrims' emotions too quickly. They found it disconcerting.

I would've given him money for his efforts, or at least bought him the ferry fare if he'd joined us again. But my scrutiny of humans changed to excited animal-tracking when I noticed hoof prints in the sand. *Could it be the horse of Gypsy Mullet?* My mind lit up. I wondered what he's up to now. Hopefully serenading his refound horse.

"What?" asked Cassie.

I must have been smiling too brightly. "Nothing. Just..."

"Just what?"

I pointed to the hoof prints.

"You found horse prints? So what?"

I nodded.

Cassie nodded. "It's just horse prints," she said.

"But what if it's Gypsy Mullet's horse?"

"Ohh, it could be," she said, waving her arms around in mock excitement. "Your friends are here. Why don't you find them? Live your dream by riding off into the sunset with them?"

Gypsy Mullet's hair streamed in the wind as I imagined him galloping along the sandy beach. A few crabs clung to his mane in delight. I decided not to tell my wife about that vision. In such a young marriage, it might not be healthy for our relationship. Probably not healthy at any time.

LSD Bill awaited our arrival in Santander. Appearing in all his disheveled glory, he ended the night crashing on our floor. In our energetic interactions, we learned how Gerta had saved him from wolves, farmers and a Nazi magician.

Waking in the night, I saw Bill had disappeared. I was glad he didn't have a drug -induced psychotic fit and murder us in our sleep.

...time warps

-

Day 19 - Santander to Boo de Pielagos
We took a bloody taxi, alright?

Cassie

Sick to my stomach, writhing around with abdominal pain, I looked down to where Bill had gone to sleep on the floor. He was gone. Only my crumpled sleeping bag was there. No note. No sign of him at all.

Already 9am, long past normal start time for a walk, I knew there was no way I could move forward today.

Sometimes you have to be strong and keep pushing to get ahead. And sometimes you just have to admit you're sick and say "fuck the Camino". James dragged me down to the street and ordered me an orange juice and a tortilla. I nearly vomited.

So. Bill had vanished. There were probably a couple of flashers waiting to show their junk to me, and I was about to throw up. No bueno.

I could see the train station across the street. I caught James' eye, then looked at the station. He knew instantly.

He picked up my pack for me, grabbed my hand, and walked us across the street. Inside the station, we realized that since it was Sunday, there wouldn't be another train for two hours. Without guilt or discussion, we walked straight up to the line of taxis in front and asked the fare to Boo de Pielagos. 15 euros. Sold.

Being in a car after so long was a strange feeling. I don't think I'd ever gone this long without being in a vehicle in my life.

As I gazed out the window at the passing industrial sprawl of Santander, I felt grateful for even having the option. But we were cheating on the Camino. Cheaters. Like the Spanish. What would Albert think of us? I let the guilty feeling linger only a few seconds more. If these were medieval times, I'd be risking life and limb to walk this extremely long and tiring pilgrimage. Given the chance of a lift for a few miles on a day my stomach was turning, would I take it? Hell yes... Any real pilgrim would, even back then.

I'd always been confused and fascinated watching medieval-themed shows like 'Game of Thrones' and 'Lord of the Rings.' Jaime Lannister declaring it was a month's march to Winterfell, or Frodo and the gang walking for a year or more to reach Mordor.

Did people really have to walk so long and far to get anywhere? How many people actually made journeys like that? What does it even mean to walk a month to a destination you could now reach in a few hours by car?

If you want to know, walk the Camino. There's no better way to expand your understanding of spatiality. To truly comprehend the implications of the combustion engine's invention and resulting globalization.

In what was supposed to take three hours, we reached Boo de Pielagos in 15 minutes. For the rest of the day, I avoided looking up at the snowy peaks and daydreamed about where the hell Bill went.

James

On our stone cold floor, only bits of bread remained from where Bill had slept. Maybe he'd become so saintly on the Camino his body had turned into sacramental bread. Was LSD Bill now the body of Christ? Could he have risen to attain spiritual nirvana? Should we all dine on his metaphorical corpse if we see him again? Either way, my pounding headache made it feel like I needed a priest to exorcise the demon drink from my soul.

To save our sanity, we took a nausea-inducing taxi to the albergue in Boo.

At the quaint establishment my headache was soothed by the owner's corgi dog licking my hair. While I played with the little animal, traditional guitar music blared from cheap speakers somewhere in the village.

Cassie took to bed to ease her pain, but I was still too jittery to relax. I left the dog to investigate the sound.

Down a few side streets, I found a little festival in full swing. Excitement flowed through the stalls selling plastic toys, candyfloss and novelties outside an open barn now blaring out flute music. The only

126

thing that took my fancy was a crappy looking straw hat to replace my lost baseball cap. Costing only three euros, the plastic bits holding it together immediately began to unravel.

As I watched the huddles of humanity laugh at the world, my hangover began to melt away. A chocolate-covered kid jumped up and tried to bite my hat, but missed. Crying in frustration at his missed morsel, he retreated to a group of revelers with babies under arms drinking cans of beer. I'd stumbled upon a proper old-fashioned fair where people could be wild, silly and raucous. Where past transgressions are forgotten for one night. Enemies now friends until the morning. A beer or five was needed to catch up with these good folk. I scanned the stalls.

My breath caught as my heart skipped a beat! Luscious locks of ferocious hair transformed this from a common festival into a momentous event. In nervous delight, my senses vibrated. Gypsy Mullet was here in all his glory! Even the flute music changed. Now it seemed to herald Fonso's magnetic aura, as if this festival was all about the mullet. I wouldn't blame them if it was.

I realized my prayers to Saint James were heard. On the sickening car ride, I'd asked for my hangover to be over, but the wise saint had actually heard the song of my heart, instead of my head. Rather than losing a hangover, I gained a Gypsy Mullet. *Glory be!*

Genuinely smiling, I approached Fonso. A red, frilly shirt billowed a little on his bulky frame. His eyes were keen, weighing up the revelers. But before I could reach my prize, another voice called my name. I turned to look into the barn. *Oh, my God!* On stage Nicu was playing the flute! Seductively, he played the instrument in one hand while the other waved me over. Surprised to be connected to Nicu in such a public display of affection, I waved back. Sternness suddenly crossed his face.

Fearful I'd caused some kind of offense, I calmed myself then continued towards the stage. His sharp cheekbones and slender lips made him look like a snake grooving in a mating dance. Slowly, as if teasing me, he put both his ring-fingered hands around the instrument. A mesmerizing waterfall of cascading music flowed through me. A force field of sound. It whispered for my toes to tap and my mind to let go.

Undaunted, my mind still sought out the higher power of the Mullet. Somehow I forced myself to look back at him, but he'd vanished. What gypsy magic was this? How could that mullet hide in the mere hair space of other mortals? *Come back to me Gypsy*, I heard the wind whisper. Disoriented, I turned back to the stage to see Nicu had started to sing, his voice like melting butter soaking into my soft head then massaging my mind. Momentarily, I was a marionette under his spell. He pointed upwards and I was compelled to look to the heavens. He pointed behind me. I turned to see Gypsy Mullet standing behind a wooden stall in the shadows. *What wonders would such as he sell?*

Breaking away from Nicu's spell, I pushed through revelers towards the stall. That tremendous mullet was so deceptive in size. Space-time seemed to warp around the hair in weird angles making it hard to grasp the actual proportions of the stall.

A petite woman stood between us waiting to be served. I needed her to move. Managing to tear my eyes away from the Mullet, I took in his wares. Polished glass bottles of all shapes, sizes and colors held tonics, ointments and salves. Some smoked. Some almost hummed. Some had little mullets attached. Holy pictures of Christian figures dangled from the top of the wooden poles, haphazardly holding the stall together. Most images dangled perilously close to his mullet. The woman left. I met Gypsy Mullet's eyes. He nodded like he knew I'd be here.

"Did you find my beautiful beast?" he boomed. Holy icons hanging about his hair seemed to be drawn into its gravity field.

My mouth was dry in anticipation. "Beautiful beast," I whispered.

His eyes penetrated my soul. Daring me to lie.

"No," I said. For a moment, my entire being wished I'd become a full-time horse detective.

He shook his head, stood up on his toes and to his obvious annoyance a few holy pictures caught in his hair. Further head shaking snapped their thin strings with ease as if to show God who was really in charge. "My beast. She may not be alone. The others may have taken her. But it is not too late." A picture of Mary the mother of Jesus stuck to his sweaty face. Without a flicker of emotion he brushed it away. Sweat beaded his brow. He perspired with the grace of an angel.

"Who would have taken your beast, Gypsy Mullet?"

His eyes flared at hearing his own name. "They are people who would have stolen my horse, Canción," he said loudly as if challenging all that could hear. "But she is swifter than the seas. She would prance on their faces for fun. But..."

"But?"

"But still..."

"But still what?"

128

"No. I won't speak of it. Won't speak of it until I see it. Take this." He snatched a clear bottle of liquid with greasy hair attached to the cork. "For feeding my horse. It is a gift for the Way."

Reverently, I put my hand out as if receiving holy sacrament. The little bottle was warm, while the hair felt like spun gold. My heart jumped. *Could it be? Pure Gypsy Mullet hair was attached?* "What is it?"

"Not what it is. When it is. Find my horse." With that he whistled. "Look at Nicu."

I turned to see him again playing the flute one-handed.

"Some say his music casts a shadow on the wind. Look to where his hand lays. Yes, pilgrim. Look. Truly look. See."

Nicu's hand resided in his pocket.

"To make such music he caresses the tonic. The same tonic I have given you. Tribes have warred. Secrets lost. But we have won."

I didn't have the heart to tell Fonso it looked like Nicu was scratching his balls, or worse.

Gypsy's next whistle was so high-pitched it startled the people closest to us and rang in my ears. Nicu looked our way, jumped off the stage, then hurried to a rusty, blue van with hay bales in the back. Jumping up with ease, he sat on a bale, then banged the side of the trailer. A slender arm drenched in bangles and painted red fingernails hung out the window. It made a fist. Smashed the side of the van. The engine revved. Wheels spun and it sped to our stall. Defying his great weight, Fonso vaulted into the trailer with ease. Religious pictures streamed from his glistening mullet as they sped off. Nicu whistled like a hawk as they vanished into the dusk.

Holding my hairy bottle tight, I whispered, "Glory be."

...buen bollocks

—

Day 20 - Boo de Pielagos to Santillana del Mar
20 km

Cassie

I was still a bit weary. The *Albergue de Peregrinos de Boo de Pielagos* (try saying that after a couple of sangrias) was a quiet and slightly luxurious place to sleep. The fantastic large dinner salads offered something delightfully different to the standard Spanish fare, and I was grateful.

After a day of saying 'no' to the Camino, and truly feeling I wanted to quit, I woke up refreshed and ready to push on. As long as I didn't have to contemplate the snowy peaks.

Today's walk undulated across gentle hills, the massive national highway never out of earshot. Not one for shortcuts unless it's to avoid pollution and cars, just out of Boo, we faced a decision:

- Stay on the Camino and walk an extra 7km (tediously along the national highway).
- Get a train for one stop to Mogro, cutting off that entire 7km.
- Take the dangerous option and cross the train bridge over the River Pas by foot, effectively saving a few bucks and still cutting off the 7km. Plus, enjoy the accompanying rush of adrenaline.

We opted for the train. It's one stop, a two minute ride. The safest option. We didn't particularly feel like dying on this day, which was a nice change.

But once we boarded the train and crossed the bridge, I saw it would've been perfectly fine to have walked. It's a double lane bridge, so if a train were to come, you'd have plenty of space to let it pass by. If two trains came at exactly the same time, you'd still be ok because it's a low bridge so you could easily jump into the marshy water below without even getting your hair wet. Lesson learned.

Halfway through the day's walk, we were entertained by watching a massive international chemical factory take shape in the distance, smoke stacks spewing god knows what, until we were standing right at its gates. Appropriately, this was our hottest day yet. Still just 78F/26C, but the sun was strong on the 25th of June. I imagined the airborne toxic particles I'd be ingesting into my unsettled stomach for the next 8km. So far, the Camino through Cantabria was a lot less beautiful than in Basque Country. The Way is maintained largely by local Camino clubs and associations, or the provincial tourist boards. In Basque Country they seemed to make a lot of effort to route the paths through as much nature and countryside as possible, avoiding roads and civilization. In Cantabria, the effort had fallen away, and much of the time we found ourselves walking along major highways on asphalt.

After a long and not-so-beautiful day, we caught our first glimpse of the picture perfect Santillana Del Mar, a small medieval village bustling with tourism and expensive restaurants. It was relieving to be somewhere beautiful and quiet, in contrast to the day's walk.

We decided over the best glass of milk I ever tasted, to rest an extra day here while I recovered from my weird stomach malady.

And seriously. You must get a glass of milk and a slice of *quesada pasiega*, the local dense cheesecake, from Obrador Casa Quevedo. I'm not a milk drinker, but this shit was goooood. Must come from happy cows. I still gave half my milk to a little dog by pouring it into a pool between the cobblestones. He happily lapped it up.

James

A tabby cat was attacking my mullet bottle. It must have rolled from the safety of under my pillow onto the floor. "Stop it, kitty," I said, as I tugged it out of the feline's mouth. We stared at each other. Disdain for my utter existence was evident in those cute eyes. I brought the bottle close. Faint smells of aged wine, church incense and now cat saliva clung to the sopping hair fibers.

Our short train journey turned into a stress fest as I thought I'd left my passport and wallet at the albergue. I frantically searched my bag until everything I owned was strewn across the tray table. *Where was it? Damn it. Would I have to go back in time again?* Next deep scan through the bag found something hard in my sleeping bag. My lost gear.

I've mislaid so much stuff already. *Why is that?* Maybe something to do with my past? I had a habit of getting lost as a child. My parents would let me run wild in the countryside. One time as a five-year-old, I'd become so lost I thought I'd never be found. This memory interests me, as I remember that instead of being afraid I was actually excited that I was lost and would never find my way home. Maybe I love loss.

In other news from the Way, I'm finally drug-free... It took three trips to the doctor and three doses of antibiotics every day of the Camino to clear my ear infection. That could be some kind of record. I was looking forward to not boiling up in the night from overreacting to the medication. Dorms already made my blood boil as it was. Damn dirty space babies.

Not being able to sleep at night in my own bed is one thing. But not being able to sleep in a dorm, night after night, is a special kind of twilight life that scrabbles at my sanity and devours memories (except how long it took to get to sleep the night before). At night, my hyper vigilant brain would ignite, then secrete adrenaline in case of any threat to my existence from the dorm's patrons, be they whisperer, roller, rooter, eater, tosser, pisser or space baby.

At times the worst feeling was watching everyone going to bed and curling up happily, fully knowing I had a long waking night ahead of me to endure. But mostly, the worst was the exasperation of trying to get to sleep and struggling against the dawn.

Occasionally, defeated by the battle, I'd just get up and head out into the world of the Camino. I've come to enjoy the solitude of the nocturnal nature walk. Calm and silent, the night air cools my overheated senses. Watching the stars twinkle, I begin to relax. These celestial giants don't bother anyone. They're just chilling out, heating up some other solar system. As the moon waxes and wanes along its gravitational journey, I begin to appreciate being the only human out and about. Only croaking toads to tell me tales.

When dawn would finally bloom, I'd take this as my cue to try to valiantly catch a morning nap. Sleepy eyed, dawn pilgrims would peer curiously at me as I walked against them, back to the albergue.

"Buen Camino," they'd say.

"Buen Bollocks," I usually reply

...torture

–

Day 21 – Santillana del Mar
Rest Day

Cassie

Rest days are important for your body. But are weird for your mind.

Even though the Camino is far from a wilderness trail, as you're constantly walking through urban areas and encountering many more non-pilgrims, a remarkable metaphysical phenomenon takes place.

It's like the Camino has its own invisible force field, and you're contained inside a tube that flows in one direction towards Santiago.

You become part of this vein of energy, and if you remove yourself from it for more than a few hours, you begin to feel like a lost fool in Spain, not sure where you are or why you're walking. On rest days, there's an opportunity to experience this. Sometimes it can be a relief, and at other times very unpleasant.

On our first rest day in Bilbao, I was lapping it up. To be autonomous in a big city for a day was rejuvenating. But this day, we're in this little tourist village of Santillana del Mar, a place without much soul, and I feel lost, wondering what my purpose is.

I was excited about visiting the Altamira Caves, which I had studied in college. They contain some of the oldest cave paintings known to man, and are often cited as humankind's earliest example of art. Just as we were about to walk in, an official told us you can't go inside anymore. The paintings are being damaged by too many human visitors. I was forced to wallow further in my endless self-reflection. I felt sickened by myself, constantly analyzing my mind and my life, wondering *what if* this, and *what if* that. It had been much more comfortable to distract myself for all those years in India thinking about soccer and Tibetans instead. I squirmed as I once again fell into a deep pool of self-indulgence.

James went to the *Museo de la Tortura - Inquisicion* when we found out the caves were off limits. I passed a bar and sat down at an outside table instead. The cool white wine was refreshing on this warm summer's day. I realized this was the first time I had sat in solitude, not a pilgrim in sight, since we had begun our trek three weeks ago.

I felt a rising wave of uncertainty. Here I was, on the Camino, the one big adventure I'd always dreamed of, and I felt like an imposter. Everyone I'd met seemed to be walking for a clear reason. Tomasino's was deciding his career path,- blacksmith like his father, or psychologist, following his passion. Bill was exploring whether to stay with his girlfriend. Others were reconnecting to nature, losing weight, or healing. Everyone seemed to be having daily mind-blowing experiences, meeting the right people, receiving cryptic messages from the universe, and feeling the legendary Camino magic. Even James, who I knew was only walking for me, was having meaningful interactions that inspired bouts of energy where he actually seemed to feel something. Even if he wouldn't or couldn't tell me, I still felt his emotions were shifting.

But me, I wasn't feeling any of it. I was enjoying the walking and nature for the most part, but nothing was really *happening*. I'd met a lot of great people, but no one had stirred my soul. I'd seen a lot of beautiful views, but none rocked my core. No signs. No messages. Nothing. I felt nothing. With Bill gone, I wasn't even laughing much anymore.

I'd felt nothing for a long time, since leaving India. My life was wide open. 36 years old, with the possibility to do literally anything. And I had not one interest, one passion, one wish or dream that I felt moved to pursue. I'd spent much of the last year watching YouTube and reading the news, completely numb to the voice inside me, once so strong.

I hoped walking the Camino would change that. But three weeks in, there was no Camino magic for me.

James

"Will you just be quiet," said one of my new companions to a sunburnt child playing at the next table. I smiled in sympathy. Oddly, for such a hot day, the man wore an extraordinarily large, black puffer jacket. It was like hanging out with the marshmallow man, if he was a posh, English bloke with a tidy mustache and beady eyes that seemed to despise life. Hatred practically steamed from his bald head. This pilgrim was ready to blow his top.

"Come on, Freddy," said his smiling lady friend Margaret while straightening her wide brimmed hat. Playfully she nudged him with her elbow. "Don't be so glum. You love history. It's half the reason you dragged me along on your silly walk." She winked at me. "Only messing."

"Ohhh, not this again," he muttered. He stood then stretched his right leg. "Feels like I've taken an arrow to the knee."

Earlier at lunch, when the three of us had been reluctantly pushed together at a table because the cafe was so busy, we'd begun to talk history. Freddy hoped the local torture museum would have information on the Spanish Inquisition and not just the cheaply deprived notions of extracting confessions from heretics so common to Hollywood. We all agreed it was hard to find reliable details about the Inquisition on the Camino. Almost as if some widely-followed religious organization was trying to pretend this part of its history never happened...

Stale skeletons hanging by the front entrance welcomed us into a well-lit museum displaying deadly and devious devices designed to cause horrific agony. Not sure what Freddy was expecting, but he clearly wasn't happy by the way he gnawed his fingernails on seeing the rusted implements, portraits of pains and gruesome descriptions, demonstrating the savage ingenuity of our species. Margaret took his hand and caressed it with her thumb to stop his nail biting.

Kids bounced in behind us, creating a ruckus. Freddy chewed the nails of his other hand. We stopped to look at a painting of a screaming man being flayed alive by scorching knives.

134

Darkly, Freddy shook his head, then spat bits of nail on the floor. "Such wicked imagination."

Margaret rubbed his arm tenderly. "It's okay, lovie."

For the first time I saw him smile as he gave her a quick kiss on the cheek. "I know," he said.

Composing himself with a deep breath, he again stretched out his right leg, then scrunched up his face in pain. Lost in memory for a moment, he shook his head then said to me, "If you're wondering, it was the army and the church that did me in." Margaret squinted at him out of the corner of her eye.

"James," he said intently. "People are being tortured as we speak. The depravity." His voice trailed off.

"The church and the Inquisition are part of the Camino," said Margaret. "We can't walk it and reminisce about saints, but pretend monsters didn't exist."

Freddy's voice began to burn with the intensity of the scorched victims we looked upon. "Monsters still exist. I've met my fair share. This place is sick." His fingers clutched at his jacket's zipper. "I'm sorry, I've got to get out of here." With that, he walked off.

Margaret gave me an awkward, apologetic smile. "Sorry about Freddy. He is trying his best and I love him more for it."

Nodding my head in concern, I waited for her to continue.

"He always talks about facing his demons, but..." She looked around. "Anything in here could have triggered him, I suppose. I better get after him"

Watching her leave I felt nauseous, as if there was bad ham in my belly. Maybe it was the plastic stench of the panic-stricken mannequins? I hoped Freddy was okay. If I bumped into them again, I'd definitely offer to buy them a drink. All that suppressed anger must be eating the man alive.

Walking deeper within, a shiver took me when I saw a painting of women accused of witchcraft cowered and screaming. My mind flashed to that dark room with the dripping water in the convent last week. There'd been a picture of a similar witch. Shadows had seemed to jump right at me. *Could this be the same witch?* Carefully, I studied her face. Examined each wrinkle. Felt like a baffled detective clutching at straws. I should really tell Cassie about the strange shadows in the bowels of that convent. I'm beginning to doubt reality.

A group of kids barreled around a corner, nearly knocking over an exhibit. With unbridled joy, they shouted and pointed at the atrocities, frightening their younger siblings with graphic tales about novel torture devices.

The younger kids enjoyed poking at the contraptions and squealed in delight prodding sharp spikes. Older family members read aloud about implements that pulled off tongues. I half expected them to take jolly pictures of each other on the rack.

Remarkably, one happy man did take a picture of his young daughter standing proudly in front of a metal bull. Apparently its inventor had won first prize in a torture design competition. A black and white poster informed me this horrendous bull was used to roast people. Terrified people would be shoved into an opening in the belly. The prize-winning part was that while they roasted to death, their screams would course through the neck of the bull and out through its nose, which created a sound like a bellowing cow. Ironically, the first one to suffer this fate was none other than its prize-winning creator. Even better, the king who commissioned its production was also later roasted.

This got me thinking about how the royal torturer of the time may have been perceived. Maybe his ingenuity was rewarded with a place at the king's table? Perhaps sitting with nobles, discussing the breaking point of their enemies? Fear of torture was a way to put dread into your enemies. It made them think twice about attacking. You never even had to use the torture device if it stopped an attack for fear of the repercussions. People will say they are not afraid of death, but everyone is afraid of excruciating pain.

Continuing to wander, I found the air cooler on the bottom floor. Slightly ajar, a heavy wooden door shook a little as if the wind blew through the building. Chopped wood scent flowed from within. Curious, I peered into the room. Sitting on a wooden chair was a mannequin dressed like a battered woman. Obviously tortured, blood ran down her face from deep wounds in her forehead. Bloodied spikes lay on the lap of her stained white dress which flowed to the floor. Little blue slippers stuck out from under her dress. Not a bad exhibit.

I pushed the door to get a closer look. The room was a cramped, glorified broom cupboard. I stepped in. Shocked, I jumped as the door crashed shut. I wasn't going to fall for any scary shit like in the convent. *Stay calm. The door just closed in the wind. But where was the wind coming from?* Cold sweat settled on my back. I didn't know if I could trust my senses. The mannequin opened its eyes. Before I could react, a smile crept across its bloodied lips.

A jumble of words poured out of its mouth. On seeing my questioning fear, it said, "Where is María?"

Frozen, I asked, "Are you okay?"

"Of course I'm okay," she said irritated. "I work here. Where's María? It's time for her to start work." She lifted her hand, then ripped the prosthetic wound from her forehead. A sickly sweet smell wafted from little pustules that had formed where it irritated her skin. She pressed one firmly, its yellow puss sticking to her fingers before she wiped it on the dress.

Surprise crossed her brow when she looked up and noticed I was still standing there. "Why are you still here? The show's over. I'm just waiting for María to take over." She looked at the yellow stain on her dress. "I'll clean my own dress," she said defensively. "You need to leave. Now."

I reached for the door handle.

"Were you attracted to my shoes?"

"What?" I looked at her blue shoes. They were dainty. "No. Why?"

"Oh. That's okay." She seemed a little down.

I opened the door to leave.

"Are you leaving? It's just people used to come to look at my shoes. People would follow me as if I was a real lady of history. Isn't that weird? They used to fall in love with me."

"I suppose." I edged further out the door.

"It's just you seem like one of them so I thought you might be attracted to my shoes?"

"No attraction to shoes happening here at all." Only my head was left in the room. "Bye."

I'd had enough torture for one day. Feeling safe and sound curled up next to Cassie was the perfect alternative.

Later in bed a thought scraped uneasily. Why am I meeting so many angry men on the Camino? Are we drawn to each other? How much in common do I have with these people?

In my dreams, I burned at the stake. All that was left of my ashes were my blue shoes that were then stolen by a child in a jester's hat.

Losing Weight on the Camino

So many pilgrims along the way list 'losing weight' as their primary reason for walking the Camino. You'd think that by burning an extra 1500 calories per day walking this would come easy, but nothing could be further from the truth. For most people, in order to lose weight you'd have to be very careful about the quality and amount of food you're consuming, not to mention the excessive beer and wine drinking that tends to happen on the journey. You'll be fitter, sure, but not much lighter. Most of the food readily available along the Camino is not diet friendly. It takes real effort to supplement typical pilgrim's menus with fruits and vegetables, and to avoid the sugary breakfasts and desserts. One trick to keep things lighter is to drink gluten free beer, which is available in most bars in Spain. You might only drink 4 carbs per beer this way, instead of 40.

Europe's Web of Footpaths

Long before the advent of railways, airports and super highways, the only way to get around in Europe was by walking or by horse. A vast network of paths developed over the course of centuries, influenced strongly by religious pilgrimage. Pilgrimage was, for most poor Europeans, the only reason ever to leave home, with many opting to walk to Santiago for their journey-of-a-lifetime. From every corner of the continent the devout plied paths, which all eventually converged on the spot where Saint James rests. Many of these paths still exist, and today it is possible to walk to Santiago from corners as disparate as Istanbul and the Baltics. Most notably is the GR-7, stretching from the mouth of the Black Sea all the way to the Straits of Gibraltar, an ancient road dating back to the Romans and beyond. Today, it is not uncommon to meet pilgrims who began walking their Caminos in Holland, Switzerland and Germany.

Beat the Blisters

Prevention. Prevention. Prevention. The best way to beat blisters is to make sure you don't get any in the first place. Invest in good socks. They should contain a very high percentage of wool. Cotton is terrible for long distance walking, because it soaks up your sweat and stays wet, moistening and thus weakening your skin. Wool keeps feet cool in the heat and warm in the cold, and dries quickly. When choosing shoes, buy them a half-size up from what usually fits. Your feet will swell everyday on the Camino, and if your shoes can't accommodate your swollen feet you will have blisters almost immediately. Figure out where your hot spots are - places on your feet that feel a bit sore or raw after a couple of kilometers walking. Before a blister has a chance to form, tackle the problem. ENGO patches are the best product out there. They are high-tech stickers that you place on the inside of your shoe, rather than on your skin, designed to minimize friction. Ours lasted the entire length of the Camino without peeling off. If a blister does begin to form, take your shoes and socks off, dry the area and clean it. Apply hydrocolloid gel plasters. They are sold everywhere along the Camino under the brand name Compeed.

Camino Tip:

You may get burnt out being around people all day. Don't feel bad about leaving your new friends to go do your own thing. They will understand and you will feel rejuvenated when you talk to them later. Also, it's good to have some alone time each day to process the deeper parts of the Camino experience. You're basically doing walking therapy. Contemplate your changing emotions without distraction. You may be surprised at what you find.

Roma People of Spain

The Roma are a European subculture of people that originally migrated from the Indus Valley region of present-day Pakistan and India in the 14th & 15th centuries. The term 'gypsy' refers to a person of Roma origin, though this term is largely considered to be outdated and is no longer politically correct in most cases.

In Spain, Romani people are largely referred to as *Gitano*. The word is derived from *Egyptano*, much like the word *gypsy*. It is believed the first arrivals in Europe came via Egypt, and due to fears of persecution, they allowed Europeans to believe they actually originated in the favorable north African kingdom rather than the far east.

The *Gitano* have a distinct culture – they practice Christianity in their own unique way, speak a mixed Spanish-Roma dialect, and largely keep to themselves, the familial lines being of the utmost importance. Today an estimated 750,000 *Gitano* reside in Spain, many remaining largely transient, as their people have for generations.

Gitanos face a considerable amount of interpersonal discrimination in Spanish society, while also contributing to various aspects of mainstream Spanish culture, most notably Flamenco music and professional football.

Cantabria Highlights

Santillana-del-Mar

This perfectly maintained medieval village might be the most charming on the entire Camino del Norte, and definitely worthy of an overnight stay. Its many fine examples of Romanseque architecture and pedestrian-only planning make for a delightful wander through its streets, lined with galleries, museums and excellent dining options. The Camino passes directly through.

Altamira Caves

Located just outside of Santillana-del-Mar, this UNESCO-recognized archaeological site houses one of the earliest examples of human paleolithic art in the form of cave paintings depicting animals. More than 14,000 years old, the delicate site is only open to five visitors per week, and you must be present at the museum on Friday between 9.30 and 10.30 am. Of all those present, five people are then chosen at random; the tour starts at 10.40 am and lasts for 37 minutes. There is a well-done replica of the cave and an interpretive center that is open to all. Closed Mondays.

Cuevas de Monte Castillo

If you missed the real thing at Altamira, visit the caves at Monte Castillo, which are open to the public regularly. These caves house the oldest known examples of cave art in the world, painted 40,000 years ago. The caves themselves are magical. Reach via a 35-minute bus ride from Santander.

Picos de Europa

As you approach Santander through Cantabria, the snowcapped peaks of Spain's northern mountains will come into view. The range offers some of the most stunning and untouched mountain landscapes in Europe, and is worth a sojourn away from the Camino proper. All the major attractions are easily accessible via public transport from Santander.

Camino Lebaniego

This offshoot of the Camino del Norte leads from San Vicente 72km to the Monastery of Santo Toribio de Liébana in the Picos de Europa. The monastery houses a relic of the Lignum Crucis, the cross upon which Jesus died. You can continue south on a marked path to connect to the Camino Frances or Camino Olvidado if you choose not to return to the Camino del Norte.

Castro Urdiales

This bustling seaside town seamlessly combines its medieval heritage with modern flare. The stunning Church of Santa María de la Asunción is perhaps the finest example of gothic architecture on the entire Camino del Norte, its flying buttresses looming over the picturesque harbor. The Camino del Norte passes directly through, presenting the opportunity for a memorable overnight stay.

WEEK 4

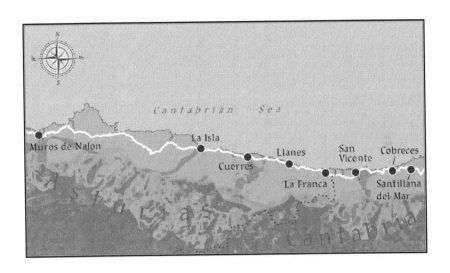

...the lizard king

Day 22 – Santillana del Mar to Cobreces
12km

Cassie

We've all heard of Einstein's theory of relativity, but take away the equations and what does it actually mean?

On the Camino, your days during the first two weeks of walking seem endless. Every dip in the road or bird on a fence seems like a sign, you remember every face you meet, and every village name. Your days are filled with wonder, and you can't believe so much happened in such a short period.

Fast forward to week three. You've been walking for more than twenty days. Now, one day is relative to twenty others, not just to two or five.

The days begin to pass quickly, and merge together. You can't remember where you slept the night before, or even a single moment of yesterday's five hour walk.

Kind of like when you were a kid. When summers were endless, and Christmas Day an epic adventure. Reach your thirties, though, and the weeks and months pass by as though they never happened. I can hardly remember how old I am most days.

If you are walking the Camino, I implore you to keep a diary. If I weren't writing it down, I would surely forget almost everything. Write. It. Down.

Today as we walked, I took special note of a white van creeping along the road behind us. I got that weird feeling someone was watching us. James had long hair, and from behind, with the pack hiding the shape of his body, he could easily look like a woman walking with me. It was super creepy.

Eventually the van sped up and went by us, perhaps realizing James was a man. It was filled to the brim with boxes and crap, like a hoarder's vehicle.

Fast forward a mile down the road, we saw the van again, skidding out from a dirt lane. He accelerated forward and pulled into another dirt road. By the time we reached his position, he had the back hatch of the van open and was fiddling around in some bushes.

We stood and stared.

But what to do? On we marched, hoping he wasn't disposing of body parts along the Camino in some kind of satanic pilgrimage ritual.

Of course, we saw him again. Another mile later, after the 'clams' diverted us off the road and onto a forest trail. Hatch open, doing something in the bushes. We walked a bit faster on to Cobreces. I'd never forget this guy's face or his van. The cautious female in me wouldn't allow it.

Living as a woman alone in India, I learned never to forget a face. I lost count how many times I'd been followed, groped, harassed and stalked. I got very good at protecting myself. My old standby when being followed, was to duck into a shop as quickly as possible. I'd stay there, talking to the proprietor, until the stalker realized I was on to him. But nature stalks were much scarier; often there was no one to help, and nowhere to hide. I was glad to be walking with James, and worried for solo female pilgrims passing by that day.

I was so naive when I first moved into the small Tibetan community in the Himalayas. I was mesmerized and hypnotized by the great show of spirituality. The prayer wheels, the colorful Buddhist flags flapping in the mountain breeze. I assumed that since these people so devoutly

144

worshipped the Buddha and the Dalai Lama, they must be a peaceful people. More enlightened than the average human. Quickly it became clear that nothing could be further from the truth.

The Tibetan National Sports Association was no different. A sham of an organization, controlled by a group of powerful old men led by Kalsang, pretending to be filled with enthusiasm for women's empowerment and equality. To perfection they played their role as poor, pure-intentioned refugees needing help from the rich foreigner to get things going in the women's sports sector.

I fell for it hook, line and sinker. I really believed in the program I'd designed, and more than anything, in the girls who were part of it. I never imagined the more confidence the girls got, the more money I raised, the more publicity we attracted, the more the men of the Tibetan National Sports Association would feel threatened, insecure and spiteful. The more love and effort I put into my job, the more animosity I attracted.

After rejecting their invitation to funnel money from the girls' program to their failing men's team, their resentment towards me grew so strong that I began to receive threats. It started with rumors I was some kind of whore, accepting money and power for sexual favors. Next, I was sequestering all the money I raised for luxury cruises and shopping. Soon, I received anonymous messages warning me to be careful, or I'd be raped. So much for the spiritual Tibetans.

I stuck it out for a few more years and pushed the team as far as I could, constantly dodging threats and interference. It fried my nerves and filled my life with fear, but I stood strong and never wavered. However, after seven years it all became too much for me to handle. I'd achieved the profound accomplishment of bringing the first Tibetan women's sporting team to play in an international tournament in North America. We attracted global news headlines and considerable disgust in Beijing. But the threats grew worse. The breathing at the other end of silent phone calls grew heavier. I had to get out.

I left India without warning, vowing to never return. I didn't get to say goodbye to the girls I'd grown to love like sisters and daughters. There was no clear end, no closure. Just an emergency booking on a flight to Ireland, and no clue what to do next. I'd married James a few months before, and should've been happy and enjoying life. But I was stuck, suddenly frozen in the years of fear and fighting, with no program to run or channel my anger and sense of purpose.

It was during these first few days back in Ireland that my world had gone dark in a pub, followed by the morning I declared I wanted to walk the Camino.

That night, after the weird darkness of the day, I couldn't help but curl into a ball in the crook between James' shoulders. And I wouldn't let go.

James

Blood dripped from my bottom lip as I slipped again on the wet cobblestones leaving Santillana. Mist was on my mind. Surrounded by its moist tendrils, it was like walking in a cloud that blanketed the entire world. Cold beads of moisture stuck to my skin and frizzed up my hair, invigorating each step. I feel younger in clouds.

Breakfast had consisted of some leftover food from the blade of my Swiss army knife, which slipped and cut deeply into my lip. Sympathy was not forthcoming from my wife who playfully mocked me for just coming off the antibiotics and now needing stitches. It wasn't that bad. Just a sharp tingle of pain whenever I touched it. Annoyingly, I couldn't stop prodding the wound. Over and over again, I'd rub my lip until blood would pool on my finger tips, only for the mist to slowly wash it away as we walked further away from civilization.

In my other hand, I squeezed the straw hat I'd bought at that village festival. Bits of its thin plastic cord holding it together were fraying everywhere. One thread had unraveled at least six feet and dragged along the ground. The cord itched my head when I bunched it under the rim whenever I wore it. Which was practically never, even though I'd gotten into the ridiculous habit of carrying the damn thing every day. Mostly the hat was curled up in my hand, making it hard to tie laces or open bottles of water. It was now a stress hat. Squeezed on every step.

Ahead, footsteps echoed eerily. Slowly a backpack materialized from the mist, preceded by its owner. Carefully treading the slippery stones. We caught up to an elderly gent, wrapped tight in a thick, green rain jacket. On his melancholy face, he sported a donut of bushy grey whiskers around his mouth and chin giving him the impression of a sour tomcat that had been kicked out of a warm barn.

Not wanting to agitate my stinging cut with pilgrim chit-chat, I thought it was best to hurry past.

"Hello," he said in a thick French accent dripping of desire to interact.

146

"Hello," I said, wincing, licking the blood from my lips. Red droplets stuck to the back of my hand where I wiped my beard. Hungry were his eyes upon my blood.

"Where are you coming from?" he said.

Caught in his trap, I said, "Santillana."

"Where are you going?"

"Santiago."

Darkness crossed his face as if I'd reminded him of some bitter sadness. "Ah, Santiago. Me, too. But it's not as good as it used to be. My name is Frank. But my friends all call me Wolfentot."

Cassie and I introduced ourselves. Falling into step, he told us in a worn out way he'd been on many Caminos around the world. "But somehow, something has changed. The spirit. The energy. The feeling of the Way is different now. Don't you think?"

"This is our first Camino," I replied.

"Ah ha. Virgins of the Way, but not in bed, I hope?"

Only slightly surprised by his remark, I answered, "We're married."

"Ah, no dormitory beds for you lovers."

I think he was just trying to be nice, but maybe his hand was down his pants. It was hard to see in the mist.

"I was married three times before," he said, brushing down his impressive side burns. "Did I tell you that?"

"No. We only just met."

"I know, but some people can just tell."

I spat blood onto the cobbles. "No. I can't tell. But three times? That's a lot. Why did you get divorced?" I bit my lip and refrained from enquiring if it was to do with his performance in the bedroom. Some people don't like to hear such jokes.

"Marriage wasn't good for me." Mist made his silence sadder. "But then I made the mistake too late and found single life is not good for me either. It's not the same as I remember."

"The same?"

"Nothing is the same, but I thought some things would be better. But it's not. They used to call me the Wolfentot, you know?"

"I know. You told us. Why Wolfentot?"

"Not Wolfentot!" he snapped. "Wolfentop! Because I was the leader of our tribe. I was top. We would Camino all over the world. I would lead. They loved it. But now, somehow. Something has changed. I used to feel the Celtic paths. The energy ley lines. Now something has

147

changed in me or in the planet. I'm not on top. I feel depressed on this Camino." Mist swirled as he just stopped to stare.

"Are you going to be alright?"

"Yes. I think so. I just need to find a purpose again. I need to find my tribe. I hear the tribes are gathering. Look!"

My eyes swiveled to where he pointed. Only a few feet away, three long-necked llamas stood watching us over a stone wall, their brown, inquisitive eyes peering out from behind the fluff.

Wolfentop clambered up on the stone wall, then tried to reach in to touch one. Skittishly, it backed away. "They used to carry my packs in Peru," he said, leaning further over the wall. "Peru is different now. Not the same. Too commercial. Before, I could feel the energy. Eat the coca leaves. Live off the land."

Instinctively, I rushed to the wall as he reached too far, barely able to catch his pack before he tumbled into the field to be softly grazed to death by llamas. Wolfentop shook his pack from my grip. "Get off me. I'll do it myself. Always have." Dejectedly, he sat on the wall. "Thank you for the company, but I'd like to be alone now. I just don't have the energy today."

Feeling a little worried about Wolfentop, we protested that we could all walk together to the next town, but he kept waving us away. "I'll find the energy soon. Then I'll run all the way to Santiago."

Mist quickly swallowed him whole. We waited for a while in a little village café to see if he would pass, but he never appeared.

The mist couldn't hold out against the sun's rays all day. After more kilometers, we were outside a church. A fresh breeze cooled the stained glass window panes.

A gaunt, impish face full of delight stuck its head out of the imposing door of the church. "Hello!" he shouted.

In reply, I gave a little wave.

Vibrating with even more joy from catching our attention, he tried to smooth down his oversized white shirt and brown pants that billowed in a momentary gust of wind. Bony fingers beckoned us. Reluctantly, we wandered over.

"Do you want to come see the bell tower?" Cassie and I looked at each other and groaned, both wanting the other to tell him *definitely no*. Ever since we met Wolfentop, we couldn't shake the gloomy mood. I declined by shaking my head.

Obviously not taking a little thing like no for an answer, the skeletal man grabbed my arm so hard he left fingernail prints, as he tried to pull me in. Cassie shrugged at my misfortune. We just didn't have the energy to protest. "Time for your first confession," I mumbled to Cassie as he half-dragged me up the aisle like a sacrificial lamb.

"Up here," he said, pulling me away from the altar. "Have you been to heaven?" Steep stairs wound upwards into pure darkness. Pain where he grabbed my arm began to itch.

Empty churches can feel peaceful. Residing in a chilly pew, I feel secure that no one will bother me.

Now my chest ached with anxiety as I was dragged into the dark by an emaciated imp that smelled of burnt fish. My discomfort wasn't alleviated by the first few steps on the stairs creaking treacherously underfoot. Incense irritated my eyes as he led us further into the blackness.

When we reached the top, I breathed a sigh of relief, causing my throat to burn and my nose hairs to twitch to maddening levels. Scores of flickering candles lined in racks did their best to scatter light through the oppressive smoke that wafted through the belfry. When I saw a gleaming money slot under the candles, the uncomfortable itch on my arm spread to my hands. In catholic culture, each coin given was a prayer for the souls of the dead. I don't mind giving money to religious orders from time to time, but I hate being asked to donate when I know it contributes to spreading the Catholic Church's anti-gay agenda or whatever else they're trying to push this century.

"Let's make a picture," our guide announced with a toothy grin.

Reluctantly, I agreed but narrowed my eyes to show I was on to him if he tried to ask for money for this unwanted tour. Dragging Cassie and me by either hand, he placed us in front of the candles. Mercifully, he didn't try to get us into any praying pose, just two quick snaps on his expensive looking mobile phone, followed by a group photo as he hugged me way too tight. And it was all over.

"Don't you want to stay here?" he asked, still crouching between us. "You can stay for free."

Before I could answer, he pulled something moldy out of his pocket. "Look what I've got," he said reverently, holding it between us. We leaned in to stare into the palm of his hand. It was a crusty dead lizard. He brought it up so close to his face, I was sure he was going to pop it right in his mouth. He grabbed my hand and forced open my palm, placing the mummified lizard carcass inside. This guy kind of reminded me of people I'd met in India, dressed in robes and with perfect spiritual lingo and poise, but really just finely trained in the art of human deception. They sit in perfect meditation pose for one hour without moving, do their prostrations and count their beads. But, really, at the end of the day all they desire is to take your money, your power, and if you are a woman, any sexual gratification on offer.

"Let's make more pictures," he said. *This is when he's going to charge us,* a sinking feeling in my tummy announced. Energy failing us again, we agreed, partially to see what would happen next.

He kept taking group photos with us and his dirty lizard in the creaking tower. One time he even wore the lizard as a mustache. "Are you sure you don't want to stay?"

We shook our heads and edged closer to the stairs.

At the church doors he pulled me back. *This is it. He's going to ask me for money.* "I have something for you," he said. He reached into his lizard pocket, then slowly handed us a clutch of painted clam shells.

"It's to remember our friendship and this blessed day." He tapped his lizard pocket then blessed himself in the direction of the altar. "God Bless all creatures great and small." He bent low then kissed each clam in our hands. Nodded to us. We nodded back. He nodded. Nodding and smiling, we slowly backed out the door.

Annoyed with myself, but relieved to leave, I pondered my paranoia that had taken away all the positives out of a genuine interaction with another human being. If I could just get a decent nice sleep, I'd surely think nicer thoughts...

I added the kissed clam to the safe place in my backpack where I kept my mullet bottle. It was starting to seem like the Camino really does provide.

...lying clams

-

Day 23 – Cobreces to San Vicente
22.6km

Cassie

It started when I was a teenager. My alarm would go off at 6am before school. I'd press snooze at least three times before my mother would have to physically remove me from my bed.

By the time I made it downstairs, I was still asleep, the definition of a zombie. Everyone in my family knew – don't talk to Cassie until she's eaten something. If anyone dared, they'd be met with the wrath of the bitchiest dragon queen from the darkest depths of hell.

As I grew older, my diet got healthier and my sleeping habits more suited to my constitution. I learned to set the alarm long before I had to get up, to hydrate properly, and to not eat much sugar. My morning 'problem' went away. I thought I'd totally conquered it.

Until the Camino.

How can mood changes due to low blood sugar be explained by Darwinism? Is the level of sugar in my blood sending a signal to my brain to develop a sudden disdain for all humans, to make it easier for me to kill them and steal their food? All in the name of living another day and passing on human-hating DNA to my offspring?

Today I woke up at 7am to the sound of three happily cackling Germans outside my window, laughing at something in a language completely unconducive to sleep. Totally oblivious I was still trying to catch some z's just a few feet away.

I wanted to kill them. Maybe not literally. Though I can't be sure.

I'm being forced to wake up way too early by chipper assholes every single morning. My diet has become Spanish, which means full of sugar, and I'm perpetually dehydrated because I'm hiking all day. My hormones felt out of whack, much like a 16-year-old.

If you're not a morning person, the Camino could be a bigger challenge for you. Get ready for pilgrims to ask you all kinds of intrusive questions about your life and where you're headed that day, right in your face, before you've even had time to pee, let alone have breakfast.

Ahhhhhh. Blood sugar. Today is one of those days on the Camino.

At least it was a pretty walk, and we didn't meet even one fellow pilgrim. But despite the beauty of the coastal landscape, I felt a heaviness wafting to me from James' direction. Something was stewing in him, and I knew he wasn't in any shape to be talking about it yet.

Upon reaching the quaint seaside port town of San Vicente, we sat at a small round table outside a cafe for lunch. James leaned back in his chair, tethering carefully on its back legs as he scanned the menu.

"What are you getting?" I asked.

"Hmmmm. I think I just want *pan con tomate*," he replied, pointing at the Spanish staple of toast with tomato.

"Sounds good," I said as the waiter bounded out the door.

"I'll have the *ensalada mixta*," I said.

151

The waiter looked at James to take his order.

Immediately, his menu began to shake as he fumbled to open it, then somehow flew out of his hands onto the ground a few feet away. His face turned beet red. "I'll have the... the... uh... bread lad. I'll have the bread lad," he stammered as he pointed wildly, searching for a different menu.

The confused waiter looked at me. "*Tostada con tomate, por favor*," I told him.

James took a big slug of beer as the waiter returned inside.

"What the hell kind of spaz was that?" I asked, snorting with laughter.

James feigned confusion, hoping I hadn't noticed his spectacle. There was no way I could've missed it. As my affectionate howls of derision continued, he realized the futility of his act. He leaned back and smiled, letting out a rare burst of giggles. "I guess I really did lose my shit, huh?"

"Bread lad?!" I managed to sneak the words in between my outbursts.

Poor James. Whatever was bothering him in his inner world was majorly affecting his ability to function in the outside world.

James

Morning. Usual snores and groans. Except this time I didn't feel exasperated or exhausted. I didn't feel anything. It was like I'd awoken from the grave. I should've been scared to death, but death is just an abstract image of eternal darkness I had no connection to. I willed a thought; my beloved old dead dog. Felt nothing. Felt myself falling. Was I paralyzed? Felt nothing.

This happens sometimes. I don't know where I go, but I come back numb. Some would call it waking up, but I'm not waking up. I feel I'm not here at all. I'm slipping away. Suddenly, claws ripped my mouth apart, letting my screams escape.

My eyes shot open to see pilgrims readying themselves for the day. No one noticed my silent scream.

I hoped Wolfentop was okay. Perhaps he was an apparition stalking the mists, or an emotional vampire? Cassie and I had little energy since our encounter. His sourpuss face did look hungry when I spat blood. Whatever creature he was, I still hoped he'd find a way to reunite with his tribe. Being a lone wolf did not suit his vibe. Perhaps he was out there now, running with the llamas from albergue to albergue, searching for marriage material, sniffing around ancient Celtic energy ley lines. In Santiago I hoped his tribe would gather.

Will they cheer his name as he triumphantly enters the cathedral? "WOLFENTOT," the monks will chant. "WOLFENTOT. WOLFENTOT. WOLFENTOT." His adoring tribe would scream to the high heavens. "WOLFENTOT. WOLFENTOT."

And he would howl louder than the clanging, cathedral bells, then scream, "IT'S WOLFENTOP! NOT WOLFENTOT! WOOOLFEENTOOOOOPP!!" before complaining these tribesmen aren't as good as they used to be, and the cathedral used to look much better before it was refurbished.

As my mind shifted to getting out of bed, stars danced in my eyes, causing a vision of my brother to appear in the constellation. 'So when will you get the courage to tell Cassie you're leaving the Camino?' his voice reverberated in my head. 'You don't want to be here.'

...dickwater

—

Day 24 - San Vicente to La Franca
21.5km

Cassie

I experienced a horrible fright as we entered a bar to have our tortilla breakfast. I was hoping to fill my water bottle in the public fountain outside. But standing before me, was that greaseball Gypsy Mullet guy, pushing his groin up into the water basin. I stood there a few feet from him, my body frozen and my eyes transfixed. His pants were pulled halfway down his thighs, and he appeared to be washing his balls. In full view of the village square, basking in the bright morning sunshine. I saw things I'd rather never see. Turns out he has two mullets.

I slept alright last night, despite the pillow. Matrimonial pillows, as they're officially called, are a Spanish thing. A Spanish thing that I do not like. At all. It's one super long pillow on a double bed meant to be shared between a couple, instead of the far more civilized two separate pillows that I suspect will do far more to keep my marriage strong.

153

The walking was sweaty today. Summer's heat was rising noticeably. After walking four hours and 17km on an ancient Roman road through the Spanish countryside (not seeing another human being), we spit out into the town of Unquera, ready to make our final push for the day.

An incredible sight greeted us. A Chinese woman was holding her two-year-old over the gutter in the pooping position, like you only see in Asia. The baby pooped, the woman looked at us apologetically, and they scurried into the restaurant opposite.

Having traveled extensively through Asia, I've seen this many times. Diapers aren't really a thing in some places. Mothers have developed an uncanny ability to detect the subtle signs their child needs to relieve itself, then promptly carry them outside and hold them in the perfect position to do the deed. No wiping required. Much of the world doesn't have a use for wet wipes or diapers -supposed baby necessities. So, no bad thing for the environment, my eco girlfriends tell me.

Of course, we did what any self-respecting international foodie traveler would do – followed mom and her relieved baby into the restaurant.

What ensued was my most rewarding meal in a long time. A full menu of assorted seafood dim sum, fresh sushi, Chinese chicken curry – all top notch and homemade by this woman whose recently pooping baby now toddled around the restaurant.

This place was so authentically Chinese in its decor, so inexpensive, and not even marked on google maps. And what's more, despite mom's handiwork in the gutter, the hygiene didn't seem too bad either. It would be a joy for any passing pilgrim to come across a gem like this in the middle of nowhere. She sold a bunch of Chinese produce inside, and even had my favorite chili sauce, which I used to buy in India from the only Tibetan monastery shop that carried it. Now every bland meal on the Camino would taste good!

We had fun speaking Span-eeze with the baby while we drank our Tsingtao beers. As we left, the pooping baby followed us, her mother laughing from the kitchen. She wanted to come.

It's amazing what a wonderful meal can do to lift the spirits when there's still 500 kilometers to go.

James

Barely in the café door for breakfast, Cassie shouted at me, "Gypsy Mullet is washing his balls in the pilgrim fountain! I saw it. Even his dick has a mullet!!"

I didn't know what to say. The man, the myth, the mullet was back in our lives, albeit balls deep in the public water fountain. I smiled. He was probably gyrating at the water spout while singing it a haunting love song. "Really?" I asked. "He has his knob out in the public fountain? That's great."

Cassie narrowed her eyes. "It is not great. That grease ball. I thought he was just getting a drink or something. Then he turned and saw me with those pirate eyes. I was like, 'Oh, God! He's washing his balls in that fountain.'"

"What did he do?"

"He apologized and pulled up his pants. He wasn't trying to flash me or anything. It seemed like he was just genuinely washing himself. Then he whistled at me to come over."

"Did you go over?"

"Of course."

I just nodded, understanding the magnetic power of his alpha mullet.

"He wants to see you," she said. "Told me to get you."

"For what?"

"I don't know," she said shrugging. "Maybe he needs a hand."

It was my turn to narrow my eyes. "You'd like me to do that, would you?"

"No. I'd like you to kick him in the balls."

"Where's he at?"

"Around the corner at the municipal fountain."

A tingle of perplexing joy jumped in my tummy when I saw him stretching his beefy calves on top of the walled fountain. Thankfully he'd pulled his tight, embroidered black trousers up. Tantalizingly, he dipped his left toes into the drinking water.

"Where have you been?" he boomed. A black overcoat draped over his broad shoulders like a heavy dressing gown.

"Walking the Camino," I said, trying to keep my composure as his mullet glistened like a beacon to the angels in heaven.

"But I was here." He looked into the water. Swirled it with his big toe. "Waiting!"

"Waiting with your balls out?"

Fire erupted in his eyes. "What?"

"My wife said you were washing your balls in the fountain. You can get arrested for that kinda shit, man. What were you thinking?"

Clouds slowly turned gray as misty rain crept into the air.

155

"Cassie," he said. "The wife you speak of. She does not understand yet the power."

"What power?"

Scooping up water that feasibly had a high quotient of his scrotum sack sweat, he ran his hands through his marvelous mane. "You and me. Me and you. We have danced this many times. A man who feeds another man's horse. This is much more than either of us truly know."

He stamped his foot into the fountain, splashing water and startling a passing pilgrim. "For my horse, she is a wild beast. For she smells the power. This is why I will tell you this. The reason your wife saw me bathe my balls in this fountain, is that they throb with the power of ancient ley lines."

"Stop," I said raising my hand. "Stop just there. Are you a pervert?"

"You are not the first to ask. But no. I am not."

"But you're washing your testicles in the public drinking water? That's kinda weird. No? Kinda inconsiderate?"

"Listen." He put a finger to his juicy lips. "You can hear them throb."

"Look, Gypsy Mullet, there is a doctor over there. You don't have to be ashamed. Is it testicular cancer?"

"Be still, Horse Feeder. Listen. This is what I'm trying to tell you. It's the power lines. The ley lines. The old Celtic paths. The ancient ways. This fountain. This very fountain is built atop one of those energy lines."

Wolfentop materialized from the mists of my mind and spoke through time. 'I'm not who I was. I need to find my tribe. If I could find the ley lines, I would run all the way to Santiago. Something has changed. Is it me or the world...?'

Shaking the emotional vampire from my mind, I asked, "How do you know this fountain is special?"

"It's a gift. My own power surges when I find the ley lines. To release the throbbing pressure I bathe my balls to cool my spirit."

"Really? And you've never been arrested for indecent exposure?"

Seemingly not wanting to answer, he resumed stretching his beefy calves.

"Does Nicu know what you're up to?"

"Nicu," he said softly, while flexing his right leg to the point where I thought the muscle would pop. "He didn't return from the festival."

"But I saw the two of you drive away together?"

"I know. I told you he is wild. I'm not ashamed to admit. He is braver than me. He left me like the hawk leaves its chick. High he prowls in the sky mountains now, while I stay safe in the cities of men. For my horse, Canción, we both keep searching. But don't you see, Horse Feeder?" He stomped his foot in the drinking water again. "This fountain. This power. She would have drank from it. She is a Breton horse. Bretons are drawn to magic. As I'm drawn to magic. As were you."

"I wasn't drawn here. Cassie told me you had your balls out and wanted to talk to me."

His eyes went wild. "Shut up. And learn. Watch the pilgrims. I wonder, have you really seen them? The struggle of walking. Hunched over like donkeys. Bearing the burden of exhaustion. Living out some saint's dreams. Then something changes. Miraculous." He kicked a load of water my way. "Suddenly life. They glow. They walk faster. They run. For they are secretly walking on the ley lines. Always, slowly soaking it up. Power lines that connect all the world. Energy centers. And I'm sure this fountain is one. I'm sure my Breton horse smelt the holy water. She drank here. Don't you see? We are close. We are so close."

Puffed up with an all-knowing smile, Gypsy Mullet traced his eyes along the invisible ley lines. For a moment I sensed reality from his perspective. The entire Camino suddenly changed. What if this whole area really did have some unscientifically proven but mystical energy coursing through its veins? That would help explain how, over hundreds of years, so many famished and injured people made it all the way to Santiago. Hair stood up all over my body.

"Yes," he said. "I see it in your eyes. Now you see."

A shiver brought me back.

Suddenly his eyes widened, then he ferociously whipped back his magnificent mullet with his meaty paw. "Police?"

I cocked an ear. Definitely sirens. Before I could open my mouth, he was quickly striding up the street. I let him go, his mullet streaming like a Greek god's in his wake.

"So how did that go?" asked Cassie. She'd moved and was now in a cafe just across from the fountain.

"Good. I think."

"You think? How so?"

"He wants to see us again."

"Oh, really? Is that actually a good idea? Where?"

157

"I don't know. He said I was part of the journey to find his horse. It got a bit confusing, really."

"Did you even ask him why he was washing his balls in the public fountain?"

Just then, a bronzed pilgrim in a cyclist's leotard reached down into the still waters of the fountain. We grabbed each other's hand under the table, both wanting to warn him but not knowing how to translate 'dickwater.'

Splashing what must have been the sweet, sour water onto his face, he merrily went on his way. Maybe it was best he didn't know he was now blessed with Celtic powers and the liquid musk of the Mullet.

...wellspring

-

Day 25 – La Franca to Llanes
20 km

Cassie

The light of a rainy morning was pierced by a rising sun basking James in an orange glow as he slept. There was a rumble of distant thunder. *Albergue Renacer* delivered an edible breakfast of whole grain bread, and nothing wrapped in plastic.

We set off, enjoying the crisp cool air, ignoring the looming black clouds. Into the forest we went. You could feel the electricity in the air, and the veil between the physical world and realms unseen was thin.

It was not long before the heavens suddenly opened. We'd walked through rain plenty of times on this Camino, but this was no mortal precipitation. This was rain from the gods. It poured down in sheets, through every crack and crevice of our ponchos. Our Gore-Tex shoes were powerless in the face of such a deluge, and we walked in puddles that had formed within them. There was nowhere to run, nowhere to hide.

So on we marched, about five kilometers in the torrential downpour. There was no relief. Finally, up ahead an albergue came into view. We ducked in under the awning, hoping to salvage some bit of dryness. Taking our ponchos off revealed we were soaked to the bone. And there was no turning back.

The rain did not let up. I checked the radar on my phone and it looked like a long day of severe storms.

Unexpectedly, a tap on my shoulder. It was one of the German girls from two days ago whose energetic laughter had intruded my morning sleep. With an outstretched hand, she offered me newspaper to stuff my shoes and absorb some of the water. I guess she hadn't felt my negative vibes toward her that day.

We were so incredibly wet. With 15 kilometers to walk and more storms on the way, daunted by the prospect of blisters or maybe even pneumonia, we hesitantly decided to do what every pilgrim considers at least once. Even if they never admit it.

We decided to cheat.

Sheepishly, we made our way to the train station that happened to be very close. Heads held in shame, we walked onto the platform. To my surprise and barely concealed delight, twenty other pilgrims, maybe more, stood guiltily there already. No one made eye contact. Everyone knew what the other was doing. Our silence sealed our pact.

The Camino gods were cheated out of many kilometers on this rainy day. And I suspect many pilgrims, for hundreds of kilometers up and down the Norte were stealing a few extra hours of rest.

We had a beautiful evening in the charming town of Llanes, a small bustling harbor with a slight bohemian vibe. Well rested and dried out, we sipped gin and tonics to the distant rumble of thunder, looking out over the sea. The storms had cleared the air of negativity, and I felt a sense of peace.

As we finished dinner, I stood to go inside to the bathroom. At the sink washing my hands, I felt a massive rush of blood push down out of my head into my abdomen, taking fragments of my vision and my balance with it. Heart pounding out of my chest, I steadied myself on the sink basin just in time, avoiding total collapse. All the energy and blood in my entire body seemed to have pooled in my gut. I had no idea why. I only had one gin. Was this a panic attack? I searched my reflection in the mirror for answers, but all I could see was spots and blobs clouding my vision.

After a couple of minutes, I felt well enough to lift my head off the sink basin, and splashed cold water on my face. My whole body was absolutely buzzing as though I was a conduit for the electric storms and lightning that had roiled in the skies.

159

I made my way back outside to James and let him know I needed to go to bed.

James

Thunder plundered our evening rest as Cassie lay half asleep next to me. Another shuddering boom rattled the windows driving the dogs crazy outside.

Overcome by possible food poisoning, my wife thought fruit would ease her symptoms. Rain was intermittent so I went straight out while it was still relatively dry.

I left the shop just as another deluge of freezing rain swept in. With no stylish bin bag poncho, I only had my crappy straw hat for protection. Soaked in seconds, I dashed through the streets, my fruit swinging while bits of my hat's cord poked me in the eye.

Scampering around in the biblical rain, I noticed I was lost in Llanes. I must've taken a wrong turn. *Damn it.* Turning back, I splashed around the town. Unable to find any reference point, I ducked into a bus stop for shelter. Wiping the rain from my eyes, I studied the bus timetable which took my attention away from the cold.

Since we began wandering the Camino, I'd observed pilgrim cash was not equally shared between villages along the official stages of the Camino.

Firstly, a village needs to catch a pilgrim's interest. A church of historical significance, a dancing priest, relics, a famed wine, a beach or a mushroom patch can all come in useful here. To snag a traveller's intrigue longer, an enterprising person would open an albergue. A pilgrim restaurant would follow to feed the ravenous hordes. Later a bar, to quench their eternal thirst. Catching and trapping the free flow of pilgrim tourism is the lifeblood of a village to be prosperous in the sparsely populated Spanish countryside.

Second, if a town is even 200 meters off the Camino, it seems to miss out on the infusion of pilgrim money that can keep a place vibrant and healthy. These non-Camino towns still make their own way in the world, envious but resigned to their poorer fate. And it will stay that way unless some unscrupulously, enterprising chancer cunningly changes the direction of the money-making clam to point to their town. Certainly, desperate business owners have been known to divert the trail blazes to trick pilgrims into becoming customers. It's a good scam. A clam scam.

Thirdly, there are the unlucky villages that are actually on the Camino but for some reason, pilgrims barely bother to stop. These are often places of unrequited love. The locals give all their passion and energy to create pilgrim facilities, but frustratingly we still won't stop. Good luck has not shone upon these places. Here, no holy men made structures to God. No blessed bones are buried under the streets. No famous steak is worth the wait.

An elderly woman crashed through the window of rain enclosing the bus stop. "Fuck this damn Camino." she said in a gruff English accent. Obviously a pilgrim with her backpack and stick, she rubbed the rain from her face. Deep, black bags under her eyes made her look so tired.

"Yeah, for sure," I said. "Fuck the Camino."

Bonded by our belligerence, we began to talk.

"I'm bailing out," she said.

"Really? You're quitting?"

Rain was my answer for the next five seconds.

"Pissing out the heavens," I said, to fill the silence.

She turned her head sideways then wiped away the blondy, white streaks of hair plastered to her cheek. "God's been pissing on me this entire trip." A gust of wind rattled the bus stop, making us wince. "I'm unhappy. I'm taking the next bus to the nearest airport and flying home. I nearly died today."

"What happened?," I said. "Are you okay?"

"I'm not. Lots of people try to kill themselves in my town. I've tried twice. Walking therapy the doctor prescribed, but it isn't working for me." She stroked her cheeks, then rubbed the bags under her eyes.

Anxiety curdled my stomach, then wafted into my throat, causing words to tumble. "Why did you try to kill yourself?"

She massaged her temples. "Too much going on in my head. I was always causing trouble for people. Just thought it would be easier for everyone if I were dead. My four-year-old nephew saved me." She paused as if to process her fate.

"We were walking along a coastal path back home when I noticed he wasn't by my side anymore. I turned and there he was at the edge of the chalk cliffs. I knew if I ran at him to catch him, he'd think it was a game and risk going over the edge. I got him, though. Took a while. But I talked him back to me. It was because I was in my head so much I'd not noticed him walk away. If he'd gone over I'd have jumped after him. We'd both be dead."

Nodding in sympathy was all I could think to do. Poor woman looked so wrecked. "Apple?" I asked.

Dismissing my offer with a bat of her hand, she said, "I didn't want to die. That nephew of mine is better therapy than any Camino. Thankfully, today I finally realised that."

Another woman emerged from the sheet of water. From under her umbrella she beamed us a grin.

"When's the next bus coming?" asked the newcomer.

"Anytime now," said the pilgrim. She nodded to herself then looked at me. "Good luck to you on the rest of your Camino."

"Fuck the Camino," I said.

She chuckled as I returned to the rain.

....cat calls

—

Day 26 – Llanes to Cuerres
22km

Cassie

Shouts of drunken men reverberating through the medieval alleyways of Llanes woke us up. It must have been a wild Saturday night as it hadn't ended by 8am Sunday. At another time, in another place, that could have been us, but the mission of the pilgrim remained wholly incompatible with dawn-lit alcohol-induced rambles.

As James washed up in the bathroom, I stood at the window trying to catch a glimpse of the hooligans making the racket. Directly below, I saw four female pilgrims, recognizable by the scallops hanging off their packs, walking quickly with their heads down followed by two of the drunken men, clearly harassing them. I could see immediately that this was no harmless party. The women looked scared, and were practically running.

With utter abandon and without a second thought, filled with the combined rage of a thousand women, I shouted at the top of my lungs, "Fuck off! Leave them alone!"

My words curdled and echoed against the stone streets and entered into every household window within 100 meters, no doubt rattling teacups as locals read their Sunday papers.

The men stopped immediately. One looked up at me about to retaliate, but even in his stupor thought better of it. This distraction gave

162

the pilgrims time to get away. My fiery aggression surprised me. The electrical current in my gut from the night before seemed to be coursing through the rest of me now. I felt ready to throw my flames down like the Goddess of Thunder on anyone who dared cross me.

As James took his time packing, I sat in a squat against the wall looking out the window again as I sipped the last of my instant coffee. I was transported back to a Sunday morning in India, 23 years old, finding my way through a tangle of tiny lanes not unlike the ones I looked down upon here. I'd woken up in a room I didn't recognize, my friend Riannon on the bed next to me. I could tell it was a guest house room by the information sheet taped to the back of the door. I tried to lift my head, but couldn't. My dress was pulled up around my shoulders, and my underwear were gone.

We'd been eating dinner and having a couple of beers at a restaurant nearby to the school where we were volunteering. The last thing I remembered was the waiter hurriedly trying to explain to us that someone had put something in our drinks. I know we laughed at the thought. *No. Not us. Not here.*

Then we woke up in that unidentified room, the brilliant morning light shining through the cheap nylon curtains. We walked home. Small talk. A little breakfast. Some TV. But we knew.

I still know, but I have no memory of it.

James and I ambled along quaint country lanes crossing cow fields, tidal marshes, and the odd beautiful beach. Asturias was my most dramatic and enjoyable section of the Norte. The landscape was raw and unspoiled, the people warm and open, and the Way mostly avoided busy roads. This was a good day on the road.

As we quickly walked along the seam of a mighty coastal range (in order to watch a World Cup match at 4pm), we finally came to the *Reposo del Andayón*. This spectacularly located B&B is a broad modern house, built of wood and perfectly perched facing the first undulating peaks of the Picos de Europa mountains.

We swung open the door to a big hug and kisses from Katrine, the elderly proprietor, whose first mission was to make us all put our packs into plastic garbage bags. I didn't blame her. We must've smelled horrible. She instructed us to take the stuff we need for showering along with our clean clothes up to the bathrooms in a wicker basket she provided.

Andayon Rest was built by Katrine in 2017. She had completed many Caminos and decided to pursue her dream of owning an albergue. She found the perfect piece of land, built a brand new, custom-designed eco structure, and ran it as a very tight ship. A ship that's filled to the gunnels with good vibes carefully cultivated by the gorgeous proprietor.

She gave us her welcome spiel, explaining the house was designed to contain all electromagnetic fields, and almost everything is made of wood and other natural materials. No phones allowed in the sleeping areas; WiFi only on for two hours, and charging can only be done inside a locked box that contains the radiation.

The place has just ten beds. It was also a *donativo*, meaning you only pay what you can afford into an honor box. Much to Katrine's dismay, we decided to scoot on down to the local pub as quickly as possible to catch Spain playing their next World Cup match. As we meandered through the perfect countryside, one bucolic lane merging into another, the clouds that were perched on the mountains for most of the day suddenly rushed down into the valley, exploding on top of us. The torrents came down in sheets, and we ran for cover under an ancient oak tree. Thunder crashed as the squall enveloped us.

I felt a lump rise in my throat. My jaw began to quake under the pressure as my stomach turned. *What the fuck now?* The rain poured down. Some heavy, secretive force began to climb its way up my spine, making a sharp turn out my mouth. I dramatically turned to James and shouted through the deluge, "I think we should have a baby!"

He stared at me, confused. I could see his eyes searching for the familiarity in mine, but I couldn't focus, couldn't soften enough to meet his gaze's plea for connection. I waited for a reply as more emotion gathered in my neck and facial muscles. He squinted his eyes further, trying to understand what was going on. I struggled to contain the absolute bomb of emotion that had exploded within me under this ancient tree.

Again, I challenged James, "Well?! What do you say? I think we should have a baby." I bit down on my lip hard, trying to steady it.

"Where's this coming from?" James looked concerned.

Now in a total state of panic, and just as confused as James, the floodgates burst. I sobbed uncontrollably. "A baby! We should have a baby!" I shook and quaked, shivering in the rain. The deep welling inside me felt like some kind of primordial power.

Inhaling sharply, James took my hand. "I don't know why you're saying this right now or what's going on with you. But my answer hasn't changed. No, I don't want a baby."

His words cut like a knife through my heart. My stomach churned even more. I turned my head wildly around, looking for something to ground me. Squatting down at the base of the old oak, I sobbed as the most immense sorrow I'd ever felt washed over me.

I couldn't catch my breath. My usually calm inner voice was starting to panic, too. *Why the hell did you just stand under this tree in the rain and suddenly blurt out that you wanted a baby? What the hell is wrong with you?*

Indeed, what the hell was wrong with me? I hadn't considered for even one second that my whole subconscious reason for walking the Camino was to establish our position on having a baby. Where was this coming from? We'd discussed having kids before, about a year ago, and agreed it was something we didn't want to do anytime soon. We'd revisit it after a few years when we were more settled. I was totally satisfied with our understanding, and hadn't paid it any mind since. Now here I was, declaring, in a sheer state of panic, I needed to have a baby, like, now.

Poor James, totally blindsided by my hysterics, stared out into the hills. The rain was beginning to lighten. Reluctantly he said, "I'm going to the pub to watch the game." He took off, walking quickly away from me. I didn't follow, and he didn't look back.

Crouched down between the oak's massive roots, I became dizzy with shock. As my breathing returned to normal, I understood the gravity of my outburst. We almost never argued. My sudden urge to have a baby was transforming into dismay over the state of my own mind. I'd upset James so much with my inexplicable, childish tantrum. What was swirling below the surface of my consciousness that made this happen?

I calmed myself down as the sky cleared, and self consciously walked to the pub, which was bursting with villagers ready to watch Spain play Russia. It was a scene. The whole village had gathered. The moment I walked in, James threw his arm around my shoulders, announcing to the huge swarm of locals I was Russian and could out drink anyone before half time. James had a funny old way of letting one know things will be ok.

Nearly late for dinner, we hurried back to Katrine's albergue. Sitting there waiting for us were the four women who were harassed in Llanes that morning. The other two in our group that night? The laughing Germans. I sat back and asked the stars why everything was so freaking weird on this day.

We were served a gorgeous dinner of gazpacho and bean and barley soup with real whole grain breads and organic butter. Fresh summer melon for dessert. The gaps that had opened up deep inside me under the tree were being refilled with love and nourishment.

After dinner, Katrine made everyone write down all the things we felt grateful for that day and add it to a jar, to be planted in the garden. And when I say 'made' I mean it. This is not an albergue where you can just keep to yourself and remain anonymous while you watch YouTube videos in bed. No way, José. You have to participate in everything fully, and Katrine reserves a wonderful glare for those who do not comply. Perfect for the day you have some kind of nervous breakdown.

Truth be told, I just wanted to crawl into bed. But this boss of a matriarch had a way of looking at me that took me back to the 1st grade when I was scared to disappoint my teacher. There was nowhere to hide, nowhere to talk to James in private. I had to squash it all away for another day, and instead think of something nice to say. I could feel the energy between us was strained, but James looked relieved not to talk about things right now. Sensing everything would work itself out for us, I was finally allowed to go to bed.

Being side-by-side with James mile after mile, in our journey through life as much as our journey along the Camino, my head and my heart did not for one moment countenance any alternative.

James

Rain can hide your tears but not your fears.

Cassie cried under the sodden, leafy branches of an ancient oak. Fear took hold of us from the realisation we had totally divergent thoughts on what had suddenly become our biggest decision – whether or not to have children. I felt bombarded by waves of her emotion. I couldn't understand why having a baby was so important right now. Under a tree. In the pouring rain. Trying to make things okay and calm the situation, I took a deep breath.

Finding it hard to look into her tearful eyes, I focused on her quivering lips. "No, I don't want a baby," I said again. "Nothing has changed. You know that I'll be unhappier with a child. I'll end up resenting it. I'll end up resenting you. I'll be a bad dad."

166

"I'll resent you more if I don't have a child," she blurted out.

Last year, we talked about kids sometime in the future. Even about adopting a child in a few years. That seemed to satisfy the situation, but now, completely, unexpectedly, we were at a jarring impasse. My body vibrated with seething anger while I tried to be loving. I forced the volcano down by keeping my face cold and voice free of emotion so I didn't explode in argument.

I felt attacked. My chest constricted. From the pain, a voice told me I was being selfish. Fighting back, I silently shouted *I don't even like kids.* They made me feel unsafe because of how I felt as a child. I'm fearful around them because they're so vulnerable. I'd be unhappier if I had a child, I had persuaded myself.

Cassie's tears streamed around her lips. *Can't we just move on?* But of course we couldn't. Part of our relationship was now trapped in this negative child energy.

I just want some inner peace. I need to slow everything down. I can't imagine a child will help this process. A strange voice in my chest whispered, *Let go.*

Let go of what? Having a baby with us all the time is more interactions everyday than I could handle. I'd melt away having to suppress my emotions by pretending to everyone I was fine.

As Cassie continued to cry, I wanted to hug her tightly. Tell her everything would be alright. But my anger and fear were now too strong. Reluctantly, I let her be.

As I walked, I was certain a child would make me more stressed. It will make me depressed. What good is that to anybody? What kind of family life is that?

In desperation, I appealed to all the gods people prayed to on this supposedly magic Way. I asked them to help us spin the cogs of our emotions and turn the wheels of intellect to create a new understanding that a child would not be beneficial to our lives. I had hope. I always have hope. It's the best melody to keep away the tune of malady.

...bed bugs

-

Cassie

Waking up in the *Andayon Rest* was an experience in itself. Katrine had her albergue volunteers swoop into the bedroom at an ungodly hour, insisting everyone get 'up and at 'em' and butts down to breakfast. I had slept so soundly and deeply that night. The kind of sleep that only comes after an hour of heavy crying the day before. A primal tension had been released from deep inside me, but replaced with a new tension between James and me. The volunteers made it impossible for me to dwell for too long this morning.

After a lovely breakfast with the gang of fellow pilgrims, I saw one of the American chicks, who I'd rescued with my unabashed shouting, had an awful blister on the sole of her foot. Kristin was a real trooper and wasn't complaining, but I could see the limp in her step. This was a great opportunity to help a fellow pilgrim. I had purchased these special stickers called ENGO patches in America. They stick to your shoe, not your foot. They are made from some space age material that creates a zero friction surface. They work. They really work. I told her to bring her shoe over and put a sticker in it.

Enjoying the morning's walk along more pretty little lanes and through rolling hills, I began to feel strange. My heart was beating way too fast and I felt nauseous. Soon, I became insanely itchy and to my horror, witnessed rising welts all over my legs, arms, stomach and hands. Some kind of severe allergic reaction. My throat began to tighten.

I'm no stranger to serious allergies, and have experienced anaphylaxis in response to an ant bite.

I rushed forward with James to our next hotel and swallowed five Benadryl tablets to stop the reaction and hopefully normalize my blood pressure. My epipen was ready if needed. I spent the remainder of the day hallucinating from the medication, seeing faces in the walls of our

168

room. I apparently watched two World Cup matches, which I don't remember.

In my chemically-induced haze, I felt a strong discomfort rise inside me again. James had barely spoken all day, and I knew things were stewing inside of him. Normally we'd have talked it out by now, but I was so disoriented and out of my body from the hives that I wasn't capable. I just wanted to roll up into a ball and die.

James

Dawn finally broke. A chill breeze raked over my skin but it couldn't cool my overheated mind. Our fight churned continuously. I pulled myself from bed with a sigh, then went onto the balcony.

Fog flowed. I presumed the world lay beyond.

Fourteen pilgrims stayed last night. The usual mix of Europeans of different ages and also the four American women Cassie had saved from the harassment of marauding drunks.

Willowy Katrine Duerinckx had an after dinner game. Each pilgrim must say why they're walking then pick another traveller. A more gentle form of the Spanish Inquisition.

I was surprised to learn that most people, when asked, fiddled with their hair, spoon or phone. I'm still realising how much the Camino is a deeply personal experience for many.

One older woman with dazzling white hair looked particularly uncomfortable. Sadly, she traced a long fingernail over her forehead's deep wrinkles, as if they were the maps to the sorrowful way she now walked. She mumbled something. We all craned our heads to listen. A husband lost. A child dead. A last stab at life before cancer catches her up. She looked around. Took a deep breath. Smiled. We all smiled back. One or two of the group gave her a hug.

Each person spoke their truth and I could see how this would help start meaningful conversations with each other on tomorrow's walk.

Everyone's attention turned to me. Before the argument about children, I'm not sure what I'd have answered. But what came up in the moment was the thought of us having a child. So I told the group, "I'm walking to understand."

Katrine's eyes prompted me to elaborate. My energy was uncomfortably stuck in my chest, so I deflected by saying the first thing that popped into my head. "On the first week of walking the Camino, I found a child's footprints that walked into a river, but didn't walk out." Confused pilgrims waited for more. "It was so weird. What I imagined

169

the boy in the river to look like had the same face I later saw in a painting in a convent we stayed in. In that same painting, I saw a witch that looked like a witch in a museum." I stopped myself before anyone could even attempt to process what I'd just blurted out, and quickly pointed at the next pilgrim.

Katrine later asked us to write down what we were grateful for today. Without pause, I wrote mental health and happiness. Self-satisfied with my crappy joke, I smiled while putting the paper in a jar.

She told us our pilgrim appreciations would be buried at the base of an olive tree, soon to be planted in her garden. I wondered, *would my lies sour their taste?*

From these two simple questions, the atmosphere was subtly transformed into the most open and honest interactions I've heard from strangers so far on the Camino. All sorts of conversations flowed; conversations that wouldn't normally take place. People cried. Hugged. Cheered. All without an alcoholic beverage. I didn't say much.

Most folk were heading to bed as Katrine approached me while I sipped on a steaming chamomile tea. Her enthusiasm ignited the energy of our conversation.

"Is it always like this?" I asked. "This open?"

"Well. Every night I have this special energy. I think of each person as my good friend and I'm really happy that they've come for dinner." She rubbed the corners of her mouth.

"I know at times people don't want to talk. But for sure, deep down people like to be understood and to connect to something outside of themselves. Some yearn for it, but are emotionally blocked. They bounce off these inner barriers, armour if you like, making themselves feel anxious and frustrated. Always feeling they're never properly connecting to friends and family."

I nodded, piecing together from her expression that she was reading my emotional state. It was uncomfortable. As if she were reading my diary.

Father Ernesto in Güemes held court and made us think of the bigger picture of the world. While Katrine wants to create a sanctuary where people connect and open up to make us feel significant as individuals.

Katrine smiled, then peered at me with questioning eyes. Was she going to ask about the child's footprints disappearing into the river? But another pilgrim joined us to make tea. I took this as a sign to avoid talking to Cassie about children for as long as possible. Hopefully this whole having a baby thing would blow over.

...relics of the past

Cassie

I think I'm allergic to the Camino. That's the only explanation. I definitely didn't pee in a patch of nettles. And I'm not allergic to my new favorite food, anchovies.

It must be the Camino.

In every heroic journey, the seeker reaches a point where they choose to enter 'the belly of the whale.' She has already come so far, overcome so much, and suddenly is faced with one final obstacle that seems insurmountable. This obstacle requires our hero to dig down deep and recommit herself to the journey's objective. It's make or break time.

My obstacle came in the form of humongous, disgusting welts covering my body.

Bed bugs.

I cried to James, spending the entire night and next morning feeling miserable. Wanting to scratch so badly but knowing it would only make things worse. My blood pumping with a potent combination of Benadryl and adrenaline, I felt crazed and desperate. I wanted to quit the Camino. There was no way forward like this. I was disenchanted and disgusted at myself. I was supposed to be a tough chick who could handle any kind of rough travel or minor challenge. But I was getting really tripped up on this Camino thing. And we still had 350 kilometers to go.

After another dose of antihistamines, I walked downstairs to the cafe in *Hotel Monte y Mar* to get some juice. An old wrinkled man with skin like dark leather and a huge grin approached me.

"Buen Camino!" he greeted me.

I wasn't in the mood to chat to another pilgrim. I wanted to curl up in a tub of anti-itch cream. I had to wait for my juice though.

He asked where I was from. He then pulled out a laminated newspaper article and put it up to my face as I leaned against the bar.

With a sigh, I took it from him and had a look. It was an article about a man who walked more than 103,000 kilometers on pilgrimages around the world.

Hmmm. I looked up at the man. His eyes were waiting to meet mine. He excitedly pointed to the photo in the article.

It was him. He was the man in the article.

The manager came out with my juice. With a chuckle, he told me I was talking to one of the world's most famous pilgrims, José Fonso Garcia Calvo. "He's too old to keep walking all the time now," he explained.

José essentially lives at this hotel along the Camino, and sits outside all day with his coffee and cigarettes offering the encouragement of 'buen camino' to passing pilgrims.

José slipped a faded clipping from a newspaper into my hand. It displayed an article explaining he'd been a fisherman as a young man. His ship hit a storm far out at sea, and of the 17 souls on board he was the only survivor. He was in the sea floating and treading water for three days before being rescued.

During the ordeal, he'd prayed to god to save him, and promised if he were spared, he'd dedicate the rest of his life to religion. When he returned to his home in Spain, he immediately set off for the Camino de Santiago with his life savings.

After reaching Santiago, he continued on, walking clear across Europe, the Middle East, and into India. He then crossed the Himalayas into Tibet, through China, and hopped a ferry across the Bering Strait to Alaska. He walked down the entire length of the Western Hemisphere before finally making it back to Spain years later.

His money was gone after just six months. He relied on the generosity of strangers for the remainder of his journey.

"Dalai Lama," he said, pointing to himself proudly.

Oh, god. The Dalai Lama?

"Dalai Lama," he grinned, now hopping up and down in excitement.

Of all the pilgrims to walk by everyday, why did José pick me to start a conversation about the world's best-known Tibetan?

Deep breath. "Did you meet the Dalai Lama?" I asked.

"Yes! Yes!" he exclaimed.

This guy must have walked across the Himalayas and into Dharamsala. Fairly impressive feat. He was beginning to win me over despite my itching.

172

I took my phone out of my pocket. Scrolling through old photos, I found it easily.

It was a photo of me with the Dalai Lama, taken several years before when I was working in the Tibetan refugee community.

Seeing this, José immediately embraced me, tears in his eyes. He hugged me and wouldn't let go. He probably told a few people every day that he met the Dalai Lama, but I'm guessing few ever whipped out a photo of themselves with the living god.

He was so moved by the picture, I couldn't help but be taken by the moment. I relaxed my shoulders and closed my eyes for a second. When I opened, my eyes met José's. They were trying to tell me something. The Camino provides again.

After bidding José farewell, I hurried back up to our room. "We must keep going," I told James.

He looked at me and smiled. "Of course we're going to keep going. You're a tough bird that might have a deadly pox, but we won't worry about that now. Onward, Christian soldiers!"

"Onward, Buddhist soldiers," I mused.

It was impossible for me to walk today because of the bites, and perhaps even tomorrow. We were starting to run short on time if we wanted to make it to Santiago.

We got the bus to the city of Gijón as quickly as possible so I could get some medicine, then reassess. This way we'd buy ourselves a couple of extra days by skipping a few stages. We'd already heard the walks in and out of Gijón were unpleasant and industrial, so we didn't feel too bad about missing anything.

I was able to get what I needed from a pharmacist, and felt instant relief when the proper cream was applied. After a nice lunch in Gijón, we got on another bus and made it to *Albergue la Naranja Peregrina*. I couldn't shake my meeting with José.

Paying attention to pilgrim chatter in the hostel simply wasn't possible. I stepped outside, realizing a song had been stuck in my head all day:

'jeete bhi lakdi marte bhi lakdi dekh tamasha lakdi ka'

Hindi was not my language, but I only had to hear this haunting devotional mantra sung once to have it memorized. It was playing from a shopkeeper's old-fashioned Nokia cell phone one morning as I strolled through the small Indian village of Bhagsu. The clear, pure voice of the boy singing stopped me in my tracks. I immediately asked the shopkeeper what it meant.

"Wood, ji. Wood. Life is wood," he said.

"What do you mean, life is wood?"

"Your own mother gave birth standing on wood. When you are born, you sleep in a cradle of wood. You go to school, and write with a pencil of wood, and the teacher beats you with a staff of wood."

"Go on, please," I urged him with my wide eyes.

"And your marriage, ji, it is sealed on a pavilion of wood, and your marriage bed is also made of wood. And when you die, madam. When you die, you burn with wood. Life is wood. Death is wood."

I have never forgotten it.

James

The rusty wheelchair smelt of stale urine and belonged on the set of a 1950's horror movie and not two feet away from my table in the dank, dirty bar. A slit in my lip stung after sipping beer from a cracked glass. It left a tangy taste of germs in the back of my throat. The tang crawled deeper. I began to sweat. At least the fat flies stopped landing in my beer.

With her eyes closed in itchy irritation, Cassie didn't get the smell on her side of our stained table. Perhaps my poor wife was lost in thoughts of children... or welts, or children born with welts.

At the table behind Cassie, a large, balding man licked an ice cream cone with unbridled delight. Sweat dripped down his furry neck. I was transfixed by his habit of rubbing his fingers through the sweat, then quickly to his lips for a swift lick.

Three pilgrims sat at a sticky table next to us. Sipping gin and tonics, they were in good spirits. One Viking-looking man with a plaited, blond beard, had his bare feet up on a creaky stool. On the souls of his feet, blisters bubbled. If they burst, it would surely end his Camino.

A headache pulsed. Fatigue washed over me. The Spanish would take a siesta. But I knew if I lay down I'd become more agitated. I closed my eyes anyway.

My mind drifted. *If I drink from my glass I'll get a throat infection. Germs everywhere. Crawling into my ear to have sex with my bacteria.* Or was I just feeling my own sense of filth from the long miles? Do we all excrete a snail trial of filth as we move through life? We've coated the planet in

174

human waste and now our offspring will suffer. I swallowed hard when I thought of children.

The words of the writer Salman Rusdhie came to mind. 'Parents pour their poison into their children.'

What poison would I pour into my kid? Its taste would probably be bitter. But before I could focus on my faults, my mind fell into a daydream. A radiant witch whispered into the ear of the drowned boy from my imagination. Still half in the water, he lay dead on the river bank.

Maggots squirmed under his cheeks where she stroked his pale skin. I wondered what poisoned words she poured into his ear?

Bastian was standing behind the witch holding a dripping, white towel. Back in that albergue we had shared with him and LSD Bill, he hadn't shut up about the peanut butter murderer. I'd just wanted to brush my teeth, but he'd swirled my blood-spit between his toes, telling me my mucus was like a brain dissolving.

Suddenly, I understood my dream. Bastian had baptized the boy too long under the water. Unconcerned, he announced, "A name can condemn a man to death."

The witch, who I now knew was the boy's mother, frantically whispered life back into his body. A fire blazed behind them, casting light on the child's now living, breathing chest.

Bastian delicately wrapped the wet towel around the witch's neck, then dragged her listless body towards the funeral pyre. The boy sat up unblinking and watched his mother burn. He looked at me.

"Hello," I said.

"You murdered me."

"What?"

"Shhhhh," he said. "You were sleeping."

"What?"

"Shhhhh. You nearly fell off your chair."

"What? What?" Confused, I opened my eyes.

Cassie smiled. "You must have dozed off." She reached over, then tenderly rubbed my boiling cheek. Potentially another ear infection. "Silly love, you're sleeping on the job. Do you want to rest?"

I shook my head and reached for my beer, then thought better of it.

Bastian? I'd almost forgotten about that strange guy and his peanut murdering anecdotes.

Next to us the three pilgrims still conversed. Feeling terribly groggy, I rubbed my eyes so hard they hurt. Again the beer tempted me. Cassie laughed at my state.

"I'll get you some water," she said, getting up.

Pilgrim chatter from the next table suddenly made sense. "Bastian," the woman had said. She definitely said Bastian! Instantly my mind focused. *Had they been talking about Bastian all the time? Is that why he was in my dream?*

Massaging my tender cheek, I glanced at the group. They fell silent for a moment watching Cassie at the bar.

Bastian's name had been said, I was sure of it. The woman who spoke it was lean and looked about fifty with short black hair and a bird-like intensity. I half expected her to snap at each passing fly as part of her tapas. She was sat with two male companions.

"Did you say Bastian?" My brain spazzing on autopilot, I hadn't meant to say the words aloud. Three heads turned to me.

"Yes," chirped the woman. "Do you know him, too?"

"Kind of." I nodded thinking of my blood between his toes. "We met at an albergue. An interesting fella."

The whites of the woman's eyes turned a little red. "Interesting? Interesting. Are you serious? There's something wrong with that man. He's dangerous."

Her voice flared giving me a slight fright. "Did you meet Jane? The tall Australian woman, with a big green and yellow pack? She warned me about him by phone."

I shook my head.

"Really? Everyone knows Jane. Bastian frightened the life out of her today, too. I know Dutch people. I'm Dutch. Bastian says he's Dutch, but I don't know if he's Dutch at all. I was walking alone." She gripped her glass. "I'm vulnerable. I'm a lone woman. We've all heard terrible stories."

Her companions nodded. "I saw Bastian on the cliffs," she continued at pace. "Just where Jane saw him. I knew it was him from the description she gave. So when I saw him staring down at me through the pouring rain, I freaked out. It was too far to go back, but I didn't want to go forward."

Agitated, she pulled the blue hood of her jacket up. "I pulled my hood up to hide, but ... I don't know. The man just felt... wrong. I prayed for someone to appear so we could walk together."

She stared at her half-drunk gin. "I'm sorry if I sound strange, but I always trust my instincts. On all my Caminos, never before has this happened. Jane told me to be careful. That he was acting crazy. But even Jane wasn't alone like me. And then I just panicked and thought he was a rapist or a murderer."

Her Viking friend put his hand on hers. "That bastard," he whispered. "It's okay. You're safe now."

She pulled her hand away from him and looked back at me. "Do you know what I did? Took out my knife. Hide it in my pocket. I was ready. Up the winding path I had to go. I thought, maybe I'll never see my kids again. And I began to cry. I kept expecting him to jump out. I was going crazy. He must have been hiding. Waiting. Because next thing, he was right in front of me. All smiles. I nearly took my knife out to him. He didn't say anything. I thought this is it. He's going to push me over the cliff."

She took a breath.

"Strange thing," she continued, then looked me dead in the eyes, "is that it was like he saw through me. As if I was a ghost. Then he asked me what I was doing. Before I could tell him I'd stab him in the stomach, he started to talk about the Bible. He said he was a friend of Jesus or something strange. The man thinks he's some kind of prophet. But just as I was about to scream, his voice changed. Softer. Like a prayer. Almost as if he was blessing me. He told me I was a caterpillar in a cocoon. Told me something about not living to my full potential. Told me my new name is Butterfly. That if I wanted a real life, I'd have to come out of the cocoon. Then his eyes dropped."

She took a sip of gin.

"I don't know how to explain it. Just dropped. When he looked at me again it was like he was seeing me for the first time. He apologized and just walked off."

Simultaneously taking deep breaths, the two men at the table nodded at each other.

"Ohh, darling," said the Viking. "I'm so sorry. Terrible man." His deep blue eyes looked at me. "You know me and little Rolphy here also met him on the cliff just after he scared Anita today? Believe it or not, he named us, too. If you can imagine such a thing. My name is Vicente but my new name is Bernadette. Bernadette? Look at my hairy hands. Do I look like a Bernadette to you? And my little Rolphy is now Jebadiah. Little Jeb, as I like to say." Rolph, a ball of muscle in a tight t-shirt, puffed up then drummed the table.

177

Bernadette continued to chat, "I asked Bastian why he was doing this. You know what he did? Told me he is the word of God and that he's traveling to Istanbul by horse. I thought, that's a long ride." He winked at Anita. "But to each their own. I didn't even see a horse. What do you think, Rolph?"

His friend just shook his head. "Don't mind him," said Bernadette,. "He's just tired. I love hearing stories about how people meet. But I'll tell you this. That Bastian. My, my... is he really dangerous? I don't know. Ha! Hold on. I'm thirsty. It's surely gin o'clock again."

Bernadette shouted an order for three more gin and tonics. "Actually. No. No." He raised a hand. "Cancel the order. Sorry. My feet are in agony. We need to drain my blisters. Rolph said he'd help."

Rolph smiled. "We're going to go back now?" he asked. "Do you want to come with us to the albergue, Anita?"

Anita snapped him a momentary smile. "Yes. It's been a long, long day."

As they readied themselves to leave, my mind fixated on one thing. The horse! Bastian stole Gypsy Mullet's horse! He'd stunk of horses when I met him. Now it made sense why he jumped into a field instead of walking on the path when he left us. *Could this be real?* That utter bastard. My eyes lit up, then I burst into a relieved laugh. All eyes turned to me.

"You enjoyed my story?" asked Bernadette, as he put money on the table for the bill.

"Sorry. I was just thinking that Bastian gave us names, too. He baptized this lovely lady Young Mike."

"Young Mike?" laughed Bernadette. "And what did he call you?"

"He called me Bones after the bones of Saint James in Santiago."

"Ohh, that's unfortunate." Bernadette laughed nervously before getting up to leave.

"Can I just ask you one thing," I said. "I'm interested in the horse part. What did it look like?"

"I don't know. We didn't see it. He said he was getting a horse."

Excited intrigue set off a dynamo of spinning energy in my chest. "Getting a horse or had a horse?"

"I don't know. I didn't see any horse. I didn't care. Sorry, but my feet are killing me."

Without further questions, I let them leave.

No way. Could Bastian be travelling to Istanbul by horse? After he left us, he must have turned back towards Santiago. Could he have stolen

Gypsy Mullet's horse? Maybe that's what he does. He said he'd walked all the way from Amsterdam to Santiago. How was he going to afford going from Santiago to Istanbul?

Maybe he just steals things? Justifying it because he's on his holy quest. *But... if Bastian is so close... then Fonso and Nicu are so close to finding the horse.* I needed to find Gypsy Mullet.

Camino Fitness

There is an old Camino adage that says, "Your first week on the Camino is your training for the Camino!" But for those who want to begin walking on their first day a bit more prepared, it's wise to avoid the serious aches, pains and blisters experienced by most pilgrims during their Camino by doing your training ahead of time. Most pilgrims aim to walk an average of 20-25km per day on the Camino, and your training should be designed to slowly bring you up to this. The first week, start with 5km a day on varied terrain. Each week raise your distance by 2km. Do yoga at least twice a week, and add in targeted core strength exercises as well.

It's vital to wear the shoes and socks you will be wearing on the Camino. During the second week you will introduce your pack to the equation. Use the pack you're bringing on the Camino. This will help you avoid the shoulder blisters many experience those first couple weeks on the Way, as well as prime your body to adjust to its new center of gravity. It can be challenging to tell the difference between a developing injury and just being 'sore' from all the new movement. If you are experiencing pain, seek the opinion of a professional immediately before continuing the fitness plan.

A bit of body and muscle soreness is to be expected, but targeted pain suggests an injury. You can train outside or on a treadmill if necessary, but try to mimic the terrain of the Camino as much as possible by using hills/inclines when you can. If you're using a treadmill, simply set the program for the distance required with varied incline. If you're walking outside, it can be very fun to plan your routes. There are plenty of easy-to-use apps to help you map it before you leave, or simply start walking and use your phone or pedometer to record your distance, and turn around at the halfway point before going back the way you came. Don't forget to hydrate as you walk. Always clear any new fitness plan with your doctor before beginning.

Camino Safety

In general, Spain is considered to be a safe country to move through, even for solo travelers and especially women. Violent crime is rare on the Camino.

That being said, unfortunate incidents have occurred, and it is important that pilgrims educate themselves and remain diligent and aware. The vast majority of illegal incidents on the Camino are nonviolent in nature - namely, theft, which most often occurs in the albergues while unsuspecting pilgrims are sleeping or showering.

Perhaps more disturbing is a string of reports coming in from various Camino routes of men exposing themselves to female pilgrims. The predictable nature of the Camino seems to have attracted this type of predator to remote areas where they can be certain females will pass by, often alone. Full on physical attacks have also occurred in remote areas, but are extremely rare.

To stay safe, monitor the Camino forums and groups as you walk, as most incidents are reported in real time. Plan ahead, and if you think you may be walking through a remote area that day, tag along with other pilgrims, as groups are rarely targeted. Above all, trust your instincts. If something feels off, get to a public space as quickly as possible and/or ask someone, anyone, for help. Don't be shy. Spanish people are very friendly and even with a language barrier you will likely be assisted.

Camino App is an initiative of the Asociación de Municipios del Camino de Santiago that allows pilgrims to leave incident reports through a mobile app in real time.

Alternatively, ALERTCOPS is an official mobile app launched by the Spanish government, which allows for the instant reporting of crimes and incidents to the National Police, or *Guardia Civil.* The app can quickly identify your location, and you can include photographs if you witness an incident while the emergency services are responding. You can chat live with an operator in English. We recommend every pilgrim have this app ready to use on their phone before starting the Camino in case of any kind of emergency.

Ley Lines

Ley lines are metaphysical connectors stretching between various energetic power points around the world called vortexes. The concept was most famously outlined by Englishman Alfred Watkins in his 1925 book *The Old Straight Path.*

Watkins hypothesized that the major megalithic monuments of Europe, built as markers of the vortexes, are connected to each other by direct, straight lines of spiritual energy, a lost knowledge that was well understood by ancient societies.

The Camino began as a pagan path linking such sites for ancient Europeans. One of the reasons so many people are attracted to walking the Camino is because of the spiritual power that still exists along it. On the Camino del Norte you may find ancient standing stones, which are said to be markers along the lines.

Along different routes of the Camino you'll find a number of unique enclaves where the energy and vibration are very high. Ancient temples were built in these spots, which were later destroyed and replaced by churches or mosques.

There are numerous reports by locals and pilgrims of unexplainable apparitions, miracles and phenomena around these points.

Asturias Highlights

Cider

No stay in Asturias would be complete without time well spent in sidrerías, found in nearly every town and village. The alcoholic drink, made from fermented apples, is the ultimate symbol of Asturian identity, and the locals take it seriously. Barmen relish in their dramatic, high pours of the effervescent beverage, and take pride in pairing each varietal with the perfect gastronomic accompaniment.

Camino Primitivo

Many pilgrims traveling the Camino del Norte choose to divert onto the Camino Primitivo near Villaviciosa, in effect gaining a vastly different Camino experience with the same goal of Santiago in mind. The Primitivo is known to be the most challenging terrain of all the Camino routes, passing through high mountain passes with less services. But you're rewarded with untouched wilderness and total peace, thick with the spirits of original pilgrims who passed this way centuries ago. King Alfonso II, who ruled over the kingdom of Asturias from Oviedo in the 8th century, undertook the first known Christian pilgrimage to Santiago using this route, with thousands flocking in his wake. You can visit ruins of medieval pilgrim hospitals on the way. The Primitivo eventually reconnects with the Camino del Norte in Arzua, a stop on the Camino Frances.

Oviedo

This ancient capital of Asturias is the very birthplace of the Camino de Santiago. The charming walled city is a cultural landmark, famous for fine dining and the flare of its sidrerías. In Oviedo's Archaeological Museum, which is housed in a 16th-century monastery, you can view the bones of a Bronze Age male, whose skeleton marinated for centuries in a copper mine, soaking up sulphate and turning ghostly green in the process, as well as the sarcophagus of one of King Alfonso's concubines. You can walk on a diversion straight to the medieval walled city from the Camino del Norte, either continuing onto the Camino Primitivo, or reconnecting to the Camino del Norte near Gijon.

Gijón

The last big city you'll encounter on the Camino del Norte before reaching Santiago, Gijón offers the opportunity for more urban pursuits before setting off into the quiet villages further on. The old city rests on a clean public beach, and affords the chance to visit Roman baths dating from 100AD, an aquarium and varied international dining options.

WEEK 5

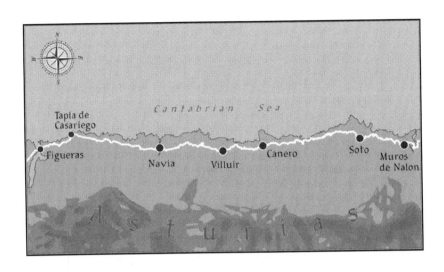

...a day for the high stool

Day 29 - Muros de Nalón to Soto
18km

Cassie

The hives are gone. The medicine had worked, with a bit of José's Dalai Lama magic sprinkled in for good measure. It was time to move forward. I wasn't allergic to the Camino, and I wasn't going to quit because of some disgusting little bed bugs.

We set off on a long walk through wilderness. Only forest today with no stops along the Way. I felt a bit faint as I climbed the hills, but essentially I was ok.

Then, the heavens burst. Lightning striking all around, accompanied by the kind of thunder that rattles your very innards. Nowhere to run, nowhere to hide.

My decision to not quit the Camino yesterday was beginning to feel a little hasty.

For four hours straight, we walked through a series of powerful electrical storms. Soaked to the bone, we stumbled into the tiny town of

Sota. The albergue here was in an old school building, cavernous and unattended.

We wrung out our clothes, headed down to the little cafe, *La Tasca de Luiso* and lucked out. On this extremely wet and cold day, we happened upon a full menu of homemade stews. Seafood for me. James chose pork. Both incredible. These stews are called 'fabas,' and are based on a broth of large white beans and tomato. This place was a gem.

As I slurped my soup down, I overheard the Dutch woman Anita ask an Irish-sounding pilgrim, "So what is your reason for walking the Way? Is it spiritual?"

Looking deep into his whiskey, and clearly disgusted by the question, the man replied by raising his glass. "Yes, well, there are certainly spirits involved," he drawled laconically.

Dutchy McDutchface definitely didn't get his meaning.

Later, I walked up to order my usual *vino blanco* mixed with *agua con gas*. The Irish guy gave me a judgmental once over.

"Ah. The Gatorade of the Camino. White wine and soda."

You can always count on the Irish to have an opinion about other people's drinking habits.

Of course, we ended up chatting to the guy and his two friends as soon as they heard James was also Irish. For a few hours at least, caught in the buzz of alcohol, things felt normal again. But I couldn't shake my awareness of the strain still felt between James and me. The Universe had done a fine job at throwing enough distractions to allow us to completely avoid talking about my outburst under the tree. I wondered if we'd ever speak about it.

I no longer felt any connection to that person who demanded, between hot, panicked breaths, we have a child. But I couldn't deny there must be some part of me, deep inside, which had spoken for my soul that day. Shaken and rattled by all the walking, finally free from my body's inner tendrils trapping around the dark recesses of my bowels. Now I feared it could never be taken back.

What would it mean for James and me, our marriage, our future?

James

Whilst drying off in a rustic pub after eating fabulous sticky stew, a pilgrim at the bar heard my Irish accent. He spun around on his stool with a massive grin and a full pint of lager, to inform me he was from Limerick City. Two men flanking him also spun around to proclaim they were brothers, from Galway.

186

It made me a little proud to see they were deeply hungover. A pale sheen glistened on their blotchy skin. Beads of sweat sat on their top lips. Dehydration made their hands shake, but they only cared about where the next beer was coming from.

"We're not drinking today," said the guy from Limerick, reverently waving his pint in the air as if it were the holy grail. He resembled an alcoholic Harry Potter, steamed up reading glasses and red cheeks blooming in delight. Of course, he had a pint. Everyone in Spain seems to drink smaller glasses of beer, but thirsty, Irish folk need that extra measure to soften their souls and senses. Empty whiskey chasers were on the bar behind them.

Outside the rain hammered down on the scuttling pilgrims that passed the front door. In Ireland we call it, 'a day for the high stool.' A day that's too wet to work outside. So your only alternative is to go to the pub and perch on a wobbly high stool while drinking beer at the bar. Well, okay, there are a myriad of other options. But many Irish folk will take the liquid diet and get the pints flying into the belly, at any excuse.

"Jesus. Will you look at that weather," said one of the Galway brothers called Rory Murphy. Since we'd started to talk, he wore a constant smile that made his green eyes twinkle above a crooked nose and face creased like a trodden carpet. His brother, wearing a Celtic football cap, looked almost identical, but had tinges of sickly green around his gills.

Slurping his pint merrily, Rory seemed delighted that the weather had hijacked the walking.

"I thought you weren't drinking today?" I asked knowingly.

"We're not drinking," said Rory, nudging steamed-up Harry Potter in the ribs. "Sure, boy, we're only having a few. Hair of the dog. Wetting our whistles."

If veteran Irish boozers are only having a few drinks, they'll consider that not enough to count as a genuine commitment to drinking alcohol. So they will just say they're not drinking today. To the shame or the honor of Ireland, it's a land where alcoholics don't have a drinking problem but instead carry their mammoth capacity to drink as a badge of pride.

These pilgrim lads had the look of seasoned boozers. Red noses and cheeks. Signs of well-fed beer bellies bulged a little under their pristine trekking jackets. Feasibly, these guys could drink the bar dry if given the opportunity. It was interesting to see such a crew in this neck of the woods. Normally, thirsty travelers of renown end up in southern Spain where the low price of booze keeps their spirits high. Down south on the Costa del Sol the only walking they'd do is from one pub to the next. Up here on the Camino del Norte, sometimes you have to walk for hours to get to the next bar. Which must have been a frightening realisation for these fellas.

I asked Harry Potter, "Why are you walking up here in the North?"

"We're on a drinking holiday, of course, boy. Our motto is, 'drink first, walk later." They gave a quick "cheers" then took long, lustful slurps of their beers.

These guys were a credit to my culture. "But why are you bothering to walk at all?" Cassie asked.

The Galway brother who'd not spoken yet opened his mouth to answer, but instead pulled his baseball cap down low, looked out into the rain, shook his head, then quietly went back to finishing his pint. He must've been dying of a mighty hangover.

Harry Potter took command again. "Old Brian here is wrecked," he said, giving his sickly buddy a playful tickle on the back of the neck. "A few more pints though, and a bit of bacon sandwich and he'll be in flying form again."

Harry Potter turned his attention back to Cassie. Opened his mouth and squinted. "You're asking why we're bothering to walk at all? Well, this is only our second day of walking. We drank too much yesterday so we didn't really get that far. And now we're a bit too hungover to continue. So you could say this is our first day." He looked at his pint and smiled. "Maybe I haven't really started walking at all." Bits of foam flew into his face as he laughed into his frothy pint. In no time we were all chuckling along with him. "Please could you get these two people pints," he said to the barmaid, pointing at us. "They're on me. We'll never walk as far as you, but you should at least try to catch up with what we've drunk."

I've always liked a good challenge. Drinking steady and sure, we all let go of the safe harbours of normal consciousness to sail the drunken seas.

Back home in Ireland, many publicans need a few patrons to be day drinking regulars to keep the trade alive and the coffers full. Brave fellas who will step up when it really matters and call a pint any time of the day to keep Ireland free. They keep the cultural pub trade afloat, regaling tourists with stories of misspent youth and articulating how they would best be suited to running the country, while lamenting the price hike of

188

beer. If any local Spanish walked into this Camino bar right now, they'd see many an Irish in his natural habitat.

And so we drank a sinful sackful of booze, while forgetting about babies and hives, but inquiring about Breton horses, unusual Dutch people and a man with a mega mullet. The Irish men knew nothing about such creatures, so we laughed about life.

At the end of the night, Cassie and I hugged and kissed and unsteadily walked hand-in-hand into the stormy night.

...citizen of the world

Day 30 - Soto to Canero
26.2km

Cassie

As usual, we were the last to get up in the cavernous schoolhouse albergue. Pilgrims hurriedly packed their things, trudging off by 8am as though they had somewhere to be.

I waited for the hustle and bustle to dissipate. James in the bunk next to me hadn't budged. He'd gone drink-for-drink with the Irish guys, and I knew it was going to be a long, hungover day.

Today there was a big choice to be had - the high road or the low. The high road, the historic Camino, would stretch on for 25km without a single chance to stop and zero services. It was a long incline followed by a long decline, up and down quite a high mountain. The low road was littered with bars and cafes, but undulated up and down the seemingly endless series of ravines crossing this coastal plain.

Since we didn't manage breakfast, and storms were brewing again, we opted for the low road. We avoided some of the undulations by using GPS to stay on the main road at times, instead of following the clams. It ended up being a pretty flat morning's walk, a life saver after the previous night's festivities. Another day of cloudy walking. In a month we had only two days I'd consider hot. I'll take it.

We soon came upon *Las Nenas*, a sprawling bar in the middle of nowhere with Tibetan prayer flags and a gay pride flag out front. Rare sights in this part of the world.

The lovely owners cooked us up some stellar burgers and fresh squeezed mixed juice. James was right as rain again.

189

Finally we made it to Playa de la Cueva. Barely. We checked into the *Hotel Canero*, which has an albergue in its basement. It's a dark, cold place - good for sleeping.

Our albergue was located deep inside one of the characteristic ravines of this coastal region, next to a sandy footpath leading to a massive beach. I rambled down just before sunset, as James was already in bed trying to sleep off last night's excess.

I climbed over a dune, and emerged onto the beach. A few families had set up camp, parents enjoying beers as carefree children ran on the edge of the sea. Everything glowed more orange as the summer sunset slowly approached. Surfers took turns on the waves, watched by patrons of a rigged up beachside bar playing reggae.

I grabbed a beer and took it onto the sand to plop down. I felt a million miles from the Camino. Alone and able to think, finally.

Just as I was about to open my can, a small group of ragged twenty-somethings piled out of a van and threw their stuff down next to me. I watched as they frolicked and bowed at the sea, taken by the beauty of the summer scene. The two girls in the group stripped off their frayed homemade dresses to reveal macrame bikinis and unshaven armpits, running towards the waterline. One of the guys started rolling a joint behind a sand pile he'd erected to protect the flakes of ganja from being blown away. The others started collecting driftwood for a bonfire.

As I watched the scene unfold, one of the guys looked up and my eye caught his. *Shit.* He smiled and practically ran over to me. He wore a pink hooded top with an om symbol, and linen knee-length knickers. His dirty blonde hair was pulled up into a bun, a few wisps becoming tangled in the string of his shark's tooth necklace.

"Greetings," he grinned through his unkempt beard. "My name is Stefan, but everyone calls me Tree."

Clearly some kind of German by his accent. This guy was the epitome of the typical backpacker in India, and looked like every friend from my twenties.

"Hi. I'm Cassie. Everyone calls me Cassie." I winked as I said it, but he didn't find it funny. I think he would've liked it if I'd said 'everyone calls me Starseed, or Parvati.'

He sat down near to me in the sand. "Oh, are you drinking beer?" he asked with raised eyebrows.

"Yes. I am drinking beer," I said. The guy was already boring me.

"I don't drink beer. It clouds the soul," he said, as he pulled out a pack of Camels and lit up.

"Where are you from?" I asked, trying hard to be friendly.

"Oh, I'm not from anywhere. I stay in a place for as long as I feel, then I move on. I'm a citizen of the world."

Oh, fucking hell. "OK, well, where were you born, and where's your passport from?"

He looked at me like I was the biggest loser who ever walked the earth. "Switzerland," he conceded. "But lately, I've been from Asia. Me and my friends only just arrived in Spain. Before we've been in Thailand and India. I think that really, I feel more from those places than anywhere else."

This fucking guy. Did he even have a glimmer of an idea what it was like to be Thai or Indian? "Cool, how long were you there?"

"I lived in India for two months and in Thailand for two months," he bragged, his chest a bit inflated. "You should go. You can study all kinds of things there. The locals really worship the divine feminine, and just understand everything about life, you know what I mean, sister?"

Did he say 'lived'? For two months? "Where in India were you?"

"The village of Arambol, on the shores of Goa."

Yep. I would've bet $100 on it. I could picture the exact street stall where he bought that awful pink shirt. Arambol was the mecca of pseudo-hippie culture in India, and totally overrun with organized crime, drugs and bastardized spiritual culture. He kept on talking as I zoned out and drank my beer a bit faster. He was going on and on about some retreat he went to where he learned to drink a glass of his own urine each morning. No doubt before he started another emotionally challenging day of THC-enhanced sun bathing.

I couldn't stand people like this. He reminded me so much of myself fifteen years ago. I would've loved this guy back then. My harsh judgment of Tree stunned me and amused me at the same time.

As I pretended to listen, I wondered what had happened to me. I had changed so much.

The sky began to darken and the bonfire was lit. I bid Tree farewell and made my way back to our room. There in the corner, hanging from the post of a bunk bed, was a tye-dyed cotton bandana that looked familiar.

Bill had been here.

I don't know what it was, but I couldn't shake the thought that I needed to see him. He must only be a couple of days ahead of us. I

191

could feel his energy in our steps. Life on the Camino was different without his presence.

James

Walking with a mighty hangover, inside my bin bag attire through the torrential rain was a dizzying experience. Rancid beer sweat excreted from every pore, making my skin itch and eyes sting.

Breathe out the bad stuff. Breathe in the good stuff...

Dehydrated, my brain seemed to vibrate painfully against my skull with every agonising step. Shakes set in, but my mind still had some post-party dopamine buzz pumping. It helped with the process of putting one foot in front of another, and making an otherwise tough trek a surreal, giddy delight.

At times we waded knee deep through submerged trails. Aquaplaning along, we found a mega-bridge that spanned the entire valley. So high above I couldn't even hear the traffic. Streams of rain created a dizzying waterfall that cascaded over its edge.

All of a sudden the sun burst through the thinner clouds, causing the giant waterfalls to dazzle. Excited, I picked up my pace to get close enough to witness spectacular, cascading rainbows pulsing within the waterfall. It all felt so wonderfully alien. As If I were exploring a new planet and had just found evidence of an ancient civilisation living in the sky.

My dehydrated brain craved liquid stimulation. I dropped my backpack onto the grass, then wrapped up tight in my bin bag spacesuit. Only steps away, rainbow water beams smashed the ground so hard they threw up stones and splashed water high into the air.

Would I be pounded to death or beamed aboard a spaceship? Stepping under the waterfall, I became one with the rainbow, then looked up to have my eyes bludgeoned with delight. I couldn't breathe, but felt totally alive.

Stepping away laughing, I reached for Cassie and held her in a drenched embrace.

All around, the lush vegetation glittered like emeralds under the intense sunlight. Reluctantly, we left the cascading torrent, walking hand in hand and joking about the alien sky race.

Onwards we marched through the bejeweled countryside.

...the divine feminine

Day 31 - Canero to Villuir
12.5km

Cassie

We shared the big, dark basement albergue with just two other pilgrims; Roberta, a shaven-headed Danish woman, and a cyclist who arrived around 11pm.

After sleeping ten hours, I wandered to the hotel cafe for some coffee before James woke up. Roberta, in her 40's and very animated, looked at me with wide eyes.

"Did you see that guy come in last night?" She was excited.

"No, not really." I'd already gone to bed.

"Ohhh," she cooed in her sing-song Danish accent. "I saw him naked. And I thought, *ohhh don't grab.*" She outstretched her arms and clenched her fingers closed several times.

Disgusted and amused, I finished my second cafe con leche then stood to round up James. Roberta beckoned me to her table before I could escape.

"I don't know how you can do it," she said, wide-eyed. "How can you and your husband share the albergue with all of us every night? Don't you need sex?" Her excitable tone carried over to the other tables, and a few people gave me a look.

I leaned down over her table, placing my palm gently in front of her orange juice. I whispered, "Don't worry, we've managed," I said, giving her a wink. She let out a horny little squeal in excitement.

No longer would locker room talk be the sole preserve of American presidents.

We only had to walk 12km today, which felt like nothing now. However, the constant ups and downs of the ravines in this particular section of Asturias were irritating and exhausting.

We lifted our spirits with lunch at the fantastic La Tiza Gastrobar in Luarca. Pad Thai with salmon and langoustines, chicken curry, and fresh home baked buns did the trick. We absolutely gobbled it down. Not only was the food delicious, there hadn't been much culinary variety of late. Beautiful meals always had a way of appearing just when we needed them.

3.5 more kilometers got us to Pilar's place, a guesthouse called *El Pajar de Lina*. She takes in pilgrims for just 15 euros per person, and we ended up with a private apartment with kitchen and living room, plus total silence. It was divine. Roberta would be proud.

Pilar let us know she was obsessed with Bruce Springsteen, who is from New Jersey, my home state. She pranced around her driveway in apparent bliss when she learned this, then scurried into her teepee in the yard to give praise to the Celtic gods.

As I hung our freshly washed laundry out to dry, I heard a shout. "Cassie!"

It was Kristin, the woman I'd given a blister patch to the other day.

"My blister is GONE! Fucking hallelujah!" she cried dramatically, arms outstretched to the heavens.

"Yep. I should be collecting royalties from Engo with all the pilgrims I'm converting," I laughed.

"Here," she said, passing a scallop shell to me. "I want to give this to you."

"Thanks, Kristin, but I'm not too into the scallop shells," I said in my trying-to-be-nice tone.

"I noticed," she replied. "You and James are some of the only pilgrims I've met who don't have one on their pack. The morning you screamed at those guys who were following us, you only did it because you could see the scallops we had, right? You knew we were pilgrims."

I nodded.

"Well, you should definitely have one of your own then."

"I don't know..." I said hesitantly. James and I felt no connection to the iconography of the Camino, and something about our egos had prevented us from fully embracing our pilgrimness.

"You know what they mean, right? The scallop shells?"

I shrugged.

"Look. The lines of the shell all start at different points, but they all end up at the same place in the end."

I ran my fingers over the lines of the shell.

"It's like us pilgrims. We come from every different point of the compass, every different situation. We all have our own stories, walk our own paths. But in the end, we all find our Way; our Camino. We all end up in Santiago somehow."

I smiled and looked up at the sky, laughing. Without another word, Kristin skipped away. When I went inside, I pushed the shell deep into the bottom of my pack where James wouldn't see it.

194

Tonight was the Night of San Juan, the official start to Spanish summer. Like so many Christian holidays, the Vatican scheduled the day to fall just after the pagan celebration of solstice, the shortest night of the year. The night that everything changes, when our world starts to spiral again into darkness.

To prepare for the collective journey, Spaniards flock to the nearest beach to build bonfires and bathe in the sea to the tune of much ritual, a relic of the pagans who once inhabited this land, mixed with typical Catholic symbology. It's believed that if you jump over one of the fires and wash your feet and face in the sea at midnight on the Night of San Juan, you'll be purified. Some even burn effigies of Judas Iscariot.

We set off from the guesthouse at 11pm, a bit of sunlight still lingering on the western horizon.

James

Roaring bonfires threatened to ignite the sky as I lay in a field. A dazzling desire to travel to the stars. A pale rider on a silver horse galloped across the moon. Milky horse prints splashing towards the horizon.

Horses clip-clopped close by. Was it Canción? A boulder dropped into my stomach. *Bastian!* His features shone as he flowed past the flames with the skittish horses.

Hopping up, I crouched to stalk my prey. His beard was bushier. His peculiar gaze showed he perceived a different world. None of the horses looked like Canción, but they smelt like Bastian. Stalking the last horse, I suddenly feared a kick so scampered to the side of the pack. One man led the way. Another walked within the pack saying something I couldn't understand.

The man in front laughed then turned his face my way. Not Bastian. Heart thumping, I focused on the middle man. Same features as Bastian... he turned his head. Damn! Not Bastian. Not anyone I knew. Disappointed, I trailed off to a wooden cabin as drops of rain began to tap dance down my face.

A few blue plastic chairs lay about. A strapping blond woman drained a can of cola. Trekking sticks lay against her leg. This woman looked powerful. As if she was a glacial flow, not needing to take the paths, instead cutting her way through mountains with sheer force of will.

Bastian is out there. I squinted through the fiery auras, scanning for the man.

"Ahhhhhh," she sighed in satisfaction. My throat became dry as I watched the last drops drip onto her pierced tongue.

"Good weather for walking," she said, in a voice obviously educated in England. With nothing else to do, I smiled and walked closer. Bright tattoos of faces and places adorned her thick arms and legs. Could it be a map of her mind?

"Good night for walking," I said. "Did you ever walk with a man named Bastian?"

Arching an eyebrow, she shook her head. "No. Do you want to sit?"

"No. Not now. I could have sworn I saw someone..."

"Are you okay?"

"No." I gave her a quick nod goodbye. Intent on my search, I let the flames guide me through the fires.

...crack houses

—

Day 32 - Villuir to Navia
17.6km

Cassie

You might be led to believe walking the Camino will be a mystical, deeply spiritual experience. You might assume you'll have hours to ponder the meaning of life, to process your childhood wounds, to meditate, to feel the fullness of multidimensional truths of the universe.

This is what I was expecting. My whole motivation for doing this crazy walk, even.

Now that we were five weeks in and 80% done, I could safely say walking the Camino has been the furthest from a spiritual experience I've ever had. I should have just stayed back home and whipped myself.

No matter how bad I wanted it, no matter how many hours I spent envisioning it. I was so busy, every day. Walking for hours, dodging other pilgrims, hand washing clothes, consuming enough calories to walk again the next day. I had no time for anything else.

I'd never been more firmly planted in the physical dimension as I was now. My lucid dreams stopped. My conscious living went out the window. I hadn't meditated in a month. Yoga? What's yoga? Every moment walking was a fight for survival. Eat, sleep, walk, wash. The meaning of life didn't matter anymore. Spiritual ascension was a distant memory.

I'd met so many pilgrims from around the world, but none had any messages for me. No one told me a story that deeply moved me or shared a part of themselves that brought clarity to the arc of my life. In fact, the majority of them seemed to have a few screws loose. It seemed a large percentage of pilgrims walk the Camino to cure their depression or escape something they can't face. It was a real shit show out there. Slogging on, up another ravine and through a dark eucalyptus forest, we laughed at the ridiculousness of it all - as more thunder rumbled in the distance.

We came into the town of Navia, arriving at the albergue, which was still shut. A folded piece of paper taped to the door immediately caught my eye. It read, 'Cassie and James.'

I hurriedly unfolded the paper to reveal a note handwritten on the back of a receipt:

'Guys, Where are you? Hopefully you're here, otherwise you will never read this. Good news and bad news. Good news is I found your poncho, James. Bad news is, the thief denied the whole thing and still has it. Anyway, missing you guys. I'm not doing well. – Beautiful Bill. PS – look behind the fountain!'

James and I read the note quickly, mouths wide open, looking at each other in disbelief. I spun around. There was a small decorative fountain with a few moldy framed images of saints and some crappy plastic roasaries hanging off it. Reaching behind, I felt the cool glass of two bottles. He'd left us Heineken.

We sat on the stoop of that Albergue, eyes sparkling and dripping with sweat, and enjoyed the best two beers of the Camino. And they were warm.

Bill was only a day ahead of us.

James

Blinding bolts of lightning tore the sickly orange sky. Dogs freaked over the ear-shattering thunder. Glowing clouds, pregnant with rain, raced to the horizon.

We talked about finding shelter. All around us, fields were tilled, but empty of crops. Streets strewn with nothing. In between thunder claps, the world went eerily quiet until Cassie remarked that a pig wouldn't be

197

terrified of thunder like a dog, and she'd like to travel with one someday. Worried it was a veiled attempt to talk about travelling with a kid, I became annoyed. I wanted to snap back that I'd rather bring a pig than a person.

Thinking I was being manipulated, my mind quickly mirrored the troubled skies. Agitated, it jumped and cracked to future arguments that would tear us apart.

None of these fights are real, I told myself. *Nothing happened. All this anger probably came from my misinterpreted meaning of a pig. Wasn't she talking about a travelling pig the night of our anniversary?*

I tried to blow my anger into the clouds, willing my emotions over the horizon. A sudden, sharp pain in my hand made me flail. *Cassie touched me!* Static electricity ignited a spark between us.

"Are you okay?" she asked, confused. "You look like you hate me."

"I'm okay. Just shocked. Felt like you were attacking me."

"Are you sure? I love you. I'd never attack you." Without fear she grabbed my hand. Slowly her touch leached the anger from my soul while we walked through lightning storms.

After many miles, my toes began to ache. Shifting the weight to the balls of my feet caused my back to hurt, so I sat on the wall near a crack corn house. Its little guardian statues watched me rest. This long, narrow stone structure on stilts with a slanted roof was used in this part of Northern Spain for storing corn and keeping it dry.

Then I saw the vehicle.. A van, open-backed, blue and beaten up.

My heart grew in that moment. Lord God above, could it be Gypsy Mullet's van? Unable to contain myself, I walked faster.

"What's the rush?" asked Cassie, trying to tug me back.

"It's him," I said pointing excitedly to the mossy walls of the next corn house.

"Him who? What?"

Juicy music trickled into my ears. Melancholy gypsy tunes.

"Do you hear him?" I said, my ear cocked towards the music. "It's Gypsy Mullet. Listen."

"Where?"

"In there."

"No way," she said, making a disgusted face. "I hope not. I don't want to see his dirty balls again."

"Listen," I said, excited. Gypsy Mullet's succulent voice turned to a sad wail. "I'm going in."

"You're an idiot."

I kissed Cassie on the forehead. "Love you, too."

Tentatively, I climbed the stone stairs, each step causing my heart to further fill with Gypsy juice. Raising my sweaty fist to knock, I noticed a hole in the door. I peered in to find him fully mulleted. Even in silence, I knew his eyes met mine. Had he heard me on the stairs?

I knocked. Silence. Pulled by an unbearable force, I pushed the door open.

My breath quickened as we locked eyes. I took a step inside.

Quickly he spoke. "Come, Horse Feeder. Come. Come. Come. I knew you would travel this way."

Rotting corn created a dense, murky atmosphere. My nose scrunched up at the over ripe smell. As I approached, his eyes shut. Time slowed. Sunlight tickled the floorboards through cracks in the ancient roof. Shadows fell in all the corners, except for where a shrine was erected around Fonso. There, candles haphazardly flickered, illuminating his glistening mullet, but also the pained look upon his portly cheeks. Holy pictures of glowing saints l hung to the wall behind him by slithers of tape. One picture that looked like Nicu flopped forward as it barely clung on by one corner. Had he hastily stuck it back onto the wall after hearing my footsteps?

Bright brown eyes flared open when I was but a meter away.

"So you find me again, Pilgrim. You still have your wife, but I am still beastless. Horse shy. No hooves to ease my Way. Does it bring you shame to see me like this? Be truthful, Horse Feeder. For I don't suffer fools."

Despite his grandiose pomp, I found him diminished. Less mullet. Less sure. It made me feel weak in my stomach. "Are you okay? I heard you singing. Do you want me to leave?" Truly, I hoped he did not.

Contemplation wrinkled his brow. Three seconds must have passed in which he studied me with a murderous glare.

Snake-like, his bejeweled fingers struck for the picture of Nicu. Our uncomfortable stare broke as he laid it between us. His lips quivered as if to cry, but instead he snarled. Slowly, he shifted his weight forward towards it, causing glittering dust to fall from the ceiling over the picture. Some flecks landed on his mullet. Sacrilege!

His ringed finger pointed to Nicu's angled features. "You respected Nicu?"

"I did."

"So I will continue to respect you, even though you have now failed to find Canción on two occasions."

I swallowed hard. I never meant to displease him. I was just walking the Camino, doing my best not to get blisters. All I ever really wanted was to get some proper sleep. Is that why he looked upon me with such hatred? Because I failed him once again? *Say it isn't so, Gypsy Mullet.*

"Nicu," he said, tracing his fingers over his friend's steep forehead, "has still not returned from the mountains. I followed the ley lines where my beast would have roamed. But I tell you this. The ley lines have lied! Impossible as it may seem. They have lied. I feel it in my waters."

Thunder boomed far away. He feels it in his waters? Is that why he washes his balls in magic fountains? Muggy heat and silence made sweat trickle down my back as I strained with the indecision of asking a question.

"Gypsy Mullet?" His eyes flared. "Do you wash your balls in a lot of the fountains?" Silence. My mouth went dry to continue talking. Swallowing hard, I tried to continue. "It's just that Cassie washes her face in a lot of the fountains. She wanted to know if she should stop? You know. Because she might get dickwater on her face. That's a bit too weird for her."

"I respect that you speak for your wife. So me and you. You and me. We shall talk about it a little more."

"Talk about the fountains you wash your balls in?"

"No. We will talk of my Breton horse."

"Okay. That's good, too. I suppose."

"As a pilgrim you must have learned something from talking to the people of this land?"

Bastian appeared in my mind, swirling my blood between his toes. Another light layer of shadow clouded Fonso's face as a candle snuffed out. "Well," I said, swallowing hard again. "I learned…"

For a moment his intense calm was unmasked. "What? What have you learned?" he commanded.

Shit. He was mentally struggling. Probably because his true companions Nicu and that horse were lost. Was he afraid to be alone?

I took a breath, felt a constricting pain in my chest, then spoke. "There was a fella called Bernadette."

Fonso creased his brow.

"He told me of a guy who might have been stealing horses to ride to Istanbul."

200

Gypsy slapped his meaty hand down hard onto Nicu's face. "Who stole my horse?"

"We don't really know if he stole a horse. No one saw it. I actually met the guy. Tall lad. He thinks he's on a holy quest like John the Baptist. Giving people new names for the Way. Bastian is his name. Do you know him?"

Gypsy shook his mullet in disgust. "Giving someone a new name? You are who you are. No new name will change this. Where is he now?"

"Well, that's the thing. It seems he didn't continue to Istanbul. He was spotted near Muros de Nalon only four days ago. You could be so close to Cancíon." More dust fell as lightning struck closer. "Maybe Nicu has already found her?"

The corn house flickered as he brushed away dust from the sleeves of his jacket onto the candles. Fonso took a heaving breath that barely held the buttons of his shirt in place.

"I knew it," he said. "The Way is the Way. It works both ways. This is why my energies throbbed with so much pain when I washed them in the ley line waters." He grabbed at nothing in the dim light. "Ghosts play games with us, Horse Feeder. For once you know something more than me. Do you believe Bastian has my horse? Will we be reunited?"

"Of course you will be reunited." *Oh, God.* I didn't want to tell him Bastian might be injecting the horse with peanut butter.

Easing his weight to the left, he caused a new batch of dust to glitter and fall. Gleaming bronze bowls, some holding pictures, appeared behind him, then disappeared as he sat upright again. *Are the bowls little shrines? That mystical bastard. I wonder what he believes.*

Noticing how I stared through him, he narrowed his eyes. "So you saw them?"

I nodded.

"Interesting. I sleep in these haunted corn houses sometimes. Spirits of nature make for interesting conversation. Other people come to visit me so I can speak to the spirits on their behalf. Some people still want me to be a savior, but I am only a seer. Today I have three ancestors sharing this house... The Mother. The Now. The All. What part of you sees them?"

Confused that he was playing a game with me, I lamely answered, "My eyes."

"Fool," he replied. "The Mother knows you." He moved to the side so I could see two bowls properly. Intricately etched on the outside of

201

each bowl were prancing horses. His portly belly obscured the view of what I imagined was another similar bowl.

"The Mother," he said, pointing to the centre bowl. It contained a black and white photo of a woman with soft, round features and piercing eyes, her curly hair so expansive it couldn't fit within the confines of the photo. He pointed to the next shrine. "The Now. You see now?" The shrine had no picture. From his coat he took a pair of scissors then cut a clump of his flowing hair.

Desecration!

Into the empty bowl, he threw the dying mullet. "The Now is always changing. The Now is always dying."

"And this bowl holds the All." He mumbled something, then turned his neck to look at it. I craned my neck to see over his belly, but the combination of dim candlelight, his bulk and his mullet meant I couldn't make out the bowl's contents. Too bashful to ask him to move, I stayed silent.

"Now," he said. "We will see what is happening in the now of the Now." Picking up a candle, he whispered words into its light, then touched the flame to the hair in the Now bowl. The fire spread rapidly, causing a mini supernova that burnt away the stink of corn, leaving a singed sensation in my mind. Transfixed, we both stared into the smoking mullet.

A calm settled in my mind. Relief I'd not felt in months travelled through my body. On reaching my toes, anger suddenly sprung into my heels and raced back into my brain. I realised the stupidity of trying to hold onto one emotion or the other, for everything changes in the now. Stop trying to control everything.

Gypsy Mullet's hand shot forward, crushing the blazing lock of hair. Something scratched in a darkened corner. My body stiffened. Was someone else here?

Opening his hand, he let the singed hair fall onto Nicu's picture. The last embers crackled over his face.

"Ley lines," he said, staring intently into his blackened palm, "have brought false prophecies before. Shrines crumble. Even my hair mumbles. Something is truly wrong. Now I can see that my beautiful beast has taken a different path."

"What do you mean?"

Fonso's energy had been low since I entered, but now his stupor lifted.

"Horse Feeder," he said slowly. "Those ley lines..." He shook his head. "No. You can go now."

"What? But...?"

His eyes were aflame again. He nodded to the door. My eyes stung. Tears welled.

Outside, under the streaming clouds, Cassie's first question was, "Did you ask Gypsy Mullet if he was washing his balls in many of the fountains along the Way?"

Cool air soothed my eyes. It was good to be back in this world. "I did ask him. But I don't know."

"You don't know? Did you really ask him?"

"I did. He just said he respected your question."

"So there could be dickwater in half the fucking fountains around here? Oh, that's just great." She spat on the ground. "I can never drink from a public fountain again."

As we walked, I tried to explain to her what happened.

"And what about the All shrine?" she asked. "What's in there?"

"His beefy bulk was in the way. I never saw it."

"You're probably better off. Bet there was a horse testicle in there. Weirdo."

...crossroads

-

Day 33 - Navia to Tapia de Casariego
22.2km

Cassie

Today we came to a crossroads and had to choose between three alternative routes. The Camino del Norte had led us to its next distinctive stage. We could feel change in the air. Our options were: remain on the inland and rather bland official Camino, head further inland away from the sea for good on the historic Camino, or take a new coastal route and commune with the sea for two more days before bidding it farewell for good. How could the Camino gods expect us to make this decision? Which way had Bill gone? Which path had Lina and the others chosen? Where was the horse Canción, and perhaps more importantly, had Bastian come this way? I could sense James was starting to obsess over it. A lonely black horse was standing at the crossroads. We stood silently side by side, looking at him for an answer. He nodded his head to the right, recommending we stick to the coastal route. So we kept on walking.

For 33 days we'd walked along the northern coast of Spain. I could say with confidence I was now intimately acquainted with hundreds of miles of the edge of the Iberian peninsula. The Cantabrian Sea had become a fixture, both in navigation and in spirit, for all of our journey.

Tomorrow would be our last day skirting the coastline, enjoying its cool breezes and epic views. The Camino turns off southward towards Santiago for the final push, and the landscapes would quickly change.

What will become of us without our steadfast ocean? Will the air change, will we feel lost?

Will the gravitational pull of Santiago finally capture us, accelerating us forward and speeding up our karma?

Despite my growing exhaustion, I felt more must still be had from this Camino business. There was something I wasn't getting. Would it manifest in the high rolling hills of Galicia? I felt ready to turn my back on our ocean companion. Something deep inside ached for a new scene.

Appropriately, our last stop on the coast was the spectacularly placed *Albergue de Peregrinos of Tapia de Casariego*. The hostel itself, despite a friendly attendant, was the most basic we've stayed in yet, with little room to breathe and no perks or extras. They get away with it though, because it's perched on one of the most breathtaking cliffs we've encountered on this journey - a true million dollar view. I sunbathed on the cliffs and watched the tide go out, revealing a sandy land bridge stretching from the mainland to a rocky island just off the coast. Some barefoot pilgrims pranced out to it as the sun began to dip. *How do they have the energy after all the walking?*

My mind went to Bill. His note haunted me. He said he wasn't doing well. No mention of Gerta. He's been picking fights with Japanese women over ponchos. I realized I was anxious to catch up to him again.

And then there was James and me. We spent hours walking together every day, but I couldn't quite bring myself to say anything about the rain-soaked fight under the tree. Every time I thought about it, a giant lump would gather in my throat. I didn't trust myself not to break down like last time.

James

Sitting on its wooden perch, the beady eyed peacock starred as us through the wire mesh cage. Baking sun reflected off its iridescent tail feathers, flowing four feet to the floor. We'd tried another Camino shortcut. Instead of getting lost on a hellish highway, this time we found ourselves on a peaceful farm.

Dozens of serene cows stood in a shed with their tails tied up so their crap would drop into channels beneath their hooves and not splash all over their clean buttocks.

Clean cows didn't feel right. As a boy, I used to visit my great aunt's farm. A lovely woman, half the size of my tiny grandmother and twice as holy. Every morning, I'd eat boiled eggs from her hens, then collect a pail of fresh milk from her ancient, stone barn that, on a hot summer day, would smell of sweet, steaming cow dung.

If terrible luck would have it, I'd see another kitten floating dead in a milk pail. It had slipped in trying to drink the creamy milk. A tragedy for my little heart each time I'd have to lift out the beautiful ball of fluff. A funeral would follow, attended only by me as I buried it in the soft earth. In those days, the milk would still be sent to the creamery for the rest of the county to taste cute death.

So much birth and death on a farm. Cows, chickens, kittens, puppies and sheep. My father told me farmers seem to get over bereavement in their family quicker than others. Be it the death of a parent or child. Living with death everyday lets one see how natural it really is. Eases the letting go.

I'd like to let go of the Camino. But here I was, scanning a barn looking for signs of Gypsy Mullet's horse. Satisfied Canción didn't hide amongst the cows, we'd wandered over to the strange sight of the caged peacock. Nearing the fence, a furious goose burst out of a coup in the next cage. Unmercifully, it honked its head off at us, thus upsetting the peacock which shook its dazzling feathers in defiance.

"What the hell's going on here?" said a voice from behind. "That's a sight and sound!"

Turning to the voice, I was looking into the bespectacled face of a pilgrim with skin the creamy glow of the full moon on a frosty night. A mischievous smile crept up his face. He pulled back his long blond hair, then pressed his forehead into the mesh fence.

"Bird friends. Let us communicate," he said in a soft German accent, while taking down the black guitar case from his shoulder. Quickly, he opened the case while the goose and peacock continued to scream and quiver. He pulled out a battered black guitar, then began to tune it.

Something impressed me about this lean guy who must've been in his late thirties. He had a calming nature, and peaceful eyes like the cows. Maybe it was that roguish smile that never left his lips. It was as if he got the joke of the Camino.

His green, tattered backpack made him tip slightly backwards to balance the instrument in his hands. He opened his mouth, then unexpectedly spewed out a tirade of honking geese noises and gyrated his hips while madly strumming the guitar like he hated it. I half expected him to jump the fence, then smash the goose over the head with the guitar.

Cassie grabbed onto my arm in worry. Giving one last intense strum on his guitar, he let out a piercing war cry then finished with a slight bow towards the stunned birds.

"This stupid guitar," he said, slightly out of breath. "I carry it everywhere but never use it." For the first time he really looked at us, then burst out laughing.

Peeking out from beneath the sleeve of his orange t-shirt, I could see the Hindu symbol of the elephant god Ganesh tattooed on his upper arm.

"My name's Michael," he said, giving me one of those namaste greetings where you put your palms together over your chest. Instinctively, I batted his hands away. I could tell he was being nice but silly. I wanted to be silly but nice.

"How dare you disrespect my respect," he said wide-eyed.

"How dare you disrespect me with your disrespect," I said. "This is Catholic country. Not the Hindu Kush. Don't come spreading your heathen religion into these lands."

"But, sir," he whispered, looking to the sky. "I am just a simple pilgrim."

"Shut up, heathen. With your fancy hair and rock and roll face. You're here to convert the children to your wild ways."

His mischievous smile returned. "You're right. To find the wild Way is why I'm walking. Are you going to Tapia, too?"

"Yeah."

"Well, let's be going on our wild way then." With that, he swung his guitar over his shoulder and case over the other, then we were off. Another Camino companion magically appearing.

Bastian and his proximity must've been on my mind, because before I could think, I'd asked him, "Have you heard of Bastian?"

"What's a Bastian?"

"A tall, scraggly-bearded Dutch man. But he might not be a Dutch man. But he might be a peanut butter murderer and a horse thief."

"Fascinating."

Nothing seemed to faze Michael. It was as if he was feeling the flow of the Camino but not caught up in its fluctuating energies.

"What about Gypsy Mullet?" I asked.

"Gypsy, what? I hope you are not one of those racists demeaning the Roma?"

"He calls himself Gypsy."

"Fascinating."

"Have you met a man named Nicu? Sharp-faced man. Always hawk whistling?"

It felt good to hear him let out a little laugh. "No."

"Have you met anyone of interest? What about the Secret German?"

"No."

"LSD Bill?"

"He sounds interesting, but no."

"Wolfentop?"

"Wolfentop. Yes. I've met him. I've had the pleasure of this displeasure. The man's a mess. He seems to be looking for something he's sure he can't find. It's destroying his energy. I've never met a man who lived so much in the past."

"His tribe is gathering in Santiago," I mused.

"We both know the tribe will not be as good as his last tribe."

"True." We both smiled.

Thinking about Wolfentop made me sigh. Or maybe I was just more tired than I realized. All this over thinking about babies and horses had worn me out.

Michael began to hum. It helped refocus my mind.

"Forget Wolfentop," I said. "I'm actually trying to find a horse. Gypsy Mullet's horse. Chestnut coloured, blonde mane with a white stripe down its face. The white stripe seems silver by moonlight. Big beast. It's a female Breton."

"You're looking for a moonlit horse? I've seen many horses, but can't be sure I've seen that one." He shrugged his shoulders. "I do know a song about a horse." He whipped down his guitar. "Stop here. Let's see if the horse is drawn to this song."

207

Would he scream, whinny and neigh? To my delight, he sang a magnificent rendition of a Christy Moore song called 'Ride On.' A shiver ran down my spine. I grabbed Cassie's hand. At times when I'd thought of Gypsy Mullet's horse, that very song had played in my head.

"Where did you learn that song?" I asked as he cocked his ear, pretending to wait for a horse.

"Off some dirty Irish guy in India who would never eat food with me. He just sat on my balcony all day eating cornflakes." Michael shook his head. "I'll never forget him playing 'Ride On" on his ipod on repeat while complaining about the lack of alcohol. Cats. He loved cats. Always with the cats. He did save lots of money only eating cornflakes. I like that. I'm Swiss. We like the money." He winked, then began to sing. "Money, Swiss. Money. Money. Swiss money. Money. Money. Swiss."

I was beginning to like this guy more and more.

"Do Swiss really love money?" I asked.

"For sure. Yes. We stole the Nazi gold. It made Switzerland great again just like Trump is making USA great again." He nudged Cassie.

"How'd you know I'm American?"

His mischievous smile twiched. "Your accent. You're a yank right? One of the chosen people of the land of the brave and free. Leaders of the free world."

Michael began to stomp his foot, then broke into the chorus of 'Born in the USA.' "Sorry if I didn't sing it patriotically enough. Like your president, my hands are a little small to play it properly."

"Ha," said Cassie. "You got that right. But he's not *my* president. He's a damn mango-Mussolini. Anyway, anyone who borrows from The Boss is alright by me. Did you know my mother dated Bruce Springsteen?"

"Really?" He arched a dubious eyebrow. "Did you know I was kidnapped in India?"

Cassie looked confused. "What?"

"Nothing. Nothing. Let's not talk about music or politics anymore," he said, putting his guitar back in its case then swinging it onto his shoulder with ease. "It slows everything down and I've got to get to Tapia."

So we picked up the pace and talked about fake Indian gurus, laughing yoga, gay monks, inquisitors and Wolfentop. After a while, fields of cows gave way to houses, which gave way to giant haystacks in the middle of a small town square.

We'd stumbled into a Sunday fair in full swing. Music blared. Kids raced around, and for some reason sawdust filled the air. Little tents selling all sorts took our fancy. Stalls swayed from the weight of bread and cheese. Michael kept whispering to me, "Money Swiss," as he swiped at piles of free samples as we circled the shops.

Next we saw why there was so much sawdust. Lumberjacks were at war, smashing their axes into thick logs, sending clouds of desiccated wood into the air. An announcer excitedly spoke of their burly exploits. Children half-heartedly clapped while a few dazed adults drank from bottles of beer and wine.

Michael tapped me on the shoulder. "Let's see if they like this. Mind my pack. Irishman." He dropped his backpack, then jumped up on stage behind the announcer. Whipping out his guitar with exaggerated panache, he threw back his head, let his blond locks flow, then began to sing a merry song I knew from *Monty Python*. A song about gay lumberjacks.

I cut down trees, I skip and jump
I like to press wildflowers
I put on women's clothing and hang around in bars...

The stunned announcer turned to see who was making such a racket, but his shift in position only allowed more space for his microphone to pick up on Michael's voice. At first people frowned, but soon most were clapping and cheering.

I'm a lumberjack and I'm OK
I sleep all night and I work all day

Invigorated by the change of tune, the sweaty men chopped faster, perhaps unaware they were working to the anthem for gay lumberjacks.

I cut down trees, I wear high heels
Suspenders and a bra
I wish I'd been a girlie, just like my dear Papa

By the end, a few angry faces were whispering in the crowd. Michael judged it a good time to call a halt to his performance. "Thank you!" he shouted. "It's been a gay old time!"

A few people cheered. A few scowled.

For the first time since we'd met LSD Bill, I thought I could hang out with another human without them grating on me after a few hours. I congratulated him with a pat on the back.

"Don't touch me, Irish," he said. "I don't want to catch the famine off you."

"Then come for a feast instead. Do you want to get some lunch?"

209

"No, but thanks. I don't want potato surprise. Anyway, the bus is coming and I've got to be in Santiago in a few days. I'm not spending all my Nazi gold on albergues. My secret is, I only walk for a few hours a day then take the bus. There is too much walking on the Camino. It's not good for your mental health." He looked to the sky, then pulled his pack onto his back.

"Anyway, great to make your acquaintance." He handed me a card. "Here's my business card. My details are on it. Keep in touch. Bye." Swinging his guitar case onto his shoulder, he walked towards the bus, then turned to namaste us.

Feeling a bit rejected and disappointed he didn't want to hang out with me, I looked at his card. Michael's face mischievously smiled back from a handstand position. He was a yoga teacher.

...biological clocks

-

Day 34 – Tapia de Casariego to Figueras

9.5km

Cassie

What happens when it's over? All these thousands of people who walk the Camino each year - what do they do when they get home? In more than a month of walking, I've talked and walked with so many people, most of whom are searching for something.

Did they find it? What if they did? Will they change their lives? Will things be different? What if they didn't find what they're looking for?

Will they give up? Search somewhere else? Most western-world humans live in a society that deprives us of our natural habitat. We've been transformed into productivity machines, and have slowly become detached from the spirit world, from other humans, and from our deepest selves.

On the Camino, many of us live more closely to nature than we ever have. Rise with the sun. Walk all day. Get the food in. Tug and push the elements. Help each other. Know each other. Sleep. Wake up and do it again.

Our feel-good chemicals, oxytocin, serotonin, they're flowing without the help of antidepressants or designer drugs. We are filled with purpose. Point A to Point B. That's all that matters, and it feels good.

But what happens at the end? There's no retreat for pilgrims, no sharing circles. No therapists or meditations. There's no one back home who could possibly understand what you've just gone through. How do you re-enter "life"? How do you process? How do you integrate?

Back to the same job. The same relationship. The same stresses and the same draining routine. How many lives will actually change?

This is what I ponder as we march today, across a strangely flat series of farm fields in the hazy heat.

Tonight we'd stay at the *Albergue Camino Norte*, a large family-run establishment with wonderful food homemade on site to order and a green lawn to lounge on. It's the last stop in Asturias before crossing into the province of Galicia, home to Santiago. Get the garlic chicken and salad.

Esmerelda, twenty-something daughter of the owners, dressed all in black, served our food. The Way was sparse here with the crowd being thinned by the three different routes. We hadn't heard much through the grapevine about the next couple of days of walking.

"Esmerelda," I asked, "have you walked the Camino from here to Santiago?"

She chuckled a bit. "No, I haven't, but I want to. On a horse. But I walk on the Camino almost every day to get to Ribadeo, the next town."

We would be headed that way tomorrow when it was finally time to turn inland. "What's the Way like tomorrow?"

Her eyes widened, excited someone had asked. "Well, you will have to cross a big bridge over the *riva*. It's an amazing bridge and I love it."

She was enamored by this bridge. "Why do you love it?" I asked.

"Well, it's so high. When I walk over it, I feel something. I feel like I am living. You know, it's a new bridge. It used to take an hour to get to Ribadeo, but now you can drive there in five minutes. But there's no bus. You have to walk if you don't have a car. It's so wonderful. And when you reach the other side, you're in Galicia."

The ancient kingdom of Galicia, now a province of Spain, and home to Santiago de Compostela, the resting place of Saint James. We were finally almost there.

James

Orange wisps of sunset streak across the sky as we sat outside our albergue around a splintered, wooden table. We sipped on a few decent bottles of wine with an American couple. It's funny how family dynamics play out. They were living in sin.

Our new drinking buddies were drained from a forty-something kilometer trek, sunburnt and joints aching. Suffering etched over their faces anytime they reached for a sip of wine. They persevered. No pain, no gain in the booze game.

Becky, still in her sweaty, trekking gear, glowed painfully from her over-indulgent flirtations with our radioactive star. Poor woman was stiff as a board and could barely even move her neck, so instead swiveled her chocolate-coloured eyes to drink in the world.

"We had to leave our families," she said, in a rising tone that made everything sound like a question. "It was truly awful. Like. Oh, God. Awful. It should be nobody else's business if we want to get married. It's our own choice. They wouldn't leave us alone. My husband's a Catholic, you see."

Fiddling with his silver wedding ring, the man opposite her was halfway through his Hulk transformation phase. His body was a ball of muscle while he peered out from black wide-rimmed glasses. Red skin peeled from his nose.

"I'm a Protestant," she continued. "My parents were so worried. They were practically freaking out that I'd convert to Catholicism if I married him."

Perhaps broken by her nagging parents, the Hulk shook his head.

"So," she said. "We just left and got married in secret. Alone in Bali. Best thing we ever did."

I respected their internal fortitude. It's not so easy to leave it all behind and go it alone. Cassie and I had technically eloped. We also had no one at our wedding. We all toasted to doing it your own way. I wondered how our early Camino crew of Boils, English Dave, Tomasino and the like were faring.

Sipping away, she continued. "This Camino is so stressful because every step for us is a lie. Right now our families are planning our wedding. We couldn't tell them we actually got married already. So we're going to have another wedding for them. A fake fucking wedding! Can you believe that? I feel like such a fraud. It's keeping me awake at night."

She grimaced as she poured wine into her glass while the Hulk picked at his peeling nose. "But it's already gone weird again," she said exasperated. "It's the priest. He's our friend. We already told everyone that he's marrying us. He's a gay black guy. But then some of my family got freaked out and told us that it was okay if he was black or gay, but

212

not black AND gay. Can you believe that? For God's sake. For my folks, gay and black is just too much. Way too much."

The Hulk tried to block out the conversation by nibbling on the dead skin he'd peeled from his nose.

"But now," she continued, "they're saying the conversation never happened. But. My God. I was technically there. We all had a Skype meeting about it, but they're denying it. Anyway, I don't want to talk about it. My mind is like so, so, so, stressed. Do you want to hear something weird instead?"

"Of course," I said, feeling a little excited about any weirdness in general.

"Last night, how well did you sleep?"

I didn't want to say anything about the armada of space babies that invaded my sleep, so I just said, "Okay," with a shrug of the shoulders. "Dorms. You know."

Eyes widening, she actually managed to turn her neck towards me. "Well. My god. I had like. The worst sleep. Don't even. Get me started." Grimacing, she reached into her bag then put a metal spoon on the table. "There was. For sure. A pervert in our dorm. A disgusting old pervert."

This did sound interesting. "Go on," I said sipping wine merrily.

"So we got to the municipal albergue. Wrecked. So I took a nap straight away. Now listen to this shit. When I woke up, I found some bearded bastard peering at me from the next bunk. Peering at me between his fingers. Like, from behind prison bars or something. I jumped up, scared shitless. But you know what? That creepy bastard just kept staring at me. Can you imagine that? Between his fingers. With his sexual face."

Thinking about space babies again, I asked, "Did you punch him?"

"No."

"So what did you do?"

"Oh, God. Not, what did I do. What did HE do. I rushed off to the kitchen. Five minutes later, I was still in there alone drinking coffee when he walked in with just a towel on. Straight away I could see he had a boner. God. I felt so sick I wanted to scream. But something came over me. In a fucking rage I just reached for the thing closest to me then whacked him on the cock with my spoon and ran off. This spoon."

We all started to laugh as she brandished a spoon bearing an embossed Camino scallop shell, she must've bought in a pilgrim's gift shop along the Way. Tourist tat. Lethal to testicles nonetheless. "Adam.

213

Stop laughing at me. You know, I'll whack you on the cock if you don't stop laughing at me." Squinting menacingly, she laid the spoon on the table.

"I hope you washed it?" Cassie asked, smiling.

Sunset rays dazzled on the spoon when she picked it up again to twirl it between her fingers. "This is a reminder," she said. "A souvenir to keep me alert. I might even melt it down to make a necklace." She burst out a snorting laugh. "I just realized how stupid I sound. Sun and wine, hey? God, we need to drink a lot tonight with this sunburn. No fucking way will we get to sleep otherwise." Bewitched by the spoon, we all sat in companionable silence for a while.

Becky's plan for an alcohol-induced coma sounded good, but had its flaws. The drunker I got, the deeper my sleep. At least for a while. Then dehydration and my overactive mind could end up making the rest of the night worse than normal. But there was something remarkably healing about being knocked out, even if I was in a drunken stupor. The next morning, I might be hungover and tired, but at least the alcohol would've allowed the eternal watchman, always alert in some hidden part of my brain, to finally turn off and get some rest. If he went off duty, even just for a little while, I felt a little healed.

Adam lost interest in eating himself, and was the first to speak. "You could have damaged that pervert's child-bearing possibilities whacking him like that." His words were uttered with a teasing smile but with a hint of venom.

"Oh, Adam. Don't turn everything into your personal quest for children. Guys, he told me today that he thinks my subconscious hit the pervert in the cock as I'm afraid to have kids." She tapped the spoon on the table. "Tap. Tap. Tap. My biological clock is ticking away. Give me a break. They want us to have kids. That's the problem, too."

My energy rushed to Becky. I wanted to defend her. Annoyance rising, I asked, "Who wants you to have kids?"

"My family, of course. Who else?"

Shrugging my shoulders, I feigned disinterest, then pretended to relax into my chair. Cassie glanced at me, then took a sip of wine.

"And him," she said, a sly smile now spreading across her face, while she waved the spoon unsteadily at her husband. "This is all Freudian to him. God. You think I'm keeping the spoon to stop myself from getting pregnant, Adam? Dope."

Adam opened his mouth to speak, but she cut him off. "He wants me to have kids, too. But at least my husband is polite about asking. My family keeps telling me I'm getting too old."

"What do they think too old is?" asked Cassie.

Jesus, I'd hoped this kids stuff would've somehow blown over. I couldn't deal with another crying mess of a fight. I needed to stop this conversation.

"I don't know?" said Becky. "35? I'm 35. Do you have kids?"

"No," said Cassie.

"Do you want them?"

"Yes."

"Then have them."

Cassie glanced at me. "It's not that simple."

"Oh, I see. Trouble in paradise." Becky swiveled her eyes to me. "What's your problem? You want to get into her but you don't want to get anything back out?" She snorted into the wine at her joke.

Anger surged. I tried to gulp it down with bitter wine.

Adam cut into her laugh. "James. Dude. Kids are what it's all about. It's kinda stupid to get married and think she's not going to want to have a baby."

"Are you calling me stupid?" Becky spluttered.

Adam raised his hands defensively. "No. No, Babe. I'm just saying. That's how it normally works. Right?"

"James," she said. "You are so like me. It's hilarious. You're selfish. Deal with it. You and Cassie got to accept it and move on with your lives. Only way. I've decided to have a baby. But not until I'm good and ready. Right, Adam?"

"Yeah, honey," he said, rolling his eyes but nervously tugging at the rim of his glasses.

All the long miles of the Camino suddenly caught up to me. All the sleepless nights on the road. With alcohol flying and emotions flowing, I couldn't stop the heat of anger rising. I banged the glass onto the table. Surprised eyes scrutinized the glass, then me.

I tried to keep the heat from my voice. "What's the point of having a baby if you don't want to have a baby? Becky, it's ridiculous to think this will make you happier. Aren't you worried you will resent Adam for making you do this? Is this some stupid society of suffering we're all just supposed to buy into here because that's how marriage works? Five weeks I've been walking this supposedly life-altering Camino. The only change I can see in us is I'm angrier and Cassie is sadder."

215

I heard a whisper within. *"Stop."*

"Stop what?" All their eyes became worried. A confrontation loomed. Fear brewed, making me want to run away. Cassie had tears in her eyes.

Selfish is right. I'd told Cassie I'm selfish. But I didn't feel selfish now. Sitting here in the dying light of the day, I just felt my old companions, fear and anger, begin to rage about the confusion of the past and future. I was alone and misunderstood. Anxious about everything. Emotions whooshed through me and I noticed my hand shook as I reached for the wine. Cassie noticed, too. And I felt even angrier for being found out to be so weak. I opened my mouth to explode, but instead just whispered, "I'm tired."

Bitterness swirled in my belly. Swallowing that whole bottle of wine would help. I just needed to be alone. Without a word, I got up and walked away.

A gnarly tree with broken branches was my resting spot. Its trunk bit into my back as I sat against it. Closing my eyes, I listened to my pent up frustrations. Heard them whisper. *"Stop swallowing me down. Let me go."*

Sadly, it was then I realised what I hoped to get from the Camino. I'd hoped to learn how to let go. I cried a little. The small outpouring of emotion changed the anger. Depression set in. I dozed for a while in a drunken stupor, not remembering what time I made it to bed.

Culinary Highlights of the Camino del Norte

Kokotxaz:	tender hake cheeks battered and fried or served in a savory green sauce. A specialty of Basque Country. Who knew fish had cheeks?
Marmitako:	Basque fish stew literally meaning 'pot' or 'casserole'. It's made with tuna, potatoes, onions, garlic and red peppers.
Torrija:	the Basque version of French toast. Brioche bread soaked in a sweet, eggy custard and pan fried.
Vino Rioja Alavesa:	wine from this geographic enclave of the Basque country is some of the most respected in the world, and shouldn't be missed.
Anchoas:	anchovies in all forms are beloved throughout Spain. They are served grilled, battered and fried, marinated in vinegar, or cured.
Picón Bejés-Tresviso:	handcrafted blue cheese from the foot of the Picos de Europa mountains in Cantabria, made with a mixture of cow, sheep and goat milk, and aged for four months inside natural limestone caves.
Fabada:	a hearty stew of beans, chorizo, pork and black pudding found in Asturias.
Sidra:	this dry, alcoholic apple drink is found all along the Camino del Norte, especially in Basque Country & Asturias.

Quesada y Leche:	this divine, custardy cheesecake is found at *Casa Quevedo* in Santillana del Mar, best washed down with a cold glass of some of the best fresh milk in the world.
Pimientos Padrón:	pan-roasted sweet green peppers cultivated by Franciscan friars upon returning from America to Galicia with the seeds. Be careful, because one-in-ten of these small, normally mild peppers are randomly spicy.
Torta de Santiago:	a sweet almond cake topped with powdered sugar often in the shape of a cross, this is the signature dessert of Galicia, since medieval times.
Mejillones Tigres:	plump Galician mussels served swimming in a tomato-based broth, found in the back alleys of Santiago de Compostela.
Pulpo Gallego:	fresh boiled octopus, cut up with a pair of scissors, often on the streetside, and garnished with paprika, olive oil and salt over boiled potatoes. A staple of Galician cuisine.
Empanada Atún:	this savory pie stuffed with tuna, vegetables and seasonings is the star of Galician tapas, best purchased in local bakeries, and delicious for breakfast as well.
1906 Cerveza	the star of the local beer scene in Galicia, this lager comes very highly rated
Percebes:	Goose barnacles harvested by hand from the rocky coast of Galicia, served steamed without seasoning. Considered to be a delicacy.

Language Barriers

Don't be intimidated by the language barrier while walking the Camino. Most of your interactions with locals will be with those accustomed to interacting with pilgrims from all over the world, so usually some basic English is spoken. But even if you find yourself trying to speak with someone who doesn't speak a word of your language, try to enjoy the process and lean on nonverbal communication - the most important of which is the smile. That being said, it's smart to make a bit of an effort to learn a few basic phrases in Spanish - the locals will appreciate your gesture.

Useful Phrases en Español & Basque

hello	kaixo (Basque)
thank you	Eskerrik asko (Basque)
Which way is the Camino?	¿En qué dirección está el Camino?
ok	Vale
Are you serving food now?	¿Para comer?
Takeaway food	Para llevar
Is there a curfew?	¿Hay toque de queda?
What time do you open/close?	¿A qué hora abres/cerrado
Any beds available?	¿Tienes camas?
Where is a supermarket?	¿Dónde esta el supermercado
Where is a chemist?	¿Dónde está la farmacia?
I need medical help.	Necesito ayuda medica.
I'm lost	Estoy perdido.

Galicia Highlights

Playa de las Catedrales

This world-famous beach lies 10km away from the Camino near Ribadeo. Massive stone arches swoop down from the cliffs to meet the fine sandy beaches below, resembling massive flying buttresses of grand cathedrals. The arches are only visible during low tide, so plan accordingly. The beach can be reached via public transport from Ribadeo, and is well-developed for tourism.

Mondoñedo

This small, atmospheric Camino town was declared a national cultural-historical site in 1985. Its main attraction is the Cathedral, dating to 1230, which reflects an unusual mixture of Gothic and Baroque architecture. The statue Nuestra Señora la Inglesa (the English Madonna) was rescued from Saint Paul's Cathedral in London during the Protestant Reformation of England. There is a pilgrim hospital dating to 1275. Sit in one of the cafes looking down at the cathedral, and soak it all in - this is the last town of historical charm before reaching Santiago.

Monasterio Santa María of Sobrado

This haunting complex of stone halls, bed chambers and worship space dates to the tenth century. The modern monks who inhabit it are welcoming to pilgrims, and have converted the old monks' quarters into bunk rooms. Of all pilgrim accommodation on the Camino del Norte, this one evokes the spirits of the medieval Camino most. Explore the abandoned corridors and the massive, empty church at sundown, and you won't be disappointed.

Camino Frances

For the last 39km of its approach towards Santiago, the Camino del Norte merges with the heavily-traveled Camino Frances in the town of Arzúa. For many who have traveled hundreds of kilometers on the Norte, the merge serves as a massive dose of culture shock. Suddenly you'll be faced with large tour groups and very well-trodden paths, enveloped in a flurry of Santiago excitement. Acceptance is the key. Sit back, mix with the other pilgrims, and enjoy the endlessly entertaining display of humanity.

Monte do Gozo

The legendary 'Hill of Joy" is the last hill on the Camino de Santiago, and the first place pilgrims can catch a glimpse of their final destination of the Cathedral of Santiago. The hill is shrouded in eucalyptus trees with lawns of green grass perfect for a final reflection before walking the last hour into Santiago. The Pope gave a sermon here in 1989, and a 500-bed hostel has been constructed for pilgrims. Visit the tiny Chapel of San Marcos for a taste of medieval Camino atmosphere.

Recommended Media

- ❖ *The Pilgrimage,* book by Paulo Coelho
- ❖ *I'm Off Then,* book by Hape Kerkeling
- ❖ *The Camino Voyage* (2018), documentary film
- ❖ *The Way* (2011), dramatic film
- ❖ Gronze.com: Camino navigation & practical route information
- ❖ Camino de Santiago Forum: thriving online community
- ❖ CaminoCoaching.org: support for preparation & integration of your Camino journey

WEEK 6

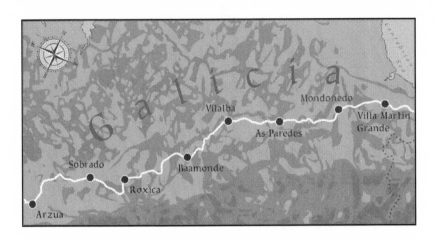

...gates of hell

Day 35 - Figueras to Villamartin Grande
24.2km

Cassie

If the Camino is a metaphor for the Catholic worldview, today we walked right up to the gates of hell.

Just as we felt the pull of Santiago, now within our reach, we faced a challenge that could finish us.

The bridge. As we approached it, I could feel the literal and figurative gravity of the situation rapidly gather strength. Esmerelda from the albergue was nuts, pure bat-shit crazy. She said she loved this bridge. I was trembling at the mere sight of it.

Named the *Puente de los Santos*, or Bridge of the Saints, it spans 612 meters (1836 feet) over a deep fjord-like estuary. Much, much too high, and much too long.

Most of its width is taken by a high-speed motorway, but on the edge they've scrapped together a pedestrian path with a waist-high guardrail. Waist-high on me, and I'm pretty short. I'd crossed other large bridges on foot before, like the Golden Gate in California, the Brooklyn Bridge in New York, and the Sydney Harbor Bridge in

Australia, but they all had fairly high guardrails and nice wide walkways. This was so narrow. If someone should come at us from the other direction, we'd have to squeeze by each other sideways. The rail was so low, a simple trip-up could send you flying over the edge to certain death.

The wind was blowing hard as we approached, and my stomach turned. I looked at James.

"You're not going to like this," I muttered as my heart started to beat rapidly.

Instinctively, I looked down and devised a plan if James should topple over into the churning sea below. I could maybe survive the fall if I kept my body straight and landed feet first. I'd grab him, strip off as many clothes as I could, and drag him to the shore. *I'm a strong swimmer, I could probably do it with the help of adrenaline.* I made a mental note of the location of a boat ramp on the far shore that I'd be able to drag him to.

"Are you ok?" I got no response. I never saw his face the whole time.

Of all the crazy motorcycle rides on mountain roads in the Himalayas, chicken buses clinging to cliffs in Central America, dangerous late night walks and god knows what else, crossing this bridge suddenly became the most perilous act of our lives.

Why hadn't anyone warned us? That damned lonely horse...

James

I'd awoken in a cold sweat accompanied by a sharp headache. Insect bites from my outdoor slumber criss-crossed my back. Yellow puss oozed from scratching them in the night. The bloody muck was hard to dislodge from under my fingernails.

I felt allergic to talking. Dodging the American couple was my main objective. I promised my wife we'll talk soon about everything. For now, we silently and slowly walked.

A monstrous bridge lay at the edge of town. I hate heights. They really mess with my mind. On seeing it, my body stiffened, urging me to go back. Shakes and growing nausea set in as I pushed forward.

Trucks roared past as I stepped onto the narrow walkway next to the thundering traffic. On my right a wire mesh fence protected us from the vehicles. On my left, an idiotically low barrier that had no chance of stopping me falling to death.

Immediately my mind fixated on jumping. I didn't want to worry Cassie, so I slowly began walking, but that only intensified my need to jump. Exhaust fumes spewed into my face from a braking truck. Engulfed in the stink, my focus wavered.

Shaking from head to toe, I forced myself not to get lost in images slicing through my brain. On repeat, I saw myself vaulting over the barrier to break apart on the water. I could barely resist the overwhelming compulsion. Breathing hard, I tried to focus straight ahead while my mind was on suicide loop.

Horribly, I became afraid to lift my feet in case those centimetres off the ground were enough to sweep me over the edge. Instead, I dragged my soles over the red, rusty metal of the sidewalk.

Only a quarter of the way, my stomach heaved, body constricting in pain. I swallowed the puke back down into the pit of my belly.

I was somehow walking again, slower now because suicidal thoughts came faster and I couldn't trust my legs to drag me to safety.

Puke rose again, stinging the back of my throat. A horrid memory accompanied the vile taste, but before I could focus on it, I swallowed it down.

I'm going to jump. A tsunami surged deep inside, bringing forth a torrent of sickening rage and confusion. Burning vomit spewed everywhere. Wind whipped some of it over the edge, while most of it dripped down the side of the fence. I dared not wipe my mouth. Hands were too much of a distraction when I needed total concentration. Cassie and the rest of the physical world fell away from my consciousness.

Pain will keep me grounded on this bridge. It will anchor me to the here and now. Violently, I dragged my knuckles across the cold, metal fence as I slowly began to shuffle forward again. Foolishly, I relaxed a little. Heard a voice hiss, *"Let go."* I smashed my hand into the fence. *I'm malfunctioning.* Looking down would be a death sentence.

Breathing hard through gritted teeth, I stopped to grip the fence about halfway. *"Let go,"* the voice whispered. The same voice I heard last night under the tree. Something was rising from the depths of my mind.

How can I let go? I pleaded. It clawed at handfuls of the sickness in my belly, pushing it into my mouth until I puked again. I edged slowly forward.

Suddenly the voice screamed, *'You murdered me!'*

I puked into my mouth. *Murdered you? Who? What am I actually puking up? What is happening here? What am I trying to let go of?*

Taking short dizzying breaths, I dug my nails into the back of my hand. I needed a stronger anchor of pain to stay on the bridge, so I

224

dragged my shoulder along the fence. Smack. Smack. Smack. Tenderized meat rapidly bruising. Focusing on the outer pain, I pressed harder into the fence. Every step made me weaker. *This is it. This stupid ending. There is nothing I can do about it.* My mind began to shut down. Overwhelmed, I saw the world through a prism of light casting horrific shadows.

An explosion in my chest. I puked again.

In a daze, I saw a ship below. Upon it, my battered body. Fireworks exploded in my mind. A few metres away, a young boy stood on the edge of the bridge. It was me. Jubilation on his laughing face showed he wasn't jumping to his death, but escaping from me. From inside me. He jumped.

Petrified, I managed to reach out to save him, but I was too slow. Momentarily, I felt relieved. It all made sense. But the realization disappeared with the dying embers of the fireworks before I could grasp the meaning. Halfway down, he began to shoot back up towards me. revolting reentry into my body. I needed to be sick again, but swallowed him down.

"You can't let go," the boy hissed. My guts seared. "Let me go. Let go."

With an organ-wrenching titanic heave, vile yellow bile burned forth as it flowed from my mouth. Suddenly, I felt a relief. An understanding. Dark anxiety in my chest lightened. Scattered jigsaw pieces of my repressed mind began to assemble and make sense. I knew that voice from the shadows of my Grandmother's house. The young voice pleaded with the Devil. I'm sorry for being born bad. Don't take me hell. I'll pray for evil people. I'm sorry. The little voice feared everyone because he was made to believe all people were born bad. No one can be trusted. All should be feared. All the while, I was sure the terrifying Devil was listening to my prayers only a shadow away. Truly, I believed all this. The word of God.

I thought of the little boy's footprints lost to the river. Now I realised as a child, I'd fixated on my own death. Terrified I'd go to hell. My death would be the Devil's embrace. All people are evil. I'm evil. No wonder I felt anxious around people. I hated them as I hated myself. People are evil. Trust no one.

The boy in the convent painting. The dead boy from my dream whispered back to life by a witch. The boy that had just tried to escape from me. All the same boy. They were all a manifestation of my own turmoil. Emotions trapped. Frozen in time, a terrified part doomed to hell. An echo constantly whispering to be saved. The terrified boy

225

needed to be protected. To be told everything would be okay. But time and again, I had swallowed his pleading voice down. Like any child whose pain is not attended to, he became frustrated, then angry. I still wouldn't, or couldn't listen, until he became enraged. I'd abandoned my inner child and now he hated me. All his pain was igniting my own issues, keeping me stuck in a destructive loop.

Sharp pain ripped through my shoulder. Surprised, I opened my eyes to see I'd been endlessly smacking into the metal while walking. Bile stung my throat and lungs, but I began to relax a fraction. For the first time in ages, I inhaled lungfuls of oxygen that freed the tension in my chest. *Just keep focusing on your breath.* Disturbed and battered, I made it to the other side of the bridge.

With the sleeve of my jacket, I rubbed the sick from my mouth. I spoke to the boy within, *"I'll protect you."* The relief in my chest spread slowly outwards, bringing with it sadness and tears. Inside I felt something smile.

Immediately, a horrible reflex kicked in and I swallowed down the emotions that would've brought on a river of tears. I couldn't be so weak in front of Cassie. How I hated myself at that moment. My mind's eye saw the boy had tensed into the fetal position within my chest. Each breath became a little more painful as my chest constricted. *"I'm sorry,"* I told him.

Deeply concerned, Cassie stood in front of me. She knew she couldn't fix me, so did the next best thing. Without saying a word she hugged me tight. Closing my eyes, I started trembling from head to toe as the adrenaline ebbed from my body. I turned my head to avoid getting vomit on her jacket. I felt safer. To feel safe was what the child wanted, too. My breath eased a little in my chest.

Pin pricks of light danced beneath my eyelids. My past was clouding my future. I've always felt unsafe around kids. I never realised I associated fear with children. They are helpless to endure all this evil. I can't even protect myself. How can I protect a child?

Poor Cassie didn't understand. I barely understood. She was just bouncing off my armour of fear and hate. Armour that disrupted our future. I was only just beginning to understand myself. At least now, I could see where the fear of having a child was coming from. *Maybe I should try to actually have a proper conversation with Cassie about this.*

My heart thumped to the beat of, *"Let go."*

"I would have jumped in after you," she said. "Are you okay?"

"Yeah. We will be okay."

In a daze we began to climb the rolling green hills of Galicia. Turning south away from the coast, I glanced back towards the fading sea, wondering if traipsing through the endless line of fishing villages and barren beaches had helped me hear the echo.

...surrender to the flow

–

Day 36 – Villamartin Grande to Mondoñedo
20.5km

Cassie

When you read the guides and online forums about the Camino del Norte, you're immediately given the impression the toughest part is the beginning, from Irún to Bilbao. Those steep ups and downs certainly come as a shock to the body and especially the feet, and quickly force the pilgrim to either adapt or cease trying.

The next few hundred kilometers feel like a breeze, and hills become barely noticeable. You'll walk 20km in five hours without stopping, and barely break a sweat.

No one mentions what happens after Ribadeo, when the Camino swings south away from the coast. Over the course of three days or so, you're forced to steadily climb a series of ever-increasing slopes to finally arrive on the high plateau of Galicia at over 600 meters (1800 feet).

This day I was wrecked. I could barely climb a hill. Every ten steps, I had to stop to compose myself, catching my breath and willing my legs to keep moving. There was no relief. Nowhere to stop. No water fountains. I was so thirsty I would've drunk dickwater from the fountain Gypsy Mullet washed his netherregions in.

I plopped myself down hard on the grassy embankment beside the path as James kept moving, and looked to the heavens for divine guidance. The wind was howling up above, the clouds racing across the blue sky. I tried to decipher the meaning of the wind's whispers as they journeyed above me, feeling it already knew the answers, but I didn't know how to hear them.

James wanted to jump off that bridge yesterday. What the actual fuck.

I'd always known life was a struggle for James. His inner world seemed a state of constant conflict. His saving grace was his ability to

227

experience joy and love just as fully as fear and pain. Always hoping to help the joyful moments outnumber the painful ones, I'd truly believed walking the Camino could be massively therapeutic for him.

But the bridge. He told me last night of this overwhelming urge to jump. Now that's a journey I never, ever wanted him to take.

At least James seemed better today. He was breathing a bit easier.

"Feeling pretty good today, I see," I said, catching him up.

"Processing," he said with a slight grin.

Yesterday he felt the urge to jump off a bridge, and today he was grinning? I struggled to catch my breath as my mind raced. Jumping from James, to the lump in my throat, to the knots in my stomach, and back again to the wind whistling through the trees above.

At last, we saw a bar appearing in the distance. No question, we had to stop.

James

Evening sunlight winked in through a grotty pub window. After such a long day of walking and over-thinking, I was done with the outside world.

Still the evening seemed to call, 'Just keep walking the walk.'

Instead, I looked deep into my wine then ravenously devoured a slice of tortilla, thinking that now I might be eating for two.

From my table, I could see out through the half-open front door. Pilgrims passed, clattering their annoying walking sticks while chattering. I thought I half-recognized some of them. These ghosts of pilgrims past haunted me with worries they'd recognise me, then try to stop and chat.

My inner child or my Catholic echo or whatever, seemed satisfied I was aware of his existence today. Negative fixations still filled my head, but my emotions were not inflamed to the point of anger because he seemed more at peace. I understood we must build trust with each other and to do this I must actually listen to my emotions. That bridge was a battle I ultimately lost because I swallowed down my pain in the end, but I learned a lot about the enemy so it wasn't a total defeat. Ironically, the enemy had turned out to be me.

Another half-forgotten, jumbled face suddenly appeared in the bar. An Asian woman, probably Japanese, her wide eyes nodded at us in a meek but friendly way. I nodded back. I couldn't remember if we'd actually spoken, but I'd definitely seen her somewhere. Nervously, she scanned the bar. Noticing our pilgrim packs, she asked if she could sit with us, presumably to talk pilgrim gossip for a while. Walking to the bar, she left her backpack at our table.

No way... "No way," I whispered to Cassie. "Look!" Sticking out the front pocket of her backpack was a Bourbon Street poncho! *Could it be mine?* Cassie's family heirloom, stolen when we stayed in the cathedral in Zumaia nearly a month ago? I looked closer. Sure enough, it seemed to be the same cheap material of my poncho.

This must be the pilgrim Bill saw with my poncho. Poor guy had been shunned by other pilgrims who misunderstood his good deed. Or maybe he was high on LSD at the time and they thought he was just a crazy guy.

This woman has stolen my poncho. Hot damn! That thieving feckstress is the reason I got soaked so many times.

Hastily, we whispered what to do. Cassie wanted to go all out New Jersey-girl style; confront her and maybe scratch her a little.

"We could do that," I said. "Or let's just see where it goes for a while. Remember she did seem to freak out Bill somehow. She could be nuts. Might be interesting."

Composing ourselves, we watched her sit down with a sigh, then brush back her jet black hair to reveal the face of a worried, wide-eyed kitten. Introducing herself as Megumi, we learned she was indeed from Japan and liked a gin and tonic. As always, I asked about Gypsy Mullet and his horse. She had no idea what I was talking about. Skittishly, she told us a story about couchsurfing at an equestrian center.

Her nails were badly gnawed. She noticed me staring, then hid them in the sleeves of her oversized yellow trekking jacket. A little flustered, she quickly excused herself to go to the bathroom.

Cassie took the opportunity to poke me in the ribs and demand why I hadn't asked about the poncho. These New Jersey girls are mad for a scrap.

"Let's just see where this goes," I said genuinely intrigued about this lady.

On Megumi's return, Cassie asked, "How are you managing with all the bad weather?"

"I am good with the weather," Megumi answered.

"Do you have a poncho?"

"Yes. Of course," she said without flinching. "Rain is terrible. No summer now." She took a sip of gin then chewed the nail of her pinky finger.

Cassie brushed back her bountiful hair. "Oh," she said. "Cool. Cause it would be awful not to have one in this weather. Did you see the guy who was walking around totally soaked? With no poncho? I was thinking what kinda weirdo walks around in the rain? All day! Imagine how much all his stuff must've got wet? That would have totally sucked, to be that guy."

Rain started tinkling on the cobblestones outside the bar. "Do you think we'll need our ponchos again today, Megumi? Is your poncho big enough to cover your backpack?" Before Megumi could answer, Cassie ordered us another round of drinks.

Cassie was not trying to be totally mean. Just protecting me. She wanted to know what this woman's story was. But my wife's inquiring smile told me she was enjoying the interrogation. She loves to know what drives the mind. Silence followed while we waited for the drinks and our Japanese guest gnawed her nails again.

"Ohhh. I have the same problem," said Cassie.

Megumi blinked quickly. "Do you?"

Cassie made a genuinely sympathetic face. "I do it when I'm feeling stressed and anxious. Or even guilty."

"Me, too." Biting her lip, she let her chin drop so her hair fell over her face. "My nerves are very bad. Life can be good, but if I always believe things will go wrong I... I just get overwhelmed. I feel I can't go on. It's so strange. It's like I freeze. I'm not myself. I'm a ghost. I have to make it right. Fix it. I could not walk the Camino if I was not prepared for the worst. I think I'm getting better, but some days I'm sure I'm getting worse. The doctor told me I have OCD. The psychologist said something else. Do you know what I mean?" Her eyes were embarrassed, but held a hopeful glint.

That probably explained why she stole my poncho. An OCD attack emanating from some fear of getting wet, combined with opportunity. Relaxing a little, I sat back to study the woman.

"I understand," said Cassie. She touched her hand in sympathy. "What do you feel you need to do now?" The interrogation had become a confessional. Sister Cassie in session.

"Now?"

"Yes. What do you think would help you to release your stress?"

She bit her nails. Looked at me, then to Cassie. Drummed her fingers on the table. Opened her mouth to speak, but instead took a drink. "Five push-ups!"

"What?"

"Yes. I need to do five push-ups." She stood up. Flicked her hair back. Leaped to the ground on all fours and started her press-ups. Breathing lightly, when finished, she swiped the gin then finished it in one mouthful. Her face scrunched up a little. "Exercise helps. Thank you for the lovely time."

"Are you really okay?" asked Cassie, now speaking in the voice of a trained therapist.

"Yes. Yes. That is me. Always the next thing. I can't help myself. Stress. Release. Stress. Release. Exercise is the best medicine. That's why I'm walking the Camino."

"Is it working?"

"Yes and no. Different on different days."

"Well, if you need to talk. You can talk to me. Where are you staying?"

Megumi smiled nervously. Exactly like me with so many other pilgrims, she needed to get away. "Thank you. I'm staying in the municipal albergue." Pulling her pack onto her back, she gave a little bow and a soft goodbye, then headed for the door.

Cassie and I looked at each other. "Thanks," I said "for trying to get my poncho back in a conniving but diplomatic manner. Remind me never to lie to you or try to keep a secret."

"Yeah," said Cassie. " zShe actually seems nice though. Fragile, too. Did you see her fingernails? Almost chewed down to the cuticle?"

"I know. Looks really sore."

"I know. And you know what else we know? She's staying in the same place as us. So plenty of time to grill our guilty thief and get your poncho back."

...forest wife

—

Day 37 - Mondoñedo to As Paredes
23km

Cassie

This morning, as usual I was first to pack up. I squatted against a wall with my pack strapped on watching James scurry about gathering his things, which always seem to end up scattered everywhere.

As I watched the other pilgrims stuff their sacks and rush to the bathroom to brush their teeth, an uncontrollable urge hit me. That Japanese woman stole his poncho. No matter how absurd, and how little material value was invested in that tattered sheet of plastic, I just could not shake the thought.

The wind gusted. Dawn's light scarcely crept through the windows. We had another day of rain ahead of us.

I looked to my right out of the crook of my eye. It was there. I could see it. She had it strapped to the outside of her pack with a bungee cord, Bourbon Street logo clearly visible.

Squatting there, body relaxed, my eyes focused on the target. I felt it inside me. It was undeniable.

Like a hawk, I watched my prey. She'd already returned from the bathroom. She was carefully placing her perfect little travel size toiletries into her perfect little toiletry kit. She zipped it up and placed it inside her bag. It looked like I'd lost my chance.

Just as she was about to swing her pack onto her shoulder, I heard, "Oh!" She quickly moved for the back door, leaving her pack behind.

She must've left something to dry on the line out back.

Without another moment of thought and with zero hesitation, I sprang up in total silence to profit from the moment. In one graceful move across the room, I lunged forward and snatched the poncho from under the bungee, slipping it stealthily under the skirt of my dress to rest inside the elastic band of my leggings.

Divinely timed, James had just thrown his pack on. "Ready?" he asked.

"Let's go," I replied, already halfway out the door.

As James walked past me and started up the hill outside the hostel door, I hesitated. Throwing my pack at his feet, I sprinted back down the hill, shouting to James, "I'll just be a second!"

I jumped through the hostel doors and stealthily pulled my own poncho off over my head. I folded it up as best I could, and quickly tucked it into the bungee cord on the outside of Megumi's pack.

We climbed up and out of Mondoñedo, which would turn out to be the last town of any charm we'd pass through until Santiago. A steady uphill stroll throughout the day would seal our place high on Galicia's central plateau. The air grew colder, and the dark clouds seemed to sit just above our heads. I felt exhausted. I'd been walking for five weeks now, and was probably more fit than I've ever been in my life. Now all of a sudden it was becoming hard to walk up a hill again.

Big fat summer raindrops plopped on the dirt in front of us, with nothing at all but two hours of empty trail in every direction.

"Shit," James muttered, looking up at the sky.

"No worries." I pulled the Bourbon Street poncho out of my skirt and handed it to him sideways as we walked, without looking him in the eye.

A few seconds passed. "So, where's your poncho, Cass?"

"I traded it with Megumi."

Without a word about ponchos, we walked most of the day in contented silence. Eventually we found shelter at *Albergue O Xistral,* an old stone farmhouse lovingly converted into a beautiful albergue complete with swimming pool. Some cold beers next to the pool were definitely called for, more so than any other day.

Landing up at a palace, I couldn't help but think I had been karmically rewarded for my dirty deed. *I protected James.* Like a satisfied mama bear, I lounged my exhausted limbs next to the pool as the Galician sun dipped down behind the hills.

James

A heavy dusting of pollen made my nose twitch. Bees laden with fine yellow powder hummed from one wild blue flower to the next, flying in and out of ditches and around the mossy trees hanging over the cobbled path.

The boy spoke to me on the Way today. As we walked, I tried to stay connected to my emotions. Yesterday, he seemed calm to the point where my feelings weren't overwhelmed. Today, the boy and I were so jumbled up emotionally, it manifested between as a pain in my chest. Our fears and hidden rage crushed together. Probing again at my emotions, I connected to the pain in my chest, then sensed him stir uneasily. Anger flared, but I found quickly that guilt lay beneath. Immediately I recoiled, hating the feeling.

Staying focused on the confusing emotional threads as they untangled, I watched in exasperation as they became entangled in tangents of other negative feelings like resentment for even being born.

A weight settled on my shoulders. My posture dropped. My steps became heavy. My chest ached. But mostly, it felt like I shouldn't ever enjoy anything. All energy seeped away from my day.

Logically, I wondered what I had to feel guilty about. A stolen poncho? It was then the boy spoke words that sliced my heart. *'You murdered me.'* I struggled to breathe. With everything else that happened on the bridge, I'd forgotten he'd said those words!

Instead of distracting myself from the guilt, I stayed connected. *I murdered you?*

In my head a silence followed. It felt like he'd hidden. Not used to the spotlight of my mind focusing on his words, my emotions had gone dormant. I was only aware of the cobblestones underfoot and insect bites itching my back. Feelings quickly returned, and I was surprised I felt less tense. It seemed I'd listened to what my feelings had to tell me, and hadn't distracted from the discomfort. Maybe some anxious energy was released. I had space for something else to flow through me.

I was finally getting to really know myself. Which was turning out to be rather weird and worrying. *Who the hell did I murder?*

At the end of this confusing walk, trees thinned on the cobblestone path to reveal a magnificent stone house that would be our albergue for the night. Newly renovated, its walls of gray blocks gleamed. Also gleaming were two muscular men wearing only their little, white underpants, washing their clothes in a bucket on the grass. Soap bubbles frothed over the rim as they jostled and laughed. Getting closer, I realised, with a smile, it was Rolph and Bernadette from that creepy bar a few days back. The Spaniards that darned each others' feet and who Bastian had also renamed. I'd assumed they would be way ahead of us.

Bernadette washed his plated, viking beard between his palms. He was cheek to jowl with Rolph, who wrung the water from his clothes into the glistening, green grass.

My smile broadened and I was surprised at how pleased I was to see them again. Listening to my emotions had made me a little more mellow towards myself, so in turn my attitude had softened towards others.

Still, it was interesting how the Camino connected people in my mind. When I saw them, I immediately thought about Bastian, who I still felt was close. My eyes scanned the area for Nicu, Fonso or a Breton horse. Not even a hoof print on the ground. The lost horse reminded me of LSD Bill. I imagined him working in an albergue with Gerta while they tried to figure out their futures. Bill made me think of Wolfentop looking for a new wife. Wolfentop made me think of the Secret German, then... tiredness took me so I went for a rest.

Later I went into the kitchen to find Bernadette still only wearing his little white pants as if he was posing in a rural fetish photoshoot for

Calvin Klein. Some nationalities are definitely more reserved than others, and a couple of people looked embarrassed or pissed off as they tried to make dinner in the cramped kitchen.

Bernadette spotted me. He trotted over, smiling as if we were reunited brothers.

"How are you? I thought we'd never see you again. How's your wife? My ego is broken!"

"Good to see you, man. Cassie's good. She's taking a nap. Your ego is broken?"

"Yes." He clapped his hands in my face. "I cannot go on. My ego is broken!" He pointed to his feet. "My steps are finished. Me and my feet don't deserve each other." Gingerly, he took off a sandal to show me the bottom of his foot.

My stomach churned seeing his blistered sole was an excruciating mess held together with gunky bandages.

"Jesus, man," I said. "Get off your feet. How did you even get here? Did Rolph carry you?"

His eyes lit up. "That would be a dream," he said naughtily while rubbing his hairy belly. "No. But he did stay up with me last night, draining my blisters with his needle." Pouting his lips, he let his chin drop. "The Camino has beaten me. I can't walk. My ego is broken. I'm ashamed to say I took the bus."

Albert's stupid saying chimed in my mind. *'All Spanish are cheaters.'* An urge took me to tell Bernadette what I heard about Spanish people so I could make fun of him, but the poor man's feet looked like they needed to be amputated.

"It's okay to take the bus," I said. "I did it a few times. You obviously can't walk any further."

Newly arrived pilgrims went a little wide-eyed as they found it awkward to squeeze past the practically naked Bernadette in the kitchen. He didn't seem to notice, just a forlorn look of defeat on his viking face.

Something didn't add up. When I first arrived, he'd seemed so happy in the grass, giggling away with Rolph.

"So you and Rolph won't make it to Santiago?"

"No. My Camino journey is over."

"Will you try another time?"

"No. My ego is broken."

"You already said that three times. What does that actually mean? You feel broken because of the pain in your feet or because the Camino has broken you?"

"No." He smiled sadly. "You don't understand. I knew all the time. I just couldn't tell anyone. I couldn't admit it. Even to Rolph."

"What are you talking about?"

"It's obvious. I'm in love with little Rolphy. Now that I can't go on, I think he will leave me here alone. He keeps telling me about his personal journey."

Sympathetically, I nodded. But this was such an odd place for an intimate conversation, with eavesdropping pilgrims cooking only inches away.

"Are you sure he wants to leave?"

"I don't know. I'm so confused. My ego..." He bowed his head a moment, pulled on his beard, then rejoined my gaze with a sparkle in his eye. "He asked me to be his forest wife."

"Oh, yeah? Right. Congratulations," I wished him clumsily. I'd heard the term a few times on the Camino. A forest wife is someone you are romantically involved with on the Camino. You spend time with them walking. Sharing everything. Knowing you'll each go back to your former life and partners after Santiago. Forest husband. Forest wife. Forest folk.

"A forest wife is real," he said, defiantly. "He's my forest husband. I always knew it would happen. Even so. Rolph is troubled. Last night when he darned my feet he even cried. I told him I can be strong for both of us. You know what he did?"

"What?"

"He started laughing, then gave me some chocolate. Said it was my little treat. He said he needed to hear that he was a loving husband. I told him, 'Little Rolphy, you are the most loving husband ever.'"

Bernadette wiped his eyes. It made me wonder what the elderly priests thought when they saw these burly, well-groomed men checking into their Catholic convent rooms together for the night. Did a few get a little angry, lonely or jealous when they glimpsed pilgrims darning each other's feet while they cried, hugged and whispered sweet nothings?

"I'm really happy for you both," I said, putting a hand on his bare shoulder. "He seems like a great guy. I hope he gave you a ring?"

He brushed my hand away. "Oh, you are just teasing me. But I am going to ask him for one. A real forest wife needs a ring."

"So what do you think will happen now?"

Bernadette pulled on his beard again. "He says, if we walk together, we stay together."

That sounded ominous. "But you said you can't walk anymore?"

236

"Now you see why my ego is broken."

Poor guy. Darning his feet had brought them closer, but now his bubbling blisters would end their relationship. "You need to talk to him," I said. "It sounds like it's now or never. You really think he'll only stay with you if you walk?" I smiled a stupid smile, then blurted out, "Don't worry, if he decides to keep walking, we'll keep an eye on him to make sure he's not up to no good."

Bernadette's hurt look brought embarrassment to my cheeks.

"Sorry," I said, lamely. "Long day."

"It's okay. As you say. It's now or never." He gave me a hug then trotted out of the kitchen, leaving more room for the pilgrims to cook and mutter about inconsiderate people needing to put on pants.

At that moment, my elbow caught a person on the arm. He dropped his glass causing a loud smash on the tiled floor. Everyone jumped back in shock. We had space again where Bernadette had stood.

"The man's ego is broken!" I said loudly. Surprised at my little outburst, I quickly cleaned up the debris while shaking my head and muttering about the state of humanity.

Not knowing what to do, I took myself to bed hoping the adrenaline would seep from my body. Lying there, I focused on my anger, letting a myriad of tangled memories and thoughts flow.

In a rush, my mind ignited. *Cassie is fucking pregnant! All her strange bouts of exhaustion. Everyone else is speeding up while she's slowing down. Bouts of sickness. Holy shit!* Some part of me must've been aware of this already but it was buried under my fears.

Curling up, I cuddled the pillow beneath my head. I always feared I'd feel resentment at this moment. Instead, it was trepidation mixed with a prick of excitement. Of course, all her symptoms might just be a coincidence. My inner child was silent on the matter. Which was a good thing, I supposed. No sibling rivalry.

Oh, Camino, what have you now put in my head? And into my wife's belly?

...storks

Day 38: As Paredes to Vilalba
16.5km

Cassie

Stepping out of the stone hostel at As Paredes, I felt the need to close my eyes for a moment and dig deep for some store of energy that must be within me. Even though we had already completed our climb up onto the Galician plateau, with a relatively flat day ahead of us, I just couldn't seem to access the power to walk. I'd never felt so exhausted. Each step required tremendous mental effort as I coaxed my legs to move forward. Meanwhile everyone else around me seemed to be moving faster and faster, their Camino-induced fitness now firmly established. Some invisible burden had set upon me, and I didn't know how to unload it.

The Way was different on this day, an ancient country road dotted with stone bridges and fields of wildflowers. The ocean was a distant memory. If I weren't so tired, I think I would've skipped all day with happiness, feeling Santiago was within my reach now, and happy for it. We were almost done, and it couldn't come soon enough. Sometimes I wondered if I could even make it to Santiago, though we were only days away.

We walked in silence. I knew James needed space to process his experience on the bridge a couple days ago, but I was grateful because I had also felt the recent strained energy that had lingered between us had finally broken.

As we meandered down the path, I heard an unfamiliar squawk to my right. I turned, and perched high on the smooth branches of a long-dead tree were two magnificent birds with long pointed beaks. They'd built a large nest of sticks and straw, and were happily roosting as we passed.

"Look!" James pointed.

"I know. Amazing birds. I've never seen birds so big."

"Those are storks. We must be on a migration route or something," James said.

Storks, I thought as we continued. *The birds that bring babies. I can't believe people actually tell their kids that.*

Just as the thought had passed from my mind, I felt a rush of adrenaline. Some primal reflex was triggered, sending an electric signal

238

from my gut to my brain that manifested as a conscious thought. Stopping dead in my tracks, I crossed my arms over my chest and felt both my breasts. They were absolutely aching. In this moment, my brain began to calculate days and weeks. I was due to get my period a week ago. I hadn't even noticed that it never arrived.

Storks. Tender breasts. Missed period. Exhaustion. Emotional outbursts under trees in the rain. It suddenly all added up.

My eyes wide and mouth slightly open, I walked beside James for the final few kilometers of the day deep in shock. I knew what this meant. I fell silent.

We checked into the albergue and headed out for a late lunch. Sitting there at the table, I didn't quite know how to broach the topic with James. My consciousness had entered into a tunnel, a smattering of different emotions continuously building themselves up around me, then breaking back down again. At the end of the tunnel, a revelation with the power to change everything. *What if I AM pregnant? James doesn't want a baby.*

The protective part of my mind jumped into the future, formulating plans. *If I AM pregnant, I'm having this baby. I'll be able to take care of it. My parents will support me. I can get a new job. It will work out.* My thoughts continued to spin into imaginary versions of my future, calculating with great detail my new life as a mother – potentially a single mother.

I told James.

We got up from lunch and looked for a green cross, marking the location of a pharmacy on the town's main drag. Approaching the door, I hesitated. I couldn't believe I was about to buy a pregnancy test for the first time in my life.

Box in hand, wrapped up neatly in white paper, we headed back to the albergue. A group of Camino friends had gathered in the back garden, drinking beers and talking animatedly. They motioned for us to join. I looked at James.

"I'll just… get this done, I guess. You go out back." He nodded.

I went into the communal bathroom, and into a stall and sat down to open the box. The instructions were in Spanish. I tried to decipher the instructions as best I could. Pee on the stick, basically. If there's only one line, life goes on as usual. Two lines, you're pregnant.

My normally steel nerves betrayed me as soon as I began to remove the plastic device from its box. My hands shook, and I could feel my heart beat stronger and faster. I'd never been so nervous in my life. I peed on the stick and just sat there, totally zoned out for a couple of minutes, my mind pausing in the calm between two very different futures. With a gulp, I finally looked down. There were two lines. Two very, very dark lines, which meant I was very, very much pregnant.

It felt like a scene from a million movies, where the young girl discovers she's knocked up and emotional turmoil ensues. I felt myself begin to panic, then just leaned back against the wall of the stall, trying to take some deep breaths. *You're not a teenager, idiot.* I had to remind myself. *You're a married, 37-year-old woman with a wonderful husband and all the resources in the world. This is not a disaster.*

What the hell is going on?

My heart was pumping so hard I didn't even know how I was feeling about being pregnant. I'd always pictured myself as a mother, and went through phases in the past when I really wanted kids. But I hadn't thought about it much in the last few years, and our semi-nomadic lifestyle wasn't exactly conducive to parenting.

Trembling, I managed to shove the instructions and test kit back into the box, emerged from my stall and washed my hands. Life already felt different. I made my way through the crowded albergue, packed with pilgrims in all stages of dressing, unpacking and taping their feet. Could they tell I was holding a secret, that there was a child inside me? I felt like the whole world must be able to see it.

As I walked out into the back garden, James, smiling from some joke one of our friends had just told, looked up. Our fate must have been written all over my face, because he came right over and took my hand. We ended up in the toilet to get some privacy.

"So?" His Irish eyes staring into mine.

I took the box out of my pocket and removed the plastic test. "Two lines. See? That means I'm pregnant." I held my breath, scanning his face for any clues of how he felt.

James

So a funny thing happened in the restaurant this afternoon. While eating a delectable meal, not because it was great, but because it wasn't another Spanish tortilla, Cassie sitting next to me, leaned over to me and whispered, "What if I'm pregnant?"

That terrifying bridge appeared. *"Let Go."* I'm about to jump. I'm leaving Cassie. But something stops me. A child standing on the railing of the bridge. Now I realise I still have a journey to take.

240

"It's okay." I'm surprised my voice is so steady, because inside I'm shaking.

"Really?"

"Yeah, that's okay. Don't worry about it." I knew she wanted to take a pregnancy test but couldn't bring herself to say it. A playful mood fluttered in my chest. *Who is this person inside me?*

My hands began to shake. Stretching out our silence, I took a long drink of tasty 1906 beer while waiting for the inevitable continuation of her inquisition. It took longer than I thought. Every thirty seconds or so, my wife glanced nervously at me. Her look, a mix of wide-eyed staring at the back of my neck and quick glances back to her drink, punctuated by a nervous wringing of her hands. On some level I enjoyed her cute torment, at least until her wide-eyed glances turned into a stare that burned the back of my neck. I couldn't keep the game up any longer, so I asked, "Do you think you should take a test?"

"Yes!" she burst out.

"But maybe," I said seriously and slowly, while sipping my beer.

"What? Tell me!"

"No. No that wouldn't work."

"What wouldn't work? Just tell me!"

"Just. You know. It's important."

"Shut up. You're killing me. Just tell me what you're thinking?!"

"Well." I looked to the sky. "Maybe. We should wait until after the world cup final?"

"What? Just tell me seriously? Are you really okay if I'm pregnant?"

A surge of nausea suddenly made me question everything. I wished she hadn't asked again. Hoping to gulp the fear down, I wanted to chug my beer but instead I felt the fear. Then felt the excitement that accompanied the fear. The complicated excitement of a totally unknown adventure.

I wanted to answer Cassie, but my chest constricted. I took a deep breath into the pain and realised it was the boy's fear, not mine. What I thought was my inner voice of reason was just echoing the boy's pain instead of my true self. He made me feel I couldn't keep the baby safe because he didn't feel safe. Relieved, the pain eased, knowing the sudden irrational fear wasn't truly my own. From now on, I just needed to be aware that everything I felt wasn't a representation of what was really happening in the moment. I needed to remember this while figuring out how to make peace with myself and let go. Jeez, I needed to remember this just so I could say, "Yes, I'm okay with you being pregnant." It wasn't the most romantic sounding line. I still didn't know if I was okay or even if she was actually pregnant, but it was a total shift in my thought process and she knew it. It must've been terribly confusing for Cassie.

I put down my glass and held her sweating hand. "I wanted to tell you in Santiago that I'd started to feel this way. Since we talked under that tree and all that crying emotion came up... I've had... I mean... I don't really know what I mean. Then there was that bridge. All sorts of emotions surfaced."

She squeezed my hand.

"Something changed in the last few days," I said. I wasn't ready to tell her yet about the kid in my chest I'd been talking to. "Maybe it was just Camino walking therapy that got me here? You know? Walking. Processing. Walking. Processing."

Her curious look told me she knew I wasn't telling her everything. But she was getting positive feedback about having a baby so wasn't going to push her luck. "The bridge helped. It messed with my mind, but connected different parts. I'm trying to understand."

"Yes," she said. "For sure, something shifted for you on that bridge. I would've jumped in after you. I was ready."

The boy relaxed and I breathed with less pain again. I felt protected. I kissed my wonderful wife. "I decided a few days ago that I'm okay with you. I mean, with us ... having a baby. It feels okay now. Just okay. I've got some positives forming. Flowing. I'm beginning to understand my stuff."

"Really? That's so wonderful." Tears began to stream down her cheeks. "I'm so happy."

"Awww," I hugged Cassie feeling the thick knots of stress in her shoulders and back. "It's okay. I love you."

"Why didn't you tell me you'd changed your mind?"

"I wanted to make it a romantic surprise when we reached Santiago."

"Really?" More tears flowed. "I'm so happy!"

Holding hands more tightly than ever, we searched for a chemist. As she bought the test kit, shock set in. Everything felt surreal. Like standing still in a dream in which our life moved too fast.

I won't lie. By this stage, I was trembling with anticipation. I just didn't know what the result would be. So I decided not to think about it until we had our answer.

Twenty minutes later, I was pulled from a pilgrim chat about Tibetan communist cats into the toilet. I couldn't read her expression.

"So?" I asked.

She took the box out of her pocket and removed the plastic test. Her hands, always steady, were shaking. "Two lines. See? That means I'm pregnant."

"Are you messing with me? Cause that's something I'd totally do."

"Shut up. I'd never do that."

"So you're pregnant?"

"YES!!"

Fecking hell... We hugged while laughing nervously.

The Camino was providing a lot lately. I fished out the pregnancy test kit from the bin. In the safe pouch of my backpack, home to the mullet bottle and the kissed clam, I added the box and mentally placed the spirit of our baby inside it for protection.

...KM 101

‑

Day 39 - Vilalba to Baamonde
20.1km

Cassie

I awoke in the dorm a different person. Now certain of what had been going on with me all these weeks, a peace had washed over me. I wasn't going crazy. The Camino was definitely providing something for me, and my body wasn't broken. I was just pregnant.

We set out for the day's walk without breakfast. We were excited to get out on the trail where we could have some privacy and talk all things pregnancy in privacy. The night before we'd called our parents, who were thrilled as can be. I think my dad in particular was pleased, secretly hoping that this would finally force us to pick a place to live and retire from our post-India lives as global vagabonds. My mother begged me not to tell anyone, as it was so early on. But on the Camino, meeting people every day that you're bound never to see again, I felt totally fine telling anyone who'd listen. James' parents had a laugh suggesting names already.

We blasted through the rather bland, flat walk, moving through several ugly towns and crossing the farmlands connecting them. "James," I said. "I just did some calculations in my head, and by my best estimate, I think I'm five weeks pregnant."

"Wow," he said, squinting his eyes as he checked my math in his head.

"Do you know what that means?" I asked. "That means I essentially walked across all of Spain pregnant." We hugged each other and laughed.

Just as the first pangs of hunger hit, we realized we were approaching Baamonde, our stop for the night. I felt so tough. A pregnant chick that just walked across Spain, and can blast through 20km without breakfast.

As we entered town and spotted the large municipal albergue, we were shocked to find a long line of people waiting outside its still-locked doors. There were twenty or so small groups of Spaniards dressed in brand new professional hiking gear and bright shiny boots. All were leaning up against their large, wheeled luggage, and looked jittery and excited.

I became hyper-aware of how I must look. I'd been rotating between the same two outfits for more than a month, and both were threadbare and forming holes. My trailrunners were becoming frayed and covered in mud. My backpack had begun to stink of days upon days of sweat and toil. James was totally unshaven and looked even worse. We felt totally out of place joining this line of catalogue-ready pilgrims.

"What the *hell* is going on?" I whispered to James.

"Look," he pointed, beckoning towards one of the concrete Camino mileage markers.

The marker indicated 101 kilometers to Santiago. The vast majority of pilgrims who earn compostelas each year only complete the last 100km of the Camino, the bare minimum required by the Catholic Church to qualify for the official compostela document. As we knew, in Spain, holding a compostela is a major qualification, and is often included on CVs and discussed at job interviews.

These people in the line were just starting out, and would aim to earn their compostela in four or five days of walking. I felt intensely annoyed.

Hey, I wish everyone could walk the Camino, even if it was just for one day, never mind forty. However, I also must admit that it felt very deflating to suddenly be in the very close company of these imposter hordes with their shiny gear. The last few days were going to have a totally different vibe.

And the worst part? Now I couldn't drink.

James

Three of us now traveled the Camino. Hopefully our baby was gestating away merrily. Hopefully it won't be a space baby.

Or was it four of us? In the night, I'd put a hand on Cassie's belly, trying to feel another heartbeat. Nothing. Next, I listened for the child inside me. Again nothing. No sign of life. Just a knowing they both were going to make themselves heard soon.

Our baby would be born to uncertain parents. Uncertain about what to do or where to live. As we walked, I tried to remember the last time I was certain about anything. *Ah, yes.* I was certain I didn't want to have kids. So before that? I was certain I didn't want to walk the Camino. So before that? My mind drifted back to my home village in Ireland, where I was certain our Camino scheme had been hatched.

A few hundred people live in the village, famous for its working windmill, muddy canal and swans.

In many ways, our Camino began in Blennerville, not least because the village actually sits on a branch of it. The Irish branch of the Camino de Santiago passes right next to the front door of the house where I grew up. Sixty kilometers further on in Dingle Harbor, medieval Irish pilgrims would board ships bound for Galicia, where they'd resume their walk.

In one Blennerville pub, with some village natives, we talked about a charity walk from Blennerville to Dingle that had been taking place for years. Drunken excitement brewed as we all made plans to give it a go.

Lads conspiratorially playing cards in the corner shushed us to be quiet. One man bristled his moustache in annoyance. "Can't you see we're gambling here? Anyway that walk to Dingle is nothing. I'd bet you'd never walk all the Camino de Santiago."

Being half drunk, it was proclaimed we definitely would - even if we didn't know where Santiago was.

One bushy-eyebrowed fella with a few chipped teeth offered us a lend of his tractor. "If it's a holy walking journey you're doing?" he said. "Well. I think that's the Lord's work. I'll be dead soon. No time for penance and I'm too tired for mass. You'll be saving me from the devil. Take the tractor. Drive her to Santiago. And she will do the Lord's work for me."

Never thinking I'd actually walk the Camino de Santiago, I blessed his pint with the promise to pray for his pickled soul along the Way.

Sitting now in another bar in Spain, only a few days from Santiago, I blessed my pint for the old fella. He would have loved the Camino, drinking his sack full of beer in each village with the Catholic faithful.

So here I am... tractorless... but the Camino had provided three items. Catholics believe God is made up by three beings. God the father. God the Son. God the holy Spirit. Strange days.

It had been a long walk. I couldn't believe Cassie had done most of it pregnant! At the beginning of our Camino in the east, near France, I watched locals in berets ordering another wine over lunch. Sounds of a contracted vowel or elongated words set the babbling scene for the fascinating humdrum of real life. I remember smelling horse, its musky scent mixed with manure dragged into bars on boots. Patches of bright paint splashed over jovial painters.

Subtle changes set in, the further west we walked. Villages had their own little quirks. From Irun with its townspeople carrying two baguettes under each arm, to the Asturian bars with hams hanging so low they greased my hair. Rioja served as the standard house wine, fading out eventually to Albariño. Bullfighters eating olives on dainty sword sticks, to cider poured three feet above the glass.

As for the here and now, wispy, white-haired men debated with varying degrees of success until their tormented whispers cursed the air. Fists banged on the table and accusing fingers waggled. It could have got raucous, but they looked each other in the eyes over their insults. I've seen it enough times now to know that respectful shouting would resume, then a few more local brews would be ordered.

A communal atmosphere prevailed here, one where people know when to quit drinking. But always another drink is offered. This affection must surely soothe the spirits of the overindulgent. The sense of community helps to keep people from turning to the dark side.

Suddenly I felt lost in time. Too much living in the lives of others. I sat up in bed. The clock read 3:25am. A barrage of baby worries had clanged me awake.

A delirium of half dreamt dreams. Voices desperately vying for attention. I took a few deep breaths trying to relax. My mind fixated on time. *With a baby, I won't have time. I need time. Not enough time.* I looked around the dorm. Many people fear the night. It's the time I feel most safe.

Babies at night. Night feeds. I'd heard they were horrendous. But the thought of soothing a baby at 3:25am actually soothed me a little. Alone,

246

we will both be bathed in silent shadows. Some nights we'll stare out at the storms. On others we'll watch the stars and talk to the man on the moon. Both wondering why we are here.

...the beaten path

-

Day 40 - Baamonde to Roxica
26km

Cassie

We woke early to get out ahead of the hordes of new pilgrims. But, as I opened my eyes in my bunk, I was accosted by a frenzied scene of half-dressed hikers furiously packing and repacking, anxiously wrapping feet, and excitedly setting out gadgets and gear, whipped up into an absolute flurry of excitement and anxiety.

We made a snap decision to aim for a very small albergue to stay that night, avoiding the popular 'stage' that most of these pilgrims would be following, hopefully earning us one more night of relative calm before our path met with the Camino Frances in a couple days. It would be a long 26km, but I felt up for it now that I had an understanding and subsequent acceptance of my delicate condition.

It was entertaining watching the behaviors of the new pilgrims. The common pattern was to walk in a big group, singing and talking loudly, for about 5km or so, or simply until reaching the next bar on the path with outdoor seating. Then, someone would go in and order a round of beer or wine for everyone, a few tapas would be gobbled down, and then the process would begin all over again. Sometimes a group of them would split off and hop into a taxi, only to reappear a few kms down the Way at the next bar. They certainly were making the Camino more lively.

The walk meandered through an endless pine forest, up and down hills and through abandoned hamlets. We climbed higher, seemingly on level with a series of massive windmills generating electricity from Galicia's constant west winds. We had reached our highest altitude of the Camino so far, and could feel it. The trees began to thin out, and we emerged onto the bald head of a long ridge strewn with boulders.

Just as we hit the highest of the hilltops, and left the hordes behind, my phone started chiming, suddenly picking up a signal after a long day of woods walking with no phone towers in sight. *Ding. Ding. Ding. Ding. Ding.* I couldn't count how many messages came through all at once. I took my phone out of my bag, surprised to see the series of messages. They were all from Bill. I stopped in my tracks and began to read aloud to James.

'You guys, things are getting crazy here. I made it to Santiago finally. When we got here Gerta told me that she thinks she is pregnant. I'm going insane. Where the hell are you? Seriously need to talk.'

"Oh, snap. Gerta is pregnant? You've got to be kidding me!" I exclaimed.

"He doesn't sound too thrilled about it," said James.

"How could he be, it would force him to confront all his bullshit," I went on.

As we continued to walk, I felt a powerful urge to forge ahead even faster.

"Why are you walking so fast all of a sudden?" asked James.

"I don't know," I said. "I guess I'm worried about Bill."

Just as I said it, we rounded a bend and saw our albergue for the night. I immediately threw my bag down and tried to call Bill. His phone was shut off.

At least the meeting with Gypsy Mullet had been eye opening.

James

It couldn't be? My heart beat faster. It was Gypsy Mullet! Only that flamboyant hair could tease the dead to dance. Under the sullen sky, he lounged against a tree. Under his scrutiny, I tensed up. Excitement brought a stupid smile to my face.

"I saw you arrive last night," he said, scratching his back against the bark. "My family is close. Follow me."

There was no way I was going to miss a chance to be with the Mullet, so I furiously nodded to Cassie that we should follow as he was already walking away.

"But that's not the way the Camino goes," she protested.

"His way has got to be better!"

"What is it with you and this guy?"

Ahead, Fonso's jacket streamed in the wind like a flag I needed to follow.

I just kept staring, while my feet were already following.

She sighed, caught up with me, then whispered. "I'm a bit freaked out about him watching and waiting for us." She pulled the peak of her pink baseball cap low over her eyes. "And what if Nicu is here? He better not whistle in my face again. What's with that ear-piercing screech, anyway?"

"It gets the attention of his horses."

"But why so loud all the time? When he's so close, talking to me?"

"That's kinda his trademark I suppose."

"His trademark? He's not whistling Dixie. It makes my eyeballs want to bleed."

"When did you get so anti-Nicu? Anyway, he's probably still in the mountains looking for Gypsy Mullet's horse."

"I'm not anti-Nicu. He just worries me."

"Worries you?" I asked, comforting her by rubbing her back.

"He looks like he's about to peck me all the time."

"Ahh, he does have rather rigid, sharp edges for a human. Those cheekbones could give you a nasty gash."

"Yeah, I know, right?"

"Fair enough." I rubbed the side of her face. "If Nicu goes in for the double kiss greeting to your delicate cheeks, you just head-butt him with the peak of your cap. But be normal about it."

"Okaaay. I think you're as strange as them sometimes."

Parked up around a bend, hitched to the blue van, was a white caravan. Raising an eyebrow, Fonso turned, then ducked inside. A scruffy black and white sheepdog lay next to the entrance. It gave a low growl as we climbed the steps. I pulled back a multi-coloured tapestry, then stepped into the caravan.

There was a lot of hair. Gypsy's mega mullet was lounging but predatory, eclipsing one side of the compartment. He sat on a red sofa that was adorned with woolen doilies along its headrest. Opposite on a similar sofa, a moustache of renown weighed down another man's face. I dared to dream. *Could it be Gypsy Mullet's brother? Gypsy Mustache?!*

"Are you, you?" I stammered.

"Hello. Sit," he said, in a voice rough and chipped like the end of his nose, his eyes flicking to the door as if anticipating a new arrival. Were we waiting for Nicu, or someone else entirely?

Between the men, an old woman sat facing us. Her purple-painted eyelids remained closed while her jet black hair draped over her high-backed chair.

A cracked, glass oil lamp sitting on a bronze base was the centerpiece of the trinketed dwelling. It lay on a white tablecloth that rested on a sturdy, wooden table.

A red and yellow striped, woolen blanket hung from the ceiling at the end of the caravan hiding a bed I imagined.

The woman opened her painted eyes slowly. A smile played on her lips, touching my heart in a homely but worrying way. She was draped in a red shirt and flowery blue skirt to the floor. Rouge made her cheeks dazzle.

"Sit. Sit. Sit," said the woman. Arms folded, she looked comfortable enough to drop off to sleep.

Nervously we sat on stools opposite her. Five bodies packed tightly around the oil lamp. Sweat began to oil my skin in the heat.

"Good morning." Her soft chocolate voice drizzled into my ear, succulent and fattening. "My name is Florica. Are you someone I should know?"

I looked to the Mullet for guidance. He returned a blank stare. "Gypsy Mullet told us to follow him here."

The Mullet expanded as he took a deep breath. "Nicu," he said. "He is supposed to be here. He has not returned. To my shame, he still searches the mountains for my horse. It will be good for all of us if this Horse Feeder and his wife have more news for us. He is the one who told me Bastian stole Canción."

Jesus. I told him I thought it might have been Bastian.

Knots in Fonso's neck showed tension as he rolled his shoulders. "Have you any new news, Horse Feeder?"

Is this the only reason we're here? I'd been giving pilgrims a description of Bastian and the horse. No one had encountered them since Bernadette and Rolph. Uncomfortable, I shifted on my stool trying to come up with something to say that could seem the least bit useful. Under their gaze, my mind went blank.

"Nothing new, I'm afraid. No one has seen them and I've asked everyone we've met."

Gypsy Mullet sighed. "Disappointing me again. You bring me nothing I can use to catch the thief?"

My stomach sank.

The mustached man tapped the lamp.

"Stefan," said the lady.

Mustache Stefan stared at me hungrily, as if I were his ice cream.

"Horse Feeder." Gypsy Mullet's voice was steel. "I tell you this. Truly Nicu was supposed to be here. I need to see and hear everything this time." He whipped his hair forward with such force, I worried he'd be hospitalized with neck injuries.

"Put that thing away," Florica whispered.

"I'm going to fix this," he said.

"But, son," she said. "It's not like before."

Shaking the caravan, he got to his feet, then ambled out the door without a word. Only the barking dog bid him farewell.

Gypsy Mullet's mother! I could have believed two women were needed to birth such a man! But here she was, his blessed mom in the flesh. I wanted to hug her.

"He is a changing man," she said. Opening her mouth wide as if to bite, she slowly turned her ear to Cassie. "You are not travelling alone? Tell me no lies?"

Nodding, Cassie smiled. "No lies. I found out only two days ago."

Stefan slowly shifted his ice cream glare to her belly. His eyes slowly melting, he nodded his approval.

"I feel he is a young soul," she said. "A new walker on the Way. Conceived in the energies. Fonso told me he felt the ley lines throb unnaturally strong within him a few days ago. I bet my troubled boy was teasing us. He knew you were pregnant all along. Let's see."

No way could Gypsy Mullet have known all along. Could he? If so, for how long?

She reached under the table. A woolen bag covered in hair, like cats used it for rutting, was placed on the table. Tattered ends frayed further as she struggled to open the buttons.

"This!" she said intently. "I bet this is what he gave you?" In her palm was a mullet bottle identical to the one Fonso had given me.

"So," I said, "you're saying he knew Cassie was pregnant all along? Even back at the festival weeks ago?"

My expectant wife squeezed my hand tightly, then said, "It's totally the same bottle, isn't it?"

"Definitely."

"Wow. That's just blowing my mind," said Cassie. "How did he know? And what are we actually talking about? What's in the bottle? Something for the baby? He told James something cryptic about knowing the time. We thought he was going on about his horse. Was he talking about my baby?"

Florica's eyes flared exactly like Gypsy Mullet's. "That horse will be the death of him. Her name is Canción. And she is death."

"Shit!" She sucked her finger tip where she'd flicked the cracked glass of the oil lamp.

Gathering her composure with a slow breath, she said, "This is your first child."

"Yes," said Cassie. "How did you know?"

"Well, young lady. Your way is not known. But I'll tell you about my first child, Fonso. He may have brought you here for more than news. My son was born under unknown stars. This meant he would be something special. We thought a saviour."

"As the midwife toiled for a night and a day to release him from me, we saw his delicate fingers for music. But as you can imagine, he was an extremely hairy baby. A sign of one who reads the secrets of the ley lines. So it came to pass that he was not a savior, but a seer. A knower of the Way. He is a complicated soul. Knowing much, but saying less. Giving clues, but sowing confusion. But since his bloody horse disappeared, Fonso's strength fades while his sullen moods darken. Hopefully Nicu will have news. Strange he hasn't announced himself at my door."

Stefan sighed deeply.

We heard a noise on the steps. The dog growled. "Out," she shouted at the animal. The dog barked. "Time for you to go. When the dog's worried, I'm worried. You don't want to be here to see what's got him worried."

I got up to leave, but got a fright as she pushed me back onto the stool. "Like Fonso you have darkness, too," she said, scrutinizing my upper torso.

A gathering storm made my chest ache.

"That horse," she said, "will be the death of my boy because he chases death. But you have death within you. Did your mother ever have an abortion?"

"No," I said, taken aback. Little bones cracked in my chest as I tried to breathe. The vice tightened. I remembered the voice on the bridge. *You murdered me!*

Still staring at my heart, she continued. "You had a twin. An elder brother. That died in the womb. You grew around it. Now he lives within you. Angry that he never got to live. Scared because you killed him."

Cassie gripped my leg. My heart beat as if something knocked on my chest. In a crazy, strange way, I half-believed her. The anger. The fear. The guilt.

I thought my negative emotions were simply some echo of my Catholic guilt. Now she's telling me it's a manifestation of my dead twin? Is that what she is really saying? It resonated. How utterly bizarre.

"You struggle with fear and anger?" she said.

I nodded, opening my mouth to speak, but she cut me off.

"No. No time for questions. I tell you the truth. Now this is what you must do to fix yourself. Listen to your twin. Deeply listen. Tell him you are always there for him. You always wanted him to have a magnificent life. Tell him it's now time to be free. There is nothing to fear. Light a candle. Let him go into the light where he is safe. Then throw the candle far away."

I opened my mouth again, but she raised her hand. "No. That is all. The dog is worried. Now so am I. Time to leave."

In the night, I woke in fright with a pounding heart from some half-remembered terror. In the dream, seas of fires raged all around. I'd worn gleaming armour and spoke to something. Was it an echo of my catholic guilt or a dead twin or Gypsy Mullet or a tumour in my brain making me half believe the madness of all of this?

Blinking in the darkness, I remembered myself as a young child praying. That was the first time I'd listened to my emotions. I was totally open to God. That couldn't be healthy... giving away all my power.

In return, God told me I was guilty and would go to hell. Did this negatively imprint even deeper fear and anger upon my raging twin who I'd murdered in the womb?

Is my twin trying to be heard by spitting all his hateful feelings at me? He needs attention because he desperately wants to live. To be set free. For me to let him go.

Florica would probably love to hear my crazy ideas. But... I definitely heard the words, '*you murdered me*' and '*let go.*'

Carefully listening for a pulse, I put my hand over my chest to feel my twin's heartbeat.

What was the Camino providing this time?

...magic stones

-

Cassie

Setting out this morning, we finally hit the landmark altitude of 700 meters, which felt positively soaring, and the highest point on the Camino del Norte. From here, the Camino would gradually descend through a series of hills and valleys until we finally reached Santiago, looming ever closer. I could practically smell the musty old bones of Saint James, and frothed at the mouth thinking about resting, relaxing and celebrating our achievement, though Bill's message still weighed heavily on my mind. I tried not to think about it. His phone was still switched off.

Moving along the path, a tall, limber Hispanic gentleman caught up to us. "*Hola!* Do you mind if I join you for a spell? Sometimes I like to pass the time by talking to people. Other times I don't."

"Yes, of course," I said.

"I'm Pepito. From Mexico City. Are you a *gringa Americana?* I can hear from your accent."

"Sure thing. Not too many Americans on the Norte. I hear they stick mostly to the Frances."

"*Es verdad*, true, true. This is my fourth Camino. I use it as a sort of therapy. I am a very angry man. But not so much any more."

James and I perked up at this. We continued to be fascinated by all things dark. "So how do you use the Camino? As therapy I mean?"

"I just walk and walk until I'm in pain. I go very fast. And I think all day about the things in my life that I'm angry about. There's so much. I whip myself up into this crazy state until I turn bright red and there's steam coming out of my ears. But I just keep walking. And all along the Way, I collect stones. Here, look."

Pepito removed a brown leather satchel from his pocket and paused. He shook its contents into the palm of his hand so we could see. A bunch of small stones of various colors, shapes and sizes tumbled out into his palm.

"I see the stones as I'm walking, so so angry. I pick up the ones that catch my eye. Then, I walk all the way to Finisterre, and when I reach the sea, I throw the stones into the Atlantic Ocean one by one.

Whatever anger I was feeling when I found it, is gone. It just disappears."

"Wow. That is incredible, Pepito. Good for you. You designed your own therapy," I said. "So that means your Camino doesn't end in Santiago?"

"No. I always continue on to Finisterre. Have you heard of it?

I nodded and was intrigued.

"Everyone thinks the Camino ends in Santiago, but the true Camino ends 100km further on. In the early days of the Camino, centuries ago, pilgrims always continued on to what was known as the 'end of the world.' They believed it to be the very western tip of humanity, a sacred spot, a power vortex. Actually, you might feel it when you reach Santiago, some kind of dissatisfaction. Like this can't be the end. That means Finisterre is calling you. Many pilgrims feel it."

Wow. James and I looked at each other. Walk an extra 100km beyond Santiago? It was hard to imagine. I changed the subject.

"You know, I'm pregnant, Pepito. We got pregnant somewhere along the Way."

"Aw, are you kidding? That's magic," said Pepito, a tear immediately appearing in his right eye. "You must give the child a Camino-inspired name. I have some friends named Camino. It's pretty common in Mexico. But it's a girl's name, not a boy's."

"Really? I would have thought it was a boys' name, but I'm no scholar of the Spanish language," I replied.

"I knew you would think that, since you're American. No actually Camino is a feminine name, because it's after the *Virgen del Camino*. You can visit her shrine on the Frances route. It's a Catholic thing, you could say."

With that, Pepito lengthened his stride and disappeared around a bend. I wondered how long it would take him to throw all his stones into the sea one-by-one when he reached Finisterre.

We descended into the village of Sobrado as the disproportionately massive spires of the *Monasterio Santa María* came into view. The sprawling medieval complex has been converted into an albergue, with dark, musty little bunks squeezed into cold stone chambers once reserved for pious monks of old. I could feel the ghosts in the place. And perhaps the Black Death.

After throwing our bags down and showering, James and I walked hand in hand through the labyrinthine passageways, slipping stealthily

255

behind a barrier to see what secrets lay beyond it. Finding what I was searching for, a long corridor led us to the grand old portico of the abbey, long abandoned for reasons unknown. The sheer size of the church was astounding, and our footsteps echoed in its vast emptiness. Any pews or altars had long been removed, its stunning stonework and stained glass forgotten. I could hear the coo of pigeons roosting somewhere in the lofty rafters, and noticed a single candle burning in the corner. Somebody still worshipped here.

I bent down and picked up a piece of chipped stone. "Here," I said to James, handing it to him. "Maybe it's time for you to start picking up some stones yourself."

"What do you mean?" he asked, studying its shape in a beam of dying sunlight that had found its way into the building.

"I heard what Gypsy Mullet's mom said to you yesterday. About being angry. And what happened on the bridge. And what the hell is all that about a dead twin? It's all related, isn't it?"

"Yes. No. I don't really know, actually." Looking at the ground, he rubbed his beard in what I knew was a sign of his rising anxiety. "Anyway, I thought you were the one who's angry? About all that Tibetan stuff."

"Don't change the subject. Yes, I've been angry. VERY angry. But at least I can admit it. Anyway, it seems to be fading now. But YOU. You're angry, and you don't even know why. How do you expect to ever be free from it, if you won't even admit it's there?"

"I'm figuring stuff out." He seemed to want to continue, but then rubbed his beard again. "Do you really think I'm angry?" He smiled a big, fake grin and opened his arms. "I'm like the least angry guy."

"Maybe on the surface," I said, reaching out to hold his hand. "But deep down you are angry, and it's all just sitting in your chest. I can practically see it. It's the reason you can't sleep at night."

With a massive, constricted sigh, James squeezed my hand and pulled me back towards the door. I heard the stone in his pocket drop onto the cold, hard floor.

We took two more steps, then he suddenly stopped. Without a word, James turned around and picked the stone back up.

James

While we waited for the head monk in the central, grassy courtyard of the magnificent monastery, Cassie asked me if I had any thoughts on what to call the baby. Pepito had planted the game in her head.

Rolling my new emotional baggage stone in my pocket, I thought about the name Camino. The stone was a tiny bit heart-shaped. I squeezed it. *Another relic to add to my collection.* On a whim I said, "We could call him Jesus."

She shook her head.

"What about the name Dilbert, then?"

Annoyed, she put her hands on her hips. "Now you're making me angry again. You really want to call the baby Jesus or Dilbert?"

"Perhaps." I looked at the grey clouds. It had been another long night.

"I had another lucid dream. About the baby. I saw it. It was energy... but like... a joker. Joker energy. It was like he was playing tricks. A happy trickster scamp. In a good way."

After the torture museum, I had a dream of a child in a jester's hat stealing my blue shoes after being burnt at the stake.

"Wow," I said, genuinely happier to think the child would be a messer. She raised her hand to high five me. I never high five people, so felt a bit of a fool. The embarrassing clap echoed around the courtyard.

"A joking lad, huh?" I said. "Good stuff." We smiled and played with each other's fingers for a few moments. My spirits rose. "At least he'll amuse us."

Cigarette smoke wafted towards us, a stinging contrast to the fresh mountain air. The culprit arrived in a cloud of tar, his brown beard stained yellowish from tobacco, bloodshot eyes of the devil. Rollies were stuffed behind each ear while he puffed on another. We edged back from his smoky aura. He pointed to the ground. I took it to mean, *stay here.* We nodded.

I heard a meow. Turned. The eyes of a tabby cat looked hopefully up at us for food and love.

"Must be pregnant," I said. "Look at the size of it." Gently I poked her in the belly with my foot. It gave a playful purr then rolled over onto its back to play. Fat nipples protruded from its fur. I knelt down, feline and human happy in our game of scratch belly. Until the fecker got too excited and nearly bit my finger off.

"Fucking hell," I exclaimed in sharp pain.

"Now. Now. No need for the profane." Turning I was surprised at the appearance of a brown robed monk towering over me.

I didn't know whether to be ashamed or laugh. To break the awkward silence I blurted out, "The cat. She's pregnant. Just like my wife!"

The monk's rosy lips shriveled. "The cat is a HE. And HE does not like being called pregnant." He pronounced his words with exquisite authority, like an upper class parliamentary Englishman. There was a slyness to his gaze. The sharp lines of his face, beard and high cheekbones gave him the look of an evil extra in a Robin Hood movie. A face both saintly and sinister.

"But the nipples," I protested, still kneeling and pointing at the cat's belly. "Those are huge nipples." The cat swiped at my hand. Smoke wafted between us from the other man's mouth.

The monk smiled. "Engorged male nipples are quite common in cats. Do get up. It's exercise time."

I got up.

"Not you. I was referring to our cat. You can lie in the grass all day." Dismissing me he turned to Cassie. "You, young lady, are pregnant. How wondrous." His saintly cheek bones smiled quite radiantly when he wasn't upset with someone fat-shaming his cat. I decided I liked the man.

"If you do not mind my intrusion, could I inquire? Did you conceive along the Way?"

"Yes." Fidgeting with her fingers, she looked a little embarrassed.

He steepled his fingers together in front of his belly. "How wondrous. Congratulations. May I ask how long ago?"

"About five weeks. We think he could be the youngest pilgrim on the Camino."

"Oh my," he purred. "Marvelous. That would be grand. The youngest pilgrim to ever walk the Way. He should get a prize."

"Well, we were hoping to get him a compostela. Do they give one to pregnant women for an unborn child?"

"You know. I feel rather silly. I should know that. Dear me. I have no idea. I don't see why not. If they don't, then they should."

"I think I might be having twins," said Cassie, bright-eyed.

Twins. When I thought of twins I would be forever transported to Florica's cramped caravan.

"Never," said the monk, giving us that holy, sly smile. "Wondrous."

"Yeah. I keep seeing them everywhere."

"Really? Well that would be momentous. Take it as it comes. Take it as a blessing. I, myself, would like to know more about an unborn child receiving a compostela."

"Jose?" said the monk. Leaning in close to the man, they began to speak quietly. Jose nodded once, took an enormous pull on the rollie, then walked off.

"In time," said the monk. "We will find out if the baby, perhaps the youngest pilgrim, will get his prize. Jose is a thorough man when it comes to research. No smoking inside of course. So he hates the work. But we all have to make sacrifices. Do you have a name or names?" He raised a bushy eyebrow. "Perhaps you may have quadruplets?"

Cassie looked at the fat cat and groaned. "I hope not! One and done."

Perhaps thinking that she would get an abortion if she got pregnant again, the monk narrowed his eyes a fraction.

Cassie didn't take any notice of his frown. "I thought the name Camino, if it's a girl. Is Camino a common name in Spain?"

The monk frowned again at the cat. "The cat won't exercise for me." He looked back to Cassie. "My apologies. Yes. There are quite a few Caminos in Spain. What if you give birth to a boy?"

"Perhaps Tiago. After Santiago. It's the Portuguese for James, right?"

"Indeed it is. I sense you are not sure of the name or the number of children. Don't worry. Remember. Take it as it comes. It's a blessing."

He looked at me. "What would you like to call the child?"

Rubbing my beard, I replied, "You know, I don't rightly know."

He nodded.

My tummy tickled. "Do you like the name Wolfentop?"

"Wolfentop?" he said narrowing his eyes. "I've never heard that name. Where is it from?"

"I don't know. It's an old name. From the mists. It's not as good a name as it used to be. I know people sometimes call my wife Young Mike. We could call the baby, Mike Junior?"

The monk's face was turning into a scrunched up question mark.

"We also thought about bringing back the old names. What do you think about Copernicus? Bombardier, or even Bonifus?"

His face snapped open in delight. "Splendid. Bringing back the classics? Have you thought about the names Pious, Innocent or Leo? These are some of our most revered popes. Our resident cat in particular could learn from Leo's sermon. Especially the words, 'Christian, remember your dignity.'"

We all looked at the fat cat licking his nipples.

The monk sighed, then smiled. "I must attend to other pilgrims." As he left he said again, "Take it as it comes. It's a blessing."

That night, I was filled with trepidation about having a child. I worried too about Cassie. Did she enjoy the feeling of having a new spark of life inside? I'd like to be able to feel what it's like to be pregnant. My mind drifted to a few other names. If it was a girl, Galicia after the province in which we now walked. Maybe Bill. There were a multitude of names we could call the young lad or lass. Suddenly, I began to sweat. Feck! Maybe we will have twins!

...camino miracles

Day 42 - Sobrado to Arzúa
22.5km

Cassie

Off we went for another day of walking amongst the swarms of fresh Spaniards - our last on the Camino del Norte. That evening we would reach the Camino Frances, and I had no idea what to expect. The Norte merges in the town of Arzúa with the most popular Camino route by far, and it being mid-July, I was honestly a bit apprehensive and, anxious even. Our weeks of walking the mostly desolate coastal paths of the Norte seemed ages ago. There was an aching in my heart when I thought back to it all.

So much had changed. When we first set off from Irun, we walked alone much of the time, rarely seeing other pilgrims until we reached the albergues at night. Our companions were the green hills, the lonely horses and the crash of the sea. There were only occasional clams and yellow arrows to follow, and no stream of fancy flashpackers. The sense of adventure had been palpable, and now it had waned to almost nothing.

Within me things had changed, too. I was now so aware of the life that had begun inside me, and somehow already felt like a mother. I looked back at all those days I spent walking, steeped in my frustration at life. It had all faded away so fast once I learned I was pregnant. Just a few short days ago, whenever I'd think about what happened in India, I'd be whipped into a full state of panic and anger. And now, it had somehow dissipated. Just like that, my life had a new meaning, and all the events of the past took on a new purpose – to prepare me to be a mother. It was only once I'd started processing everything walking on the Camino, it was only then that the child chose to come to us.

I was so excited to reach Santiago, now only two days away. And I worried about Bill. I could feel him somehow, energetically reaching out for us. I kept trying to ring him, usually once or twice a day, but his phone seemed permanently shut off. But I couldn't shake the awareness that he needed us, or that perhaps, we needed him.

Reaching the rundown town of Boimorto by midday, we were faced with a decision. Here it's possible to bypass most of the Frances route, and head towards Santiago without the need to merge onto the most popular stretch of all the Caminos. In many ways this sounded appealing, but the Frances would get us to Santiago faster. I think my sense of urgency to get there and find Bill had kicked in. We quickly decided to keep on the main path.

Walking into the town of Arzúa felt like approaching the outer gates of a carnival set up in a field. Still a couple of kilometers out, we felt the buzz in the air. Everything would be different now.

Finally taking our first steps onto Arzúa's main drag, we were confronted with throngs of pilgrims walking in from a different direction. Large groups, some clearly led by guides, blocked the sidewalks. Outdoor restaurants competed for space, tables filled with loud foreigners and giant platters of burgers, pizzas and french fries. Pilgrims still in the day's walking clothes spilled out of bars and onto the streets, some dancing and celebrating as if they had just completed the Iditarod.

The Norte was made up mostly of solo pilgrims, or sometimes couples, mostly from northern Europe. The Frances was much more diverse, with huge groups of Koreans and Chinese, lots of Americans, and a never ending stream of Spanish. The atmosphere was fiesta-like, and wine was flowing everywhere. Many carried large DSLR cameras and fancy walking poles. The restaurant menu boards were in English, and tailored to the American or English palette. This town was the Disneyland of the Camino.

We strolled around a while, gawking at the changes. We had complete culture shock. The girl working the desk at the albergue told us it was especially crowded in town today because the Festival of Saint James was to start in a couple of days. It was Santiago's biggest event of the year, and many pilgrims scheduled their walks to arrive in time for it.

We would be completing our Camino in stride with the biggest crowd of the year.

The mystique of Gypsy Mullet and the lost spirits who seemed to swirl around in his midst began to fade. And how would we ever find Bill in this messy heap of humans, especially if he'd lost his phone?

The thin vein of the Norte had collided with the main artery, and the beating heart of Santiago was pumping us towards it. Might as well go with the flow.

James

Look at all those dirty pilgrims. Infamous Arzúa, where the honourable Camino del Norte meets the infamous Camino Frances. Both routes headed for the pilgrim mecca of Santiago. Here, my unwashed brethren flourished. Their walking sticks clicking, backs aching, blisters bursting. Hoards of pilgrims on procession. Milling and spilling about.

After a power shower at the hostel we found a seat at restaurant Casa Nena. Excited voices burst in the door as thirteen women poured in. Ranging in age from a bespectacled, bubbly youth who bounced arm in arm with an 'old mother Hubbard,' to everything in between.

American accents bombarded us with quick-fire questions. Even before they sat down, we learned they were teachers and they learned we'd conceived a baby on the Camino.

One young, boisterous blond with opal eyes, who was fairly drunk, shouted, "It's a Camino miracle!" In a gushing show of cute melodrama, she told everyone she'd waited so long for romance on the Camino. Quickly, she became bashful when she was inundated with cheers of, "You need a Camino miracle tonight!"

God. I knew this Camino miracle bullshit would happen but I didn't know it would be my fault. If my brother was here, he'd be laughing his head off.

Wine was ordered by the bottle. Large measures poured. These giddy ladies were tipsy and loving life.

In our shared pleasures of eating, drinking and jabbering, we learned the women were getting credits for future teaching positions by walking.

"Walking and drinking!!" Most cheered clicking glasses.

Nice work if you can get it. The Irish lads we met a while back would love this group. Their mingling would create possibilities for many more Camino miracles.

Obligatory selfies seemed to be the norm here, accompanied by zoomed-in pictures of bowlfuls of food. Cassie and I were cajoled into countless photos with people we'll never know. More drinks were ordered even before they had finished the ones in front of them.

Normally, I'd be into the energy of the drinking part of this merriment. But too fast, our peaceful Norte had morphed into intense moments plastered onto pictures for other people's posterity. At times over the last month, it felt like I was sleepwalking. We needed to reawaken slowly, not have our bed set on fire.

Making lame excuses about injuries to treat, we left as the women ordered more wine. A chorus of "Camino miracle," echoed after us.

By 2am, I was still over thinking twins to the rumble of snores, so decided to go downstairs.

Uncomfortable on a soft armchair, my mind wandered to Gypsy Mullet. That Florica was a strange woman. *A dead twin?* I laughed out loud at the thought.

This Camino had gotten me all messed up. But I felt I shouldn't laugh because I could be desecrating the dead. And the dead lived within me! An articulate zombie fetus. I laughed again. Confusing guilt arrived. I tried to ignore it, but its weight sank me further into the armchair.

Again I wondered about Gypsy Mullet. What would he do? Actually, no. This Camino is a Catholic pilgrimage so... maybe I should ask what Jesus would do? *Hmmmm.* He walked the desert for 40 days and 40 nights, talking to the devil. He beat up a tax collector. He hung out with twelve guys. He heard voices in his head. But mostly, I remembered him from the Bible as being kind.

Kindness. I need to be kinder to myself. That could help. Taking a few deep breaths, I cultivated a kind nature by thinking about stroking animals. Then, like Florica had said, I focused inwards hoping to hear from my twin. *Okay, speak ye strange parts of me that want to be heard. I promise this time I'm listening.*

Faintly, I heard the words *Love. Love. Love.* I smiled. Then I felt a punch to my chest as I heard *Die. Die. Die.*

I opened my eyes. *God damn it. Am I just schizophrenic? Is the only thing I'm going to learn from Camino walking therapy is that I need real therapy?* Some weird stuff happened on that bridge. Or did I just have a nervous breakdown? And maybe the competing voices within, chanting Love and Death, are just brought on by sleep deprivation?

Gritting my teeth, but smiling at the absurdity of it all, I scrunched up my eyes. Florica said the solution was to listen to my dead twin. Was I supposed to light a candle and burn it, or write a letter and burn it?. What am I supposed to write? Die. Die. Die. Love. Love. Love. Love? He has to have more to say than that, surely? What about when he said, 'You murdered me.' *Am I supposed to write that down? What if someone finds the note before I burn it? It could get me arrested!*

In my pocket, Cassie's anger stone pushed uncomfortably against my leg. I took it out. *What can you soak up, Mr. Stone? Pepito pushes all his anger into your type. Do you have room for mine? Perhaps you have room for a whole life's worth of anger? You see stone, my twin would like to relocate after I murdered him. Can you safely mind his soul?* I rubbed its sleek surface.

Damn it, Florica! Now I felt compelled to ask my mother if she could ever have been pregnant with twins before and one may have died. That was going to be a fun conversation... *Thanks, Florica. Thanks, Camino.*

Santiago Basics

The final marker on the Camino de Santiago is a scallop shell etched into the stone in the middle of the Plaza de Santiago, at the foot of the Cathedral. Sop up your achievements and sit back, delighting in the arrival of fellow pilgrims.

If you get lucky, a local musician will be playing the bagpipes, ensuring an ample supply of joyous tears.

The daily pilgrim mass is at 12 noon, and worth attending even if you're not Catholic. Inquire as to the schedule of the botafumeiro, the giant, swinging incense censer, as it isn't in use for every mass. Backpacks are not permitted in the cathedral, so check in to your accommodation first. After mass be sure to walk down into the chambers below the altar to get closer to the grave of Saint James.

Pilgrims can pick up their compostelas at the Pilgrim's Office, five minutes from the cathedral. Depending on the time of year the wait can be quite long, but there is now an electronic queuing system in place. You do not need to get it on the exact day of your arrival, but bring your passport and pilgrim credential.

The Museum of Pilgrimage and Santiago is also worth a couple of hours. There are informative exhibits covering the entire history of the Camino plus multimedia experiences.

Pilgrim House Welcome Center offers free programs focusing on Camino reflection and spiritual integration, and additional support in the form of printing, storage, cooking facilities and local guidance.

We recommend staying in the old city, or as close to it as possible. The cavernous albergues with hundreds of beds are quite the experience, but there are many smaller hostels and even five star hotels available.

Off the Beaten Path in Santiago

Santiago de Compostela is an enchanting city with hidden corners far from the maddening crowds of tourists who come in by the thousands to visit the shrine of Saint James.

Expand your horizons beyond the cathedral, and take a walk down to the trail that follows the green banks of the Río Sarela, passing abandoned mills and quiet residential areas, ending with a grand lunch at Mesón O Almacén (you won't be disappointed), afterwards looping back around to town via the Camino Finisterre.

At sundown, position yourself in the Plaza de la Quintana, under which according to local legend, a medieval monk, who had fallen in love with a nun of the convent of San Paio, met her every night secretly, traveling through a tunnel beneath the Quintana stairs that joins the convent to the cathedral. The lovers planned to run away and marry, agreeing to meet in the plaza disguised as pilgrims. The monk waited for her in the shadows, but she never came. Since then, every night he returns, hoping to see her. If you look close enough, you'll see his shadow.

Afterwards, grab a beer at O Bandullo do Lambón, which stocks an incredible diversity of microbrews from all over Spain and the world before hitting the back alley tapas bars of the Old Quarter.

The next day, go on a hunt to discover the Lost Street of Santiago. Long ago, there was a street between Rúa do Vilar and Rúa Nova known as Rúa de la Balconada. It has now been blocked off, without any entrance. The street was closed after the murder of an archbishop by the enraged father of a beautiful young girl whom he had abducted.

This street can only be seen from above from the high rooftops in the old section of Santiago.

Finisterre, Muxía and The Coast of Death

Finisterre, literally 'end of land,' is the stuff of legends. Ancient Europeans believed this area was the farthest western edge of the world, and many undertook pilgrimage here to watch the sun sink into the Atlantic long before Christ walked the earth. Local pagans, worshiping the sun, held out until the 12th century as Christianity spread into the region, and today many locals still whisper of ancient legend and lore.

High on Cabo Finisterre is the hermitage of Saint William, built over a megalithic ceremonial site. Enclosed within the compound is a long, flat stone upon which barren couples copulate in order to conceive, harnessing the power of the ley lines believed to converge here.

This entire wild coastline is known as the Coast of Death, for more reason than just symbolic. Hidden rocks and dangerous currents have led to countless shipwrecks and drownings up and down the coastline, including many pilgrims who had gone for a swim.

The Santa Compaña is a procession of tormented souls. It is led by a living person carrying a torch, followed by several souls of the dead carrying lit candles. The souls can't be seen, but they can be felt as a sudden cold breeze or the smell of wax. The living person leading the procession is compelled by a supernatural force, not remembering anything the following day but feeling unrested. If you see the procession, you must draw a circle on the ground and enter inside it or lie face-down until the procession passes. If you don't do this, the curse will be passed to you.

At the site of the shrine in Muxía you'll find the Pedra de Abalar, or 'rocking stone,' a massive slab of granite at the edge of the sea that teeters back and forth. It's believed that standing on the stone can heal disease, induce fertility, or determine guilt versus innocence. It is said that Mother Mary visited James the Apostle at this site before he began his journey through the Iberian peninsula.

WEEK 7

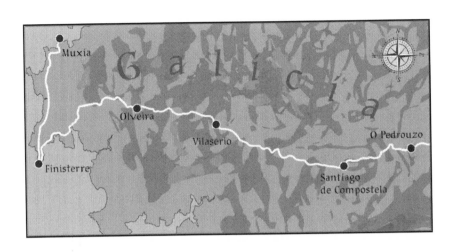

...the boulevard is not that bad

Day 43 – Arzúa to O Pedrouzo
19.7km

Cassie

Jesus freaks, out in the street. Damn. I felt out of my Camino element.
Our first day walking on the Frances reminded me of a scene from a
movie. Every few minutes we passed some kind of major Camino-
themed distraction. Nuns handing out free refreshments. Suspicious-
looking monks distributing religious pamphlets. Walkers dressed in
medieval pilgrim-garb, self-flagellating as they crawled at a snail's pace
towards the bones of their saint. Posters for restaurants and albergues in
Santiago glued to most trees and poles. Hari Krishnas in their saffron
robes, dancing around like fairies. American evangelicals offering to save
your soul with an on-the-spot prayer.

The technicolor religious madness stood in sharp contrast to the
large gangs of animated pilgrims, stopping for a beer at every chance
they got, giddy with laughter and consumed by the lure of the carnival
scene. James and I trod forth, mesmerized by the endless stream of eye-
candy as the Camino wound its way through flat forests and farms

converted into makeshift bars and cafes. Wooded groves and clumps of bushes were strewn with dirty toilet paper, bloody bandages and energy bar wrappers. Some of the Camino distance markers were even covered in graffiti.

We sat in the garden of the iconic Casa Tía Dolores, decorated with hundreds of empty beer bottles, and watched the strange world roll by. Then, my phone rang.

"Hello?"

"Cassie, is it you? It's me, Gerta."

"Gerta? Uh. Hello! What's up?" I was shocked Gerta would be calling me. We weren't necessarily confidantes. I hadn't heard from her since the text warning of the flasher.

"Well, I hope you are doing well and everything. Where have you guys reached? I'm in Santiago," she said, her voice audibly shaking.

"We'll make it to Santiago by tomorrow I think. Are you ok, Gerta?" Immediately, I made the snap decision not to blurt out anything about her possibly being pregnant. She probably had no idea that Bill had told me.

"Yes, I guess I'm ok," she said, unconvincingly. "But I'm calling because I'm searching for Luka. Are you guys with him?" I'd nearly forgotten that Bill was just a nickname given by Bastian. He had a real name, and it was Luka.

"No, Gerta, he's not with us. I heard from him about a week ago, but nothing since. I think his phone is shut off."

"Yes, I think so, too. I really need to find him. We reached Santiago together, then he suddenly disappeared. I don't feel right about going home to Germany until I've found him."

Deep breath. I'd felt that something dramatic was happening with Bill. "Well, we'll meet you as soon as we reach Santiago tomorrow and help you find him. Where are you staying?"

Hanging up, I felt my heart begin to ache for poor Gerta as I pieced together the information I had gathered. Gerta must've told Luka she might be pregnant once they reached Santiago. After walking together for the entire Camino, it seems he freaked out and abandoned her there without saying goodbye. *Oh, Bill. What the hell are you thinking?*

All I knew was, I needed to find him. Not just for Gerta's sake, but his own.

James

Clumps of humanity banded together are the Way of the Frances.

270

We found our space, but soon ran into a busy photoshoot. The model was a wise eyed donkey that shivered under the pressure of pilgrims wanting to get too close. Its owners were three hippie guys wearing leather waistcoats. One Zeus-like, bearded hippie had a tray full of jewelry to sell. Pilgrims poked at the bits of metal and wood, enquiring about their origins.

Interested only in the donkey, I learned they'd found him years ago in terrible health. He was bought from a farmer for 40 euros. Now it travels everywhere with them. As they said, "Good for karma. Good for business."

Feeling content to hang out with the donkey saviours, we sat against a tree, watching humanity stream by to the promised city.

"Did you think anymore on names?" asked Cassie.

"What about Pompadour?"

"Shut up. No Pompideeeers." We laughed, but unease creased her pretty face.

"What's up?"

"Nothing."

"What's going on with you?"

"I'm okay."

Grabbing her leg playfully, I said, "Tell me what's going on?"

"It's nothing. Well. It's really annoying. Some people are so crazy, you know? I checked the Camino forum to see if anyone had answered my question about a baby getting a compostela for completing the walk. And you know what? There were people commenting that I shouldn't care about the compostela. They said I should be at home praying for the health of my baby. Not be so selfish as to walk the Camino and put the baby's health at risk. Can you believe that?"

She pushed back her hair in frustration. "I feel like I'm doing something wrong. Another guy told me I was lying. That I couldn't still be on the Camino if I thought I'd conceived in Cantabria. It never occurred to the ignorant bastard that I could be walking slower because I'm pregnant. What kind of crazy person counts the days someone has been walking just to make them feel bad about their unborn child on a web forum?" Cassie looked down at her belly in sadness. "Am I doing something wrong?"

My jaw grated at being so helpless to stop my wife and kid from hurting. To try to protect her from the world, I put my arms around her shoulders. "It would seem Camino trolls don't live under bridges, they lurk in the online forums." Massaging her leg, I reassured her that

271

nothing could be better for the baby than its mother being healthy. "This walk is a perfect beginning. Don't let these cowards ruin what you've achieved. They are so unaware. Anonymous little Hitlers banging keyboards, with no consequences for their actions."

We decided if we were going to get abuse from invisible people, we might as well amuse ourselves by trolling the trolls and get some proper outrage spewing. We posted that we wanted our child to be adopted by someone we meet along the Way. Our preferred candidates would be two lesbian nuns. So if two nuns are available, we'll drop him off at a religious orphanage along the Way. The only stipulation is they must call the child Gypsy Jesus. I was looking forward to seeing what replies we got to that question.

That night, in bed, I took Cassie's phone as I wanted to see for myself what she'd read on the Camino forums about the baby. At the top of the page, I'd found that she'd received more comments from a bunch of ridiculously reactionary netizens, too wrapped up in their own bias. But further down the page, things took a turn for the better. There were replies that Cassie must not have seen yet. People were sending us genuine love and affection with their words of encouragement and congratulations. Some people were just happy we'd found time for sex! One guy, who worked in the pilgrim office in Santiago, had even offered to help us get a compostela for the baby when we arrived.

The funny thing is, the compostela didn't even matter that much to us. It just seemed like a nice present for the baby. A reminder for when he's older that he'd walked almost the entire breadth of Spain.

All those positive messages were having a strange effect on me. Having others talk about our baby changed my perceptions. The baby was real! I curled up tightly around Cassie. *Thank you, internet humanity.*

...clam central station

-

Day 44 – O Pedrouzo to Santiago
19.4 km

Cassie

My eyes shot open earlier than usual. There in my bunk, I felt the familiar excitement of a child waking up on Christmas morning. Could today really be the day we reach Santiago? This was it, the final push.

We'd originally planned to spend one last night out on the trail at the large barracks hostel just outside of the city. This would allow us to reach the cathedral early in the morning before the hordes, and avoid long lines at the pilgrim office to get our compostelas. When I looked at my phone while dressing, I could see a new text from Gerta. *Are you here yet?*

She was clearly desperate. After her call yesterday, I suspected I couldn't afford to wait any longer to help find Bill. I could feel him out there somewhere. Even in my delicate state, 20km felt fine, so I told James I wanted to push forward strong and make this the last day. He agreed. I felt I could practically skip all the way to Santiago.

We headed out early, easily passing by the groups of new pilgrims, most of whom were limping at this point. I looked down at our legs. Slowly but surely, they'd become so toned and strong over the past weeks. Our feet were weathered and invincible, our shoes perfectly molded to them. The skin on our arms and faces was tanned and leathery, adjusted to the Spanish summer sun. I didn't feel the weight of my pack anymore. I'd never felt healthier in my entire life. A physical transformation had taken place, and I was only now noticing. *Delicate state, my ass.*

The final day took us up and down wooded hills, the buzz growing stronger with each passing minute. We moved quickly through the gauntlet of freaks, priests and bars gathered like sentinels at every crossroads, competing for the attention of passing pilgrims. Finally, the trees began to clear and we stood on the precipice of a broad hill, underneath statues of pilgrims. This was the famed Monte de Gozo, where for centuries pilgrims would finally get their first glimpse of the Cathedral of Saint James. Sure enough, I could make out the triple spires of the ancient church in the distance, surrounded by the stone buildings of the small city of Santiago de Compostela, which sat daintily in a green valley surrounded by hills.

Loads of pilgrims had stopped here to take selfies and group photos, giddy to find themselves at this landmark. James and I just looked at each other and kept walking. We'd be there in no time now.

As the trail descended out of the hills, we entered the edges of Santiago's urban sprawl, passing by shopping malls, chain restaurants and down a series of busy highways. These last few kilometers were unrecognizable as part of the Camino, and suddenly I no longer felt like a pilgrim, just some anonymous city-dweller walking down a sidewalk. We decided to try and get a couple of beds at the massive *Semenario* hostel, which could house more than 300, just before entering the old city. We were lucky to get them, the priest at the desk told us. The place would be full that night.

I threw my bag down and texted Gerta. She was sitting at a cafe somewhere in the center. Looking urgently at James, I said, "OK, I've got to go meet Gerta and see where to start with Bill. You coming?"

"I think not," he said, pondering. "She might tell you more if it's just you girls. Go ahead and I'll meet you later."

"OK. But let's agree not to walk up to the cathedral without each other. We have to finish the Camino together, hand-in-hand. Promise?"

"Deal."

"Meet me near this fountain in a few hours." I showed him the location of *Praza de Cervante* on my phone. "There's a bunch of bars and stuff."

Without even a shower, I practically ran down the steps and out the door, pointing myself towards the spires. I found Gerta sitting with Lina at a table tucked under a green awning in some unnamed courtyard deep in the old city. Lina looked leaner, tanned, and somehow more confident than the last time I saw her. Gerta looked sadder than ever. As I approached, they both shot up from their seats in unison, faces momentarily shifting from alarm to relief.

"Cassie!" cried Gerta, hugging me as if we were long lost best friends. "It's so good to see you finally. Are you ok? You guys never caught up to us."

"Yeah, I'm fine," I said, thinking this was not the right moment to mention I was pregnant. "What the hell is going on? Sit down. Tell me everything."

"Well, everything was fine. Wonderful even. Luka and I walked all the way to Santiago together. It was magic. I - I don't know what happened."

She was speaking so fast. Her eyes swept quickly back and forth as she spoke. I took a deep breath, hoping her subconscious might take it as a sign to do the same. It did. She went on. "Luka was amazing, in every way. It felt to me that we were falling in love. Then, when we reached Santiago, I told him that I missed my period. I thought, hey, this is not so uncommon. I'll just tell him and we can take the next steps together and then decide what to do. But no. We walked back to our

274

hostel that night, and he was gone when I woke up in the morning. Bags and all. No note. No nothing. His phone is shut off." Gerta looked like she was about to start sobbing.

"Hmmm," I said, placing my hand flat on the table. The girls' beers looked pretty delicious at this moment. *Sigh.* "How did he react when you told him you missed your period?"

"He seemed fine, fine as you could expect. A little shocked of course, but fine. He held my hand as we walked back for the night."

"Well, I last heard from him five days ago, it must've been the next morning after he found out. He texted me, asking where we were, and said he needed to talk. After that, nothing. I've been trying to call him every day."

Clearly disappointed I didn't have more to share, Gerta and Lina sat in silence for a moment. I started to formulate a plan. "Gerta, do you have any idea where he might've gone? Who he might be with?"

"No, not really. But I'm not leaving here until he comes back. I can't. I don't know what to do," she said, her voice quivering.

The three of us sat, glumly. I looked at Lina closely for the first time since we sat down. She looked like she was about to cry, too. "And what's up with you, Lina?" I said, redirecting my attention.

Her eyes opened wide in surprise "Me? Well, it's Boils. Cassie, he kissed me! I'm in love with him."

Boils. The 50-something Finnish businessman I spent a couple of days talking to on the trail, who serenaded us on our anniversary night. *She kept walking with him? Hmmm.*

"OK, so if you're in love with him and he kissed you, what's the problem then?"

"Cassie, we walked together for the entire duration of the Camino. All day, every day. We became so attached. I don't know how it happened. We argued a lot, too. But I started to have feelings for him. Nothing happened though, until we reached Santiago. The night we got here, he pulled me into a dark corner of a bar and kissed me like I'd never been kissed before. My knees went weak."

She was practically frothing at the mouth recalling it. "Go on, Lina. What next?"

"Cassie, Boils is married, remember, with three children. He has a whole life in Helsinki! The next day, he disappeared as well. He blocked my number on his phone and blocked me on Facebook. I looked through Gerta's phone, and I can see that he's in Madrid now, with his wife! He must have met her there!" She groaned at the mere thought of it.

"Oh, boy," I said, trying to find the words. "Listen, if he would block you and leave you like that with no explanation, you don't want him anyway, Lina. Trust me. Forget about him."

A tear fell from her cheek. "I know, you're right, Cassie. I decided that I can't go back to Germany like this. It would ruin my whole Camino. So tomorrow I will take a bus to Lisbon and walk the Camino Portuguese all the way back here. To erase what happened. Start over again. And forget about him forever."

Sheesh. I spent my own Camino thinking I had some serious drama going on, but compared to these chicks, I had it easy. I didn't miss the desperation and pain of unrequited love, and gave a silent *thank you* for being happily married. I wanted to help. I turned my attention back to Gerta.

"Listen, I feel like Bill - I mean Luka - is still around somewhere. I don't think he went home to Austria. I'm going to do whatever I can to find him. I'll be in touch."

I gave them both a good long hug and set off to meet James. I'd been in such a rush to meet Gerta that I scarcely noticed the beauty of Santiago spring up around me. We hadn't even officially finished the Camino yet!

The city seemed to be carved from one giant stone, each church, house and business flowing seamlessly into the next, separated by secret alleys and passageways that echoed with laughter and the clinking of glasses. Each approaching bend surrendered a clue to what lay on the other side, whether a slice of orange light beaming down from the midsummer sun, or the whine of a bagpipe reverberating across the masonry. As I navigated my way through on this Saint James' Eve, I knew there was even more to discover in this city built upon ancient bones.

James

When we arrived at the steps of the colossal seminary hostel in Santiago, I rested on my new walking stick I'd found along the Way. In full view of my fellow pilgrims, I'd triumphantly turned to survey the city of Saint James. The stick bent under my weight then snapped. With a humiliating thud, I hit the ground.

Pilgrims laughed all around. Again, I remembered my brother laughing at the thought of me doing this ridiculous walk. It was in this stupid moment, I realised I'd made it! I'd walked the bloody Camino! I laughed. My legs turned to jelly. My Camino flashed before my eyes. *Pilgrims. Pubs. Poncho. Nuts. Hills. Grandmother. Horses. Mullet. Murder. Conception.*

Pilgrims lifted me from the ground to live again. *But what now?* What would I do with my resurrection? Relax and read a book on fatherhood or resume my quest for a missing horse?

In the somber convent dorm, I found pilgrims in varying degrees of disrepair, bandaged and moaning. This was not the place for celebratory merriment I was expecting. I added my broken stick to others in the corner.

I'm going to be a dad! Shocked by this thought again, I quickly showered then ran away to start my new life as a horse detective.

I followed the bronze clams embedded in the pavement. Pilgrims were either giddy to be finishing the Camino or maintained looks of deep contemplation as they made their way into the old part of Santiago where the cathedral resided.

It seemed the Catholic version of God was not what they worshipped in this medieval city, but rather the hallowed clam. Everywhere, street signs, shops and even wall tiles were printed with clam shells. As I wandered further into the crustacean's domain, I found its image printed on t-shirts, dog jackets, hats, lollipops, cakes and craft beer labels.

Restaurants sold what pilgrims dreamt about when they arrived too late for dinner on those cold, wet nights on the road. Menus del dia with tantalizing broths. Fish stews. Sizzling meats. Two for one beer. Wine by the bucket. Music. Dancing. Laughing. Loving. Santiago was a city of free tapas. For every drink ordered, a complimentary snack appeared. On ten euros a day, you could have five beers and five small meals. Not to mention all the free Santiago cake and sweets passed out at confectionary shops.

In one narrow street, I stumbled into a group of singing, hippie pilgrims banging drums while half-dancing along the cobblestones. They sang rowdy songs of welcome and reward, so I followed close and let their river take me where it would. My horse sense was keen, but I spotted no beast peering out from between the thronged stalls and curious alleys.

Tables laden with wine and coffee lined most streets. Aproned waiters tried to catch my eye, but I was more interested in petting the dogs of the homeless. Buskers wailed for coin while some white-haired old men dejectedly sat behind cardboard signs proclaiming their ill fortune.

Priests in dusty, black cassocks and sparkling white collars wearing backpacks, who looked like they'd just finished the Camino, took my interest. So I waded from the hippies to the holy. People parted for the clergy, so it was easy to solemnly follow in their wake until we reached a tightly-packed square which felt very close to the bones of Saint James. A fountain sat in the square's centre. Sure enough, I was in *Praza de Cervantes*.

In the midst of the clamouring masses, I spotted a dingy, black bar called *A Gramola*, with an empty table and two chairs out front. I plonked myself down with a satisfied sigh in the shadowy haven to survey the sacred.

No horses roamed the mobs as I ordered a 1906. No Bastian either. No mega mullet. No Bill. Cassie could be close, talking to Gerta. Bill could be spying on me right now. If I told him of my recent adventures, he'd probably tell me he saw my dead twin using Saint James' bones to play the drums.

A loud bang on the bar's murky window gave me a fright. Turning, I was surprised to see three Goths, laughing loudly when they saw I wasn't who they thought I was. I smiled back. *Who was I supposed to be now? A dad!* Sickly, sweet scents of children's candy filled the air. I couldn't be sure if I was imagining it.

The beer arrived. Its bubbly embrace invited me to suck it down in one gulp. I refrained. Over the last few days, I'd been drinking slower or choosing fizzy water. I held the cold glass to my hot ear. Closing my eyes, I savoured the refreshing bubbles bursting over my tongue. It chilled my chest then hit my empty stomach giving me an immediate beer buzz. Jelly legs stopped wobbling as the rest of my body relaxed. *Ahhhhh. We did it! We really made it!*

From the moment of serenity came a horrible feeling I'd lost something. With my eyes still closed, I tapped my pocket and was relieved my wallet was still there. Still, something definitely felt missing. Like a revelation I hadn't grasped. But for now, I wasn't going to go full Wolfentop and spend my time lamenting the loss of something I couldn't explain.

Fiddles played in my mind. Opening my eyes, I saw two women in beautiful white gowns sitting on high stools, playing beside the decorative, drinking fountain. Their long, blonde, bouncy hair fluttered a little in a breeze that didn't touch my shady spot.

An overly enthusiastic band of young girls appeared from around the corner. Puffy hair bouncing, arms bopping and all smiles. They half-drowned out the fiddlers with their boombox while dancing to a choreographed version of the 90's dance song *Macarena*.

The breeze gusted, causing hats to fly while table umbrellas threatened to follow. Wind even reached me, hotter than it seemed it should be. Chaotic energy swirled, throwing up bits of rubbish and dust that blew into dinners and faces. Hippies passed with horns and handstands. Elderly priests shuffled past, holding their caps on their heads.

Santiago was a heady cocktail. Intrigued by what show would miraculously appear next, I ordered another beer and waited for Cassie.

"Love husband," said Cassie. "Let's go straight to the main cathedral square. I want to see what all the fuss is about." Cassie had developed a pregnancy glow. She looked beautiful. It would be a privilege to walk hand in hand towards pilgrim central.

After passing a bagpiper, we reached the cathedral square. My body filled with anticipation. We stepped in… But we were nearly run over by a train! *A fucking toy train!* Boop booping loudly, its little blue carriages carried dozens of tourists.

So this is it. After six weeks of walking. A toy train...

Letting the train pass, we waded into Clam Central Station. In the middle of the square we looked down at the very last clam etched into the stone. "You caused me a lot of trouble," I whispered.

Cassie poked me in the ribs. "Are you talking to that clam?"

"Yes."

"Leave the clam alone and give me your hand." She took my hand and put it on her belly.

"Can you please move for a minute?" said a red-cheeked woman, wrapped in a green scarf. She held a camera and was insistently nudging another woman towards us to take pictures over the clam.

I rubbed Cassie's tummy. For at least enough time to take a breath, I felt we'd earned this hallowed spot above the last clam.

We held hands and took in the cathedral's magnificence.

After five breaths. "I'm starving," I said.

"Me, too. Let's get out of here."

279

From my seminary bed, our dark room glowed eerily. Another thunderclap of a sparkling firework burst over the city. Cassie had become tired, so we'd left the celebration of Saint James' Eve while the night was still young.

I couldn't stop thinking about the cathedral square. Pilgrims in particular. Something was amiss in the atmosphere and energy of that whole place. I didn't know what it was. Felt at a loss to explain my feelings... loss... That was it. They seemed lost. They have no purpose. The Camino is over. Game over. Go home. The thin blankets on my bed suddenly felt so heavy. What was the point of it all? Tears welled in my eyes.

Slowly, my mind focused on a time years ago when I stayed in a Tibetan monastery. The rows of hard beds were much like the ones here, but there the freezing, Himalayan wind rushed through every crack in the windows and doors. The wind bit into my back as I'd half-heartedly tried to meditate. Even our Buddhist teacher, peering at us with one eye from time to time, would pull his red robes tighter about his wrinkly frame. Back then, my hand had been ripped open by a mountain dog. The Tibetan monks had wrapped it up, but the infection had taken hold.

What did I learn there? Could it help to stop this fearful sadness now? Remembering my promise to listen more to the voices inside, I hugged myself tightly as more fireworks exploded outside.

Again, I tried to grasp the faint feeling of a disappearing memory of revelation I'd felt in that monastery long ago. I'd practiced subtle-body meditation there, a technique designed to open a door within, leading to a dimension of nothingness. During that time, I felt I was lucky to achieve this space for even a fleeting moment. If even that... I still don't know if I'd really achieved the subtle state. I did gain space from my emotions for a few moments. At the time, that's what I desperately needed.

Now here, in this tearful state, I tried to bring myself back to the time. Ever so slowly, I attempted to enter the void. To timelessness. To nothingness...

At the grimy bar in Santiago today, I sensed a feeling of loss. Thought I'd lost my wallet, but now I knew it was something more.

Suddenly it became clear this new fear was not having control over my own destiny. With a child comes a loss of freedom. At the bar, my mind constantly showed me different lives I could lead, but I hadn't been taking notice. I was too wrapped up in horse detecting and Santiago's merriment. I could have so many different lives if I wasn't having a child. Go with the party priests. Go with the pilgrims. Go to the mountains. Go with myself. Go nowhere.

I was in mourning. Crying was a way to wash away my old life and the lives I would never lead. My tears cleansed and strengthened me, readying me for something new.

The Buddhist monk taught me to observe my emotions. To surrender. With fireworks exploding, I realised, I was comparing my life now with an infinite amount of other possible lives I could lead. Today my mind had become terribly stressed and overloaded trying to process so many lives lost at once. It brought on my depression tonight.

The words of the author Mark Twain arose. *Comparison is the death of joy.* I realised I needed to stop comparing my potential other lives to the one I have now. I'm becoming a father. *Let go. Be with this life. Stay focused on it.*

My mind was struggling to let go of my old life. It mourned for the ones I'd not lived. I needed to stop trying to control everything, stop grasping and lamenting for the energy of the other lives. My way was with my family. Getting up, I walked to the bed where Cassie slept. I hugged her as blue fireworks lit up the room.

...shadowy figures

—

Day 45
Santiago

Cassie

On Santiago's highest and holiest day of the year, I shot up from my bunk. "Wake up, you. Let's get down to the square." I implored James, realizing he was next to me in bed.

"Uggggh. Why so early again?" He did his best to ignore me as he croaked from under the sheet.

"We have to get our compostelas, and I don't feel like standing in line for hours because I've got things to do. It's going to be mobbed today."

We packed up our things quickly to move into a different hostel down in the city. Immediately upon getting out the door, basking in the brilliant morning sunshine, we walked towards the cathedral, following the last of the scallop shells. Spanish mornings are quiet, all the shutters still closed. This day was no different. We stopped at a bar and shoveled *tortilla* into our mouths.

Approaching the large main plaza of the city, set at the base of the commanding cathedral, we could only see a few meandering tourists taking photos and a few drunk stragglers who hadn't quite made it home from the night before.

Our Camino was over.

"So where is this compostela office, anyway?" asked a bewildered James.

I led him to the west side of the square where a smaller chapel stood. It was an absolutely ancient-looking relic, that in my mind was somehow more impressive than the grand cathedral just in front of it. "I think it's just down here..." My thought was cut off.

Coming up a stone ramp from the street below was a sight to behold. A darkly bearded man, wearing a sombrero, chugged up the walkway. He was pulling a large homemade cart filled with all sorts of curiosities, mainly large bags of what appeared to be trash piled up, nearly toppling out the back. Tied with bungee cords to the front of the wagon was a tent, a makeshift stove and a few blankets. The man looked weathered yet relaxed, a true testament to the benefits of living outside the hassles of mainstream society. As he passed us by, I noticed a little sign taped to the caboose of his rig. *Camino Wife Wanted. Inquire Within.*

"Hey. Hi. *Buenos dias*," I said as I shuffled towards him. I couldn't help myself.

"*Buenos dias, amiga.* I made it to Santiago for the most special day of all. It is a good day to be alive."

"Where are you coming from?" I asked, looking down the street he'd just come up.

"I walked through the night from the fair banks of the Río Tambre, just to see this sight on this day," he gestured towards the cathedral. He could read the inquisition in my face. "I mean to say, I'm coming from Muxía, amiga. On the Camino Finisterre."

"Ah, you're coming from the Camino Finisterre. Is that it there?" As I asked, I could see a yellow arrow and a scallop blaze pointing down the way he'd come.

"Yes, indeed. Probably my favorite Camino of them all. I've walked all of them, you know. That's what I do. I ply my way to and fro on the

282

various Ways of Saint James, picking up what rubbish I can and living the life of a saint," he explained, winking.

"Wow," I said, eyes widening. "How long have you been walking?"

"Four, going on five years now, *amiga*. But now I am getting a bit lonely. I'm searching for a Camino wife to join me. Know anyone?"

"I'll keep my eye out for you," I said smiling. Then, a thought hit me. He was coming from the Camino Finisterre. *What if Bill had gone that way?*

"You didn't happen to notice a tall guy, from Austria, walking out that way, did you? He's pretty noticeable. Loud, outgoing. Here." I took out my phone and showed him a photo of Bill cutting up his LSD on the albergue floor in Bilbao.

Squinting through the morning glare, he looked carefully. "Hmm. Yes. I do believe I've seen this person. A few days back, he was walking towards Muxía. He asked me for a rolling paper."

"Wait, seriously? You really saw this guy? And where the heck is Muxía?"

"Everyone thinks the end of the Way is Santiago. Then they learn that the end of the Way is actually Finisterre. But only the truly devoted come to know that the real end of the Camino is at Muxía," he said, almost whispering. He looked deeply into my eyes, cementing the sanctity of his secret in my heart.

"But you are certain you saw this guy?" I asked, pointing at my phone again.

"Yes, *amiga*. I am sure." He paused a moment, assessing the space around me as though he was reading my aura. "Seems like you better get going if you're going to find him in time."

"In time? In time for what?" Now I was starting to get worried.

He just smiled. "*Vamos!*," he said, pointing down the road towards the west. "And let me know if you find me a wife."

I went quiet as we walked the rest of the way to the pilgrims' office. I knew James was trying to read my thoughts, but he said nothing. As we emerged about an hour later, we found ourselves back in the main square. Around the corner, people were lining up to go inside for mass.

We decided to split up for a while. I needed to sit down and think properly, and James wanted to wander and people watch. I knew he could sense that a process had started inside me, and that I needed to let it play out.

"I'll meet up with you later," I said, blowing him a kiss.

"So does that mean our Camino isn't over yet?" asked James. He looked exhausted but I could see a twinkle rising up in his Irish eyes.

I shrugged, and said nothing, then turned to leave him. I walked straight into the cathedral. The cool air wafting up from its bowels made me shiver.

Never religious, and certainly not Catholic, my mother made an attempt early on in my childhood to instill her wholesome Presbyterian values in me. But soon enough soccer became the religion of my Sundays, and there was no time left for church. I never bought the stories I heard from the Bible, anyway, and didn't even believe in Santa Claus as a child. It all seemed like a fairy tale to me, designed to comfort the heaving masses of confused and unfortunate people. Not until I reached Asia and studied Buddhism did I actually begin to understand what religion was all about.

I took a seat at the end of a crowded pew of the faithful. As mass began, I felt a mysterious protective force wash over me. The holy dirges sung in the clear, true voice of a nun in the rafters might as well have been a Sanskrit mantra. Like Tibetan Buddhists, the Catholics were clinging tightly to strings of prayer beads, and incanting on their knees, with eyes closed and heads bowed. In front of me was a statue of Jesus, a man who dedicated his life to teaching morality to anyone who'd listen. Didn't the Buddha do the same thing? And James. Good old Saint James. Inspired by his friend Jesus, he escaped Judea and came all the way to Galicia – to the very end of the world – to further spread the teachings. *How the hell did I end up walking this crazy pilgrim path to the place where his bones lay?* I could feel their presence below me, from somewhere deep in the viscera of the ancient church.

As the Spanish priest's sermon ended, several more robed monks emerged from behind the altar. One of them lit up a large pile of powdered incense that had been poured inside a massive, shining censer, as the others immediately hauled it up into the rafters by a thick rope. The men began to pulsate in perfect time with one another, powerfully nudging the now smoking thurible into a rhythmic back and forth motion spanning the entire length of the medieval cathedral. It was thrilling to watch it sail over the heads of the hundreds of people in attendance, all perfectly trusting that the monks wouldn't lose their grip.

The buzz of feeling the air move as the massive botafumeiro soared above my head gave rise to a tangible fear. *Please don't let it be a girl.*

Suddenly I was back in Pemba's father's house. The sweet-smelling corpse under a white sheet, just feet away. The monks were gathered on the other side of the room, wrapped up in their scarlet red robes to keep out the Himalayan chill, rocking back and forth to the rhythm of their

284

lowly-sung mantras. The never-ending cloud of incense burned the back of my mouth. The sandalwood mixed with pine, supposedly purifying the space, setting the soul of Pemba's father at ease. My throat swelled from words left unsaid.

This world is not safe. Please don't let it be a girl.

After he punched me in the face that day, my fate was sealed. I swore, never again. I escaped soon after, and never looked back. But did I run too fast? Did I miss the lesson? Would my unborn daughter be doomed to repeat my own mistakes, karmically bound to the truths I'd run away from?

Please don't let it be a girl.

The heaving botafumeiro stirred the air just above the crown of my head. Each time it passed, I felt a pounding in my throat, and a choke around my heart.

Bill. I must find Bill.

I wandered the city as light faded into night. It seemed like everyone in the city was hopped up on booze except me. Tired, but not ready for bed, I sat on some stone steps behind the cathedral with a cone of *gelato*. As the sugar took hold and the endorphins kicked in, I realized there was someone across the plaza staring back at me.

But it wasn't. It was just a shadow. I could make out the outline of a pilgrim, perfectly projected onto the outside wall of the massive sanctum. But there was no person casting it. It seemed to appear from thin air. He was wearing a hat and a cloak, and carried a bindle over his shoulder. He looked to the west.

Bill was so much like me when I was 21, setting off for the first time to travel the world. I craved the same freedom he did, open to every chance I had to learn something new and expand my mind. My eager naivety gave me the confidence to go to India and start Tibet Women's Soccer. I didn't think much about consequences in those days, and understood so little about the dark side of humanity. If I'd been more experienced, I probably would have never gone. Then a lot of shitty things happened. A lot of scary things. A lot of dangerous things.

No. Our Camino was not over yet. Sure, James and I could fly home now, compostelas in hand. But the higher purpose of this walk had not yet been realized by either of us. So much was still left unsaid. I had to find Bill.

We had come so far. We might as well keep going.

James

A stray firework of thought ignited a neuron, exploding me into consciousness. Pain shot through my ear. *What the hell was I dreaming about?*

Cassie stood over my bed, flapping about. Must be time to finally get our compostelas.

All was going well as I spoke to one of the many receptionists behind the wooden counters in the packed pilgrim office. All around, excited chattering and deep sighs of accomplishment more than made up for the smell of funky feet lingering in the air.

My worries commenced when the receptionist with her freckled eyelids, shook her head.

"You have not stamped some of your days," she announced, tapping her pen on her plump red lips.

Damn. How was I supposed to respond? This simple task was beginning to get messy. Hating the thought of confrontation, I began to sweat.

"Did you walk all the way?"

"Of course," I said a little too quickly.

She squinted at me, then leaned to her left to consult her neighboring colleague on the matter.

What should I say? I heard they could be strict here. People didn't get their *compostela* just for taking one bus ride. We definitely skipped a good few kilometers on public transport while tending to our various ailments of body and mind.

Turning back, she stared me right in the eyes. "You know you need to stamp the passport twice a day in the last 100 kilometers? You have not done so. Also," she tapped my credentials with her pen, "it appears you didn't stamp it here about two weeks earlier. Why didn't you get stamped?"

"They didn't have one," I said quickly. "Actually. No. Now that I think about it... You know. I think I just forgot in the morning."

"Really?"

I licked my dry, lying lips. *How could I get out of this? Why don't I just tell the truth and say we took rest days. Just tell her my wife is pregnant.*

"I took rest days," I blurted out. But unfortunately it was at the exact moment she was about to stamp it.

She pulled the stamper back. "What did you say?"

286

Damn it. Now I was afraid I'd mess it up if I said anything more. "I said... nothing."

Her freckles danced. "No, tell me. What did you say?"

"Nothing. Just...talking to myself...talking and tired."

She squinted at me. "Are you okay? Do you need water? What did you say? It's okay."

What if it's not okay? Sweat dribbled down my back. "Nothing. Nothing. Really nothing."

"You should maybe drink some water."

"My wife is pregnant."

Her eyes widened in confusion. "That's nice."

"I mean. My wife became pregnant on the Camino. As we walked. That's why we skipped some days."

Her face lit up. "Wow, that's amazing. Congratulations." Leaning over to her colleague, they both nodded and smiled. "A Camino baby," she said.

"It's a miracle," I said, cringing.

"So I can give you a compostela now and leave space for the baby's name? And I'll give you another certificate to show how far you walked. You can pay for the tube over there. What are you going to call the baby?" She had her pen raised in anticipation.

"I don't know. Just leave it blank. It's an unknown baby."

The thud of her stamper was music to my ears. "Congratulations, James, and to little unknown Baby."

"Yeah. Good times for all."

She handed me the certificates, but did not let them go. "Will you walk again?"

"Yes. No. I don't know."

"If you do walk again, be sure to stamp all the days." We stared at each other, then she let go of the papers.

Spaced out, I turned to see Cassie was already finished. "How did it go?" she asked.

"Fine."

"You got the baby thing?"

"Yeah, look. She left a space for the baby's name."

"Why are you sweating?"

"Because," I said, wiping my brow. "Just. Nothing."

"Why are you mumbling?"

"I'm not mumbling. It's just loud in here. Did you get the other certificate thing?"

"Other one?" she asked. "No. What is it?"

"I don't know."

"So why did you get it?"

"I don't know. She told me to get it."

"What did she tell you to get?"

"This." I handed her the certificate I'd not even looked at yet.

"Ohhh, that's cool."

"Is it?"

"Yeah, it shows how long you've walked and where you began. So let's go. It's too hot in here."

"No," I said. "I have to pay the guy."

"What guy?"

"I'm not sure," I said, scanning the area. "Him. I think. Behind the counter by the door."

A frustrated looking man wearing a blue baseball cap with a sharp face, who could've been Nicu's son, shook his head as I approached his counter. I rooted in my pockets for money, then produced a five euro note. Hoping this was enough, I waved it at him. In deeper frustration, he wrinkled his brow.

Oh, no. What the hell have I done now?

He tapped his cap, then gave me a curt shake of the head. It was then I noticed I was at the wrong end of the short but complicated line to pay. Someone behind cried out in pain as I stepped back onto a probably blistered toe. As I turned to apologize, the lady said it was okay and I could cut in front of her. I wish she hadn't. The desk guy was having none of it and gesticulated angrily that I needed to go to the back of the queue. In my shame sweat, I hurried to the end of the line.

My tired and pregnant wife eyed me suspiciously. "What are you doing?"

"Queuing. What are you doing?"

"Waiting for you. Why are you acting like a crazy person?"

Opening my mouth to argue, I instead muttered, "Saint James' Day is always crazy. Crazy time of year."

"You're acting distinctly unusual. Your face is all red and sweaty. You look like you just came out of a sauna."

"No. No. I'm fine. Just Saint James' Day energy. Can't you feel it?"

"No one else is acting like a sweaty weirdo."

Before I knew it I was in front of young Nicu.

"Yes?" he asked.

My mind went blank. *Fuck. Why am I here? What am I actually paying for? I don't know why I'm here. How do I tell him that?* He tried to hand me a tube. Vigorously, I shook my head. Dismissing me as crazy, he looked over my shoulder, hoping I'd just go away.

Frantically, I said, "I need the.... the thing. The thing for 5 euros. The thing." I waggled five euros at him. In confused desperation, I put my passport and credentials on the counter.

Cassie hissed in my ear. "Stop it. You're spazzing." But it had gone too far. My overheated mind was beginning to frazzle. I couldn't stop waving the money at him. Suddenly, he tried to snatch the money just to get rid of me, but my elbow knocked my passport and credentials off the counter. Just as I dropped down to pick them up, he grabbed hold of the money. The note tore between us.

Full of apologies, I popped back up, but then dropped my passport again. *Why am I here? What am I supposed to be paying for?* Unbearable tension took hold as I felt all the eyes in the office on me.

A hammer struck my brain. I jumped up. It's three euros. I'm not here to get another certificate. I already have both. I'm here to get a protective tube that he already tried to sell me. It's 3 euros for the tube. I wilted in relief at knowing how to continue in life. Frantically scrabbling in my pockets, I found 3 euros and handed it over..

Sweating like a wet sponge, I exited in disgrace.

Cassie spent the next two minutes laughing so loudly at me, the security guard had to tell her to be quiet. But she couldn't stop, and, infected by our plight, the security guard succumbed to helpless laughter.

"I love you more now," she said, wiping tears from her eyes. "There is nothing I love to see more than you spazzing out." She began to mimic my previous ordeal of tearing the money, and bouncing up in front of the counter like a madman.

Trying to hold back my laughter, I shook my head in mock disdain.

Finally our deed was done. We had a compostela for the baby. Possibly the youngest pilgrim of all time. We both walked out laughing.

Cassie headed for the church. Contemplating my Catholic guilt was not part of my plans today, so I headed back to the hostel to shower.

On entering, I found a deeply tanned woman arguing with the receptionist.

"But, I know. I'm sure," she said, taking the wide-brimmed, red hat off her head. A few thin braids were woven into her brown hair. "I'm totally sure. I have a booking."

"We are sorry, Miss. Your booking is not here." The screen was turned towards the woman. They both ran their fingers over its surface looking for her name.

"Screw this," said the tanned woman, kicking her green backpack next to her. "What am I supposed to do? Everything is booked. Can't you do anything for me?"

She was right to be angry. On Saint James' Day, every bed in the city would be booked. She could be sleeping out in the cold tonight. Tears of frustration welled up in her eyes.

"Come back later, miss," said the receptionist. "A guest might cancel their booking at the last moment."

Crushing the red hat back onto her head, she glared at all of us, then hauled her pack onto her back and walked out.

By lunchtime, I'd found a shadowy archway to drink a few cans of beer with its city's boozers as I'd done many times in life. A trembling old woman arrived. Maybe she was a pilgrim with her big brown trekking boots but her yellow jacket hanging to her knees would be impractical for hiking.

Faces turned away from her needy gaze as she tried to catch anyone's eye. Tears began to stream down the wrinkles of her sunburnt face.

On noticing my concern, she strode over and opened her palm. Glass marbles dappled in a swirling kaleidoscope of colors.

"They stole my bag," she said in a hoarse German accent, as she used her free hand to push her long white hair behind her ears.

"Who?" I asked.

The lady said nothing. Just used her thumb to push the little balls about in her hand then raised her arm higher.

"They stole my bag," she said again in a pleading voice.

The marbles made a slight clicking noise, which clicked my brain into action. She wants to pay me in marbles to find her bag.

Maybe it was St James who whispered some kindness, for I plucked a green marble with blue swirls from the old lady's hand. "Who stole your bag?"

Smiling, she put the rest of the marbles into her pocket then walked off.

My drinking crew shrugged as if to say she's crazy.

I followed. The people of Santiago seemed to move a little out of her way. A few times I noticed beggars narrow their eyes as the old lady passed. Did she live here on the streets?

Studying her back I found her somehow strange and familiar. She was like a secret that had come to the light. In some unsettling way, it felt as if I were following my future self.

Further we walked into thinning alleys, until the lady stopped and peeped around a corner. Not knowing what danger lay ahead, I peered around her to see a bedraggled group lounging about, chatting, smoking and sipping from cartons of wine.

This sacred city was as good as any to be a beggar in. People must be quite generous at the end of their Camino, feeling positive about life and with trekking equipment to donate.

Before I could decide what to do, the lady gave a little yelp then rushed forward. A dog roused and barked wildly, but before the group could react she was past them and hauling on a backpack that lay against a nearby wall.

"Crazy Daisy has lost her marbles," one guy said. Some laughed. A vicious glare was her response, then she was gone.

Were some of these people former pilgrims? Did they just stop here to live in the city? If I just stopped here that would be so much easier... Just stop everything.

The vice loosened in my chest. I took an enormous relaxing breath. *Could I die here and be reborn? To surrender to the city? To become a familiar stranger forever walking in circles?*

Returning to the hostel, I found the same woman with the red hat sitting out front.

This is ridiculous. "You've still got nowhere to stay?"

She shook her in frustration.

After finding Cassie sitting in the lobby, I explained my plan. She couldn't wait to be my accomplice.

I went outside again and asked the woman her name.

"Pleasant." She loved my plan. I tapped the front window. Without so much as a second of hesitation, my wife got up and walked over to the reception desk and said a few words. Behind the counter, the prickly receptionist immediately looked shocked. In a frantic burst, she rushed off to some back room behind the desk. Cassie gestured for Pleasant to scoot into the dormitory.

Sprinting in on our tiptoes, we tried desperately not to laugh. And before anyone noticed, I hid Pleasant behind the curtain of my bed.

Later, tucked up for the night next to my wife, I whispered. "We're going to Finisterre tomorrow, aren't we?"

She giggled then sighed.

"So what did you say to the receptionist, anyway?"

"Well," she began, smiling mysteriously. "I told her I'd seen a horse wander into the back garden."

We fell asleep smiling in each other's arms.

Our Camino wasn't over yet.

...alchemy

-

Day 46 – Santiago to Vilaserio
31.8km

Cassie

I didn't sleep much. Worries hardly ever keep me awake, but I couldn't stop thinking about Bill, wondering if he really was out there on the Camino Finisterre. I lay in my bunk, studying a map of the route. Ninety kilometers or so til the end of the line, the true terminus of the Camino. We could do it in three days, I reckoned. It would be tough, but we could do it. My rational mind kept interjecting. *Are you crazy, pregnant lady? You're going to keep walking? Like 30km a day? To find some angsty psychedelic kid from Austria? Take the bus!*

It was a logical consideration. But what if Bill hadn't reached Finisterre yet, or was already on his way back? Walking was the only way to make certain we'd intercept him.

Unlike the path into Santiago on the Camino Frances, the walk leading back out towards Finisterre avoided any signs of urban sprawl. Within minutes, we were climbing through eucalyptus alongside a little river, bidding farewell to the spires of the cathedral one last time upon reaching the top of a hill. The first hill rolled quickly into a second, and then a third. Up and down, the sun beating on us, I was regretting the decision to keep going so fast. James didn't look happy either. He was starting to limp. There were less services on this path, and we hadn't seen a bar or cafe in hours.

A couple of pilgrims approached, walking towards us. They must have already reached Finisterre and were returning to Santiago. The pair glowed, oblivious to my aching feet and racing mind. What had they found out there, to the west?

Back during the Camino's medieval heyday, much of the world was obsessed with the practice of alchemy. Homegrown scientists and the world's greatest scholars all vied to be the one who could figure out the formula that would transform base metals into gold. As the notion spread across Europe and Asia, the meaning was adapted. Long before, in response to violent suppression by the Vatican, pagan masters were forced to code their spiritual knowledge with metaphors and symbols, so they could record and secretly spread their practices. The meaning of the term alchemy melded into the process of spiritual ascension, the transformation from disconnected, miserable human to radiant being of light and truth. True alchemy is just the process of enlightenment, in code.

Maybe alchemy is what it's all about. We are all here just to design our own chemistry experiment to produce the perfect potion. A little of this, a bit of that, mix in some drama and emotion, and bam - you've found your way to happiness. But there's no one mix that works for everyone. We each have to discover our own unique formula.

We raced forward as fast as we could, despite our aches and pains. Perhaps my alchemy was part blister, part backache. Part hopelessly trying to find a crazy young Austrian for no apparent reason. My life once had purpose. Now my life had devolved into one long walk that seemed like it would never end.

Those seven years in India were spent mostly racing around, supporting a Tibetan girl in need, seeking another donor, striving for every opportunity to get our team involved in soccer matches and tournaments. Dodging dirty looks on the streets of Dharamsala amidst swirling rumors that traveled faster than the wind whipping through the prayer flags overhead. Under constant harassment, the tightening in the pit of my stomach became familiar, and the false display of strength I'd mastered became second nature.

Every morning, to the tune of human thigh bone trumpets and loud, guttural chanting, I'd rise from my bed and scoot out into the towering pines, walking fast and strong up the steepest hill in the still-sleeping Himalayan village. I'd march faster, hardly able to catch my breath, pounding down on the path, increasing my resolve with each step I took. After twenty minutes, the high peaks would emerge from behind the face of the foothills, and the morning sun would shine off the fresh snow above. I'd finally stop and take a real breath for the first time that day. Then I'd turn, facing downhill, and run as fast as I could, nearly out of control. I'd sprint with all my power, jumping branches and debris, ignoring stares from passing villagers carrying firewood on their backs. I'd run, and run, until I reached the outskirts of town again, and the heavy reality of my day's inevitable challenges settled back down on top of me.

"James?" I said through labored breaths as we climbed yet another long hill.

"Yep."

"I'm scared the baby is a girl."

"Why would you be scared of that?"

James

Sneaking Pleasant out of the hostel had been easy enough.

For breakfast, the three of us celebrated by eating tomato toast in the morning sun while collectively basking in a job well done. Nearby, a signposted clam pointed our way to Finisterre. They called it, The End of The World. Bill lay that way. Hopefully, we'd catch up to him before he fell off.

Sipping orange juice, I admired a droopy-eyed priest with lipstick smudged all over his left cheek, staggering up the road towards us.

"A definite stag priest," said Cassie. We nodded. But then again, maybe he was a real priest. It would be perfect camouflage for an actual man of the clergy to go buck wild and get away with it in Santiago. Perhaps he preferred shaking his money maker in the cathedral while sipping champagne from a nun's shoe.

The priest stumbled as he passed our table. I reached to catch him, but he pulled his arm away. "Never forget," he slurred, wide-eyed. "Never forget."

"Forget what?" asked Pleasant.

"The planet moon. Pelagius. 8:14. He will rise again. They are coming."

More priests in various states of disrepair were struggling up the road. A more hungover crew I'd never witnessed. Stale booze wafted over us. Some still clung on for dear life to crosses as if they were life buoys keeping them afloat in their personal ocean of pain.

What would the monks who laid the foundation for the first Cathedral de Santiago have made of these fine creatures?

After finishing breakfast, we three promised to meet somewhere else someday, then said our goodbyes.

Onward Christian soldiers. Our Camino transformed into tracking down Bill. I'd like to see the guy again, but maybe it was fine for him to make his own way in the world. Cassie had other ideas. Ideas that quickened our pace.

Outside the city, I found a lemon on the ground. An invigorating aroma shot into my nose when I scratched into its thick rind. Its zestiness gifted me a sense of constancy. Maybe lemon trees had always lined the lanes of the Camino Finisterre? I wondered what tales an ancient lemon would share? With a citrus voice in my mind as I walked, I tried to remember the myths I'd learned from other travellers.

Finisterre. Taken from the Latin words *finis*, meaning 'end', and *terra* meaning 'Earth.' It's said to be situated on the Coast of Death. The name derived from the many shipwrecks, caused by the fierce storms and dangerous rocks lining the length of this wild Atlantic coast. Old records show the route from Santiago followed the stars of the Milky Way all the way to Finisterre. A place where the living could get closer to the land of the dying. The gateway to the afterlife, where the sun went to die each day.

My Catholic guilt had been right to worry. This sounded a bit too much like we could be walking straight into hell.

At the end of our walking day, we watched the sun die from our farmhouse albergue. The proprietor had those wizened, witchy features from fairy tales. She also happened to be the loveliest little woman I'd met since my grandmother. Arms open, she gave me the best hug I've had in ages as we arrived at her front door, transmitting genuine warmth and gratitude. Cassie had tears in her eyes when she pulled away from the hug. The old lady noticed this, then with tears in her eyes too, pulled Cassie in for another loving embrace.

Nourished by homemade pumpkin soup and kindness, I fell into a dream that, for the first time in ages, didn't deal in death.

...istanbullshit

-

Day 47 - Vilaserio to Oliveira
20km

Cassie

The day it all ended, I answered the call even though it was a blocked number. I'd just arrived in yet another cheap hotel room in India, fresh back from Canada after taking a team of refugee girls to represent their country (that was no longer recognized as even being a country) in an international soccer tournament. The frenzy of interviews, film crews, endless photographers and phone calls from top reporters had exhausted me, but was worth it for the increased exposure of the Tibetan cause. Now, the girls had all scattered back to their refugee settlements scattered across India, and I found myself alone for the first time in a month, prepping my next move.

But the phone rang, and I answered. On the other side, nothing but heavy breathing. The slow in-and-outs sounded wet with angry testosterone, raw and real and dripping with danger. I couldn't hang up, stunned motionless by the fear that had risen from my gut and spiked my throat. After what seemed like eternity, the breath revealed its voice. 'You best be careful, Cassie-la. You best be very careful." Then click.

His voice was unmistakable. This man was the head of a nation's entire sports program. The guy in charge of Tibetan sports had just threatened my safety. In India, anything is possible. For the cost of a simple meal, people are willing to hurt others. And the police don't seem to mind, in exchange for a bottle or two of whisky.

So this was it. Taking the team to Canada had finally done the trick. It was just too much for the men to handle, a women's team being the first to play in North America, getting all the media attention, donors and admiration of supporters around the world. This is where it would end.

I called James, back in Ireland, waking him up. "What should I do?" I asked.

"Cassie, you know I'd never tell you what to do."

He spoke so strongly. His voice was clear and raised slightly in volume.

"But if you think you are in danger," he said "Come home. Now. You don't take the risk of being attacked, or worse."

296

Emotions filled my throat and furled my brow. By this time, over 1000 young Tibetan women had joined the soccer program. My jaw began to tremble. "I can't just leave..." I didn't know what to say, how to comprehend what James had advised. But what he said was true. And every cell in my body knew it. "The girls... what will they do?"

"You can still be in contact with each and every one of them, Cassie. You can still be there for them. They are stronger now. You always said that, in the end the Tibetans will have to do it for themselves. The girls have real expectations they should be treated equally now. You've reached your goal with them. It's not the first time you've been threatened. We both feel something sinister is brewing. You get out, right now, if you feel, for even one second, that your life's in danger. You promise me that, Cassie."

Without thinking, I hung up the phone, logged on to the internet, and booked a flight for the following day. Just like that, in the span of five minutes, Tibet Women's Soccer was dead.

These memories shot through me as I slowly sipped my coffee. While pilgrims shuffled out the door of *Albergue Casa Vella* that morning, the pain was palpable. It was impossible to hold my shoulders up, the burden was so great.

I watched the albergue grandmother whisk around the room, sweeping the stone floors, clearing breakfast plates, and intercept every person before they could walk out the door. She embraced each pilgrim as if they were her child.

When it was my turn, I tried to sneak past. She was too quick, and the pull of love too strong. She grabbed me by the shoulders and hugged me close, even tighter than the night before. She could feel the pain inside me, and she pulled me in closer. She whispered some magic words only uttered by Galician mothers in the darkest nights as they held their babies. It was impossible to hold it in. The giant tears again streamed down my face as she finally let me pull away.

I turned and started walking.

James

A hawkish whistle echoed through the green hills. Squinting through my fingers, so as not to be blinded by the sun, I studied the trail ahead. All I could make out was a few horses milling about.

Cassie and I stared at each other. *Could it be Nicu?*

The sharp shadow of a man appeared, his silhouette practically cutting the grass as he edged closer. It was Nicu! He was striding towards us in a black hat and wrinkled shirt as if he'd just come from the horse races.

"Nicu," I said before he noticed it was us.

Surprise turned to smiles, then words sped out of his mouth. "I didn't think you had it in you!" Grasping me by the shoulder, he smacked me on the back. He gave Cassie two quick pecks on the cheek.

"Congratulations to you both. Miracle of life."

How the hell is he here? I thought he was still tracking Gypsy Mullet's horse? I'd never seen him so excited. Maybe being away from the intense dourness of Fonso had done him good?

A few neatly trimmed horses waltzed between us. "See," he said. "The beasts even come to celebrate your baby. I'll introduce you to my travelling family."

"This is Octavia," he said. The muscular, chestnut-coloured horse neighed from the force of his playful slap upon her rump. "And that's Cantante. And this is Rojo. See those wild, red eyes? Beautiful. And this mare is Balada. She's like lightning." Balada, a dusty white colour, eyed Cassie curiously.

"Balada smells you're with child," said Nicu excitedly.

Feeling rather giddy from all the attention from Nicu, I asked, "Where have you been? The search party has been out for you for ages. Fonso is waiting for you a few days back. And how the hell did you know Cassie's pregnant?"

Rubbing his hand over the arm of his wrinkled shirt, he looked to the clouds. "I've been away. And Gypsy Mullet was the one who told me of your good fortune."

Somewhere close, I thought I heard the faint whips of scintillating flamenco guitar. Balada wandered back to sniff Cassie, then whinnied.

"Quiet down, girl." He patted her roughly, then eyed Cassie's belly. Pursing his lips to whistle, he tilted his back, but instead said, "Fonso has changed. He was fighting with some kind of nightmare when last we spoke. He's confused. He's a different man when he's confused. It was best I left."

I remembered Fonso's sadness. How he'd seemed so much smaller when I'd met him in the corn house.

A protective anger arose, and I felt a strong, illogical need to defend Gypsy Mullet. "What do you mean he's different?" I said loudly. Each of

298

the four horses stared at me. Balada stopped sniffing Cassie. Silence reigned, except for the slashing of tails. "Where did you see him?"

"Finisterre."

Excitement bubbled within. "But that's where we're going."

"I know."

"How?"

"You're a pilgrim walking west from Santiago. Only two places to go. Muxía and Finisterre. And you don't look like Muxía people."

"Hold on a minute," I said, raising my hand. "I thought Gypsy Mullet was going after Bastian to find his horse? It's not that long ago there was talk of Istanbul."

"Bastian? Istanbul? Istanbullshit, if you ask me. But Gypsy Mullet believed you. And that's why it's worrying." He stroked Cantante. "Fonso believes Cancíon still lives. But he also knew she could not be in Finisterre. But he kept traveling to Finisterre anyway. Can you believe it? That place can be the end of men. He wouldn't leave that horse for anything."

Gypsy Mullet was in Finisterre! Hills seemed to close in around us, but the sky above never looked more open.

I looked Nicu in the eyes. "So did you find Cancíon?"

"I wasn't sent to find the horse. When Cancíon went missing, I stayed with Fonso. Sometimes he becomes different if he's left alone for too long. It has always been. Where the horse goes, Gypsy Mullet follows. That's his life. He turns dark without this way to follow. And his way was taken from him. Fonso was getting darker by the day, so I decided to find that horse to save him from himself."

Lowering his head, he spoke a little quieter. "I couldn't find Cancíon. I followed the ley lines. I searched the hills. Asked everyone I knew along the way. Poor Cancíon has disappeared." He shook his head. "That horse bound us, but beat us." He pushed down his crumpled shirt. "Anyway. I'm too long in the wild away from my wife. My daughter is three. Nearly ready to ride her own horse. I need to be there for that." Proudly Nicu stared at the horses then looked at Cassie and winked. "My travelling family goes with me to meet my family." He looked towards Finisterre. "The end of the world awaits you. Oh, and I'll tell Gypsy Mullet you're coming."

He dove in to give Cassie a couple of kisses, then shook my hand with such vigor I feared he'd dislocate my shoulder. "You'll be fine," he said. "Nothing to fear from fatherhood."

299

...sore middle toes

Day 48 - Olveira to Finisterre
32km

Cassie

It was a steep climb out of the valley leaving Olveira. The trees began to thin out, and I could see the hilltops were bare and windblown. The sky held a subtle shimmer, hinting that the sea was near.

We paused at a fountain next to the dirt track as a young woman with a giant backpack approached quickly behind us. She looked terrible.

"Only about 20km more to Finisterre," she said between deep breaths.

"Yep, almost there. Where you coming from?"

"Santiago. I'm coming from Santiago," she replied.

"No, I mean where did you sleep last night?" I asked.

"I didn't," the woman said, scratching her head. Her black, curly hair was becoming matted, and her ankles were caked with dried mud.

"You didn't sleep? Are you ok?" I could see now that she was trembling a bit.

"I got to Santiago, and I didn't feel anything, ya know? So I just kept walking. And I didn't stop. I guess I'll keep walking until the end." Her eyes were bright and wide open.

"But you must be exhausted. That's like... 70 kilometers or something," I said.

"Can you feel your big toe?" she asked.

"Um. Yes."

"Can you feel your little toe?"

"Yep. I can feel it," I said, wondering what the hell she was getting at.

"OK. But can you feel your middle toes?" she asked, raising her eyebrow at me.

I sighed and tried to bring my awareness to the three toes in the middle. "No, actually I can't."

"So you've got two choices. You can either smash your middle toes with a hammer right now, or you can concentrate a bit every day, until you can feel them on your own. Your choice."

"But you're assuming I want to feel my middle toes. What if I don't care?" I asked.

300

She shrugged and wiped some sweat from her cheek, leaving dirt behind.

James and I sat on a boulder, watching her in silence as we drank water. She pulled a sausage out of her pocket and hurriedly ate it. As she turned to continue up the path, she stopped and looked at me. "In my personal opinion, the middle toes are worth it."

We watched in silence as she disappeared over the ridge. James just looked at me and shook his head. "She should come babysit for us sometime."

Hours later, as we walked on a flat track through a scrubby pine forest, ozone and saline scents danced on the air. "The sea is around the corner. I can smell it," I said to James excitedly.

In perfect time, a seagull's caw echoed nearby. James stopped in his tracks, motioning to a clearing uphill from us. "Follow me."

We walked up into the opening, and sure enough, just through the trees, we saw the unmistakable blue of the Atlantic. I dropped my pack and sat down on the grass. "Let's just stay right here, where the mountains meet the sea. Forever," I said.

James squatted down next to me, surveying the plot. "We can build a custom albergue, right here. We haven't seen one all day. We'd be filling a large gap. Right where you get your first sight of the ocean. They'd all want to stay at our albergue," he said, winking at me.

"Yes!" I replied. "It will be a perfect albergue, with sun beds and a courtyard, a separate room for snorers, and one for early risers. And I can bake for everyone, and you can work with the really wacky ones on solving their problems. And I'll be like that Galician grandmother, welcoming everyone with hugs and love, making them cry with relief. That's who I want to be."

"Our life can be the Camino." said James, standing up. "Bastian can be our security guard and his job will be to steal the super space babies from their beds in the middle of the night. English Dave can be the receptionist! Nicu can be the whistling alarm clock."

"Yes! And Bill can be the drug dealer! And Father Ernesto can come bless the place!" I added.

"Gypsy Mullet can do live flamenco shows every weekend," said James wistfully. "People can stay as long as they want, as long as they don't talk to me too much!"

The fantasy made my blood pump.

We began to descend to sea level down a long, steep grade. My knees were killing me, and James was limping harder than ever. We'd made it to Santiago unscathed, why were we now killing ourselves on this final stretch? *Fucking Bill.*

We passed through a series of pretty seaside villages, and finally, there it was in the distance. It was unmistakable. Finisterre. The lighthouse stood like a sentinel upon a dramatic rocky outcropping at the end of a promontory of rugged land. This is the spot believed to be the very edge of the world for so long, and it looked the part. We watched as mist was born from waves crashing against the base of the headland, slowly rising to sit on the hilltops. Between us and it, nothing but a long sandy beach.

Arriving at the lighthouse, we saw several pilgrims, but no sign of Bill. I asked a few, showing them a photo. No one had seen him.

We checked into the municipal albergue, and I asked the attendant if I could see the register of who was staying there. Sure enough, Bill's name was there. But he'd checked out that morning.

"James!" I shouted across the bunkroom.

His shirt was half off in preparation for his shower. "What?"

"Bill was here! But he left this morning. I can't fucking believe it!"

"But we'd have seen him if he left. We didn't leave the Camino all day," he pointed out.

"Ya I know," I said. "But what if he kept going? To Muxía. That guy in Santiago said it's truly the *end of the end* of the Camino."

"You've got to be kidding me," said James. He knew what was coming next.

I took out my map. "It's less than 30km. I can do it in one day."

James turned to face the open window, his eyes closed.

"You don't have to come. I think I'd like to go alone. To give me time to think about everything."

He was still facing the window.

"It's fine," I continued. "I don't mind at all. And I feel strong. And if I start to feel weak, I'll just bail out. I've got to find him, ya know? I just have to try."

James finally turned around, rubbing his eyes in amused exasperation. He approached me. Then smiled. "If you have to go, go. Go get the guy. I'll be right here waiting."

James

Finisterre was in the distance. The end of the world. Only a few kilometers of sandy shore separated us from the gates of hell. Empty footprints in the sand led the way. But I couldn't bring myself to step onto the beach. *What's going on here?*

Cassie pushed me gently forward. "Come on. Let's go."

I didn't budge. My legs had stiffened. Waves sizzled in and out on the shore.

As so many times on this journey, I remembered my grandmother.

"It was when you saw only one set of footprints, it was then that I carried you." This verse hung over the cooker in her kitchen.

Cassie pushed harder onto my backpack for me to move, but I was lost in my Catholic upbringing. That verse inspired awe in me as a child. Sitting next to my grandmother in church was the first time my little brain tried to comprehend duality. Unseen and seen. Someone unseen can carry me? Something invisible can help me in life? What is this magic? Is the priest a wizard? Excited, I held on tight to the pew in case it flew away. A painting of Adam and God almost touching fingers hung close. It made me think that if I wanted to know magic, all I needed to do was touch God. What a revelation, that inspired me to want to truly believe.

Cassie tried again to push me forward into the footprints in the sand. Things that meant nothing a moment before meant everything now. A whispering breeze blew leaves across the beach. *Could these be the footprints of my dead twin? Could he be older than me and unseen? Had he been the one carrying me all these years?* I stepped into the footprint. Felt an odd tingle. Amused that my mind wanted to take it as 'a sign,' I said a little prayer of thanks to my twin for helping me. Out of respect, I dodged the rest of the footprints.

Upon reaching Finisterre's lighthouse, Cassie went to see if Bill was close by. My prize was the Mullet.

Instead of finding Fonso gyrating at the gates of Hell, I found a scruffy herd of goats slowly climbing a steep hill. Momentarily, my legs buckled and vision blurred. I needed to jump.

Grey clouds rolled in as I crushed the anger stone. I looked to the heavens for the onslaught of demons. *So this is it? The end of the world.* After all the strange stories I'd heard about the Coast of Death, myths began to mingle with my imagination. Unsatisfied with the mundane, my sense of self remained at the lighthouse, but another part of me went exploring for the portal to the Other World. Breathing deeply, I closed my eyes.

Acrid smoke brought me back from the dead. Its stink reminding me of Gypsy Mullet's burning hair in that corn house. Nicu said he was here, but where? If I did get tangled in his Mullet-verse again, then this walk to Finisterre would've been totally worth it.

Another puff of smoke wafted my way. Following the stench further down the hill, I was intrigued to find its source – a burning black hoodie and some black socks.

Next to the fire was a young guy hacking away at his long, blonde hair with scissors. He threw the locks into the flames with wild abandon like they were the source of all his terrors. Utterly focused on cutting and burning, he didn't notice me. I hoped he was trying to conjure a creature from the flames.

Seemingly satisfied with his ferocious grooming regime, he wiped his hands on his t-shirt, then took off one black trekking boot. Into the fire it went. Stinking demons hissed from the damp shoe as the laces glowed. Was he hungry? I'd heard of starving people eating the leather of their shoes. Perhaps he was cooking up a size 10 lunch.

Still deep in his state of liberation, he took off the other boot. Bending down to root in his ragged, black backpack, he pulled out a bottle of beer, cracked it open with his teeth, and spat the cap into the flames before pouring the rest into his disgusting boot. He sighed, then looked to the heavens. A state of conviction settled on his face. Head back. Boot held high. Beer splashed into his mouth. Dripping with boot beer, he shook his head furiously, laughing loudly.

A man exorcising his demons needs space, I reasoned, so decided to leave him be. Finding more melted boots near the lighthouse, later I learned it wasn't just this guy burning his stuff and re-evaluating his life on reaching the end of the Camino. Happens to a few of us, by all accounts.

I left him a packet of nuts on a rock, then scrambled about the clifftops looking for more curiosities. Finally, I found an ancient black dog sleeping. Foam spray from the waves crashing off the boulders below, rose and fell in sync with the dog's breathing. The ferocious guardian of the underworld made me happy, so I sat next to it. I took Cassie's anger stone from my pocket. The dog sighed in satisfaction as I rubbed the stone up and down its back.

...karmic acceleration

Day 49 - Finisterre to Muxía
28km

Cassie

I didn't dare wake up James before I set off that bright morning. In his mind, he was at the end of his journey. He'd finished the Camino, a pilgrimage he'd never really wanted to take, and had only done so because he loved me. I could hear in his breathing he'd fallen into a deep sleep. Maybe for the first time in over a month.

Packing my things, my fingers grazed against something hard on the bottom of my pack. I pulled out the scallop shell Kristin had given me weeks ago. Why had I been so hesitant to tie it onto my pack? I realized, despite already walking hundreds of kilometers of the Camino, I'd somehow felt like an imposter when she presented it. I hadn't appreciated that I, too, had been swept up by the current of the Camino, and wasn't ready to admit I was as pilgrimy as they come. I zipped up my bag and tied the shell on.

Sneaking quietly out the door, I was reminded of so many times in the past when I'd struck out on my own to a new place, a new country perhaps, alone and ready for anything, and nothing. The difference this time is I wasn't really alone anymore.

We worked together in India for nearly five years, on and off, before we finally got together. He was my next door neighbor for a while, up on that hill in the forest, surrounded by meditating monks. We shared movies and a few beers once in a while, and sometimes I'd do his laundry. Not because my gender expected it, but because I was one of the few people in the area lucky enough to have a washing machine. But he mostly stuck to himself.

A few times I'd awoken in the night, hot and confused, with James on my mind. His fierce blue eyes would invade my dreams, but the message he shared would dissipate as my consciousness returned.

At soccer camps, we'd often kick the ball around together, and end up on the dusty pitch wrestling each other. He once took great pleasure in smearing a hearty slice of cream cake in my face at a team birthday party that descended into a food fight, and I'd regularly give him a friendly kick in the shins whenever he strayed too close to me on the soccer field.

Then time was up. I was in yet another doomed relationship. One afternoon, he came by to pick me up for a soccer camp meeting. The Canadian guy I was dating at the time stuck his head out the door as James pulled up, and asked if he could join. James walked up the steps towards me. Grabbed my hand. And told him no.

He was holding his head so high that day; his back was strong and sure. Ecstatic electricity entered my palm as he guided me down the steps and over to his motorbike. As I climbed on and wrapped my arms around his waist, I knew this was finally it. How could I have been so blind? For so many years? How had I not seen the greatest love of my life was right under my nose, living just next door? In that minute, everything changed. We were married three months later, high on the Rock of Gibraltar, at the most southern tip of Spain.

The path linking Finisterre to Muxía, at the most western point of Spain, was devoid of other pilgrims, even now, at the height of the summer season. I walked for hours without seeing another soul, rambling through aromatic eucalyptus groves, past tiny hamlets and over steep hills from which I could catch glimpses of the grey-blue Atlantic. It occurred to me it might be the last time for a long while I'd be able to hike alone like this.

The energy on this obscure Camino offshoot was different, too. The pulsating rhythm I felt pumping me towards Santiago, and then Finisterre, had waned almost entirely. It was just like a normal path in the woods. But something else was motivating me to keep on walking.

Walking faster than I had on the entire Camino, I remained perplexed as to why I was doing this. I had no idea what I'd say to Bill when I found him. If I found him. He could've easily run further off by now, back to Austria, or to some other far off place where he could disappear for real. That's what I would have done when I was his age.

Finally, the village of Muxía appeared below. Beyond it, on the tip of a small peninsula separating the open sea from a calm fishing port, I could make out the *Santuario da Virxe da Barca*. This Catholic shrine was built over the site of a Celtic altar, and was one of the last holdouts of pagan spiritualism in Spain. The power of this spit of land was undeniable. I imagined all the ley lines of the world converging on this one tiny point. On Christmas Day, 2013, Mother Nature had concentrated her own energies here, when lightning struck the 500-year-old building and fire tore through its heart.

As I started downhill towards Muxía, a family rounded a bend towards me, heading the opposite way. "Good afternoon," said a polite little girl no older than three, with pigtails and a scallop proudly strung around her neck.

"Good afternoon to you, too," I replied with a smile, looking up at her parents. "Are you walking the Camino? Is *she* walking the Camino?"

"Yes, she is. And she loves it. She sits in her buggy sometimes, but she mostly walks like us," replied her mother. Dad nodded proudly. "We came all the way from the French border."

"That's amazing," I said.

"We got bored listening to people telling us we wouldn't be able to travel once we had kids. It's actually way more fun with her," said Mom, smiling down at her daughter as they moved on down the trail.

Skipping forward as I traversed the descending ridge, a massive stone sculpture came into view. The monolith, seemingly split in two by some invisible, shattering pain, dwarfed scatterings of random pilgrims below, waiting for their turn to have a photo with it.

I scrambled down the rocky headland path towards the scene. My heart stuttered as I reached *the end of the end* of the Camino. A more pristine spot on this Earth could not exist. Deep within me, some muscle, tensed for seven weeks, finally relaxed.

It couldn't be. Were my eyes playing tricks on me?

There, leaning up against the base of the sculpture was the unmistakable figure of LSD Bill. I closed my eyes in relief then looked up at the sky. *Thank you.*

Emotion began to pool in my jaw and throat. It felt I'd been chasing him since the beginning of time itself. As I approached, I set my gaze on Bill, trying to grab his attention from a distance. He still hadn't seen me.

He was now strolling around the outside wall of the church, rolling a cigarette, and staring at a young brunette. Close enough to make out facial expressions, I saw him wink at her as she walked by with some other pilgrims, flashing his infamous grin. She looked back at him, doe-eyed. I watched as the age-old flirtation ritual played out before me. *He doesn't waste much time.*

Finally on level ground, I came up behind him. "Bill. Hi." I half-smiled, not sure how he'd react. My heart was pounding.

He turned, and his jaw dropped open. "Cassie! What... what are you doing here?" He looked up the path behind me, searching for James. "I thought you were just getting to Santiago." Exposed in his shock at seeing me, his jaw quivered.

"Give me a hug, you idiot," I said, pulling him in tight.

"I had a feeling you were going to show up," he said, hugging me hard, his voice cracking.

"Really?" I asked. But before he could answer, he'd already loped halfway down the rocky shoreline towards the sea. I watched as he sat down on a flat boulder, his broad, bony back arched as he folded over himself, his face into his hands.

Slowly, I approached and sat beside him.

"It's all just too much, Cassie. It's better if I just disappear." His face was buried in his hands still.

"Disappear??" I asked. "You mean kill yourself? Or run off with a band of gypsies? Nothing ever really disappears, Bill." I sighed.

"I didn't walk the Camino so this would happen. I never should have left Austria."

"So why *did* you decide to walk the Camino? The day I met you it seemed like you were walking for adventure, for freedom. You'd totally opened yourself up to the flow of the road, ready for anything. I'd never met someone so ready to surrender. Look at you now."

He lifted his head slowly, his gaze creeping out between his shoulders curled forwards towards the frothy sea. Tears streamed down his cheeks.

"Freedom. What a joke. I went looking for it, but now I'm in prison."

"Maybe. But I think not."

"Come on, Cass, what are you saying? I took off from everything back home, to feel free again, and now I've just ended up in an even worse situation."

"How do you know it's worse? I thought you were happy with Gerta. You walked the whole Camino together. Is it so bad to imagine having a child with her? Being happy with her? Anyway, you don't even know for sure that she's pregnant, you jackass."

If he replied, I couldn't hear his words above the crash of the waves.

I ploughed on, determined to have my say. "When you chase after freedom, you're opening yourself up to all the possibilities of the world, I think. And you don't get to choose what happens. That's the whole point. *Anything* can happen. That's why most people in this world cordon themselves away in their houses, watching television, playing it

308

safe. Because they don't want to open themselves up to all the possibilities, because it's too scary. You did the opposite, man.

"You said to the universe, go ahead and show me what you've got. And now you've got it. So have some faith, Bill. You chose to let life roll, with all the beauty and drama and uncertainty it could muster, because you believed in it, because you trusted it. So trust this."

Bill looked up at me finally. "Go on," he demanded, appearing anything but persuaded.

"I don't know, Bill. I have no idea what I'm talking about, really. But I'm just thinking, maybe the Camino is like Dharamsala."

"Dharama-what?"

"Dharamsala. The place in India where James and I met. Where I lived for years. It's a crazy little town. So much life. I remember meeting a woman at a chai stall on a mountain road. She was wearing white robes and told me that when you're in Dharamsala, your karma speeds up. The place is jam-packed with Buddhist and Hindu monasteries and temples, and thousands of monks and other holy people who spend all day just praying for the enlightenment of others. All that praying, all that mental energy, it speeds up everyone's karma. We all have to learn our lessons in life, and the faster we learn them, the faster we achieve enlightenment."

"This isn't India, Cassie!" Bill was looking alive again.

"But the Camino's the same! Thousands of years, the devout come here from all over the world, walking up and down the Camino, praying the whole way, some with every step! Plus, all the churches, the holy relics, the monks and nuns. Saint James himself, even! Every person who decides to walk this thing, it's an act of prayer in itself! So on the Camino, maybe your karma speeds up, too. That's why there's so much drama, and crying, and anger, and emotion. That's why you meet the people you meet, see the things you see, and that's why they always say that the Camino provides!"

Bill threw a stone into the sea. "All the ups and downs to fill a lifetime get squeezed into this one Camino experience; that's what you're saying?"

"Yes! And it might suck while it's all unfolding, but in the long run, it's for your own good. And *that's* what you signed up for, Bill, when you decided to do the Camino. You signed up for rapid, karmic evolution of your withered little soul. And that's what I signed up for, too."

Bill stood, reaching out to help me up. "Want to get a beer?"

"Yep. But I can't."

He looked at me with disappointment as we swung our packs on.

"I'll explain later," I said, gesturing towards town.

"Oh, and Cassie? Where the fuck is James?"

"He's looking for Gypsy Mullet in Finisterre," I said with a grin.

"You mean you came here alone?"

"Yep. Just to find you."

Bill nodded to the sky, finally understanding something.

Gulls screamed above us as we rounded the headland and approached the charming row of seafood restaurants and fishermen bars. The sun was getting low in the sky and the village was coming alive.

Bill stopped abruptly and turned to me, placing his hand on my shoulder. "Cassie, do you mind if we skip that beer, actually?"

"I told you I can't have one anyway."

"Good," he said, without asking why. "Because I've got to get walking."

"Where you going?" I asked nonchalantly, but knowing already.

"Santiago," he said. He pulled me in for a hug, then headed purposefully off towards the hills, turning one last time to give me a wave.

That night in an empty albergue bunk room, I had a lucid dream, one of those rare ones during which you feel fully conscious and in control of your actions within the dream. One that you have no trouble remembering the next day and feels as real as any interaction in waking life. I was sitting in a beautiful green garden, and from behind a tree emerged a woman with dark blue skin wearing a crown of orange and red flowers. Her wild black hair was on fire, the flames framing her beautiful face as her big round eyes pierced mine. She approached me, gently placing her hand on my shoulder.

"Would you like to know the sex of your baby?" The blue woman asked.

"Yes," I replied.

"All you have to do is approach the flame and look deep inside. Then you'll know."

Standing on a pedestal in a corner of the garden was a large white pillar candle. I walked towards it, bent down, and stared deep into the black void at the center of its flame. A vision appeared of a laughing newborn, clearly a boy. As soon as I opened my eyes that morning, I was 100% sure that a male baby grew inside of me.

James

The heart sees what is invisible to the eye. Those were the words I had engraved on Cassie's wedding ring. But now I left my wife to meet a mullet. Actually, she left me. All I know is we were both pulled by different invisible threads of emotion.

Nicu had indeed told Gypsy Mullet we were arriving, for a spindly-lettered note had been left at the albergue informing me where to meet him. Down a cobbled street, I found Bar Galería.

I ordered a 1906 beer from the bandana-wearing barman dressed as a pirate, and found a spot by the window overlooking the pier. Outside, fishing boats puttered about the harbor. In a wicker chair, I swallowed down swirling excited trepidation.

Arriving early, before the other person, normally makes me feel less anxious. Taking in more of Bar Galería, I observe grizzled bar jockeys, drinks in hand, straddling their wooden mounts at the counter. A few already gripped the reins of their pints for the long ride ahead.

The bar was decorated like a kitsch memorial to the God of Everything. The impossible number of artifacts deserved a curious glance if not a full blown archaeology dig. One part of the ceiling was covered in ancient records and tinsel. Rotting acorns. Wind up watches. Typewriters. A diving suit dressed in a dickie bow. Shells and hats. Dried fish. Faded maps. Puppets. Muppets. The walls were covered with such a wealth and weight of memorabilia and books, it felt as if the bar would fold in upon itself.

Rays of dim sunlight began to percolate gently through dusty windows highlighting the shadowy premonition of my meeting with Gypsy Mullet. He'd ride right into this very bar on his beast, trampling all before him, bar flies thrashed by Canción's furious tail. Bastian tied to her back.

To say a hush overcame the bar would do sound a disservice. Because as Gypsy Mullet walked towards me, it was as if silence sang. The Master of Mullets had arrived. Each neck craned to see those strains of timeless hair. Without making eye contact, he sat opposite me. Flecks of light burned in his brown eyes.

He raised a hand. Other men would have called it a paw. The young barman hurriedly poured steaming water into a glass, followed by what looked like whiskey. Quickly he brought it over to our table. Its smoky wood aroma wafted between us.

Taking a quick sip, Fonso placed the glass on the table. What poise. A brew like that would've removed the lining of my mouth. I couldn't think what to say.

"Nicu gave word you were seen on the Way. I felt it good we see each other one last time." A pinging noise rang around the bar as he clicked the glass with his long fingernail. His mother had pinged the oil lamp the same way. He seemed agitated. Not for the first time, I wondered how could anything ruffle such a colossus.

Maybe the whiskey fumes gave me Dutch courage, for I fired my words. "Why didn't you tell me you knew Cassie was pregnant? It would have been nice to know."

"Would it? Would you have changed anything?"

"Maybe." I thought about it. "Well. Actually. Yes, I would. She would not have drunk alcohol for starters."

He pursed his lips as if to concede. "I apologize, but I can't be all things to everyone. This is the stupidity only intelligent people fall into. Anyway. The baby is well, but your wife is long suffering."

"Why?"

"Because of you." He gave me a playful punch on the shoulder that nearly drove me out the window.

Was I reading this right or was he trying to be friendly, even jovial? All I knew was I got my first touch from the Mullet, and that was as much as anyone could hope for in this short life.

"Where is your beautiful lady?"

I raised an eyebrow, trying to match his own enigmatic nature. "Her own path drove her ever forward." I paused to look out to sea. "To save a soul."

He nodded.

Were we speaking the same language? Hard to tell. He gave a mischievous wink, then a quick whistle and downed the shot of steaming whiskey.

"Nicu is well?" he asked.

"He seemed better than ever. Better since he left you." I laughed. Fonso did not. I began to redden under his scrutiny. As if my inept existence amused him, he shook his head briefly, then raised his meaty paw. Another steaming beverage soon arrived.

"Nicu is well?" he asked again, in a firm voice that trampled on the timbers of my chest.

"Yes, Nicu is well." I took a long swig of beer. "What can I say? Nicu seemed happier than I've ever seen him. He really seems content."

312

"How?"

"Free. Full of life. Whistling away. Traveling with a load of horses to bring to his daughter. It's her birthday soon. He was happy for me and Cassie." A painful constriction in my chest made me want to talk about what his mother had said about my dead twin. Instead, I held the stone tight in my pocket.

"Happy for you," he said in a mocking voice. "Happy for you? You don't even know what the word means. I know Nicu. He may seem happy to you. But he is not happy in himself. That makes a world of difference. Did you like his horses?"

"Indeed I did."

Fonso just nodded. "Nicu has a kick like a mule. Don't be fooled. He's a wild man to be stuck in the mountains for so long. After Canción disappeared, our friendship was not the same. I lost my way. My horse, Canción…" He looked out the window towards the sea.

"Did you find Canción?" I asked.

"Did you find *your* way?" he snapped. He pinged the glass, but didn't take a drink. "I couldn't follow her anymore. This Bastian you told me about. I inquired. He is a man who knows a person's true name while going backwards in life. To my knowledge, this means he knows the future." Without flinching, he downed the drink in one shot. "I'm sure my mother told you she thinks I'm a seer? Well I know a seer when I hear one. This Bastian better leave us all be." He looked out to the mountains. Clouds rolled down like so many trampling horses.

"So you gave up?" I asked.

"No."

"So? Where is the horse?"

"Canción is dead." A sad smile passed his face. My fingernails scratched the stone surface. He put his hand in the air to order another drink. I felt nauseous. In silence, we both watched the trampling clouds as the barman poured the liquid.

No way. Could Bastian have killed the horse somehow? He just seemed like a man on a mission. A crazy zealot right out of the Bible. But then again, murder had been on his mind. Could he have ridden the horse to exhaustion, or worse? The hippie vagabonds we met just before reaching Santiago had bought that dilapidated donkey then nursed it back to health. Someone would surely have taken pity on Canción and helped her?

"I didn't want to talk about it," he said. He took a quick sip. Whiskey fumes wafted. "I didn't even tell Nicu. For my shame, I left my friend searching." He sighed. "That beast was the wildest. She knew the Way. Now she is ruined and battered beyond belief. Perhaps now she is more free than ever." He smiled sadly at the clouds.

I wanted to tell him everything would be okay. Instead I took another long drink of beer. I felt so tired. We'd walked so far. For sure, the strange thoughts of Gypsy Mullet and his lost horse had given me extra motivation to continue on the Way. Now the horse was dead. I felt Fonso wouldn't want any condolences. He would swat them away like flies. Finally, I asked, "How long is she dead?"

"Not long after you fed her. Not long after we first met at the fountain in Basque Country."

"So what happened?"

Pinging the glass much gentler, he replied, "Canción would not have wandered off alone. How could she just disappear? Something terrified her that night and she ran far away. I heard that she bolted out in front of a truck."

Light glinted in his moist eyes. Too proud to cry, he took another drink. I held back my tears in respect.

"The end of the world is a good place to say goodbye," he said.

I nodded.

Deep silence followed. This was the real end to my Camino. The journey of a dead horse and a new baby. Nothing accomplished but life and death.

"I'm sorry," I said. It dawned on me I might be getting this whole thing wrong. "You think something or someone terrified her?"

Fonso stayed silent.

"But why didn't you tell Nicu about Canción's death?"

"He expects too much. Cared too much. Coattails and horsetails do not mix."

"I don't really understand."

"You don't, do you? I've wondered deeply if my beast would have been better served being fed by someone other than you."

My heart sank and he waved his hand as if to dismiss me. Immediately he saw in my eyes how hurt I was.

"Sorry, James."

A trickle of laughter fell from his mouth. "You expected a reunion where we would enjoy? As if we were old comrades. You do understand that the end of one thing should be taken as a mourning process? And now I choose to spend my freedom by mourning with you."

I shivered into realisation. We were at some kind of funeral wake. He is sharing Canción's spirit with me. Maybe in his culture they have the same custom as we do in Ireland, where at the funeral wake, death is not mourned, but celebrated. The best stories from the dearly departed's life are spoken. We were in this bar to celebrate Canción's life.

Darkness was in his eyes. No, he didn't want a celebration. If that was his desire there would be others here. Canción was to be let go, not propelled back in painful existence with tall tales. He's here because I'm just some guy who was kind to his horse. Maybe the last person who was kind to his horse. The veneer that I was something more in his life sadly stripped away. I began to feel more relaxed. I didn't have to pretend to be special anymore. Still, he chose me. An image of the dream, where I saw my child as a joker, flashed in my mind.

"Energy is strange," I said.

"What?"

"Do you want children?" I asked.

"What?" He snorted so hard it shook the table. "Did Nicu tell you that?"

"No."

Absentmindedly, he began to scratch the table. "I'm mourning the death of my horse. The death of that freedom. I'm trying to replace it, but definitely not with a child."

"Why are you smiling?" he asked.

"You're scratching the table like it's a horse."

He let his thick neck hang backwards. "Give this man a drink," he shouted. "He's not making any sense." Two more drinks were poured by the pirate and plonked on our table.

My need to be special to Gypsy Mullet abated. I felt more at ease, so asked, "Fonso, why are you really here?"

Narrowing his eyes, he again looked out to sea. "The end of the world calls us all at one time or another. Freely letting go of one life is like suicide, then we move into another. Even you could figure that one out. I didn't want Nicu and my family to see my heart was dying. Let them live their lives. I am true to myself. It's why I spend the time with you."

He clinked my glass.

"So what is…" I began to say.

"What is your fucking problem? Can't you leave me alone? I did not come here to see you. I came here to meet my lover, Carmen. My way is lost, but we need not cry about it forever in a corn house."

315

His lover! Nicu really didn't know Fonso at all. Did anyone really know him? This was a woman I wanted to meet.

Pointing a thick finger at my chest, he said, "In my mother's house I could see who you should and could have been."

He pinged his glass. Finished the drink. Paw went up. Another glass was filled then brought straight over. "I was ordained to be a savior, but am reduced to seer." He spit the words bitterly, then tapped his feet together. "No hoofed feet to save my horse. Change has been my path from the beginning. Some changes are better than others. I'm good with change, but that does not mean I *feel* good with change." His mouth lay open, but he swallowed down the rest of his words with steaming alcohol.

Again, my rational mind tried to assimilate his fantastical belief that he was a seer of the still unknown. Drifting to a mystical mind-frame, I thought he spoke about the freedom taken from us all. He was trying to tell me who I could have been. Was he trying to tell me I'd be better off alone? Had he seen a catastrophe? Or could he have been jealous of my future happiness because his was snapped away? Or was he just getting drunk and this was all show?

Something clicked. *He really does want a child! That's it.* Or at least it may be it. He is hoping to fill up a little of the hole left inside him by the death of his horse.

"You can be the godfather to my kid if you want."

"I'm not staying long enough for that," he shot back.

Was he suicidal?

"With Carmen, or?" I asked.

"Yes. With Carmen."

"To...?"

"Stop asking questions. You whip my mind like my nightmares where I see Bastian whipping Canción to death. You are fearful that a child will take away your freedom. You presume you will resent him. I'm here to meet you now. Not just for death, but for life. Carmen is pregnant. I wanted to spend time with you. The friend of my horse. For a meeting of life. Share our tangled way. But you disappoint me. You seem to be so fearful." His eyes narrowed, then he stroked his magnificent hair. "As for me, I still have to make my decision. To be or not to be. With Carmen."

More confused love on the Camino. For how many other couples over the centuries had this played out?

316

I opened my mouth. He raised a hand. Another drink was prepared. "No," he said. "This time I am not calling for a drink. I'm telling you to shut up. I like you, but I see you cannot help me in my decision."

A need not to fail him again sprang from my stomach, causing my voice to almost shout out that I could surely help.

But he stood up. Not a wobble from the alcohol. "Thank you for the drinks." Out the door he marched, each patron eyeing him sideways as he left.

Cloud horses wandered on the hillsides. The first thing that crossed my mind made me smile. It was so stupid. But for once my mind fixated on a positive. Gypsy Mullet said he liked me. *He really likes me.* That almost made the whole walk worth it.

After a few more quiet beers, I walked out into the cool night air with nowhere to go and nowhere to be. So I walked past the main pier, beyond little houses prowled by cats and gossiping neighbors. I found a flight of stone stairs leading to a beach laden with lit lamp posts.

On the moist sand, I lay down. In my lightheadedness, I named it the Tesla beach because of the rows of light bulbs that lit the shore.

Who exactly is Gypsy Mullet? Why is he always in my life of late? Was he just a distraction?

Bulbs lit up the waves. Little fish crackled about. After such a long time walking, I'd surely learned something? Understood some magic? All that walking. Talking. Contemplating. Always emotions moving internal while perpetual motion of the Universe reigns external. Constant change inside. Constant change outside. Change is the only constant. Change is the nature of the Universe. To change and change again. If one is good with change, one is good with the nature of the Universe. So does that mean if I'm good with change, I'm closer to God?

If that's true, then I never really needed to set foot out the door to be on an adventure. I'm ever changing every day. For all is motion.

I scratched the back of my head into the sand.

Life. I always thought it was happening over there, somewhere. Some adventure that needed to be chased. To be explored. But really, everything will change anyway, whether I sit back and lay here forever or walk with it.

Bulbs illuminated the waves. Bulbs illuminated the crabs on the sand. Bulbs illuminated life. But I still felt myself in the dark.

317

...tiago

Cassie

The more ground you can put between that which has hurt you and the goddamn here and now, the better you're gonna feel. There is no more effective way to cover lots of emotional ground fast than by walking the Camino. But you better not be walking to forget. You better be walking to feel it, every little smidgen of pain and anger and hurt and tragedy in you. You better walk it, pound it right out of your very soul with each new step, until you wake up one morning in a crowded, stinking albergue and realize it really doesn't hurt so much anymore.

If you walk to forget, it will only get worse. Your pain will find all the dark folds and crevices within your mind and body to hide and fester for all the days of your life. You'll never be free. The pain will find a way to show its unforgiving fury over and over in different forms, until one day you wake up and punch a horse in the face, or discover you're dying of some mysterious incurable disease.

You can only walk so far before it all catches up to you. That's what freedom does.

Carry your pain like your scallop shell. Wear it like a badge, and wear it proud. It's the most important thing you can pack. Every bend in the road, every person you meet, will have a way of coaxing the truth out of you, laying on a healing balm more powerful than years of therapy.

Your load will grow lighter and lighter as the Way goes on.

A tree on the hill overlooking the shrine at Muxía called me to her that morning. She was gnarled by the salty spray of the sea, fertilized by the secret prayers of countless pilgrims who'd made it to the *end* of the *end* of the Camino. I sat beneath her, and as the tears flowed, I began to smile, then laugh.

By trying to block out all the bad feelings, I'd also blocked out the good. And there was so much good. For the first time since I left India, I smiled when I thought about my wild adventures there. A massive thump of love burst straight through my heart, decimating the black lump that was living inside and gagging me for years, finally rushing up into my forehead like a northbound train. It felt like I'd been going through life wearing dark glasses indoors, and they'd been removed for the first time. My laughter rolled harder and louder as the sun's morning rays shimmering on the ocean bore witness.

Kora is one of the most significant aspects of Tibetan culture. Devoutly Buddhist, these good people believe that every circumambulation of the temple, stupa or holy mountain counts towards one's eventual liberation from the painful cycle of life. Living amongst them for all those years, I figured it was symbolic. Kneel to pray. Prostrate towards the statue. Count the prayer beads. Spin the wheels. Hang the flags. Circle the temple. Round and round they go, some of them dozens or even hundreds of times a day.

The truth was staring me in the face this whole time. I'd been on my own *kora* all these years. Walking and walking. Circling the sacred truth, hoping if I just kept going round, it would slowly purify me.

It was time to enter the temple.

Tiago and I boarded a bus headed for Finisterre, back to James, back to the path life had laid out in front of us.

Back to feeling happy.

James

Drenched in misty rain, I waited for Cassie on the slippery rocks below the lighthouse.

Two feet away, another fire faintly burned. No real warmth. Only gusty wind keeping its embers aglow. Cold waves slapped the rocks, sending spray from the belligerent sea towards my shivering body.

Uncomfortable feelings, I now knew were not my own, arose with the waves. Painfully, they constricted my chest, making me feel like my life was wrong. My way was wrong.

To fix my life, all I needed to do was run away. To be filled up by some unknown adventure. To chase the highs that made me forget the lows. The need to change my life has always been strong. The pull to leave always wins. A longing that will never stop unless I release it. Looking into the dying embers of the flames, I thought it was finally time to give it a try. "Time to go free, my tortured twin," I said. Who was I talking to anyway? Florica had pulled the idea of my dead twin to the surface of my consciousness. Whether she uncovered it or created it, I don't know, but I wanted to set him free.

Following Florica's instructions, I'd bought a white candle in town. Taking it out of my pocket, I anxiously sliced it down the side with my fingernails. I whispered to the dying embers. "I'm sorry you were murdered. I'm sorry you had such a crap life trapped within me." I put the wick of the candle into the fire. "I'm setting you free. I'm giving you all my power. Now use it to travel wherever you want." Wax melted as I pushed the candle deeper into the embers. The candle flamed into life. "I love you."

Feeling the heat on my palm, I protected the light as I walked closer to the sea. I flung the candle as far I could. Sadness took hold as it extinguished in a moment, barely making a splash in the vastness of the ocean. The mist quickly stole the lingering smoke.

Waves crashed. A few tears. But I didn't feel anything change within. I could just fall into the ocean. The portal to the land of the dead was only steps away. A gust of wind pushed me further towards the edge.

I needed an anchor. The stone in my pocket suddenly felt heavier. I gripped it tight. Imagining the soul of my dead twin had entered the safety of the stone, I took it out. "You know a baby is coming," I said to the stone. "But if I let you go? Who am I?"

I threw the stone out to sea with such force, I stumbled forward. Pushing myself up, I sat back and felt a peculiar sense of ease.

Scrambling back up to the embers, I waited. A baby will soon be here.

A cluster of hair appeared. I wiped my eyes. By God's gift, could it be Gypsy Mullet?

Cassie emerged steadily into view, long, curly hair dancing in delight on the ocean wind. At that moment, I loved her even more. Her integrity and strength. The child she carried.

We wrapped around each other, mist running down our lips as we kissed. Without a word, she pulled me towards the fire. She removed my wedding ring clasped to the chain around her neck, then gently took my hand. Cassie put the ring on my finger. "Do you?" she asked.

"I do."

"Well, what are you waiting for? Do me, too."

"Here?" I made a grab to kiss her.

"Excited you are," she said then kissed me deeply. She handed me her wedding ring. "Do me, you fool. Marry me."

"So, do you?" I asked.

"I truly do." We didn't need any flames to feel the warmth.

"Do you want to see what I found as I walked up here from town?"

"Nice clam," I said, pointing playfully at the scallop shell tied to her pack. "Where did you get it?"

"Oh, I had it all along," she winked.

We slipped a few times on the wet stones, then walked over the grass to where she led.

"Hello," a voice boomed. Mist turned to mullet as Fonso loomed into view, his face as stern as ever. "I'm only here because your lady spotted me while I was making my escape with Carmen. Cassie made me promise that I'd wait, so that you could meet her."

From behind his bulk Carmen appeared, small and sultry. Her eyes raged to live. In greeting, she nodded. I nodded back. Gypsy Mullet smiled. No introductions were given and I knew they'd never be needed.

He rested his hand on Carmen's shoulder. "New ways we have to live. We will go much further than the end of the world."

They turned and walked into the mist. I held Cassie's hand. I imagined no God nor woman would ever truly tame that mullet.

Fonsos's voice boomed. "I'm calling my child Tiago."

Cassie squealed in delight. "I told him *we* would call *our* baby Tiago!" She looked at me. "Are you crying?"

I wiped my eyes. "No. Just a bit of stray hair."

Routes of the Camino de Santiago

There are way too many Camino de Santiago routes to describe them all here, but we've given our descriptions of the seven most popular routes. Remember, the Camino de Santiago is not a single path – it is a network of many trails fanning out all over Europe, all convening in Santiago de Compostela in northern Spain.

CAMINO DEL NORTE

The Camino del Norte is an 840km trail that begins at the French border and travels nearly the full length of the northern coast of Spain before turning inland towards Santiago. You are seldom out of sight of the sea, so beach lovers tend to unite on this path.

The Norte is known for its challenging terrain, with lots of ups and downs through the coastal ravines, and even some long stretches walked on sand. You are rewarded with the best food found on any Camino, with fresh seafood galore and the visionary cuisine of the Basque people, passing through foodie capital of the world San Sebastian. In 2019, 18,491 pilgrims completed the Norte, which is just as long as the popular Camino Frances but with no crowds of pilgrims to speak of.

However, if walking in the summer it's best to plan ahead and book some of your accommodation in seaside towns, because you'll be competing with the Spanish holidaymakers to get rooms. History buffs will also appreciate this Camino, as sections of it are among the oldest of any Camino, connecting medieval seaports where pilgrims would arrive from the north of Europe to the main Camino routes. There are some stunning cathedrals and pilgrim hospital ruins along the way, as well as ancient Celtic sites.

The Norte is a perfect mix of nature interspersed with charming towns and ample opportunity for swimming. The climate is best for walking in June/July/August while the inland Caminos are ridiculously hot… the Norte stays quite green and cool! The Norte embodies the adventurous, the sea-loving, the food-loving and the pilgrim who wants to avoid the crowds of the Frances.

CAMINO FRANCES

All hail, the Camino Classic! The Camino Frances is the most famous and well-known of all the Caminos, and rightly so. A whopping 183,404 pilgrims completed it in 2019, making it by far the most traveled of all the Caminos. The 780km path actually starts in the French Pyrenees, the first couple days spent descending into Basque Country as you unceremoniously cross the Spanish border.

Enjoy the green hills while you can, because soon the Frances will begin to cross Spain's high and dry plateau called the Meseta. The stretch of dusty plains will seem endless until you finally begin to climb up into the green hills of Galicia as you approach Santiago. But with the green comes the crowds….

The majority of pilgrims JUST WALK the final 100km of the Camino Frances, and you'll have to deal with the sight of all the shiny new hiking boots and carnival atmosphere as you try to continue your inner journey started in the relative solitude of the Extremadura. Every few kilometers there is a bar or restaurant to stop at, and virtually every business within a stone's throw of this route caters to the every need of the pilgrim.

There are also some wonderful cities to stop in along the way with some interesting historical sites. You'll never really be alone on the Frances, and are guaranteed to make many new friends.

The vast majority of Camino books, movies and documentaries feature the Frances, so it's very easy to plan and get a sense of what it will be like before you arrive. It's a great first

Camino, but beware of doing it in the popular months of June-July-August-September, as you'll have to deal with maddening crowds and races for beds in the albergues. The Camino Frances embodies pop culture, newbie-enthusiasm, social merrymaking, and the desire to do things in the 'classic' way.

CAMINO PRIMITIVO

The elusive Camino Primitivo – the original Way – the path forged by King Alfonso II in the early ninth century. It would be impossible to walk the Primitivo without taking into account its unique lore.

Violent wars were being fought between Christian and Muslim armies throughout the Iberian Peninsula, and meanwhile it had become too dangerous for most European pilgrims to travel to Jerusalem to save their souls. Luck would have it in year 814 when a hermit discovered the grave of Saint James in present day Santiago de Compostela. When King Alfonso II got wind of it, he became the first official peregrino by trekking from the seat of his kingdom in Oviedo to the grave, where he erected a shrine, later to become the cathedral.

In his wake thousands of pilgrims began to do the same, in a time when the very heart and soul of Christianity was in grave danger. Eventually an economy sprung up along the route, and the Camino de Santiago was born. By traveling the Camino Primitivo, you're following in these early pilgrims' footsteps.

Their path was difficult, undulating up and down high mountain passes and through rocky ravines, mostly because it was more secretive and safer back then. Beginning in charming Oviedo, the path winds its way 330km to Santiago, and is the most challenging of all Caminos in both terrain and services.

Some days you are forced to walk very far distances because there is nowhere to stop, or even to fill up water. You are rewarded with jaw-dropping views over the Cantabrian

Mountains and your own private visit to ruins of pilgrim hospitals from centuries past.

Many pilgrims opt to begin their Camino on the Norte at Irun, taking a brief extension to Oviedo to then pick up the Primitivo. The Camino Primitivo is for the athletic, the determined, the one who wishes to push him or herself to the limits. It's for the history buffs, the mountain lovers, and those who enjoy the solitude of nature.

VIA DE LA PLATA

The Via de la Plata translates to 'the Silver Road,' and is an ancient path laid out by the Romans to reach the silver mines in the north of Iberia, and likely even earlier. It is the longest in length of all the Spanish Caminos at 1000km, and is a silent and desolate road with only about 3% of all pilgrims choosing this route each year.

Despite the low numbers, the way is marked well with good services for pilgrims, though some of the stages are very long between accommodation options. You'll begin in the wonderful city of Seville, and can enjoy the pure Spanish culture of the cities of Caceres, Salamanca and Zamora to break up the endless days of walking across Spain's high and dry Extremadura region.

The terrain is fairly easy, with not much climbing, but it is difficult in the sense that the stages are longer due to low frequency of services. The winters are very cold and the summers are very hot, so it's best to travel in spring or autumn. The last week or so is spent in the green hills of Galicia, when you will finally merge with the crowded Camino Frances, a culture shock after the solitude of the previous weeks.

Via de la Plata is for the hardcore pilgrim with a lot of time, for those who love solitude and harsh conditions, and for those who want the experience of traveling through the heart of

Spain's interior away from the maddening crowds with only birds of prey as your companions.

CAMINO INGLES

The Camino Ingles is considered to be the shortest route to finishing a complete Camino, being only 122km in length. It connected the seaports of Ferrol and A Coruna to Santiago de Compostela, and was traditionally traveled mostly by pilgrims coming in on ships from the British Isles, starting in the 11th century.

The Ingles is a merry, easy-going way, passing through charming seaside towns with gorgeous views of the ocean and fresh seafood, then climbing up into the green hills of interior Galicia, through some lovely nature. In 2019, 15,327 pilgrims walked the Ingles, keeping it free from crowds but populated with enough pilgrims to still benefit from the camaraderie.

Unlike all the other Caminos, except for the Portuguese, it DOES NOT merge with the Frances before entering Santiago, so your final approach to the holy city is more peaceful and less touristic. This is a great route for pilgrims of all fitness levels, and a wide variety of accommodation is available. In the summer months it stays cooler on this Camino than some of the other routes, too.

The Camino Ingles embodies the jolly, the fun-loving, and the pilgrim looking to complete a FULL Camino in as little as four or five days. It's for the sea-loving, the easy-going walker, and those interested in following in the footsteps of northern European pilgrims who would have arrived by ship.

CAMINO PORTUGUESE

The Camino Portuguese is the second most popular of the Camino routes, with 21,768 pilgrims completing it in 2019. The official start is in Lisbon, making it 616km long, but most pilgrims opt to start in the city of Porto, cutting it to just 240km.

The weather on this route is less extreme than other Caminos, being moderated by the Atlantic Ocean, and the way stays green and cool in summer with plenty of rain.

There are a couple of interesting variants on this route, a coastal trail for the beach lovers, and an inland spiritual trail for those more interested in religious pursuits. This is a great route for those who have already traveled extensively in Spain and want to experience something a bit different, especially the Portuguese cuisine. The terrain is varied, passing through some gorgeous nature, but there is a lot of road walking, too.

The Camino Portuguese is for the seasoned pilgrim, those craving variety, for the spiritual and for the sea-lovers.

CAMINO FINISTERRE

AH! The only Camino that DOESN'T end in Santiago. Only hardcore Caministas know that Finisterre is the true end of the Camino, and you're extra cool if you've caught on to the fact that end of the end is actually in Muxía.

The Camino Finisterre is 89km of Galician bliss. An easy path undulates up and down long slopes, through lush eucalyptus forests and through charming little hamlets. Most of the people you meet on the Way have just completed a longer Camino route and have opted to add a few more days on at the end, so by default many are focusing on the inner journey, trying to integrate everything they've just experienced and preparing their mind and spirit for returning back to the real world.

It's a sparsely populated Camino, with 24,979 pilgrims completing it in 2019, but it's gaining in popularity fast. The Camino Finisterre is especially interesting for those looking to delve deeper into the pagan roots of the Camino, as this was the path ancient Celts would travel to reach 'the end of the world,' which was thought to be the Cape Finisterre. If you've just come off of a longer, inland Camino, when you crest that hill on the fourth day and get your first glimpse of the blue Atlantic Ocean and the 'Coast of Death,' the joy is palpable.

Upon reaching the Finisterre lighthouse it is customary to burn your Camino clothes and boots in a ceremony marking the end of your great journey and then spend a few days in the laid back beach town celebrating and eating seafood. But for those pilgrims who STILL don't feel like they've reached the end, there is a little known extension of the Camino that takes you another 30km to Muxía, the site of a very holy chapel on the rocks, built over the remains of a pagan altar. This feels like the true spiritual end of the Camino for many, and if you still want to go further, you'll have to walk straight out into the sea!

You are thoughtful, determined, and you definitely want to do what it takes to fully process the psycho-spiritual implications of your Camino – and, you're reluctant to hurry home!

The Camino begins when you decide to do it,
and it lasts for the rest of your life.

About the Authors

James Ryle and Cassie Childers met in the Indian Himalayas in 2011, leading to a long collaboration with the Tibet Women's Soccer program, a women's empowerment NGO operating in the Tibetan refugee community until 2017. Together they worked to introduce soccer to Tibetan women for the first time.

James worked one-on-one with players providing performance-enhancing therapeutic tools and interpersonal support, drawing from his love of the sport and time spent as a hypnotherapist in Ireland. Cassie conceptualized and managed the program, orchestrating the first meeting of Tibetan and Chinese athletes since the 1949 Chinese invasion of Tibet, sparking a wave of sports diplomacy of immense geopolitical significance. Today, due to their efforts and the incredible spirit of the young players they coached, Tibetan women in exile play soccer regularly.

Via their business Ascension Therapy, the couple now works to help others overcome their past and align with their ideal future both online and in person.

Cassie also coaches pilgrims from all over the world to prepare for and integrate their Camino de Santiago adventures with a special focus on the inner journey.

ascensiontherapyclinic.com
caminocoaching.org

Made in the USA
Middletown, DE
10 December 2020

27130342R00203